SCRIPTURE AND HERMENEUTICS SERIES

VOLUME 8

THE BIBLE
AND THE
UNIVERSITY

The Scripture and Hermeneutics Series

Series Editors
Craig Bartholomew
Anthony Thiselton

Consultant Editors
Ann Holt
Karl Möller

Editorial Advisory Board
James Catford
Fred Hughes
Tremper Longman III
Francis Martin
Gordon McConville
Christopher Seitz
Janet Martin Soskice
Nick Wolterstorff

VOLUME 8

THE BIBLE
AND THE
UNIVERSITY

— *editors* —

DAVID LYLE JEFFREY
C. STEPHEN EVANS

— *series editors* —

CRAIG G. BARTHOLOMEW
• ANTHONY C. THISELTON

Copyright © 2007 University of Gloucestershire
and the British and Foreign Bible Society

First published 2007 jointly
in the UK by Paternoster Press, an imprint of Authentic Media,
9 Holdom Avenue, Bletchley, Milton Keynes, MK1 1QR, UK
www.authenticmedia.co.uk
Authentic Media is a division of IBS-STL UK, a company limited by
guarantee (registered charity no. 270162)

and in the United States of America by
Zondervan
5300 Patterson Ave SE, Grand Rapids, Michigan 49530

11 10 09 08 07   7 6 5 4 3 2 1

British Library Cataloguing in Publication Data
A catalogue record for this book is available from the British Library
ISBN 978-1-84227-072-1

Library of Congress Cataloging-in-Publication Data
The Bible and the University / editors,
David Lyle Jeffrey, C. Stephen Evans.
    p. cm. — (The scripture and hermeneutics series; v. 8)
Includes bibliographical references and indexes.
ISBN-13: 978-0-310-23418-0
ISBN-10: 0-310-23418-2
    1. Bible—Influence. 2. Education, Higher. 3. Church and college 4. Universities and
colleges—Religion
I. Jeffrey, David Lyle, 1941- II. Evans, C. Stephen.
    BS538.7 B575 2007
    220.09—dc22
2007016774

Cover Design by Gert Swart and Zak Benjamin, South Africa
Typeset by WestKey Ltd, Falmouth, Cornwall
Printed in the United States of America
Printed on acid free paper

Dedicated to Rosemary Hales, for her sterling and personable administration of the Scripture and Hermeneutics Seminar

Contents

Preface

The Bible and the University is the final in a series of eight volumes that the Scripture and Hermeneutics Seminar conceived some ten years ago; the first volume, entitled *Renewing Biblical Interpretation*, was published in 2000. There is nothing arbitrary in the move from the ambitious goal of renewing interpretation of the Bible as Holy Scripture to a volume on the Bible's role in the university: Scripture is God's word for all of life and not 'just' for the institutional church and the believing theologian. The Bible claims to tell the true story of the world and can only be excised from the variety of disciplines in the modern university to our own detriment and that of our neighbor. The university is hugely significant in forming students for their royal stewardship in God's world, although sadly one of the legacies of modernity is the privatization of religion and the relegation of Scripture study to a 'leisure' activity.

Religion, however, and its significance for public life – including that of the university – will not go away. Indeed, particularly since the events of 9/11 religion has once again forced its attention upon the West. While the West's struggle with militant Islam is daily on the front pages of our newspapers, however, a remarkable and possibly more important development, the phenomenal growth of Christianity in the South, is for Western observers with a post-Enlightenment perspective hard to see, let alone take seriously. We are all in debt to Philip Jenkins for his books *The Next Christendom*[1] and *The New Faces of Christianity*[2] for drawing this seismic religious shift to our attention.

Jenkins notes that at the end of the second millennium many statistics were compiled about that millennium but religion received little attention. He suggests, however, that 'it is precisely religious changes that are the most significant, and even the most revolutionary, in the contemporary world. . . . We are currently living through one of the transforming moments in the history of religion worldwide.'[3] During the twentieth century the center of gravity in

---

[1] Philip Jenkins, *The Next Christendom: The Coming of Global Christianity* (New York: Oxford University Press, 2002).

[2] Philip Jenkins, *The New Faces of Christianity: Believing the Bible in the Global South* (New York: Oxford University Press, 2006).

[3] Jenkins, *Next Christendom*, 1.

Christianity moved steadily south, to Africa, Asia and Latin America, and in these contexts it continues to experience phenomenal growth. Christians are in a majority or have sizeable minorities in many countries in the developing world, which are the fastest-growing countries in the world, countries such as the Philippines, Nigeria, Mexico, Brazil and China. If we extrapolate from present statistics to the year 2050 'and assume no great gains or losses through conversion, then there would be around 2.6 billion Christians, of whom 633 million would live in Africa, 640 million in Latin America, and 460 million in Asia. Europe, with 555 million, would have slipped to third place.'[4]

Surprisingly, few in the West have noticed this 'creation of a new Christendom . . . Southern churches remain almost invisible to Northern observers.'[5] The result is that hardly any analysts are wrestling with what it means for Western civilization that what was once its basic religious scaffolding, as David Lyle Jeffrey points out in his fine introduction, is increasingly held outside the West!

Intriguingly, the type of Christianity exploding in the South is predominantly of a biblically orthodox character, while maintaining a strong social conscience. Jenkins has explored this in detail in his *The New Faces of Christianity*. As a subtitle to his chapter on 'Power in the Book,' Jenkins quotes Martin Luther: 'The Bible is alive – it has hands and grabs hold of me, it has feet and runs after me.' This is how Southern Christians experience Scripture, as the living and true Word of God. And this believing approach to the Bible has not, as is so often the case in the West, been wedded to political conservatism seeking above all to entrench the status quo: 'Across the global South, it has commonly been church leaders who most visibly struggle for reform, democratization, and human rights; who most publicly denounce tyranny, at whatever risk to their personal safety.'[6]

Jenkins notes that in terms of the future relationship between God and the world, the greatest change is likely to involve our Enlightenment-derived assumption that religion should be segregated into a separate sphere of life, distinct from everyday reality. In the Western view, religion may influence behavior in what is often, revealingly, termed 'the real world,' and faith might even play a significant political role, but spiritual life is primarily a private, inward and individual activity. For Americans particularly, the common assumption holds that church and state, sacred and profane, are wholly separate enterprises, and should remain so. In most historical periods, though, such distinctions do not apply, and are even incomprehensible. In recent decades, the politics of much of Africa, Latin America, and Asia (and one might add, of

---

[4] Jenkins, *Next Christendom*, 3.
[5] Jenkins, *Next Christendom*, 4.
[6] Jenkins, *New Faces*, 142. See his examples, 143ff.

Eastern Europe) have been profoundly affected by religious allegiances and activism, as clergy have repeatedly occupied center stage in political life. If in fact Christianity is going to be growing sharply in numbers and in cultural influence in coming decades, we can reasonably ask whether the faith will also provide the guiding political ideology of much of the world.[7]

So much of Western Christianity has capitulated to the privatization of religion that it is hard to imagine what this might involve. What does it mean to follow Christ in the world of the arts? What does it mean to follow Christ in education, politics, marriage and sexuality, economics, globalization, and the like? In most of our Western universities these questions are unimaginable but in terms of global development they are crucial. It is time for us to recover a sense of Christ's lordship over all of life, to say with conviction of Jesus that 'This man is the secret of heaven and earth, of the cosmos created by God.'[8]

This volume explores the sorts of steps such a recovery of the Bible for the university might involve. There are already signs of recognition of the need for cultural recovery of biblical literacy.[9] Our hope is that this volume will supplement such attempts and help Christians in both North and South to reclaim Scripture as God's Word for all of life, never simplistically, but truly.

I am most grateful to David Lyle Jeffrey and C. Stephen Evans for editing this volume, as well as to Katherine Jeffrey for her sterling work on the copyediting. The consultation out of which these essays emerged was hosted by Baylor University in May 2006 and we are thankful for its financial and administrative support of the event.

Without the support of the British and Foreign Bible Society there would not have been a Scripture and Hermeneutics Seminar and its contribution, along with that of the other partners in the Seminar, needs to be noted. One aspect of the Bible Society's support was the provision of administrative oversight in the person of Rosemary Hales, whose thorough administration and commitment to the communal nature of the project were exceptional. We are therefore delighted to dedicate this volume to her.

This collection marks the conclusion to the eight-volume series as initially conceived. However it does not mark the end of the work of the Seminar. While we do not intend to keep producing a volume each year there are plans underway to sustain the community engendered by the project and to develop further initiatives. To keep in touch with the work of the Seminar readers are encouraged to visit our website at www.sahs-info.org.

---

[7] Jenkins, *New Faces*, 141, 142.
[8] Karl Barth, *Church Dogmatics* 111/1 (Edinburgh: T&T Clark, 1958), 21.
[9] See, for example, the lead article in *Time*, Canadian Edition, April 2, 2007, 28–34, entitled, 'Why We Should Teach the Bible in Public School,' by David van Biema.

I warmly thank all the scholars who have participated in our nine consultations over the past decade, including my series co-editor Anthony Thiselton, and pray that our loaves and fishes, as represented in this Series, may be multiplied to good effect by him who is indeed the Word made flesh.

In Christ,
Craig Bartholomew
Easter 2007

Contributors

William J. Abraham is Albert Cook Outler Professor of Wesley Studies and University Distinguished Professor at Southern Methodist University and Perkins School of Theology. He is the author of *Waking from Doctrinal Amnesia: The Healing of Doctrine in the United Methodist Church* (Abingdon, 1995), *Canon and Criterion in Christian Theology: From the Fathers to Feminism* (Oxford University Press, 1998; new edn. 2006), *Divine Revelation and the Limits of Historical Criticism* (Oxford Scholarly Classics, 1982), and *Crossing the Threshold of Divine Revelation* (Eerdmans, 2006).

Robert F. Cochran, Jr. is the Louis D. Brandeis Professor and Director of the Institute on Law, Religion, and Ethics at Pepperdine University School of Law. He is the author of eight books and over 40 articles and book chapters. His books include *Faith and Law: How Religious Traditions From Calvinism to Islam View American Law* (New York University Press, forthcoming), *Christian Perspectives on Legal Thought* (Yale University Press, 2001) (with Michael McConnell and Angela Carmella), and *Lawyers, Clients, and Moral Responsibility* (West, 1994) (with Thomas L. Shaffer). Professor Cochran is the founder of Pepperdine School of Law's Union Rescue Mission Legal Clinic.

C. Stephen Evans is University Professor of Philosophy and Humanities at Baylor University. He previously taught philosophy at Calvin College (where he also served a term as Dean for Research and Scholarship), at St Olaf College (where he was also Curator of the Hong Kierkegaard Library), and Wheaton College. His sixteen books include *Why Believe?* (Eerdmans, 1996*)* and (more recently) *Kierkegaard's Ethic of Love: Divine Commands and Moral Obligations* (Oxford University Press, 2007), as well as *Kierkegaard on Faith and the Self* (Baylor University Press, 2006).

Scott Hahn is founder and president of the St Paul Center for Biblical Theology. He currently holds the Pope Benedict XVI Chair at St Vincent Seminary in Latrobe, PA and is Professor of Scripture and Theology at Franciscan University of Steubenville. He earned his Ph.D. in Systematic Theology from Marquette University in 1995; a revision of his dissertation will be published next year in the Anchor Bible Reference Library. His scholarly writing has appeared in the *Journal of Biblical Literature*, *Catholic Biblical Quarterly*, and *Currents in Biblical Research*. Dr. Hahn is editor of *Letter & Spirit Journal* and the *Ignatius Study Bible* and is author of more than a dozen books including *The Lamb's Supper* (Doubleday, 1999), *Letter and Spirit* (Doubleday, 2005), and *Understanding the Scriptures* (Midwest Theological Forum, 2005).

David Lyle Jeffrey is Distinguished Professor of Literature and the Humanities in the Honors College of Baylor University, and Professor Emeritus of the University of Ottawa, Canada. He is author of *People of the Book: Christian Identity and Literary Culture* (Eerdmans,1996), *Houses of the Interpreter: Reading Scripture, Reading Culture* (Baylor University Press, 2003), and primary author and general editor of *A Dictionary of Biblical Tradition in English Literature* (Eerdmans,1992). He is currently working on a commentary on Luke for the Brazos Theological Commentary on the Bible.

Byron Johnson is Professor of Sociology and Co-Director of the Institute for Studies of Religion (ISR) and Director of the Program on Prosocial Behavior at Baylor University. He is also a Senior Fellow at the Witherspoon Institute in Princeton, New Jersey. Recent publications have examined the efficacy of the 'faith factor' in reducing crime and delinquency among at-risk youth in urban communities, and the impact of faith-based programs on recidivism reduction and prisoner re-entry. Along with ISR colleagues he is completing a series of groundbreaking empirical studies on religion in China.

Roger Lundin is the Blanchard Professor of English at Wheaton College (Illinois). He is the author and editor of a number of books on nineteenth-century American literature, hermeneutics, and the intersection of religion and literature; they include *There Before Us: Religion, Literature, and Culture from Emerson to Wendell Berry* (Eerdmans, 2007); *From Nature to Experience: The American Search for Cultural Authority* (Rowman & Littlefield, 2006); and *Emily Dickinson and the Art of Belief* (Eerdmans, 1998; 2004). He is currently editing a volume of essays that have grown out of the work of the American Literature and Religion Project, which he directed from 2000–5.

Glenn W. Olsen is Professor of History at the University of Utah, Salt Lake City. A specialist in medieval Church and intellectual history, he has published on a wide range of ancient, medieval, and modern topics including the history of biblical exegesis. His books include *Beginning at Jerusalem: Five Reflections on the History of the Church* (Ignatius, 2004). He is an editor of *The Catholic Historical Review* and of *Communio: International Catholic Review*.

Robert Roberts is Distinguished Professor of Ethics in the Philosophy Department of Baylor University. He works on 'psychological' aspects of ethics. His most recent books are *Intellectual Virtues: An Essay in Regulative Epistemology* (Oxford University Press, 2007; with Jay Wood) and *Emotions: An Essay in Aid of Moral Psychology* (Cambridge University Press, 2003). Forthcoming (2007) is *Spiritual Emotions: A Psychology of Christian Virtues* (Eerdmans). He has published papers in the *Philosophical Review*, the *American Philosophical Quarterly, Philosophical Studies, Philosophy and Phenomenological Research*, the *Journal of Religious Ethics*, and *Faith and Philosophy*.

David Smith is Director of the Kuyers Institute for Christian Teaching and Learning and Associate Professor of German at Calvin College in Grand Rapids, Michigan. He is co-editor of the *Journal of Education and Christian Belief* and the *Journal of Christianity and Foreign Languages*. He has published widely on Christian education, including the recent books *The Gift of the Stranger: Faith, Hospitality and Foreign Language Learning* (with Barbara Carvill, Eerdmans, 2000), *The Bible and the Task of Teaching* (with John Shortt, The Stapleford Centre, 2002), and *Spirituality, Justice, and Pedagogy* (co-edited with John Shortt and John Sullivan, The Stapelford Centre, 2006).

John Sullivan was for twenty years a secondary school teacher at all levels, from the classroom to Principal, in the north of England and in London. Since 2002 he has been Professor of Christian Education at Liverpool Hope University. Author of *Catholic Schools in Contention* (Veritas, 2000), *Catholic Education: Distinctive and Inclusive* (Kluwer, 2001), co-editor of and contributor to both *The Idea of a Christian University* (Paternoster, 2005) and *Dancing on the Edge: Chaplaincy, Church & Higher Education* (Matthew James Publishing, 2007), he has also published (in the UK, USA, Europe, and Australia) more than sixty chapters and articles on religion and education.

Dallas Willard is Professor of Philosophy at the University of Southern California, where he has taught since 1965. He has held visiting appointments at UCLA (1969) and the University of Colorado (1984). He specializes in Ethics and the Theory of Knowledge, but has written extensively also on Logic and the Philosophy of Mathematics, primarily in connection with the works of Edmund Husserl and "Phenomenology" (e.g., *Logic and the Objectivity of Knowledge*, 1984.) In addition to work in Philosophy, he writes and speaks in the area of Christian thought, especially as it concerns spiritual formation. His most recent book is *Renovation of the Heart* (2002). At present his writing project is a volume entitled: *The Disappearance of Moral Knowledge in the 20th Century*.

Al Wolters is Professor of Religion and Theology/Classical Languages at Redeemer University College, Ancaster, Ontario, Canada, and has been co-editor of two previous volumes in the Scripture & Hermeneutics Series. His other publications include *Plotinus 'On Eros': A Detailed Exegetical Commentary on Enneads III.5* (1972), *Creation Regained: Biblical Basics for a Reformational Worldview* (Eerdmans, 1985), *The Copper Scroll. Overview, Text and Translation* (Sheffield Academic, 1996), and *The Song of the Valiant Woman: Studies in the Interpretation of Proverbs 31:10-31* (Paternoster, 2002). He is currently working on a commentary on Zechariah.

Abbreviations

AB	Anchor Bible
AUSS	*Andrews University Seminary Studies*
BBR	*Bulletin for Biblical Research*
BCOTWP	Baker Commentary on the Old Testament Wisdom and Psalms
BIS	Biblical Interpretation Series
BibInt	*Biblical Interpretation*
BJRL	*Bulletin of the John Rylands University Library of Manchester*
BR	*Biblical Research*
BRev	*Bible Review*
BZNW	Beihefte zur Zeitschrift für die neutestamentliche
CBQ	*Catholic Biblical Quarterly*
CBR	*Currents in Biblical Research*
CTJ	*Calvin Theological Journal*
EvQ	*Evangelical Quarterly*
EvTh	*Evangelische Theologie*
FAT	Forschungen zum Alten Testament
HBT	*Horizons in Biblical Theology*
HCOT	Historical Commentary on the Old Testament
HS	*Hebrew Studies*
HTR	*Harvard Theological Review*
HUCA	*Hebrew Union College Annual*
HvTSt	*Hervormde teologiese studies*
IJST	*International Journal of Systematic Theology*
Int	*Interpretation*
JBL	*Journal of Biblical Literature*
JBR	*Journal of Bible and Religion*
JBTh	*Jahrbuch für Biblische Theologie*
JETS	*Journal of the Evangelical Theological Society*
JR	*Journal of Religion*
JSNT	*Journal for the Study of the New Testament*
JSOT	*Journal for the Study of the Old Testament*
JSNTSup	Journal for the Study of the New Testament: Supplement Series
JSOTSup	Journal for the Study of the Old Testament: Supplement Series

JTS	*Journal of Theological Studies*
MT	Masoretic Text
Neot	*Neotestamentica*
NIB	*The New Interpreter's Bible*
NICOT	New International Commentary on the Old Testament
NIGTC	New International Greek Testament Commentary
NIVAC	The NIV Application Commentary
NTS	*New Testament Studies*
OTL	Old Testament Library
ProEccl	*Pro Ecclesia*
QD	Questiones disputatae
RBL	*Review of Biblical Literature*
RevExp	*Review and Expositor*
SBLMS	Society of Biblical Literature Monograph Series
SHS	Scripture and Hermeneutics Series
SJT	*Scottish Journal of Theology*
SNTSMS	Society for New Testament Studies Monograph Series
SubBi	Subsidia Biblica
ThTo	*Theology Today*
TLOT	*Theological Lexicon of the Old Testament* (3vols.; ed. E. Jenni, assisted by C. Westermann; trans. M.E. Biddle; Peabody, MA: Hendrickson, 1997)
TRev	*Theologische Revue*
TynBul	*Tyndale Bulletin*
VT	*Vetus Testamentum*
WBC	Word Biblical Commentary
WMANT	Wissenschaftliche Monographien zum Alten und Neuen Testament
WUNT	Wissenschaftliche Untersuchungen zum Neuen Testament
ZAW	*Zeitscgrift für die alttesamentliche Wissenschaft*

Introduction

David Lyle Jeffrey

Almost simultaneously with the Baylor Consultation of the Scripture and Hermeneutics Seminar in early June, 2006, there appeared an article by Hector Avalos, of Iowa State University, on the home page of the Society of Biblical Literature, arguably the pre-eminent academic guild for biblical scholars in the world. Under the heading, 'SBL Forum,' and titled 'The Ideology of the Society of Biblical Literature and the Demise of an Academic Profession,' Avalos decries the 'ever-growing irrelevance of biblical studies in academia,' and in particular chastises what he regards as a subservience of the university discipline to religion. He is outraged that 'biblical studies is still functioning as a handmaiden to theology and faith communities,' albeit in what he regards as a self-deceived fashion, because of a latent ideological reflex which seeks to justify academic study of the Bible in terms of 'the idea that the Bible bears "higher" ethical or religious lessons . . . as compared to those found in the texts of other cultures.' This weak sentiment, for him, as for others in the academy today, constitutes a bogus, fifth-column sort of apologetic for a 'religiocentric mythos' and as such should be exposed as perpetuating notions that are 'alien and irrelevant . . . for the modern world.'

Coming as it does from an officer of the leading professional society in biblical studies, this article sends a strong distress signal concerning the paradoxical divorce of formal biblical study at the beginning of the twenty-first century from the historic ecclesiastical traditions which have preserved and handed down the texts of Scripture and its rich exegetical and critical commentary. Further, it expresses a loathing for the entire academic enterprise effectively constituted by the divorce. According to Avalos, we ought to recognize that 'the Bible has no intrinsic value or merit. Its value is a social construct, and the SBL is the agent of an elite class that wishes to retain its own value and employment by fostering the idea that biblical studies should matter.'

It would be difficult to find for any discipline in the university today such a radical manifesto for professional annihilation. Ironically enough, the vehemence this SBL-sanctioned statement expresses can perhaps best be understood as an unintended consequence of the modern discipline's own much-vaunted determination to keep a firm and prophylactic distance between the Bible as an object of critical study and the Bible as a subject of faith. This divorce Avalos now believes has proven impossible to maintain – or is so badly maintained that any intellectual seriousness in biblical study now appears to some in the field to grant to the discipline an unwarranted legitimacy. The ironies are trenchant. Throughout the past century, the rule of practice in the academic work of the Society of Biblical Studies has, in fact, been for scholars to 'leave their faith at the door.' Most have. But even that rigor, Avalos seems to say, has not sufficed to reduce the status of the Bible to being just one more cultural artifact among many, which in his view is the only way it should now be treated.

We have a different view – and, accordingly, we have considerably more hope for the future of biblical studies. The present collection of essays, the result of a collaboration of scholars associated with the Scripture and Hermeneutics Seminar, is the final volume in a series of eight which have, each in their turn, grown out of international seminars conducted over the last decade in full consciousness of the impending bankruptcy of much that has passed for normative in the Western academic pursuit of biblical studies. The first rule of practice for our own group of Protestant and Catholic scholars has been self-consciously counter to the watchword of the SBL: in the words of Craig Bartholomew, our principle has been, 'You must NOT leave your faith at the door.' For the authors of this collection, as for those of previous volumes in this series, the pertinence of faith to our understanding of the challenges posed by Scripture and its tradition could hardly be greater than now it is, in the rather harsh light of so evident a crisis of confidence in our academic culture.

The abiding concern of the distinguished convocation of scholars who have contributed to SAHS over the last decade, mostly from the disciplines of biblical studies and hermeneutics, but including also, as the topics invited it, philosophers, literary critics, intellectual historians, historians of religion and, in this volume, social scientists and historians of education, has been to examine and begin to remedy notable aspects of the modern failure of academic biblical study. For us, that includes failure to have been as fully useful to the wider Christian community – notably the Church – as we believe ought properly to have been the case.

This last volume in our series addresses a particular aspect of that deficiency, namely, an increasing tendency to practice the formal disciplines of biblical studies too much in isolation from the other intellectual disciplines of the university, including, lamentably, even those that have most obviously grown up over the centuries as an outgrowth of the serious study of Scripture.

There are, of course, historical reasons for the isolation and eventual compartmentalization of academic biblical study. Not all of these, it should be recognized, are the fault of departments of religion and theology, and certainly not all have been without rationale and fruitfulness. But the resulting lack of mutual awareness of the connections among our disciplines has led to real loss in the intellectual conversation within the university, and in particular to a loss of focus and perspective on the deepest purposes of a university education. Our own work has been thus necessarily self-critical. Out of it, however, we have hoped to make amends to some small degree, and, in the process, to bring about something of a modest anamnesis, a renewed sense of the integrative richness and capacious generosity of a liberal education in which what has been historically the university's most important intellectual wellspring can once again be recognized and utilized in a less partisan, more holistic way.

The task is not an easy one, as indeed the present volume – with its focus on the relationship of the Bible to a whole range of university disciplines – should make abundantly clear.

The Bible in Intellectual History

For one thing, there have always been objections to our topic. Many take the form of one of the most famous – 'What has Athens to do with Jerusalem?'[1] Tertullian's famous question has been often quoted and repeated, typically to characterize the early Christians as somewhat philistine, suspicious of art and learning. There is a similar passage in St Jerome's letter to Eustochium (Epist. 22.29–30), and every student of later antiquity is familiar with it; it relates the troubled dream of this great fourth-century scholar in which 'the Judge of all' accuses him of being not a Christian but a Ciceronian – conveying thus a remembered guilt which Jerome, in this instance for pedagogical purposes, confesses. Near the headwaters of Anglo-Saxon literature we hear the theme again, adapted now by Alcuin, likewise a formidable scholar, admonishing with authority the monks of Lindisfarne: '*Quid Hineldus cum Christo?*' – 'What has Ingeld to do with Christ?' (Epist. 169). Though the alien attraction that concerns Alcuin is Anglo-Saxon pagan epic, while for Tertullian and Jerome it is the literary legacy of Greece and pre-Christian Rome, the point is evidently the same. '*Caveat lector!*' all three seem to say: a grave risk of theological adultery attends upon dalliance with pagan authors. It is as if they reiterate the epistle of Paul to say that the true philosopher of Christ will keep himself pure and

---

[1] Tertullian, *De Praescriptione Haereticorum*, 18; cf. *De Spectaculis*, 4, 26, and 30, Ante-Nicene Fathers, vol. 3.

unspotted from the world, and certainly 'teach no other doctrine' (1 Tim. 1:3–4).

Typical modern citations of these famous injunctions continue to implicate much of Christianity in a certain dour abstemiousness where the liberal arts are concerned. They assume a desire to separate, even cordon off, humanistic learning from what are sometimes taken to be more 'appropriate' spiritual preoccupations. In such a characterization the wall of separation constructed for early and medieval Christianity can seem almost as steep as the rhetorical barrier erected between faith and rational discourse by advocates of liberal learning since the Enlightenment, whose august latter-day guardians of purity, facing from opposite ramparts, include such venerables as Edward Gibbon, David Hume, and, in his 1809 decision to separate the study of theology from the other humanities disciplines at the new University of Berlin, Wilhelm von Humboldt.[2] Nor should we dismiss such tactical moves (perhaps on either side) as entirely misinformed concerning biblical counsel in the matter – the ancient voices were echoing St Paul in his still more extreme warning to the Corinthian Greeks about both syncretism and idolatry: 'What has Christ to do with Belial?' (2 Cor. 6:15). The modern separationists thought of biblical piety itself as the contaminant. They all thought they had warrant.

But have such selective proof-texts, however motivated, accurately measured the character and method of the biblical influence on humanities education in Western intellectual history? Here we are on much less firm ground.

Genetically speaking, the subsequent development of the humanities disciplines in Western culture cannot be fully understood apart from an appreciation of scriptural husbandry and, if we use the term somewhat flexibly, a kind of ecclesiastical mothering which, together, have birthed and nurtured Western intellectual life down to the present age. In brief, I want to support and extend the thesis of Robert Wilkens when he says that any notion that there was a 'Hellenization of Christianity' should by now be regarded as having outlived its usefulness – indeed, 'that a more apt expression would be the Christianization of Hellenism, though that expression does not capture the originality of Christian thought nor the debt owed to Jewish ways of thinking and to the Jewish Bible.'[3] But how, we may ask, through the centuries-old and ongoing diaspora of the Jewish peoples whose ancestors wrote the texts, and

---

[2] See the discussion by S. Prickett, *Origins of Narrative: The Romantic Appropriation of the Bible* (Cambridge: Cambridge University Press, 1996), xiv; 180ff.; and his *Words and the Word: Language, Poetics and Biblical Interpretation* (Cambridge: Cambridge University Press, 1986), passim.

[3] R. Wilkens, *The Spirit of Early Christian Thought* (New Haven: Yale University Press, 2003), xvi. Wilkens is, of course, correcting the attempt at 'de-judification' of the Bible by Adolf von Harnack.

despite their minimal demographic presence throughout Western Europe in particular, did this way of thinking persist? The subject is massive and fundamental; in this present essay there is space merely for a few cryptic observations.

Authority and Wisdom

One is obliged to recognize, as N.T. Wright does in the third volume of this series, the decisive role of St Paul. As apostle to the Gentiles, he proclaimed the teaching of Jesus and the twelve in an overwhelmingly Hellenistic context. While at times he would accommodate his message to his audience, as in the Areopagus speech in Athens or in the rhetorical shape of his letters to the churches, in his views of the nature of God, the role and place of human potential as reflective of God's image in God's world, he remained fundamentally Jewish. This shaped the ways he discussed not only the resurrection of the body, but his wider views of the relation of body and spirit and the nature of human sexuality, for example, far more profoundly than did any norms of Hellenistic culture. That these Jewish views had an inner logic that proved coherent, cogent and compelling for centuries of readers of St Paul is now evident. Though relatively few converts after the first generations would have been conscious of the degree of it, Mediterranean, European and North Africans learned to think in a Jewish way about fundamental theological, social and moral matters, and it soon showed up in their own writings.

Nor can we adequately trace the shaping of Western intellectual culture in the humane disciplines without considering a certain North African bishop, in particular through his enormously influential *De Doctrina Christiana* (*On Christian Doctrine*).[4] It may be, in fact, that the prominence of Augustine's text in the Western history of both hermeneutics and educational theory has, as much as any other influence, helped to shape the way in which the Bible has come to be institutionalized in Western culture – even when invisibly. Augustine's relation of the goals of Ciceronian education to a biblical order of reasoning about language and truth was so successful that his book became a touchstone for more than a millennium of later humanistic authors. The list of texts indebted to it is long, but certainly includes Cassiodorus's *De Institiutione Divinarum Litterarum*, Rabanaus Maurus's *De Institutione*, Hugh of St Victor's *Didascalicon,* Bonaventure's *De Reductione Artium ad Theologiam,* John Wyclif's *De Veritate Sacrae Scripturae,* translated sections in the preface of the Wycliffite Bible, as well

---

[4] Trans. D.W. Robertson, Jr. (New York: Bobbs-Merrill, 1958); see, for useful commentary E.B. English, *Reading and Wisdom: The De Doctrina of Augustine in the Middle Ages* (Notre Dame: University of Notre Dame Press, 1995).

as later writings of Erasmus, Petrarch, Salutati, Milton, J.H. Newman, and C.S. Lewis, to name just a few. Even this abbreviated list should renew our appreciation of an enormous contribution to Western intellectual culture that derives, essentially, from one magisterial attempt to develop a method for reading the Bible.

Augustine's pedagogical strategies regarding the disciplines required for an intelligent reading of Scripture became in some ways more influential than his specific exegesis, helping the Bible eventually to transcend theology and become not only the historical foundation for humane learning in the West, but also the procedural and methodological basis of nearly all scholarship in the humanities. Textual criticism, philological analysis, poetics, language theory, narrative epistemology, historiography, anthropology, positive law, and natural law are all among the immediate beneficiaries.

With regard to the goals of education Augustine does not, at one level, seem to differ much from Cicero: eloquence and wisdom are the enduring *desiderata*. But though himself a teacher of rhetoric, Augustine is emphatic that eloquence is instrumental, not an intrinsic good. Why is this important? Well, because divine wisdom is essentially the burden of Scripture's content and superior wisdom in the life of the reader is its ultimate purpose. Acquisition of this wisdom, in turn, provides a more reliable platform for a distinctive and superior grace in utterance: 'one speaks more or less wisely,' Augustine argues, 'to the extent that he has become more or less proficient in [the Holy Scriptures]' (4.5.8). Wisdom, rather than Ciceronian eloquence in itself, is the ultimate justification of all higher learning. Meanwhile, biblical language constitutes a special order of eloquence, 'fitting for those of higher authority' (4.6.9). These convictions also have had an incalculable influence on Christian intellectual culture.

Authority and the Book

For Augustine, as for his teacher Ambrose, on a biblical view truth is truth, regardless of where it comes from (2.28.28; cf. Thomas Aquinas: '*studium philosophiae non est ad hoc quod sciatur quid hominess senserint, sed qualiter se habeat veritas rerum*' [*De caelo*, lib.1.1.22, a 8]). We can also expect there to be a harmonious accord between the Book of Nature and of Scripture, rightly placed and understood (2.39.59). Obscurity and figurative discourse in relation to the 'big questions' is neither a failure of language nor a means of Gnostic exclusion; even in Scripture itself it can be an artfully deliberate means of *inducare, educare*, leading to the Truth (2.6.7–8). The appropriate method of learned investigation is thus hermeneutically ordered – patient unfolding of the layers of meaning 'hidden' in the text, separating 'fruit' from 'chaff' – the prototype of what would be called a millennium and a half later, by professional readers long secularized, 'explication de texte.'

But here is the point too often missed: classical learning, indeed all types of learning in the monasteries and other communities of Christian education, was organized around a *studium* whose central preoccupation was with the Bible as a foundation for *all* learning. It was the study of the Bible – principally but not exclusively in Jerome's Latin translation – far more than the study of Cicero and the classical authors generally that spread Latin literacy *and* produced also a textual tradition in several European vernaculars. Moreover, we can say confidently that not only was the Bible in such a fashion made foundational for general humane learning in European culture, but that without it, much of Roman secular learning and many of the ancient texts themselves would not have survived to be a part of our culture at all.

The liberal arts as we know them did not begin to emerge in their familiar form in Christian Europe until the work of the polymath Boethius (480–525 AD), the Roman Christian whose treatises on arithmetic, geometry, astronomy, and music are foundational for what he himself was first to call the *quadrivium*.[5] (None of these particular Boethian works, however, survive.) Grammar, rhetoric and logic – the *trivium* – had been standard for some time. But Boethius, though a layman, was also a biblical theologian, author of five major *opuscula sacra*, and these, along with his *Consolation of Philosophy*, make of him one of the last Roman thinkers to stand firmly astride two worlds, Roman and Christian, culturally speaking. His Lady Philosophy is not a reincarnation of Athena, or Mentor, or Vergil as Dante portrays him, but of Dame Chôkma in the biblical wisdom books. Though in his *Consolation* the epistemological object is a recollection of human dignity and freedom, the transcendent wisdom that Lady Philosophy personifies is, in effect, an ontological presence of transcendent being.

From thence onward to the nineteenth century it is difficult to find a major European humanist whose intellectual formation was not in some way grounded in study of the sacred page. Hugh of St Victor considered this legacy from his vantage point as a master in the cathedral schools that were growing up in France, and which would be the chief institutional means by which monastic scholia were within a century to be supplanted in intellectual importance by the rise of universities and the disputation they encouraged.[6] For Hugh, in his magnum opus on liberal education, the *Didascalicon*, the 'seven to be studied by

---

[5] On Boethius, see M. Colish, *Medieval Foundations of the Western Intellectual Tradition* (New Haven: Yale University Press, 1997).

[6] Hugh of St Victor, *Didascalicon de Studio Legendi*, trans. J. Taylor as *The Didascalicon of Hugh of St Victor: A Medieval Guide to the Arts* (New York: Columbia University Press, 1961).

beginners' were assigned thus by the ancients because they were found to be not merely of 'higher value,' but 'the best tools, the fittest entrance through which the way to philosophic truth is opened to our intellect.'[7] This instrumentalist approach regarding the arts presupposes a still higher intrinsic good; Richard of St Victor, one of his students, comments that 'All arts serve the Divine Wisdom, and each lower art, if rightly ordered, leads to a higher one. Thus, the relation existing between the word and the thing requires that grammar, dialectic and rhetoric should minister to history.'[8] We can still hear Augustine's voice in Richard's prose; the liberal arts function like signs in a meta-language that it is necessary to learn if we want a full-bodied engagement with human wisdom as it comes to us, both in history and ultimately in Sacred History, of which, on the Christian view, all other story is anticipation or refraction (*Didascalicon*, 6.3).

A century later, Bonaventure takes the whole instrumental hierarchy of learning here implied and turns it round so that all of the arts are both a means of common grace and a trace (*vestigium*) of that Divine Wisdom of which human flourishing is an axiom. In his *De Reductione Artium ad Theologiam* Bonaventure accordingly traces all of the arts, and particularly the liberal arts, to what for him is the ultimate source of our knowledge, human and divine, namely Scripture as articulated divine Word.[9] By *artes* Bonaventure means secular or empirical knowledge as distinct from the knowledge of God; on this view all knowledge is a light, or means of understanding, but the highest of all lights – superior to philosophical knowledge, to the knowledge arrived at by sense perception, and to the mastery of the mechanical arts – is the 'light of Sacred Scripture.' Yet, he writes, the 'Wisdom of God which lies hidden in Sacred Scripture is hidden in *all* of knowledge and in *all* nature. In this light, 'all divisions of knowledge are handmaids of theology' (26). Here, in short, is yet another medieval affirmation of the providential unity of reason and revelation, faith and reason – making explicit to the reader that Sacred Scripture is the key to any possible unity of prospect.

The confidence late medieval intellectuals expressed in this view of the interconnectedness of liberal learning or the products of reasoned investigation with biblical revelation and its progressive understanding in the Church is enduringly impressive. Whether in Alfred the Great, Thomas Aquinas, Thomas More or the great Dutch humanist Desiderius Erasmus, this confidence was itself presuppositional to intellectual life in the Renaissance, and, we might add, it was still regarded by the humanists of the Renaissance as

---

[7] *Didascalicon* 3.3. The notion of the seven liberal arts as pillars of wisdom (cf. Prov. 9:1) rather than wisdom itself – that is, a corpus of instrumental goods – is persistent.

[8] Richard of St Victor, *Doctrinale* 17.31.

[9] Trans. E.T. Healy (St Bonaventure, NY: Franciscan Institute Press, 1955).

liberating. On the one hand, John Calvin will say that once we have acknowledged the Spirit of God to be the 'only fountain of truth' it will oblige us 'not to reject or condemn truth wheresoever it appears,' but whenever anything is found which is 'noble or praiseworthy,' to trace it to the hand of God, whether the work be done by fellow believers or not (*Institutes* 2.2.15–16).[10] On the other hand, Renaissance humanists were chief among those who sought recovery of the Scriptures in better critical editions and historical commentary alike; the rallying cry of Erasmus was '*Ad fontes!*' – back to the sources – and to the evangelical humanist movement he led, in which figures such as John Colet, Jacques Lefevre d'Etaples, Johannes Reuchlin and even, in his own fashion, Martin Luther played a part, we owe the dramatic recovery of Scripture to a wider intellectual discourse which became vernacular in the sixteenth century.

A Flourishing of the Disciplines

What we witness in such a vigorous renewal of commitment to Holy Scripture is very far from a narrowing bibliocentrism. It is evidence rather of renewed primary engagement with the actual foundation of Western intellectual culture, evidence that Scripture continued to occupy a unique ontological as well as hermeneutic status in humanistic, university discourse beyond the high Middle Ages well into what we think of as the Reformation. This is not meant to imply that the *ipse verbum* of Scripture is everywhere obtrusively present in phrasing or citation as we might find it in the early monastic writings,[11] or over the centuries in the Scripture-saturated writings of such figures as Bernard of Clairvaux, Jeremy Taylor, John Bunyan and John Milton. I refer rather to the presuppositional and teleological framework of such disparate scientists as Robert Boyle, Isaac Newton and Henri Poincaré, or philosophers such as John Locke, Blaise Pascal, Soren Kierkegaard and Jacques Maritain, poets such as William Cowper, Goethe, Charlotte Bronte, the Brownings, T.S. Eliot, Paul Claudel, not to mention legal thinkers such as Henri de Bracton, Sir Edward Coke, F.W. Maitland and Sir William Blackstone. Yet here again, even a thumbnail list is indicative for both the intellectual and spiritual history of the university.[12]

---

[10] John Calvin, *Institutes of the Christian Religion*, 2 vols., trans. W. Beveridge (Grand Rapids: Eerdmans, 1947; 1981).

[11] Wilkens, 26; Henri de Lubac, S.J., *Exégèse Médiévale: les quatre sens de l'écriture* (Paris: Aubier, 1964), 4 vols; vols. 1 and 2 *passim*.

[12] On the legal writers, see D.S. Davies, *The Bible in English Law* (London: Jewish Historical Society of England, 1954), 3–23.

In all of these authors, biblical allusion and plenitude of biblical idiom is a reflex of something deeper. In areas of study as diverse as theology, science, mathematics, poetry and law, the Bible has in the Western tradition become what a Platonist might call the 'intelligible object,' but which I would prefer to call rather an *ontological object* of intellectual reflection – invisible but present – even when the immediate epistemological object is apparently something else.[13] In fact, the presence of Scripture as ontological object often can be felt even when the Bible or biblical tradition is being explicitly challenged. A notable instance is the opening scenes of Goethe's *Faust I*, where we find the ambitious professor Faust determined upon a translation of John's gospel superior to that of his Wittenberg predecessor Luther; his real intention, en route to mastery of all of the arts, is revealed to be subversive of the authority of the original biblical text. Though Goethe's theological challenge is explicit, the text of Scripture remains critically 'present' throughout his great Romantic drama; it is of the highest order of tribute to Scripture's vital presence as ontological object that all Goethe's ambitions may be summarized as a wish not merely to translate but actually to rewrite the Bible.[14] The same sort of thing, but here in respect of overt intellectual biography, might be said of Rousseau's *Confessions*, in which biblical language is employed to subvert both biblical precept and the intrinsic procedure and methodology of Augustine as a benchmark orthodox reader of Scripture; Rousseau intends a kind of rascal's reading of Augustine's *Confessions,* even (and perhaps especially) if it reveals, *de facto,* an infernal reading of the same Bible with which Augustine had been in intimate conversation as with the veritable Word of God.[15]

Yet not all outgrowths of Romanticism's triumphant subjective have required such gestures. For example, much closer to some of us, in the Southern Agrarianism of Cleanth Brooks, Robert Penn Warren and Allen Tate, and with a genteel belletrism to equal any in modernism for its eloquence, a species of methodology originally evolved for biblical study was silently appropriated for secular literary criticism. The 'New Critics' purloined much more than they admitted from biblical critics and academic apologists for Luther's independent Bible reader.[16] Even in Brooks's *The Well Wrought Urn* the presence of the

---

[13] C.D. Broad, *The Mind and its Place in Nature* (London: Routledge and Kegan Paul, 1925), 141ff., defines an ontological object as 'the real or existing object of an act of knowledge as distinct from the epistemological object,' its 'object envisioned,' whether veridical or illusory.

[14] Jeffrey, *People of the Book: Christian Identity and Literary Culture* (Grand Rapids: Eerdmans, 1996), 255–59.

[15] See A. Hartle, *The Modern Self in Rousseau's Confessions: A Reply to St Augustine* (Notre Dame: Notre Dame University Press, 1983).

[16] On the New Critics as borrowers of the stance of Luther's independent Bible reader as well as some methods of their contemporaries among biblical scholars, see Jeffrey, 91-96.

Scriptures and biblical criticism is palpable. Though epistemologically speaking not the envisioned object of the critic's act of knowledge, the Bible's imputed authority and acculturated method inform the critic's work powerfully as onto-logical object, a silent warden of an ostensibly secular critical enterprise. The New Critics' attempt at a rigorous detachment from the explicit influence of the Bible was accordingly transient; in the work of Hans Georg Gadamer and Paul Ricouer, to take but two examples from the next phase of literary and philo-sophical hermeneutics, the return, *ad fontes*, was again plainly visible.

Ad Fontes Redivivus?

Nowadays, gaining a significant place among both European and North Amer-ican scholars is a self-conscious and explicit resuscitation of the hermeneutic practice of the Fathers, for example, in *ressourcement* theologians such as Hans Urs von Balthasar and Henri de Lubac. In the *ressourcement* work especially we find the early hermeneutic rediscovered, articulated between the discourses of philosophy and theology and, via the vast *collegium* of biblical reading in its plenitude, offering a 'new ontological discourse' in which human nature is re-inscribed in divine nature.[17] But this evidence of intellectual recrudescence is far from limited to Christian theologians and philosophers. In literary theory the work of Robert Alter, Meir Sternberg, David Damrosch and others has in the last two decades put on center stage the hallowed Jewish traditions of Bible study as an introduction to modern comparative literary theory and criticism. These efforts have in turn morphed rather quickly into a renewed effort to study the biblical texts in their own right outside of the dominant professional religious strictures. In the work of Burton Vizotzky and Aviva Zornberg, among others, we see biblical texts applied to a kind of new secular humanistic discourse for the marketplace.[18]

'The Bible *as* Literature' and 'the Bible *in* Literature' have both, since the 1970s, emerged to great prominence. But it might more truthfully be said that

---

[17] J. Milbank, The Suspended Middle: Henri de Lubac and the Debate Concerning the Supernatural (Grand Rapids: Eerdmans, 2005), 5.

[18] E.g. B.L. Vizotzky, *The Genesis of Ethics: How the Tormented Family of Genesis Leads Us to Moral Development* (New York: Crown, 1996); A.G. Zornberg, *The Beginning of Desire: Reflections on Genesis* (New York: Doubleday-Image, 1995). In 'The Bible as Literature in the 1980's: A Guide for the Perplexed,' *University of Toronto Quarterly* 59 (1990), 369–81, I give a review of prominent titles from that decade. Much of this work is speculative, some even specious from a scholarly or theological point of view, but the obsession is persistent. H. Bloom, *Jesus and Yahweh: The Names Divine* (New York: Riverhead Books, 2005) is just one among many more recent examples.

this development has been emerging since the establishment of vernacular literature as a university discipline under Matthew Arnold in nineteenth-century Oxford.[19] In the twentieth century Arnold's program to resituate the Bible as perhaps the greatest English literary (rather than religious) foundation was continued by structuralists such as Roland Barthes and Northrop Frye; later still, psychoanalytic readings and a plethora of aesthetic and post-structuralist engagements with the Bible began to be published every year by academics from a wide diversity of disciplines, including philosophy, history, anthropology and, of course, a variety of Western secular literatures.

To be sure, the prevailing political currents in Western universities have been contrary in academic arenas as well as public rhetoric and in law. Even in American churches and synagogues, biblical literacy is said to be at a low ebb. The symbols of biblical foundations are regularly attacked in the public square, and media characterization, as often because of ignorance as of malice – is typically adversarial. Yet within the university there are signs of a continuing recrudescence of consciousness concerning the value of the Bible and biblical tradition to a flourishing for the liberal arts. Some of this is occasioned by critique of the current state of college education from within the university, especially for our failure to maintain our focus on the redemptive and broadly humane purpose of a liberal arts education. *The Decline of the Secular University* by C. John Sommerville (2006) and Harry Lewis's *Excellence without a Soul: How a Great University Forgot Education* (2006) are among the latest installments in an ongoing postmortem. Both lament our failure to retain the values we have traditionally associated with biblical wisdom at the heart of the liberal arts curriculum.[20] Sommerville's call to the academy has about it the bewilderment of a biblical prophet who cannot quite believe that from his own mouth such words are proceeding: 'The academy needs to learn to speak theologically,' he writes, 'This undoubtedly sounds alarming, but. . .' if we are honest, he admits, 'we have been really creating a tacit but unfortunately barren substitute for it all along.' Yes. And what we have found to our cost is that the secular substitute, lacking transcendence, fails to provide anything like an ontological object sufficient to ground and integrate the curriculum. According to Sommerville, we need most urgently now to get over it, and to recognize that 'the concepts of religion and of the human will survive, witnessing to an ultimacy we can't ignore' (32). Stephen Prothero's book, *Religious Literacy: What Every American*

---

[19] See Prickett, *Word and the Words*, 63–65.

[20] Similar notes, though from different angles of political conviction, are discernable in M. Nussbaum, *Cultivating Humanity: A Classical Defense of Reform in Liberal Education* (Cambridge, MA: Harvard University Press, 1997); and M. Berube, *What's Liberal about the Liberal Arts: Classroom Politics and 'Bias' in Higher Education* (New York: Norton, 2006).

Needs to Know – and Doesn't (2007) has been widely and approvingly reviewed for its unflinching exposé of the nearly grotesque biblical illiteracy of even religiously observant Protestant, Catholic and Jewish university students; what Prothero shows is that we are operating at present from a position of massive cultural deficit where knowledge of biblical foundations are concerned, and that education in many other disciplines suffers as a result.

In looking back over Western university education in the twentieth century, it seems clear on any number of accounts that attempts to pursue the liberal arts as though they were in themselves intrinsic goods have not been sustainably fruitful. One reason for persistence in this confusion is surely the tendency of modernist Western educational culture to the commodification of knowledge. But, as the poet Charles Tomlinson puts it, we have discovered repeatedly that 'Facts have no eyes.'[21] In our sometimes enthusiastic preoccupation with *techné* at the expense of *logos*, promoting technical excellences more narrowly appropriated rather than the acquisition of a synthetic intelligence, we may thus have run into our own version of the error forewarned against in one of the earliest defenses of the liberal arts, by Martianus Cappella. In his ninth-century *De Nuptiis Philologiae et Mercurii* Martianus argued that the Ciceronian goals of education, *eloquentia et sapientia,* cannot be successfully realized without a perseverant reference for meaning to the higher and integrative wisdom of Sacred Scriptures such as Augustine and others had championed.[22] In retrospect we can now see, perhaps, a little more clearly what Martianus saw, namely that it was this 'turning of the many toward the One' in regard to the arts that allowed for the predominant riches of the biblical *studium* to become a constantly flowing fountain, irrigating all of the other arts.

As with most types of effective irrigation, much of this has been most effective when least ostentatious. From the fountain of the biblical *studium* flowed not only a high order of widely applicable interpretative skills (*techné*), but also and more fundamentally a continuous renewal of confidence in the capacity of knowledge crowned with wisdom (its *logos*) to correct and regenerate intellectual culture. Whether in the medieval university, in the dissenting academy of the eighteenth century or the American liberal arts college movement of the nineteenth, this recurrent stream has been until recently the lifeblood of vital educational development in the Western world.

To recapitulate: in our meditations upon the role of Scripture in relation to the humanities we began with something of the history of the relationship. Then we moved on to attendant matters of inherited language, ontological status, and hermeneutical methods. Each is of critical importance; none has

---

[21] 'Observation of Facts,' by C. Tomlinson, in *Selected Poems, 1951–1974* (Oxford: Oxford University Press, 1978), 8.

[22] Ed. F. Eyssenbardt (Lipsiae, 1866).

received more than a preliminary notice here. But I wish to conclude with a comment on that higher goal towards which Scripture, more than Cicero, has pointed our traditions: *chōkma, sophia, sapientia.* If there is anything we need now to learn from the fruitful centuries of previous practice in the humane disciplines, it is that we cannot long thrive without a centering of our efforts upon the getting of wisdom. Hugh of St Victor already in the twelfth century acknowledged the hypertrophy of disciplines with which we are far more familiar – and the growth of what he called the 'appendages of the arts.' Hugh warned that those who 'willingly desert truth in order to become entangled in these mere by-products of the arts, will find. . . exceedingly great pains and little fruit' (*Did.* 3.4). We, who have experienced a far more prolix hypertrophy of the disciplines and perhaps more than a little entanglement in the painful by-products can report a confirming experimental result. The corrective for Hugh was to recognize explicitly the instrumentality of the humane disciplines to an intrinsic and higher good, namely wisdom in the learner of an abiding, life-changing and personally transcendent *gravitas.* We, who practice the humane disciplines and teach out of them, can perhaps do worse than to remind ourselves from time to time that we are not simply in the knowledge industry, but that we have, more compellingly, an obligation committed to the getting of wisdom.

Postscript

The cover art for this volume is appropriate to the essays that follow in several ways. It is the center panel of a triptych, the Mérode altarpiece of the last decade of the fifteenth century, generally if uncertainly ascribed to Robert Campin, or 'Le Mâitre de Flémalle,' and one of the best-known pieces in the collection of the Metropolitan Museum of Art in New York. As with most altarpieces that have the Annunciation as primary subject, the painting makes a direct connection between the biblical account in Luke (Lk 1: 26–38) of the proclamation to Mary of the Word made flesh, and the ongoing proclamation of the Gospel in its liturgical context.

The painting is striking in several ways most pertinent to our reflection in this volume. For one thing, the angel Gabriel appears to declare the Virgin's blessedness not, as in most contemporary representations (e.g., those of Roger van der Weyden, Petrus Christus, etc), in a marriage chamber, but in what appears rather like a study – even a room at the university. The anachronism should not be regarded as naiveté. This scene would have been understood by the artist and his audience as historically impossible, just as impossible as the Virgin's reading from a codex rather than a scroll: the painter's intent is to make a point about deeper meaning that transcends the literal level of the precious narrative. Whereas typically in art the Virgin is found kneeling at a *prie dieu*, attentive to her book of hours, and reading, as a medieval Mary would, in *lectio divina* her daily Psalms, here, like many a teenager given to serious reading in any culture, one supposes, she is seated on the floor, using the bench as a mere elbow rest; she is so wrapped up in her reading that she is not yet fully aware of her visitor. But the book is not a book of hours; by its size and heft, the painter invites us to regard it as Scripture. Moreover, there is a second such volume on her table, on top of a book bag which has a scrip of student notes sticking out, evoking the classic medieval iconography for the four evangelists themselves in their 'study' or cell, as of similar representations of the great doctors of the Church, such as Augustine and Jerome. Moreover, the cloth with which Mary protects the book is not only a reminder of its holy status as Word of God or, as some have thought, a suggestion that, like a medieval student, she is protecting the binding of a treasured book; it is also proleptic, a reminder of the swaddling cloth to come, signifying thus the relationship of the Word of God proclaimed to the Word made flesh in Christ Jesus.

Mary's youthful faithfulness is suggested by the *talit,* the Jewish prayer shawl on the special rack behind her, as, by the conventional lily on the table in its vase (pitcher), her virginal purity is more conventionally identified. But theologically speaking, the artist's finest touch is, of all elements, the subtlest. The candle by whose light (cf. Ps 119:105) she has been reading (Torah) has just been blown out by Gabriel's beating wings; the smoke still rises, even as her eyes, intent upon the sacred page, have begun to turn to see what has broken her concentration. And the homunculus gliding down the beam of new light toward her (cf. Ezek. 44:2, in the exegesis of St Anthony of Padua and St Bonaventure), bearing the Cross to come, is only the most obvious suggestion of the way we, too, are to see this definitive moment in the history of salvation as antimony, a harbinger both of inward joy and of the sorrow that attends the way of the Cross. Yet we should not fail to see that this artist has unusually chosen to show us Mary at precisely the point *before* she hears the divine proclamation; we see her thus as one still in preparation, reading the Scripture, intent upon the Law, and now about to be surprised by Grace.

This painting, from a moment in time before the Church in Europe would be rent asunder, has in our context today a special poignancy. On the one hand, we see in it why St Ambrose of Milan regarded Mary's humility and receptivity as a 'reader' of the divine Word as a virtue which 'commends the Mother of the Lord to those who read the Scriptures and, as a credible witness, declares her worthy to be chosen for such an office' (*De officiis* 1.18.68–69). We also understand in this remark of a distinguished reader of Scripture in the ancient Church why it is that Mary has so often since the rise of the Christian university in the Middle Ages been the patron saint of universities as places of learning in which 'study of the sacred page' has been recognized as the foundation of all other learning.

There is much of enduring value in this painterly characterization of reading – especially where Scripture is the text – for those of us who inhabit academic communities which tend to read less for understanding than for mastery, or to employ the tools of criticism less to provide communal access to truth than as exercises of our personal will to power. If the formal academic study of the Bible is on times anything like so hard as suggested by the SBL 'manifesto' with which we began, it may be because too many of us have forgotten how to 'ponder these things' in our hearts.

1

The Bible, the University and the God Who Hides

Dallas Willard

Human beings stand in their world condemned to act, and to act on the basis of whatever ideas, images, beliefs, impulses, desires and emotions they may have in the moment of action. We have no choice about that. We *may* have some choice about what ideas, beliefs, impulses, etc. will be available to us in future situations where we must act. That will largely depend upon what is given to us from the world we come into and what we are prepared to do now. But whatever world we come into, the human problem is *to find in knowledge a solid basis for action*. This problem cannot be solved by individuals on their own. Each one may contribute to the solution, and none can be totally passive. But the standing sources of knowledge and wisdom available in and through our social world are indispensable to the individual as well as to groups. The university is such a 'standing source.' What individuals could do on their own, starting from nothing, in the area of mathematics or anthropology, for example, would amount to very little. What they can do by accessing the knowledge and practice already acquired, and available in various forms in their social world, is very great, and a potential source of much good that is otherwise impossible. This applies to all areas of knowledge, but especially to the area of practical wisdom: How to live? That is where the Bible comes in. Or should.

It is of the nature of human knowledge, in whatever field, to grow transgenerationally and to deposit its gains in various ways that make accessible to any subsequent generation the learning of the past. But knowledge is indeed power, and reputation for knowledge gives authority and the right to act and direct others, individually or through policy. This leads to struggles between individuals and groups to *control* knowledge: to possess it, keep it away from others, to sell it at a price, to defend its status as knowledge and to attack the claims of others who advocate alternative sources of knowledge. If one thinks only for a minute one realizes how common these struggles are today on the national and international, political, social and moral, scenes. Consider, for example, the issues surrounding nuclear technology, 'alternative medicine,' gay 'marriage' – not the mention the primary question of what God wants of us.

Sources of Knowledge

In the history of the Western world there is no more continuous and momentous struggle over knowledge – who has it and who does not, and what it is – than that between the institutions of the Christian religion and alternative sources of knowledge that arise out of the Renaissance and early modern science and its developments. As the centuries rolled by, these alternative sources of knowledge progressively developed a freestanding intellectual class and took over the institutions of education. The progressive secularization of those institutions culminated, during the late nineteenth and twentieth centuries, in the rejection of religion and its institutions as sources of knowledge about reality and life, and, very largely, as sources of wisdom to guide life. As a part of this process the Christian Bible lost its long held position in Western culture at the center of higher education, as the fundamental avenue to knowledge of ultimate reality and of what is good and right. But the Bible did not go away. It is still here. And, for all the sound and fury, nothing has replaced it as a source of knowledge about life. There is nothing that remotely compares to the biblical figures, stories and teachings as a presence that frames our thought and practice. One has only to look at the facts of street-level culture – TV and cinema, art and magazines – to see that this is so. Yet, the institutional authority concerning what counts as knowledge in our world, the university system with its professional off-shoots, does not accept the Bible as a source of knowledge about life and reality. What happened? Did someone discover that it is not such a source?

I want to say immediately that this was *not* discovered by anyone. Many things were discovered in the course of the historical process referred to, and many things that had been *claimed* to be known by religious leaders and institutions were found out to be false or ill-founded. We gained a great deal of knowledge about the Bible and the church as historical realities. But what really happened to put the Bible in its present position with reference to higher education can be roughly described as follows: A broad-based cultural development occurred, beginning in the 1600s and onward, that created *a set of secular myths*. These became dogma (things unquestionable and unquestioned by those 'in the know') in circles of higher education during the first 60 years of the twentieth century – a period in which, not incidentally, higher education was institutionalizing itself as a freestanding profession, with sub-professions for each academic division.[1]

A favorite mode of secular myth-making is telling a story which supposedly lets you in on the secret of how something came about, in a way that leaves you to think some previously unquestioned teaching is false. This strategy was perfected in the nineteenth century by such thinkers as Nietzsche, a master of retrospective 'debunking.' (Recall his story, told in *The Genealogy of Morals* as well as other works, of how resentful slave-priests inverted the healthy moral values of classical Greece and Rome to make sickly, repressive, Judeo-Christian values supreme.) But one also sees this mode of 'explanation' very clearly in the story — repeatedly presented on Public Television during Christmas and Easter as established truth, or at least an academically 'respectable' position — that the Apostle Paul is responsible for inventing and transmitting the views about Christ that became orthodox Christian teaching. *The Da Vinci Code* is entirely nested in a set of secular myths about religion, the church, and the non-resurrection of Christ that are accepted as authoritative by those 'in the know' and lie unquestioned in the mind of people whose view of truth is shaped by bestsellers and movies.[2] These myths are usually accompanied by powerful images of a pure and brave individual standing against corrupt and oppressive institutions.

The central teachings of the Christian religion (just take the main points of the Apostles' Creed, for example), and the position of the Bible as a source of knowledge, were themselves re-categorized in the late modern period as 'myths' or fabrications, and disengaged from serious knowledge and inquiry. They were replaced by a set of secular stories that have gained the status and power of accepted 'expert knowledge.' Under this re-categorization, the central teachings of the Bible about God, the kingdom of God, and the life, death and resurrection of Jesus Christ, are not matters to be taken with intellectual seriousness. If you do so take them, you *may* be a nice person, but….

Now I reiterate that discoveries of various kinds *were* made, and that these undermined many traditional religious claims, especially about particular teachings and institutions within Christian faith. (One recalls Lorenzo Valla's [1406–1456] momentous discovery, by examination of texts, that the so-

---

[1] You will find most of these secular myths, as I have called them, nicely traced and sympathetically summarized in A.N. Wilson, *God's Funeral*. See also H. de Lubac, *The Drama of Atheist Humanism*.

[2] Including, notably, the new James Cameron sensation, *The Lost Tomb of Jesus*. For an illuminating and humorous take on this type of reasoning, see Charles Lamb's delightful essay, 'Dissertation on a Roast Pig,' first published in the *London Magazine*, September 1822, and republished many times: See Lieder, Lovett and Root, *British Poetry and Prose*, 272–75.

called 'Donation of Constantine,' upon which the church rested its claim to temporal authority, was a forgery.) And Christian personalities and institutions did much to disenchant, or even to disgust, thoughtful people. (One thinks of the brutal but largely truthful chapters 28 and 37 concerning events in Christian history in Gibbon's *The Decline and Fall of the Roman Empire*. Or of Bertrand Russell's many polemical writings on the history and nature of religion.) But none of these amounted to disproof of central Christian teachings, or of the Bible as a reliable source of knowledge, when rightly used, about the most important matters of human life. What we were left with was a set of unsubstantiated 'stories' that eventually gained authority in the institutions of higher education, and had the effect of repositioning Christian and biblical teachings beyond the pale of indispensable sources of knowledge and wisdom. (Nothing better illustrates this than the writings of Ernest Renan and David Strauss, easily accessible in A.N. Wilson's *God's Funeral*.)

The Bible as a Source of Knowledge

What are the issues concerning which the Bible still stands, I claim, as an indispensable source of *knowledge*? (That, of course, is not the same as a source of faith.) They are few but fundamental. Most fields of human knowledge and inquiry have little to learn from the Bible in terms of detailed matters of fact. We can be thankful, in fact, that God did not give Moses or the prophets the multiplication tables or the table of chemical elements, for then we would not be able to teach them in public schools (given current anxieties about the separation of 'church' and 'state'). There are a few basic questions or issues, however, which every society and every individual must answer, if only by how they live. To these, Christ and the Bible offer answers or solutions whose truth can be known through fair inquiry, and which will stand up in the face of the most serious critical examination, since they have been tested over time in the life of humanity, and invite thorough comparison with all alternatives. The questions we must answer, if only by living, are these:

1. What is reality?

This abstract sounding question is actually the most practical question of all. Answers to it determine everything else. Higher education as it now stands pretends not to deal with this question, and does not deal with it *officially*. That, in a way, is quite appropriate. For there is no 'department of reality' to be found in the university. Every 'science,' as Aristotle noted long ago, isolates a particular part of 'what is,' and devotes itself to understanding that. None deals with reality as a whole.[3] This is a simple fact that can be verified by inspection of the cognitive contents of the various sciences. However, the university does *assume* answers to the question about reality, because it offers to prepare people for life. And it is a fraud if it omits some reality that seriously impacts life. (How would the university look if it turned out that there was a God and the single most important thing in life was to live in harmonious relationship with him?) In assuming the irrelevance of God to every field of study, as it routinely does, it offers a teaching about reality, willy-nilly. As Noah Porter, President of Yale in the 1880s, pointed out, every field teaches theology, if only by assuming the non-existence or the irrelevance of God to its subject matter. It does so by claiming *adequacy* for its treatment of its subject matter.[4]

The biblical tradition teaches that reality consists of a personal God and his kingdom (all he arranges for), and that every subject matter of human thought, along with human thought itself, exists within that overarching reality. It clearly indicates that this personal reality can, at least in part, be known, though it also can fail to be known. That is permitted. People can be and often are without knowledge of God. One can – multitudes can – choose to neglect it or purposefully put it out of mind, at least for a while. God does not jump down our throat. Like all knowledge, knowledge of him must be sought.

The university system does not try to answer the general question about reality, and is not equipped to do so. It has no 'theory of everything,' of a kind popularizing books in speculative physics misleadingly claim. But it does by its practice make assumptions about reality as a whole, for which it then fails to take intellectual responsibility. It allows itself to do this, and finds itself 'responsible' in doing so, because of certain stories, myths, and rumors in current circulation. Sometimes these are intellectually incoherent, such as that there was nothing and then there was a Big Bang – or just a very tiny bang. But told often enough these stories *seem* okay. We get used to them. And of course the 'God' route to reality also poses hard intellectual issues. No doubt of that. And, even presupposing knowledge of God and his kingdom, many questions remain about what is 'real.'

---

[3] See the opening lines of Aristotle's *Metaphysics*, Bk. 4: 'There is a science which investigates being as being, and the attributes which belong to this in virtue of its own nature. Now this is not the same as any of the so-called special sciences; for none of these others treats universally of being as being. They cut off a part of being and investigate the attributes of this part; this is what the mathematical sciences for instance do' (trans. W.D. Ross).

[4] See G. Marsden, *The Soul of the American University*,127–28.

2. Who is genuinely well-off?

Who has the good life, the blessed life? Practically, what kind of life should I aim for? Here too the university system assumes answers of various kinds, but does not try to defend them. It assumes answers by what it requires its students to do, and by what it tells parents and society *it* will do for its students and for society. But just as there is no 'reality department,' there is no 'the-good-life department' in the contemporary university. One of the background myths of university life is that there are *many* ways that life can be good. You would think there is one waiting for you around every corner. But when you ask people to give the details on *just one*, very little is forthcoming, and what is presented looks more like a collection of whims and images than a coherent and well-thought-out picture based upon reality as individuals must live in it. Sears offers 'the good life at a great price.' Then there is Starbucks. Is 'the American dream' the good life? Or a life of consuming lots of things? Or a life of public service? Is being liberal or conservative enough? Why *do* winners of elections sing: 'Happy days are here again'?

If you were to sample thought and practice in the colleges and the few universities of the 1800s or earlier, you would find that – except for a few 'advanced' thinkers – the *picture* of the good life that was dominant was overwhelmingly theistic. It was a life lived 'under God.' And this was understood, where genuinely understood, largely in a biblical way, in the manner of the Twenty-Third Psalm and the Lord's Prayer, which everyone knew. Such biblical texts were generally taken as representations of a reality that some people, at least, *knew* to be the case. Or so it was widely thought. The good or blessed life was life in the hands of God. Anyone alive in the kingdom of God is 'blessed,' as Jesus taught. (And at the time he was generally assumed to be a person who *knew* about things, and communicated that knowledge to the world.) This life in the kingdom was an 'eternal' life, in which the individual knew God and his son Jesus Christ, a knowledge gained through an interactive relationship with God in Christ (Jn. 17:3). In the university today there is simply *nothing of this kind with respect to the good life*, religious or otherwise. And there is no serious attempt at it. That is one reason for the prevalence of the flippant and cognitively empty response: 'Oh, there are *many* ways life can be good.'

3. Who is a genuinely good person?

This deep and troubling question seems to press more heavily upon the individual than the previous question about the good life. People desperately want to be good, even though they are prepared 'if necessary' to do what is wrong. To question someone's goodness knifes so deeply into them that this dimension of moral evaluation has almost totally disappeared. It is too sensitive to deal with seriously (even in a provocatively titled book such as Simon Blackburn's recent *Being Good*). And yet the issue remains on the field of human concerns just because *everyone* wants to be, and to be known to be, a morally good person. A notion of moral goodness is profoundly tied to people's sense of worth, to their mental and physical health and to the possibility of genuine community – not least in the university. Yet here too, the world of higher education has nothing to say, or *certainly* nothing to teach, on this subject. There is much talk of rights and of 'ethics,' but of a kind that cannot speak about human goodness or, for example, differentiate between being a good person and a bad person in a professional context. The onlooker might conclude that all human beings are good and that there is no such thing as human evil. That, I think, is pretty much the assumption of higher learning. This is one of the most intriguing features of what is called ethical theory in the university context. It has nothing to say about evil. But how could it be otherwise, since it has nothing to say about who is good?

Of course the biblical teaching when carefully studied centers human goodness on the *agape* kind of love originating with God and extended to and through human beings. The good person, on the biblical view, is the person who is permeated by *agape* love. That kind of love is spelled out in many ways and in many places in the Bible. Love that (in the manner of Christ, who else?) goes the lengths of sacrificial care to the point of death serves as a moral point of reference for human goodness that has few if any serious rivals anywhere in world cultures. The attempt in Western thought from, say, Kant and Mill, to put moral duty and human goodness on any other basis is, to this point, simply a failure, as the latest outstanding efforts (Rawls, MacIntyre, Levinas, etc.) amply testify. As we shall see later, this failure in ethical theory goes hand in hand with a progressive redefinition of what counts as 'knowledge' in the university setting.

4. How does one become a genuinely good person?

This, once again, is a vast and intractable human question. It has obsessed human beings from the point in human development when tribal answers ceased to close it off. Before then, to become a good person was simply to conform to the customs of the tribe. (That type of answer has never totally disappeared, of course.) But what to do when those answers no longer suffice is the problem that gave birth to ethical theory in Socrates, Plato and similarly ancient 'wisdom' figures. It was the one they were *most* concerned to answer, and in pursuit of which they worked out their answers to questions 1–3, above. They thoroughly understood its profound implications for human life, and their successors in the second century and beyond recognized the superiority of the Christian solution to this problem. The problem lives on today in the concerns of our society about *character formation*, everywhere from the lower grades to penal institutions. Nowadays it is often discussed in religious circles – and other contexts where 'human transformation' or 'healing' is at issue – under the heading of 'spiritual formation.' And this problem always intersects with 1–3. Its solution will depend on the answers to the first three questions. That lies in the nature of the case, as any extensive inquiry will verify.

While this fourth question is, arguably, the most urgent for parents and those in places of public leadership and authority, it is the one most earnestly avoided by the magisterium of higher education today. This fact is itself worthy of an inquiry and of development that can't be undertaken in this essay. But it is a fact. Sometimes leaders, such as Derek Bok, have suggested that higher education *ought* to deal with it, but such suggestions never get off the ground. Partly this is because to do so would presuppose a body of moral knowledge to undergird the project, whereas no such body of moral knowledge is now recognized as existing, least of all by university faculty and their guiding lights. And partly it is because the understanding of psychological processes – and of the human self – remains in such a bad way. Another part of the explanation lies in the fact that university faculty have long since disowned, along with the *in loco parentis* role, the project of getting people to be good. A final reason that proposals such as Bok's get nowhere is that such projects are associated with exhortation or, God help us, even *preaching*. We faculty merely help people *think*, you know, and trust them to come to their own conclusions; and any conclusion *they* come to is to be accepted as 'right for them.' We would not want to do anything to intrude upon that individualized process or its outcome. We would not even think the thought that their outcome might be an *error*. It is after all *theirs*.

Now this is very far from how question 4 was approached by traditional colleges and universities as they entered the twentieth century. They, of course, thought they had answers to questions 1–3, largely biblical answers, that amounted to knowledge, and that it would be grossly irresponsible of them *not* to institute and carefully supervise answers to the question of how one becomes a genuinely good person. They normally thought that it was their responsibility to turn out, at least in the sense of 'finishing,' genuinely good people. One of the many excellent things about George Marsden's *The Soul of the American University* is the detail he provides concerning how American colleges of the past carried out this responsibility: what they corporately put into the project of character formation. At the heart of the biblical answer to question 4 lay the idea of the imitation of Christ, or at least of obedience to him. (Even today you will hear non-believers on university campuses criticizing Christians for not being Christlike.) Although this corporate effort often led to quite deplorable versions of self-righteous legalism and Pharisaism, that was generally not the intent. Rather it was hoped that the individual student would be inwardly transformed into a person pervasively possessed of intelligent *agape*. And means of discipline and grace were brought into play to bring *that* about, frequently with remarkable success.

A few clarifications

Now I need to point out a few things I do *not* mean by what I have said about the Bible as an indispensable source of knowledge, and to give some other clarifications. First, I do not mean that just by *studying* the Bible to understand, in a scholarly way, what it says one can come to knowledge on questions 1–4. I suppose it could happen, for when you read the Bible (even not necessarily seriously) you may be drawn into a dynamic field of meanings and influences where God is present, and then, as it were, 'all bets are off.' But you wouldn't want to count on the knowledge in question coming by mere intellectual study. You have to *put into practice* some of the central things you find in the Bible by studying it, or by hearing about it. You have to let yourself be absorbed, to some degree, into the kind of living you see when you study the Bible. You must meditate on the words of the Bible and think deeply about them, and see how what is talked about in the Bible matches up with life.

Second, you probably will not come to know 'on your own.' The Bible lives in a transgenerational community. What one generation sees unclearly and through symbols makes itself present to later generations more fully and forcefully. The Bible itself is fully present only in a historical process. You have to consider that transgenerational community and you have to look at its contemporary alternatives. You come to know the reality of what the Bible talks about by, in some measure, familiarizing yourself with the historical community in which it lives. The *knowledge* that comes from the Bible – as distinct from mere information – will rarely be given without intelligently experiencing some particular form of that historical community. We do not here call that community 'church,' because that is considerably too narrow a term for what we are talking about. But 'church' is relevant, and should not be too readily set aside.

Third, a great deal that is discussed in the Bible will not become a subject of knowledge in our present circumstances. St Thomas Aquinas and many others have insisted that many articles of the Christian faith, while not contrary to reason, are things of which we cannot now have knowledge. Knowledge is a special kind of mental condition, and not everything we can think or believe can be known. 'A man's reach exceeds his grasp,' it is wisely said.[5] Here I have carefully restricted our concern to the four specific areas indicated. My claim is

---

[5] By R. Browning, in his '*Andrea del Sarto*' (1855).

that within these areas, if we use the Bible rightly, it can *guide us into knowledge*. The overall pattern of thinking and experiencing with the Bible that, I say, can guide us into such knowledge is something I have described in my article, 'Language, Being, God, and the Three Stages of Theistic Evidence.'[6] That article, however, does not go into the details of confirmation that comes from *putting the central teachings of the Bible into practice in a communal setting*; such confirmation is a major part of the basis of thought and experience that enables us to represent God as he is. Knowledge of persons is based upon interactions with persons. You don't have to 'buy it before you try it,' and you'd better not. But you do have to get close enough to what you're dealing with to genuinely consider it.

Fourth, knowledge is not the whole of what we as human beings need. It can make us arrogant. But the Bible is of course fully aware of this, and responds to the need expressed by question 4 by abundant teaching on what is needed *in addition to* knowledge, if one is to live in the knowledge of God.

At this point let us pause to get the picture. The institutions of higher education in the Western world were very largely formed around Christian and, mainly, biblical answers to questions 1–4. It was understood that these answers constituted *a body of Christian knowledge*. Within the last century or so, those answers were successfully re-categorized in the public mind so that they are no longer generally regarded as knowledge of how things are, but as, at best, historically created myths with certain emotional and practical associations for people within the Christian community. They have no significance for the guidance of life for people generally. Presently, many who identify with the Christian traditions, in a more or less serious way, agree with this depreciation of Christian knowledge, largely because the 'church' generally takes its direction from the university in intellectual matters. To summarize my point so far: *In the place of the Christian answers, the 'modern' intellect and the university system and its offshoots have developed no generally credible alternative answers – nothing that you could seriously teach as course content and grade students on, or publish in a peer review journal as a 'finding.'* So the university lives without intellectually responsible answers to 1–4.

A Brief History of 'Knowledge'

In order to see what has happened to bring us to this point, we have to look at what might be called the history of 'knowledge,' from, shall we say, Descartes to postmodernism. For most of human history the primary source of knowledge with regard to the four questions has been authority: the authority of people who are older and of people in positions of power. The authority of the

---

[6] In Moreland and Nielsen, *Does God Exist?*

positions and the authority for what was claimed to be knowledge were usually said to come from God, and, all humor aside, it is hard to imagine a better authority than that if God is really the source. But of course authority is not always what it claims to be, and in late medieval and early modern times a lot of 'authoritative' teaching was found to be false. Everyone then knew that, whatever it was, *that* teaching couldn't be knowledge. People turned to rational method or 'reason,' in Descartes and after. This in turn became an authority that proved to be capable of results that were false. And finally we as a culture turned to sense experience or observation as setting the boundaries of reality and knowledge – not, of course, totally excluding authority and reason, but placing firm boundaries, it was thought, on what they could claim. This was empiricism, primarily in the form given to it by John Locke and then – quite differently – by David Hume.

The process was complicated, of course, but the outcome was the emergence of types of methods that characterized the particular sciences, especially mechanics, then later physics and chemistry, biology and so forth. These methods achieved great things in their proper areas. A vague but powerful idea of 'scientific methodology' came to the fore, and claims to knowledge had to be measured by their conformity or lack of conformity to 'scientific method.' This became a very powerful force against traditional knowledge in all its forms – and, of course, in many respects it was a very beneficent force. But, like all claimed sources of knowledge in the past, it overreached and became imperialistic. It neglected the long-standing idea, stemming originally from Aristotle, that the subject matter of the inquiry must dictate the method of the inquiry, and not the other way round. Largely because of its practical applications and benefits, the method appropriate to the 'natural' sciences was eventually taken by many to be *the* method of knowledge. And anything not derived by that method, or something arguably like it, was rejected as not being genuine knowledge at all; what in the past had been regarded as knowledge, but was now regarded as pseudo-knowledge because of its 'unscientific' character, was rejected as non-existent or at least of no significance. The effect of this shift on human life is devastating. For most, if not all, of the things that matter most to human beings are not subjects of anything like scientific methodology, and hence, if the reigning assumptions about knowledge are true, they are not subjects of knowledge and perhaps do not even exist – they are at most, in contemporary language, just 'constructs' of the human mind or language. This is postmodernism in its most basic epistemological sense.

What this meant for *institutional policy* in the American universities has been carefully studied by the historian Julie Reuben. In her indispensable book, *The Making of the Modern University*, she tells the story of how theology and then morality were forced out of the fields of knowledge – out of 'course content' – by the *institutional* developments of the leading universities of this country. She does this on the basis of careful study of the internal documents and the public speeches and writings of university presidents and other leaders of education. The story is in fact not terribly complicated. Theology was dropped from course content because so much of what theologians taught *was* just tradition, usually keyed to a particular denominational group, and hence really did not amount to knowledge at all. As what 'had to be held,' it was not open to question or research. The theological distinctives maintained in the colleges (some of which were really trivialities) had to be dismissed, but in the process they took the more fundamental issues of Christian theology – 'mere' Christianity, as C. S. Lewis called it – with them. (Post-Civil War industrialization and the professionalization of public life was, in any case, moving education more toward scientific and technical expertise.)

The teaching of morality had been largely based, rightly or wrongly, upon the theological teachings, and so it too was progressively swept from course content, and finally, administratively, over into 'student life.' The story Reuben tells of the progression – in which administrators first looked to the natural sciences as the teacher of morality (after all, their goal was truth, was it not?), and then to the social sciences, and then to the arts and humanities, each in turn opting out of the job – is itself an outstanding contribution to knowledge. But the overall point of the story, as Reuben brings out clearly, is that what was happening was not just a rejection of theology and moral teachings, but *a shifting of the understanding of knowledge itself*, and of research, in such a way that moral teachings no longer could count as cognitive content for which students or faculty could be held responsible. The somewhat later emergence of philosophical non-cognitivism in theology and morality, in the forms of existentialism and logical positivism, was really an expression of what had *already* happened institutionally. She does not say this, for her research does not reach right up to the present, but this is also certainly true of the later postmodernism, in its philosophical forms. It is a philosophical expression of what has *already* taken place institutionally.[7]

The effect of the historical progression in Western intellectual life and in higher education to the present is that knowledge itself, along with truth, disappears from the university setting *as a goal*. All that remains is *interpretation* and *theory*. 'Truth' is the butt of constant cynicism and ridicule, if it is so much as mentioned. The top of the line now is a *research* university, and what validates

---

[7] As Hegel famously said: 'Philosophy, as the thought of the world, does not appear until reality has completed its formative process, and made itself ready.... When philosophy paints its grey in grey, one form of life has become old, and by means of grey it cannot be rejuvenated, but only known. The owl of Minerva takes its flight only when the shades of night are gathering' (concluding the 'Preface' to his *Philosophy of Right*).

you as a faculty member is not knowledge but research. Being renowned for knowledge would be a very marginal compliment. What research could be without knowledge and truth (or at least falsity) has never been explained, but in the hands of the highly influential critical theorists (Frankfurt School etc.), research is just one type of *social ferment*. This view is nicely presented in Jean-François Lyotard's book, *The Postmodern Condition: A Report on Knowledge*. The 'report' – a study produced at the request of the 'Conseil des Universites' of the Government of Quebec, which asked for an account of the state of knowledge in the Western world – is, frankly, that *nothing like knowledge as traditionally understood remains at the heart of the universities*. Instead we have investigative 'ferment' governed by paralogy and power. (Paralogism: 'fallacious or illogical reasoning; especially, a faulty argument of whose fallacy the reasoner is not aware [*American Heritage Dictionary*, 1981].) Lyotard's *Report* agrees with much now said about the current processes and standards of academic life by other postmodernist writers, such as Richard Rorty. As descriptions of current academic life in general, I must say that they are largely correct. This means that what one is responsible to in 'research' is not truth or knowledge or old-fashioned logic. Such notions are frankly boring and/or pretentious. Rather, what is 'interesting,' 'challenging,' 'provocative,' and so forth – purely social phenomena – are rewarded by attention, at least, and possibly by position and money.

In the first of *The Screwtape Letters*, C.S. Lewis has Screwtape advise his protégé, Wormwood, not to try to use *argument* to keep his 'patient' securely on the road to Hell. That might have worked 'a few centuries earlier,' Screwtape says, when 'humans still knew pretty well when a thing was proved and when it was not; and if it was proved they really believed it…and were prepared to alter their way of life as the result of a chain of reasoning.' No longer, the advice continues:

Your man has been accustomed, ever since he was a boy, to having a dozen incompatible philosophies dancing about together inside his head. He doesn't think of doctrines as primarily 'true' or 'false,' but as 'academic' or 'practical,' 'outworn' or 'contemporary,' 'conventional' or 'ruthless'. Jargon, not argument, is your best ally in keeping him from the church. Don't waste time trying to make him think that materialism is *true*! Make him think it is strong or stark or courageous – that it is the philosophy of the future. That's the sort of thing he cares about.

The condition of the 'patient' here described is precisely the one celebrated in the academy today, though of course the jargon is changed. But freedom *from* knowledge, truth and argument (in the normative sense it still had in Lewis's day) has even greater play now, and methodology that has the appearance of discipline is very often the reflection of an investigative fad inculcated by some glittering personality – phenomenology, structuralism, post-structuralism, deconstructionism, analytic philosophy, 'ordinary language,' 'conceptual analysis,' and so forth. One draws comfort and assurance that one's work is somehow 'okay' because it fits into the flow with some such social tendency. (Of course there are individual exceptions to all of this.)

The greatest issue facing the individual in the academy today is whether there is really anything more to it than that. This issue is much greater than that of the place of the Bible in the life of the intellect. One does have to make one's way, and that means coming to grips with how things are. How they *really* are. How they *truly* are. How one *knows* them to be. Rorty, famously if not fatuously, says that 'truth' is what your colleagues allow you to get away with saying. Is that so? Or is it just another thrust in the social flow of professionalized academic life? Clearly he thinks it is true, which must mean, then, that it is something that his colleagues allow him to get away with saying. It depends on who your colleagues are. But of course he believes his statement is *true*, and not just permitted. He believes that his saying presents the situation in academic life *as it really is*, and on the basis of appropriate thought and experience. If it were 'true' in the sense he states, it wouldn't be worth stating, and few people would care. But he really does care, and he thinks he has achieved valid insight into how things are. That, of course, is *knowledge* in the time-honored sense in which knowledge is necessary to human life.

We do not really have time and space here to go over the process that led from St Thomas Aquinas to Descartes, to Hume and Kant, and on to Rorty and Lyotard. The process historically culminates in a condition – *truly* the postmodern condition – where we do not have knowledge of knowledge, there is no acceptable truth about truth, and methodology is, with little exception, a matter of a modish practice with no point of reference above the surrounding social flow. Some really helpful explanatory and critical writing has been done on this process, notably the works of Edmund Husserl (especially *The Crisis of European Sciences and Transcendental Phenomenology*) and Michael Polanyi (beginning with *The Tacit Dimension*). Neither thinker comes through the cacophony of twentieth century thought very clearly. But what they have to say on the fate of knowledge and truth in the contemporary university, and the baleful effects of core confusions about science, knowledge and truth, makes them necessary companions for anyone concerned about the integrity of the university and the intellect, especially for anyone concerned about religion and the role of the Bible in the intellectual life.

For our present purposes, what must be done is to establish – or at least to offer – a workable idea of knowledge that is suited both to ordinary life and to work in any professional setting. We need to understand knowledge in such a way that both its presence and its absence can be recognized and dealt with by the people who pay for the university and upon whose backs the intellectual rides through life. It must be an understanding that motivates serious efforts toward knowledge, such as is relevant to our initial questions 1–4, as well as to all matters of technical detail in any specific area where one has to be responsible. It must be one that accounts for the fact that we as academics do possess knowledge, which we discover, learn, communicate to our students, test for in our students, and evaluate degrees of in an oral examination or a research project or book. It has to make sense of our selections of course content and of how we grade papers. That is our business as university faculty. Here 'postmodernism' has no more legitimate place than if one were landing an airplane or negotiating fringe benefits or repairing automobiles. I believe this formulation meets the need: *A person has knowledge of a certain subject matter if they are capable of representing it as it is on an appropriate basis in thought or experience.*

Knowing vs. Not-Knowing

If you reflect on how you draw the distinction – as you certainly do – between knowing and not knowing, for yourself and others, and between those who do know in a certain area and those who do not, you will see, I think, that this understanding of knowledge is the one we apply. That does not mean that such application is always easy – though often it is – or that we are ever infallible in our applications. Often we do not know whether we or someone else, or humankind generally, has knowledge on a certain point. But there are many clear cases, and these guide us to a reliable understanding of what knowledge is. Some further observations:

(a) When someone represents something *as it is not* – and this itself is something we frequently know happens – then he or she does not *know* with reference to that particular subject matter. Such failure is, in large part, what led to the breakdown of confidence in the authority of ecclesiastical institutions in the late medieval period, and it is the key to how we grade papers and evaluate physicians and automobile mechanics. However 'good' they may be in other respects, when they 'get it wrong' they do not know. You cannot know a thing that is in fact false. Reputation for knowledge does not guarantee knowledge. And being wrong with regularity undermines one's status as an authority for knowledge.

(b) Knowledge, when real, guarantees truth. But neither truth (as in a good guess), nor the best evidence humanly available, taken separately, guarantees knowledge. There is no general characterization of 'an appropriate basis in thought or experience.' One of the illusions of the ages is the quest for such a completely general, fail-safe characterization: what John Dewey called 'the quest for certainty.' You can know and not be 'certain' and you can be certain and not know. Certainty is neither a necessary nor a sufficient condition of knowledge.

(c) Knowledge does not require or guarantee infallibility. We often know in cases where, given appropriate circumstances, we could be wrong, though we are not. This is actually the usual case in ordinary life. It does not imply that we do not know, just that we might not: it is *possible*, even though we do have knowledge, that we are representing things as they are not or that our basis is not adequate, or both.

(d) The possession of knowledge (not just true belief) confers the right, and often the responsibility, to act, to lead, and to prescribe policy. It confers authority, including the authority to teach. Most of what human beings know they know by authority. That is still true today. Good authority is essential to human life. Good authority is always open to question, which need not be an attack. It accepts the fact that it might be wrong. The familiar bumper-sticker that says 'Question Authority' is fine, so long as that includes 'Question This Bumper Sticker,' for questioning authority has now become an authority in its own right, and one which usually goes unquestioned, or even resists being questioned.

(e) Knowledge, or presumed knowledge, routinely leads to arrogance. What it involves is so important that people cannot, without great grace and intentionality, divorce their ego from it. To be out of 'the know' diminishes us in our own eyes and before others. To know is to be in a 'better' position than those who do not know. Thus the Apostle Paul's statement that 'Knowledge puffs up.' Well he knew! And thus 'humbleness of mind' was for him a primary ethical virtue. The arrogance humanly associated with knowledge and truth is, curiously, one of the factors which has led to their being overtly disowned in intellectual settings. We still believe, generally, that arrogance is bad. But overall, arrogance seems to have diminished little as a result of our abandoning knowledge and truth in favor of 'research.'

(f) Knowledge as such, knowledge and truth by their very nature, do not rule any particular area of life and reality out – or in – as domains of possible knowledge, and they do not restrict knowledge to what is attained by some particular method. Any decision about what can be known or not, and how or not, is to be settled by examination of the facts of the case. Whether there can be knowledge of God, for example, and whether the Bible might be somehow central to the way such knowledge is to be attained, are matters to be settled by inquiry, and inquiry in general is not something one can lay *a priori* limitations on. Inquiry is a muddling sort of thing, full of unexpected discoveries, accidents and inspirations. Honest history of science makes that clear in the case of the particular sciences. For most subject matters inquiry is transgenerational, and something one could never write a methodology for.

In our day, particularly, there is a great illusion in the university and culture about *the* 'scientific method,' and about whether something is 'science' or not. There is, we may be sure, no such thing as 'science' in general, and to proclaim that something is or is not 'science' or 'scientific' – especially if it is a question or an issue – has no bearing on whether it has to do with knowledge and truth. Things have been 'scientific' – taken to be the best science of the day – and also wildly false. Geocentrism was not just a stupid mistake, but the result of serious science. One of the things for which we are indebted to postmodernist thinkers is their blowing of the whistle on the illegitimate claims of 'science' to have a corner on knowledge and truth – or on 'the' method or methods of research. There are of course scien*ces* (not just science) and they all have a legitimate subject matter and proven methodologies regarding that particular subject matter. But intellectual work will always be much broader than the particular sciences, and intellectual method will always have to be dictated by the particular subject matters in question. To try to characterize an 'adequate basis in thought or experience' in terms of methods derived from some particular science or sciences is at best groundless, and can be something little short of idolatry. In any case, it is always an error. And we must never allow the politics of knowledge (and reputation for knowledge) to escape our scrutiny. Reason is a fragile human capacity that has little power to resist social pressures, even if it calls itself by a fashionable term such as 'scientific inquiry.'

(g) In general, knowledge does not offer itself freely or mechanically to those in the human condition. One should not be surprised if this is true of the knowledge of God, or with respect to the four questions we have enumerated as central to human need. Man is an essentially challenged being, always on a path, *Homo Viator*. There is therefore some point (though also some danger) to Lessing's saying that if God offered him truth in one hand, and pursuit of truth in the other, he would take the pursuit of truth. (In this way, of course, he is presenting us with a truth he has, and is not 'pursuing.')

Knowledge and truth are things that have to be *endured*. Stories such as Faust, Frankenstein and the Sorcerer's Apprentice well up from deep within the human psyche. They deal with the threats of unleashed desire when empowered by knowledge. Perhaps a good way to think about the expanse of human history is to see it as an extended opportunity to form collective and individual character that can accept and can safely use knowledge when it comes. (We're obviously not doing so well with this, one might think.) The principle of the 'fullness of time' applies broadly to human affairs and innovations.

Knowledge of the God who Hides

This we must accept, then, as a general principle about knowledge: It is not always good to have it, and it needs to come in suitable ways. There are special considerations when it comes to knowledge of God, and these suggest some things that might lead to a theology of the Bible itself, as it actually exists among us. Suppose for a moment that there is such a God as the Bible reveals: one of unlimited intelligence, power and love, with the highest possible intentions for humanity and creation. How would he be present to a humanity in flight from him? One might at first think: *overwhelmingly!* (We might imagine Jesus going back to Pilate or the Chief Priest after his resurrection and saying: 'Now, shall we have that conversation again?') But would that accomplish what he has in mind for human beings in his cosmos? What would the result be? People intimidated into submission, no doubt. Cringing cinders. Robots. Persons totally dominated by fear, unable to have a vision of good to be accomplished or to take initiative toward it. Not a notably glorious outcome. Not a community of love inhabited by the Triune God himself, absorbed in a tremendously creative team effort, with unimaginably splendid leadership, on an inconceivably vast plane of activity, with ever more comprehensive cycles of productivity and enjoyment, where power and character are forever adequate to each other. Imagine that God seeks people to involve as his admiring and trusted and trusting co-workers in a cosmoswide, cooperative pursuit of a created order that continuously approaches but never reaches the limitless goodness and greatness of the triune personality of God, its source. He wants to grow us to the point where he can empower us to do what *we* want. So the character of our wanting is what he must deal with by *how* he comes to us. The diffuse and fugitive presence of the Bible on earth, which we see to be the case, might not be such a bad idea.

C.S. Lewis again gives us (in *The Screwtape Letters*) some language that seems to capture the delicacy involved in God making himself known to bring people to himself:

> You [Wormwood] must have often wondered why the enemy [God] does not make more use of his power to be sensibly present to human souls in any degree he chooses and at any moment. But now you see that the irresistible and the indisputable are the two weapons which the very nature of his scheme forbids him to use. Merely to over-ride a human will (as his felt presence in any but the faintest and most mitigated degree would certainly do) would be for him useless. He cannot ravish. He can only woo. For his ignoble idea is to eat the cake and have it; the creatures are to be one with him, but yet be themselves; merely to cancel them, or assimilate them, will not serve.... Sooner or later he withdraws, if not in fact, at least from their conscious experience, all supports and incentives. He leaves the creature to

stand up on its own legs – to carry out from the will alone duties which have lost all relish…. He cannot 'tempt' to virtue as we do to vice. He wants them to learn to walk and must therefore take away his hand…. Our cause is never more in danger than when a human, no longer desiring, but still intending, to do our enemy's will, looks round upon a universe from which every trace of him seems to have vanished, and asks why he has been forsaken, and still obeys' (Letter VIII).

God is not obvious, not even in the Bible, which offers so many opportunities for man to go wrong – as history and contemporary events surely witness. This is an undeniable fact, which is absolutely consistent with the further idea that he can be found, and found in the Bible also. By seeking. *Deus absconditus* is a deep theological principle. Isaiah cries out in amazement from his own experience: 'Truly, Thou art a God who hides Himself, O God of Israel, Savior!' (45:15). He reveals himself, and uniquely in the Bible, but in a way that allows him to be hidden to all but those who resolutely seek him (30:20, Job 23:9–10). One can deny God. That is a choice. But it is a choice that *he* has made possible. It would have been a mere trifle for him to have made it *im*possible.

Sir Robert Anderson says, opening chapter 13 of his *The Silence of God*, 'When faith murmurs and unbelief revolts, and men challenge the Supreme to break that silence and declare Himself, how little do they realize what the challenge means! It means the withdrawal of the amnesty; it means the end of the reign of grace; it means the closing of the day of mercy and the dawning of the day of wrath.' It means human life as we know it is *over*.

The distance of God, his *un*obviousness, is God's way of making himself available without destroying us. Job, who certainly knew the hiddenness, comments on God's works in nature, and then exclaims: 'These are some of the minor things he does, merely a whisper of his power. Who then can withstand his thunder?' (26:14). It was well-known biblical wisdom that no one can see God and continue to live. The sight would kill the human being who had the experience. Men have died from much less. Imagine 'getting intimate' with our sun, hardly a speck of God's nature and power.

But it is also true that God wants us to *want him*. He does not want to be present where he is not wanted. That is the way it is with spiritual beings, God or man. There was a famous discussion between Father Copleston and Bertrand Russell. Toward the conclusion Copleston asked Russell what he would say if he died and found himself standing before God. Russell replied, 'I would ask him why he did not give me more evidence.' If the hints above are on the right track, God might well answer that that would not have allowed Russell to follow his desires. What those desires were are fairly obvious from Russell's own autobiographical writings, and now also from those who have written his biography: they were not pretty, to say the least.

Now if we were to develop a theology about the Bible from these suggestions, we might come to say that the position of the Bible in the world, and in
the university today, is *exactly what God has chosen*. We suppose that had he
wanted something different – if something else would have been more suitable
– he would have arranged that. Perhaps not in every detail, but in general for
sure. Let us think the thought that the nature and position of the Bible in our
world is exactly suited to God's purposes with his project in history. It is a communal, transgenerational presence which fans out across the world in many
forms, and allows, but does not impose, growth in the knowledge of God, or of
human well-being and well-doing, for those who seek to know him. It allows
human responsibility for the earth to have a guide, but also allows human
beings to worship and serve themselves and other idols – indeed, to do this with
Bible in hand and in mouth. Humans are even allowed to make the Bible itself
a kind of idol. (Think of what it would mean for human affairs if someone actually had the 'originals.')

The epistemology of the Bible, how it provides knowledge of God and
human life, must follow the theology of the Bible. The Bible comes through
human history like a comet comes through space, dragging a great tail: a great
tail of causes and effects, of historical events and institutional accretions, of
interpretations and misinterpretations, encompassing and trailing a solid core
of knowledge. The knowledge that comes through the Bible is gentle. It fans
out through personalities, families, events, art works and national symbols and
rituals. It does not just state truths and invite us to verify and know them; it uses
every possible mode of projection and presentation to draw us into the reality
of which it speaks: image, story, art, metaphor, ritual, event, not just *in* the
Bible but projected from it into the rich texture of life around it.

My primary concern is to state that the Bible is a source of possible knowledge with reference to the Christian answers to the questions 1–4. Perhaps it
provides much more than this, but I am purposefully setting aside other issues
to concentrate on it as a source of knowledge. My claim is that one can come to
know – in the sense of 'know' explained above – the truths of the Christian
answers, as explained above, to the four major questions of life. I do not claim
that people can be forced to know the truth of those answers, or to believe
them, or even consider them. But if one is willing for those answers to be true,
and if one also seeks to know them through all available avenues of authority,
reason and experience – including, of course, careful study of the Bible itself –
then they will be able to represent God and the well-being and goodness of
man as they are, on an appropriate basis of thought and experience. The intellectual dogmas and myths of our age do not even *begin* to show that this claim
about knowledge and the Bible are false.

The Task of the Christian Intellectual

Now we might ask: What is to be done about our current situation by those who agree with me and who also are involved in the university and its intellectual and social life?

The first thing we must do, in my opinion, is to work out in our own mind a view of what knowledge and truth are and how they relate to our academic and intellectual business. This is not a peculiarly Christian project, but concerns, in John Henry Newman's language, 'The Idea of the University.' I do think that Christians might be in a better position to address it than almost anyone else, because they have a place to stand *outside* the university, in the historic Christian tradition and its institutions. To be sure, this tradition and these institutions are far from perfect, and often fly off the track of truth in the service of God and of human good, but they also retain objectively testable points of reference that transcend the political, economic and social currents in which the university is currently submerged. When you look honestly at that tradition, is there anything to compare with it and its witness to history, everything considered?

Now it is true that very few universities, as they now stand, and very few institutions that are identified as Christian, would dare to take and defend the position, as institutions, that there is a body of Christian knowledge ('mere' Christianity in some specification – let's leave aside the 'denominational distinctives'!) that can be taught *as* knowledge and implemented in practice *as* a unique, irreplaceable and vital resource for corporate and individual life today. The idea of the Bible as a source of knowledge about anything would be even more outrageous. The power structures of the academic professions and the socialization of faculty as they go through graduate school hermetically seal the mind against any such thing, making it unthinkable.

But that is, after all, contrary to the fundamental ideal of fair and thorough inquiry. So those individuals who do believe that the Bible is a source of truth about the fundamental issues of life must assume a scholarly idealism in their life and work, and present their views when and where it is appropriate, in the spirit and humility – dare we say the *intelligence*? – of Christ. I do not think this should be done in an attitude of evangelism or apologetics. It should be done in exactly the same attitude of inquiry that characterizes intellectual and artistic work at its best in any context. Good work is what is needed, whatever the field, with patience and with confidence that the God who has come to us through the Bible will be with us and act with us. We should not be bent on *making things happen*, in my opinion, but should leave that entirely to God. Then we should do our best at what we do. And where the Bible is in any way relevant we include it because it is relevant to our subject matter.

We also, as Christian intellectuals, have a standing in the community, in our church connections, perhaps, but also in other venues. We can write and speak

to the larger public that is not bowed down under the standards of 'respectability' and intellectual self-righteousness from which the university now irratio-
nally suffers. Here we must not forget what God can do in conjunction with us
to disrupt the power of the secular myths mentioned earlier.

Finally, there is no reason to think of the universities as *the* institutions of
knowledge in society. They have their place, but knowledge is far too important to be left to the universities. Christian institutions, speaking generally,
have failed their calling as institutions of knowledge, from the Sunday school to
the Divinity School. They – and the Christian pulpit – now stand obsequiously
before the universities and the professions, in servile complaisance. It is a tragic
situation, for the very matters on which 'the church,' to speak loosely, is supposed to bring knowledge are the ones that the university is, by its own admis-
sions, incapable of dealing with. It was never called to be the light of the world
or to be the guide of human life. It only caught *that* idea of itself while it was
operating under the aegis of Jesus Christ. It has stumbled into a position it does
not have the spiritual and intellectual resources to handle. I expect this to
become increasingly obvious in years to come.

Bibliography

Anderson, R., *The Silence of God* (Grand Rapids: Kregel, 1978)

Aristotle, *The Basic Works of Aristotle*, ed. R. McKeon (New York: Random House, 1941)

Blackburn, S., *Being Good: A Short Introduction to Ethics* (Oxford: University Press, 2001)

De Lubac, H., *The Drama of Atheist Humanism*, trans. E.M. Riley (New York: Sheed and Ward, 1950; repr. Ignatius, 1995)

Hegel, G.W. F., *Philosophy of Right*, trans. S.W. Dyde (London: George Bell and Sons, 1896)

Horkheimer, M., *Critical Theory: Selected Essays,* trans. M.J. O'Connell, et al. (New York: Herder and Herder, 1972)

Husserl, E., *The Crisis of European Sciences and Transcendental Phenomenology* (Evanston, IL: Northwestern University Press, 1970)

Lewis, C.S., *The Screwtape Letters* (New York: Macmillan, 1962; many other editions)

Lieder, P.R., R.M. Lovett, and R.K. Root (eds.), *British Poetry and Prose*, 3rd edn. (Boston: Houghton Mifflin, 1950)

Lyotard, J.-F., *The Postmodern Condition: A Report on Knowledge* (Minneapolis:University of Minnesota Press, 1984)

Marsden, G.M., *The Soul of the American University: From Protestant Establishment to Established Nonbelief* (New York and Oxford: Oxford University Press, 1994)

Polanyi, M., *The Tacit Dimension* (Garden City, NY: Doubleday Anchor, 1967)

Reuben, J.A., *The Making of the Modern University* (Chicago and London: The University of Chicago Press, 1996)

Willard, D., 'Language, Being, God, and the Three Stages of Theistic Evidence' in *Does God Exist: The Great Debate*, ed. J. P. Moreland and K. Nielsen (Nashville: Thomas Nelson Publishers, 1990)

—, *The Divine Conspiracy* (San Francisco: HarperSanFrancisco, 1998)

Wilson, A.N., *God's Funeral* (New York and London: Norton, 1999)

2

Scripture and Christian Theology
William J. Abraham

An Important Platitude

It is a platitude in Christian theology that Scripture plays a pivotal role in the origins and warrants of Christian doctrine. Until the modern period this platitude was pretty much central to the heartbeat of theology in the West, that is, in both Protestant and Catholic theology. To question this basic epistemological assumption, that Scripture is the crucial if not the only norm of Christian theology, was to be outside the pale.

This disposition to look to Scripture as a foundation for theology fitted nicely with an epistemological conception of Scripture. Scripture was read first and foremost as both source and norm of Christian theological proposals. The very sense of canon was articulated in terms of Scripture being a criterion; and Scripture also fixed the reference for canon, in that the canon was constituted by Scripture. This did not preclude appeal to other epistemic norms, such as tradition, but tradition was carefully subordinated to the canon of Scripture even in those communities that gave a high place to tradition. Effectively, tradition was a hermeneutical norm for getting at the meaning of Scripture.[1]

To be sure, other sorts of readings were permitted, so that one could read Scripture for devotional purposes, seeking in Scripture food for the soul, encouragement for the journey of faith, and comfort in sorrow. Indeed it was impossible to eliminate such appropriation of Scripture because, after all, Scripture is the foundation text for Christian preaching. Preaching necessarily has devotional overtones and aims; preaching is not simply lecturing, but is a practice aimed at cultivating the life of faith. Yet, as can be seen in the long-standing polemic against allegorical readings of Scripture and against pietism, such readings were often frowned upon. At the very least, devotional and

---

[1] The turn to tradition was, of course, a dead end, requiring the development of papal infallibility as a way of resolving disputes between rival interpretive traditions.

homiletical usage of Scripture should presuppose a literal sense of Scripture as the normative foundation for Christian faith and practice. To this end theologians created the discipline of biblical studies in order to ensure that the foundational work on which they relied was executed with proper skill and care.

The Creation of Biblical Studies

An epistemological vision of Scripture clearly shaped the curricula of Protestant faculties of theology. In the Reformed, Lutheran, and Anglican traditions it was agreed that one should begin one's theological studies by learning the relevant original languages and then settle in to a detailed study of the scriptural texts. The result was the founding of intellectual disciplines devoted to a book. So we have chairs of Biblical Studies, of the Interpretation of Scripture, of the Old and New Testaments, of Biblical Languages, of Biblical Theology, and so on. It is surely odd in the extreme that we have professors of a book, or even parts of a book. Yet it strikes no one as incongruous that this is the case, for the oddity made sense in a theological world where the initial and indispensable work in Christian theology lay in the careful study of Scripture conceived as a norm that gave us access to the full round of truth about God and everything else insofar as it related to God. Other disciplines in the world of theological encyclopedia, that is, church history, systematic theology, practical theology, and the like, were always secondary if not parasitic on biblical studies. Some sub-disciplines, like philosophical theology, were entirely optional; indeed philosophical theology might well be treated with hostility because it can readily become a rival 'fundamental theology,' where fundamental issues are treated as lying outside the purview of biblical studies.

The epistemological primacy of biblical studies was confirmed by the ready place given to Scripture by systematic theology. Indeed over time the loci of systematic theology were expanded to include complex *prolegomenae* whose primary purpose was to lay out and defend a vision of Scripture as the critical norm for all theology. This looks straightforward on the surface; after all, the task of the systematic theologian lies on the other side of biblical studies, so let each be done in its own time and season. However, this leaves systematic theology unstable and secondary. The theologian must not only await the findings of biblical studies but also be constantly prepared to revise the content of systematic theology. Clearly this leaves the structure and content of systematic theology up for grabs. Theology must now come to terms with a permanent revolution in its domain.

My favorite piece of evidence for this enduring disruption within theology is the impassioned plea that shows up in the Scottish tradition. I invite the reader to pause and ponder what will happen once we follow the mandate of the hardy writers of the Scot's Confession (1560).

> If any man will note in our Confession any chapter or sentence contrary to God's Holy Word, that it would please him of his gentleness and for Christian charity's sake to inform us of it in writing; and we, upon our honor, do promise him that by God's grace we shall give him satisfaction from the mouth of God, that is, from Holy Scripture, or else we shall hereafter alter whatever he can prove to be wrong.[2]

There is, of course, no end to the altering, as the subsequent history of Protestant theology makes clear.

Initially the acute difficulty that this kind of plea introduces into theology can readily be concealed. So long as biblical scholars buy into the favored creedal or confessional commitments of the day, biblical scholars and systematic theologians can paper over the revolutionary consequences of an epistemic conception of Scripture, and this was successfully done for centuries. However, once a serious clash between biblical scholars and theologians arose, the cat was out of the bag, and it was always going to be a challenge to catch her and put her firmly back in place. Cats are, after all, promiscuous and elusive by nature.

In reality modern biblical studies arose as a massive effort to get free of the strictures of systematic theology. Systematic theology came to be seen as a narrow-minded parent that undercut the freedom of the biblical scholar. Happily, the rebellious children could move beyond rebellion and appeal to a core conviction of the parents, for biblical scholarship was set up by theologians in the first place precisely to discover the content of Scripture. Once established, the core problem for biblical scholarship was this: systematic theology was seen as placing constraints on the study of the Bible that undercut the proper study and place of Scripture in Christian theology. The constraints were of two radically different kinds. One constraint was derived from theories of inspiration that required that the study of Scripture be conducted with a hermeneutic of epistemic generosity, that is, that Scripture be read, say, as historically, morally, and theologically inerrant, infallible, reliable, or in some other praiseworthy manner.

A second and very different constraint was that Scripture should be read in such a way as to underwrite the ancient creedal faith of the Church or of the pertinent confessions of modern Christian denominations. Biblical scholars therefore came under suspicion if their findings were incompatible with this or that first-order vision of Christian theology. Yet Christian theology itself required that biblical studies be primary, so biblical scholars had theology itself on their side; they were simply carrying out the academic mandate set for them

---

[2] Quoted in B.A. Gerrish, *Saving and Secular Faith, An Invitation to Systematic Theology* (Minneapolis: Fortress, 1999), 61.

by an epistemic vision of their materials. Thus from the beginning it was clear that biblical scholarship had the upper hand in the debate with theology; theologians by their own canons of thinking had agreed on the foundational nature of Scripture, so those who studied Scripture had to be given the first if not the last word in theology.

The Unexpected Disaster

It would be tedious and beyond my competence to unpack the story that unfolds within the horizon I have just sketched.[3] We cannot appreciate the hopes engendered by the rise of biblical studies as a logically distinct but not separate sub-discipline within theological studies without a creative act of imagination. Nowhere is this clearer than within Protestantism where the scholarly industry in and around Scripture has been so impressive. The end result, however, has been disastrous for theology. The outcome is now clear: biblical studies no longer acts as a feeder discipline for theology. It has become a region of expertise on its own that is carefully guarded by the scholarly guilds. It is rare in the extreme for a theologian to be allowed to teach a course on Scripture; in most cases theologians would, as a matter of professional conscience, refuse that option where it given them. More importantly, there are simply no secure results that the theologian can now rely on in the foundations of his or her work. We simply have a Babel of voices in the biblical studies guild; and theologians are in no position to adjudicate the alternatives.

Karl Rahner captures the crisis clearly:

> When you [biblical exegetes] simply leave the work of bridging the gap between exegesis and dogmatic theology conveniently to us, and we poor dogmatic theologians want to take up this work (and have then to concern ourselves also with exegesis, since a bridge crosses from one bank to another) then you are the first to shout – admit it – that we dogmatic theologians understand nothing about exegesis, and that it would be far better if we left it alone rather than dabbling in it in a clumsy sort of way! Who then is to do this job that must be done? You behave rather strangely sometimes in this matter. On the one hand, you complain that too little attention is being paid to the Scriptures, that there is too much scholastic theology and not enough biblical theology. But then, when it comes to the point where it would be necessary to show how and where in the Scriptures the Church's teaching finds its expression or at least its ultimate basis, you begin to excuse yourselves and declare that even with the best will in the world you cannot find anything in the Scripture which would serve as a basis for the teaching of the Church.[4]

---

[3] J. Barr's *The Concept of Biblical Theology* (Minneapolis: Fortress, 1999) is a landmark study, the fruit of a lifetime's ruminations.

[4] K. Rahner, 'Exegesis and Dogmatic Theology,' in *Theological Investigations*, vol. 5 (London: Dartman, Longman, and Todd, 1966), 71–72.

The general situation is, of course, complicated but we should note two factors that confound the dilemma. First, in the modern period of biblical studies the drive to read the text as functional atheists was very powerful. In order to be truly academic, historical, *wissenschaftlich*, critical, and the like, students of Scripture had to bracket their theistic and confessional commitments.[5] To be sure, this was more of an ideal than a reality. Many scholars, like Martin Kähler and Adolf Schlatter in Germany, or like the disciples of the great trio, J.B. Lightfoot, B.F. Westcott, and F.J.A. Hort in Britain, never bought this line.[6] Moreover, most Scripture scholars have been practicing Christians and have done their work both motivated and informed by their faith. Yet the general reality has been that Scripture scholars methodologically have had to describe and explain the phenomena of the text as if God does not exist. Anyone who challenged this, like Brevard S. Childs in the last generation, had to mount a massive counter-paradigm that traded on theological convictions that are inevitably contested and controversial.[7] In any case, internal differences along theological lines simply made matters worse by increasing the number and voices of Babel. In reality biblical scholars have diverged both on the method and results of their work from the beginning.

Second, with the rise of postmodernism in biblical scholarship the old ideal developed by figures like Ernst Troeltsch and Van Harvey has come under heavy fire.[8] The tendency now is to celebrate the diversity of voices with gusto and thus to make a virtue out of necessity. Indeed the old ideal is vigorously attacked for its sham self-criticism, in that its claims to neutrality and objectivity are interpreted as power plays that mask the discriminatory racist, classist, and sexist impulses that lie below the surface. Thus the very idea of looking for any kind of stable meaning in the text is excoriated. Ironically, the editors of *The Postmodern Bible* make the point with pleasing clarity when they explain the title of their work in terms of shared

---

[5] For a spirited reiteration of this tradition see J. Berlinerblau, *The Secular Bible, Why Nonbelievers Must Take Religion Seriously* (Cambridge: Cambridge University Press, 2005).

[6] For the latter, see S. Neill and T. Wright, *The Interpretation of the New Testament, 1861–1986* (Oxford: Oxford University Press, 1989).

[7] The contested and partisan character of Childs's position becomes patently clear in P.G. McGlasson's *Invitation to Dogmatic Theology, A Canonical Approach* (Grand Rapids: Brazos Press, 2006), a text endorsed with enthusiasm by Childs himself. What McGlasson wants to propose is a revisionary return to *sola scriptura*, with Augustine, Barth, and Childs operating as a privileged canon of theologians who provide the horizon for scriptural interpretation.

[8] V. Harvey provided a brilliant restatement of Troeltsch in his *The Historian and the Believer* (Urbana: University of Illinois Press, 1996), originally published by Macmillan in 1966.

suspicion of the claim to mastery that characterizes traditional reading of the texts, including modern biblical scholarship…by sweeping away secure notions of reading, by radically calling into question the apparently stable foundations of meaning on which traditional interpretation is situated, by raising doubts about the capacity to achieve ultimate clarity about the meaning of a text, postmodern readings lay bare the contingent and constructed character of meaning itself.[9]

So, where once it was at least assumed that there were texts with stable authors and meanings to be understood, this assumption is now under suspicion if not outright rejected.[10]

There is, of course, an easy solution to the dilemma I have sketched that is immediately open to the theologian. Let the theologian join the ranks of postmodernism and develop a theology to fit the new data emanating from the guild of biblical scholarship.[11] What is interesting about this response is how modern and traditional it is. It buys into the traditional assumption that Scripture is foundational for theology, for this provides the warrant for taking the current orthodoxy in biblical studies seriously; and it accepts the modern assumption that the task of theology is to take the findings of biblical scholarship and move from there to a theology that will be credible in the light of the epistemological regime of the day. What is trumpeted as new and cutting edge is in fact stale and suffocating.

The Really Deep Problem

I have not, however, quite hit bottom yet. The deep problem that has befallen us is not the cacophony of voices that render the faith hopelessly unstable and erratic, with a shelf life of a generation or two. The real disaster is the loss of the gospel in the Church.

It is hard to know how to state what I am after succinctly and persuasively but suffice it to make two points. First, the good news of the arrival of God's

---

[9] *The Postmodern Bible*: The Bible and Culture Collective, ed. G. Aichele, et al. (New Haven: Yale University Press, 1995), 2.

[10] It is interesting that even J. Collins, one of the great contemporary champions of 'historical criticism,' feels under pressure to deal with the postmodernist crusade against meaning. See his exceptionally interesting *The Bible after Babel; Historical Criticism in a Postmodern Age* (Grand Rapids: Eerdmans, 2005).

[11] Interestingly there is both a conservative and radical way to make this move. Thus conservatives have turned to postmodernity as a way to reinscribe their confessional commitments in biblical study; some, like the Pentecostals, have cleverly made hay of their marginal and oppressed status as their ticket to a seat at the table. The radical alternative is not to find a niche inside diversity but to revel in the reality of diversity as something intrinsically beautiful.

kingdom in the life, death, and resurrection of Jesus Christ through the working of the Holy Spirit is simply drowned in a sea of conflicting opinion. The gospel becomes simply one more option among others rather than being the radical, transforming Word of God. In this context the kind of fierce confidence that Paul displays, for example, in the first chapter of Galatians, comes across as hopelessly dogmatic and intolerant. Second, any formation that takes place will not involve initiation into an agreed vision of Christian faith and life but initiation into an arbitrary, parochial, sectarian version of Christianity. At a time when the Church needs to recover its evangelistic nerve, Scripture studies and theology together offer a variety of exotic stones when the convert looks for bread. At a time in Western culture when the Church needs a trumpet sound she shows up in public as a noisy brass band whose members play from radically different scores. At a time when the Church has learned to take seriously the seeker, she has nothing to offer but the satisfaction of spiritually untutored desire.

We have reached the end of an era in Protestantism where both Scripture and theology are concerned. Theologians innocently created biblical studies as the foundation of their own work; biblical studies then undermined theology from within by systematically cutting theology off from its constitutive norm; both biblical studies and theology then in turn undermined access to the gospel for the ordinary believer. It is no surprise that in these circumstances varieties of fundamentalism, evangelicalism, and Pentecostalism continue to flourish within Western Protestantism. The popular preachers of these expanding movements have found a way to speak to the felt needs of people with an air of scriptural authority. Ironically there is a strange symbiotic relation between these traditions and biblical studies, in that they provide much of the motivation and cognitive dissonance that fuels the continuation of biblical studies in the academy.[12] We have a bizarre self-destructive dance in which theologically motivated, epistemic conceptions of Scripture drive Christians to engage in intellectual work that undermines both theology and personal faith from within.

Retracing Our Steps

By this stage some readers will have already begun to tune out. They will be tempted to dismiss what I have proposed as apocalyptic rather than sober, as exaggerated rather than accurate. So let me approach my concerns from a

---

[12] A nice example is the recent work of B.D. Ehrman who was driven to biblical studies by his fundamentalism and is spending a career sorting out what to do after losing his faith. See *Misquoting Jesus: The Story Behind who Changed the Bible and Why* (New York: HarperSanfrancisco, 2005).

different angle. I propose to go back towards the beginning of biblical studies and revisit a manifesto that casts light on our current difficulties. The advantage of this strategy is that it also allows me to indicate both the central problems I want to highlight and where we may have gone wrong. I have in mind returning to the remarkable inaugural address of J. P. Gabler given at the University of Altdorf in 1784.[13] James Barr notes that Gabler's inaugural address is often mentioned but seldom read.[14] My intuition is that Gabler captures a crucial turning point in the discussion; we can readily detect in his work precisely the assumptions that took us down the wrong track.[15] Once these are articulate I can lay out the changes that are essential for the future of theology and its relationship to Scripture. To anticipate, I shall argue that what theology mistakenly gave away, she can now take back, and that she can do this without ignoring the incredible gains to be garnered from the historical study of Scripture.[16] However, the retrieval of Scripture, if it is to avoid the vain repetition of the modern and postmodern period, will require radical changes in the vision of Scripture deployed, the scope of canon, and the task of theology itself.

The problem that Gabler set out to resolve is one that is familiar to all acquainted with the history of scriptural interpretation, namely, there is little agreement on what Scripture actually teaches. Nobody would be bothered with this if we were dealing with any other canon of texts, but in the case of Scripture this is disastrous given the normative status attributed to Scripture in theology. Gabler opens his address with as good a statement of this element in the discussion as any.

> All who are devoted to the sacred faith of Christianity, most worthy listeners, profess with one united voice that the sacred books, especially of the New Testament, are the one clear source from which all true knowledge of the Christian religion is drawn. And they profess too that these books are the only secure sanctuary to which we can flee in the face of the ambiguity and vicissitude of human knowledge, if we aspire to a solid understanding of divine matters and if we wish to obtain a firm and certain hope of salvation.[17]

---

[13] In his 'An Oration on the Proper Distinction between Biblical and Dogmatic Theology and the Specific Objectives of Each.' See J. Sandys-Wunsch and L. Eldredge, 'J.P. Gabler and the Distinction between Biblical and Dogmatic Theology: Translation, Commentary, and Discussion of His Originality,' *SJT* 33 (1980), 133–58.

[14] *Concept of Biblical Theology*, 642, n.16.

[15] How far Gabler's work is representative or historically influential need not be decided here.

[16] I use the soft term 'historical study' rather than the term 'historical criticism' in order to signal that I am well aware of the contested character of the latter. As we shall see, we need deflationary moves all along the line in our future work.

[17] Sandys-Wunsch and Eldredge, 'J.P. Gabler,' 134. It is astonishing how readily Gabler is treated as an Enlightenment rationalist in the secondary literature.

The problem, of course, is that despite this agreement there is contention. 'Why these fatal discords of the sects?' Gabler explains this discord along four lines. Scripture is often obscure; people read their own opinions into the text; they do not distinguish between religion and theology; and, if they do, the problem arises 'from an inappropriate combination of the simplicity and ease of biblical theology with the subtlety and difficulty of dogmatic theology.'[18] The problem that Gabler has identified is nothing new in Protestantism, for it was present from the beginning of the Reformation and was the cause of endless intellectual and political trouble in Europe for centuries. In the nineteenth century it haunted brilliant, sensitive souls like John Henry Newman and John Williamson Nevin, causing theological and spiritual burnout for years before they found a way through it.[19] Gabler shows no signs of being haunted or suffering from burnout. He is confident that there is a clear way forward. His solution involves tackling the four sources of disagreement already identified. I shall begin with the last two and then look briefly at the first two.

One element in the solution is to get clear on the distinction between religion and theology:

> religion is passed on by the doctrine in the Scriptures, teaching what each Christian ought to know and believe in order to secure happiness in this life and the life to come. Religion, then, is everyday, transparently clear knowledge; but theology is subtle, learned knowledge, surrounded by a retinue of many disciplines, and by the same token derived not only from the sacred Scripture but also from elsewhere, especially from the domain of philosophy and history. It is therefore a field that is advanced by careful discriminating observation that experiences various changes along with other fields. Not only does theology deal with things proper to the Christian religion, but it also explains carefully and fully connected matters; and finally it makes a place for them with the subtlety and rigor of logic. But religion for the common man has nothing to do with this abundance of literature and history.[20]

---

[18] Sandys-Wunsch and Eldredge, 'J.P. Gabler,' 135. It is crucial to note that Gabler takes divine revelation and divine inspiration with radical seriousness. He is clearly trying to nuance these notions in ways that will take into account God's accommodation to the needs of the times and to allow for genuine human action in the case of divine inspiration. But these moves assume a hearty commitment to both divine revelation and divine inspiration.

[19] Newman's agony is well captured in his *Apologia Pro Vita Sua* (London: Longmans, Green, Reader, and Dyer, 1875). Nevin provides a searing and devastating critique of North American Protestantism in his *Antichrist, or, The Spirit of Sect and Schism* (New York: J.S. Taylor, 1848). Nevin took five years to figure out whether he should or should not swim the Tiber; in the end, unlike Newman, he did not.

[20] Sandys-Wunsch and Eldredge, 'J.P. Gabler,' 136.

It is important to note here that Gabler is not in any way disparaging theology; on the contrary he sees it as essential to the Christian faith; and he intimates that it is a field of study not to be undertaken by the fainthearted who have no time for subtlety, learned knowledge, philosophy, history, and rigor of logic. Yet Gabler rightly notes that there is something spiritually unsettling about this for the ordinary believer. In the end this kind of work can only be for the intellectually elite. Moreover, given its nature, it is inevitably marked by the idiosyncrasies and culturally relative situations of the theologian. Theology has a history and a chronology, moving from the discipline of the Fathers to the 'scholastic theology of the Middle Ages, covered with the thick gloom of barbarity,' to the light of the doctrine of salvation at the Reformation, on to the Socinian and Arminian factions of later times. Even within the Lutheran Church alone we can hear a plethora of voices.

Gabler has surely put his finger on a critical problem, one that is readily dismissed today in theological rants about the easy simplicities and certainties of fundamentalism. The problem is simply that ordinary (and not so ordinary) people turn to Christianity looking for salvation, for hope, for a way forward in the darkness, for happiness in this life and in the life to come. If they turn to theology, they will soon be swamped by the ephemeral and changing judgments of the theologians. We might say that theology has become soteriologically dysfunctional; rather than give us food for the soul it offers elaborate menus and recipes; rather than lead us to God it leads into theological studies.

Gabler's solution is to offer the seeking soul not theology but religion. Here they can find the simplicity they rightly desire. More formally, what is needed is not dogmatic theology but biblical theology, a form of inquiry marked by 'simplicity and ease.' So religion and biblical theology are the solution to the difficultly thrown up by theology. In addition the biblical theologian can provide an invaluable service to the dogmatic theologian by identifying that material from Scripture that is the foundation for her subtle, complex, rigorous work. The crux of the proposal is this:

> we distinguish carefully the divine from the human, that we establish some distinction between biblical and dogmatic theology, and after we have separated those things that refer most immediately to their own times and to the men of those times from those pure notions which divine providence wished to be characteristic of all times and places, let us then construct the foundation of our philosophy upon religion and let us designate with some care the objectives of divine and human wisdom. Exactly thus will our theology be made more certain and more firm, and there will be nothing to be feared for it from the most savage attack from its enemies.[21]

---

[21] Sandys-Wunsch and Eldredge, 'J.P. Gabler,' 138.

We have already crossed over into Gabler's solution to the first two problems we mentioned above, namely, the problems of obscurity and of eisegesis. We are also beginning to sense that a mushy bog is beginning to show up beneath our feet, for it is beginning to look as if the simplicity of biblical theology is a highly qualified simplicity. What we now want to know is how to get access to religion by the method of biblical as opposed to dogmatic theology.

Happily, Gabler hammers on undaunted. What is needed is a comprehensive study of Scripture that will use the relevant philological skills, make appropriate distinctions between the Old and New Testament, put each author in the proper period, pay attention to the reflection of time and place, look at whether we are dealing with historical or didactic or poetic material, read below the surface of the text, sort out mention of an idea from proof of an idea, and so on. Clearly this whole operation is replete with a network of challenges in and around these issues at every step of the way. And we must then add to it a second challenge, namely, the task of sorting through this wealth of material and finding what is universal across the differences. 'Each single idea must be examined for its universal ideas, especially for those which are expressly read in this or that place in the Holy Scriptures, but according to this rule: that each idea is consistent with its own era, its own testament, its own place of origin, and its own genius.'[22] Once this is done, 'then finally there will be the happy appearance of biblical theology, pure and unmixed with foreign things, and we shall at last have the sort of system for biblical theology that Tiedmann elaborated with such distinction for Stoic philosophy.'[23]

Karl Rahner should now be happy. The theologian is off the hook on exegesis for it has been handed to him by biblical theology.

> As soon as all these things have been properly observed and carefully arranged, at last a clear sacred Scripture will be selected with scarcely any doubtful readings, made up of passages which are appropriate to the Christian religion of all times. These passages will show with unambiguous words the form of faith that is truly divine; the *dicta classica* properly so called, which can then be laid out as the foundational basis for a more subtle, dogmatic scrutiny.[24]

And what are the tasks of the dogmatic theologian at that point? Gabler mentions two. First, the theologian works out a harmony between the findings of Scripture and the principles of human reason.[25] Second, the theologian

---

[22] Sandys-Wunsch and Eldredge, 'J.P. Gabler,' 142.

[23] Sandys-Wunsch and Eldredge, 'J.P. Gabler,' 142.

[24] Sandys-Wunsch and Eldredge, 'J.P. Gabler,' 143. The '*dicta classica*' are the new proof texts for systematic theology. Gabler's traditionalist underwear is in full view at this point.

[25] It is clear why Gabler is so easily treated as a terrible rationalist of the Enlightenment, but seeking harmony between the truths of Scripture and reason is a long-standing

elaborates on the foundations supplied by biblical theology, 'according to the variety both of philosophy and of every human point of view of that which is subtle, learned, suitable and appropriate, elegant and graceful.'

Back to the Crisis Again

In reviewing Gabler from our current situation it is clear that his solution, however creative and fruitful it may have been in the history of biblical scholarship, does not solve the problems he set out to resolve. The obscurity of Scripture remains, as does the constant danger of reading our own opinions in the text.[26] The methodological flaw represented by the distinction between religion and theology is obvious on its face. Biblical theology turns out to be utterly similar to dogmatic theology in that it also involves a host of skills, materials, practices and ancillary disciplines. So the simplicity at this level is a chimera.[27] So too is the simplicity by way of results: we are confronted with the same sort of development, difference and diversity that has cropped up in the history of theology. Biblical studies, like theology, has a chronology and a history. Moreover, if we take Gabler's results, we will have already cooked the theological books in advance, for Gabler has in fact committed himself theologically in the way he handles the canon of Scripture itself.[28] To put the matter

---

practice in Christian theology that cannot be confined to the dark days of the Enlightenment. It is also surely intrinsic to any serious theology.

[26] It is currently hoped that reading the text from the underside or from the margins will save the day; this too is a forlorn hope, as we can see when we note how this kind of reading so readily fits with and is generated by the prior political and theological commitments of its proponents. Of course, it is always possible for biblical scholars to see through all this and still learn to play this game with great sophistication and concealment.

[27] Yet the ideal dies hard. Consider the requirements for an educated clergy laid out by P.C. McGlasson: 'That education must include full proficiency in Greek and Hebrew; a complete grasp of church history in its setting in world history; comprehensive training in the canonical shape of both Testaments of Scripture; firm grounding in biblical and dogmatic theology; wide exposure to the history and contemporary work of biblical exegesis; practical training in the art of pastoral care; and genuine understanding of the mission of the church in the world.' See his *Invitation to Dogmatic Theology*, 158. Amazingly, given McGlasson's emphasis on preaching, not a word is said about homiletics. However, what is really interesting is that the norm articulated here (even if we take it as a counsel of perfection) is a recipe for intellectual and theological self-deception and illusion.

[28] Of course, the whole enterprise depends on theology for it is the Church and theology that supplies the Scripture in the first place. The tortured contortions on what to

technically, Gabler has in fact elected for a vision of canon within the canon in his interpretation of Scripture. Thus his goal is to unearth by painstaking exegetical and historical work the universal ideas that can be extracted from Scripture. This is where he settles when he sets out to find the unambiguous, clear, certain, undoubted, foundationally appropriate teaching of Scripture that the theologian is to carry back to the office.

Thus Gabler in the end lands us right back where we started. By its own intentions theology created biblical studies in order to carry out the first, foundational phase of her work. Biblical scholarship gladly took on the service for which it was created; but in time it took on a life of its own, becoming a field of inquiry that could neither in principle nor in practice deliver the goods. We might say that biblical studies is no longer in the business of taking orders from the theology department; thus theology by setting up Scripture as its canon of truth has self-destructed from within. While theologians may still have an order department, the orders are no longer being filled in or dispatched. In handing over their Scriptures to biblical scholars, the theologians have lost their Scriptures, and thus, by their own norm, they are bereft of the resources they identified as constitutive of their work. The wake is in full progress even if the date of the funeral has been postponed.

It is the spiritual effects of this development that are truly devastating. Where before we had the sects of theology, we now have the sects of biblical studies. And as the sects multiply, those who seek after God are left wandering on the hills without help for their souls. The gospel is now swamped by experts in biblical studies as much as by experts in theology. In Gabler's terms, there is no religion to which the hungry soul can turn. Spiritual darkness and hopeless insecurity have enveloped us on the other side of Enlightenment. Distrust, suspicion, anomie, boredom, one-upmanship and dogmatism stalk the theological landscape. In the meantime local churches have become market churches in a move that mirrors the shift from the nation state to the market state.[29]

Turning to the Future

The solution to the tragedy in which we are enmeshed strikes me as simple. What theology gave, she should now take back. Thus she needs to reclaim Scripture. However, in reclaiming Scripture she needs to reclaim an older and

---

call the Old Testament ('Hebrew Scripture,' 'The First Testament') make this point all too clear.

[29] The shift is presented in a work of great erudition, if not genius, P. Bobbitt's *The Shield of Achilles, War, Peace, and the Course of History* (New York: Alfred A. Knopf, 2005).

much better vision both of Scripture and of her work. I can only begin to map out what is at stake here, but we can begin from Gabler himself.[30]

Gabler exposes, if only faintly and confusedly, a very different vision of Scripture that is also central to Protestantism, albeit perhaps most prominently in the despised world of pietism that has been given such short shrift in theology. The different vision of Scripture that Gabler hints at comes out in two ways. It emerges explicitly in the recurring concern with salvation that runs through his address. Here is one of his hints: Speaking of exegeting the apostles, he confidently notes that 'it may be finally established whether all the opinions of the Apostles, of every type and sort altogether, are *truly divine*, or rather whether some of them *which have no bearing on salvation*, were left to their own ingenuity.'[31] The key phrase here is 'which have no bearing on salvation,' a feature of the text that Gabler identifies with the 'truly divine.' This hint surely dovetails with the other concern that crops up, namely, the fact that people turn to Scripture as a sanctuary where they can get a solid understanding of divine matters, and where they might obtain a firm and certain hope of salvation. They do not turn to Scripture simply because it may be great literature, or because it helps sorting through their questions about ancient Near Eastern antiquities; they turn to Scripture in order to become wise where salvation is concerned.

We can surely see here a rival vision of the function of Scripture, namely, Scripture is to be seen as a place where human beings can find deliverance and salvation. What is at work here is a soteriological as opposed to an epistemological conception of Scripture. On this analysis Scripture functions as a complex means of grace to awaken us to our spiritual diseases and draw us to living faith in God. It is precisely this soteriological vision of Scripture that needs to be retrieved and put to work in the present situation. It needs also to be extended to become the heart and soul of theology itself, for once we abandon the epistemological conception of Scripture we also undermine the standard vision of theology that we have inherited in the West and that still haunts the landscape. Theology set up biblical studies as a feeder-discipline because of a vision of its own task as a kind of *scientia* with appropriate foundations; Scripture was conceived precisely in such a way as to supply the foundations. The way forward is to stop thinking of canon in this way, to revisit what constituted its referent, and then to think through afresh what we should be doing in theology. Ancillary to this we need to develop a new sub-discipline in theology and philosophy, namely, the epistemology of theology, in order to

---

[30] I have developed a more formal vision of what is needed in 'Canonical Theism and the Future of Systematic Theology,' in W.J. Abraham, N.B. Van Kirk, and J.E. Vickers (eds.), *Canonical Theism*, forthcoming from Eerdmans.

[31] Sandys-Wunsch and Eldredge, 'J.P. Gabler,' 143 (emphasis mine).

address the issues that first generated the vision of Scripture as a criterion of truth in theology.[32]

We can, of course, think of other options. In broad terms we can think of three very different responses to the crisis I have identified. First, we can simply give up Scripture as the foundation of theology and find other foundations for theology in reason, experience, tradition, or whatever, and start all over again. I have argued elsewhere that, if we keep this option in mind, modern theology can profitably be read as a wild goose chase to find the right foundations for theology. That goose chase should be called off once and for all.[33] Second, we can give up the search for foundations, find some other way to think of the epistemology of theology, and then start again from scratch. It is clear that this option is flourishing in biblical studies, in philosophy, and in theology, so we can expect to hear more from those who favor this way forward. Third, we can go back in and try to rework our vision of Scripture as norm and then go back to work all over again in theology. No doubt this will mean a new vision of biblical studies where the theologians will have to lend significant help, but so be it. Perhaps theologians should simply take to doing biblical studies themselves, acquiring whatever skills they need to get the job done.[34] An attractive variation within this option is to shore up the problem of divergent interpretations of Scripture by the formal adoption of a vision of papal infallibility or something that is its functional equivalent; that is, by seeking out an epistemic office and mechanism that, under the tutelage of tradition and the sense of the faithful, clearly tells us what Scripture really teaches on critical matters of faith and morals. It is clear from the wonderful flowering of Scripture scholarship in recent Catholicism that this option has already borne much fruit.[35]

---

[32] The crucial epistemological issue lurking about here is a robust vision of divine revelation.

[33] This is the central thesis of the latter part of *Canon and Criterion in Christian Theology* (Oxford: Clarendon, 1998).

[34] I suspect that it is this, or something akin to this, that is fuelling the new commentary series by Brazos Press; the lead volume is the remarkable commentary on Acts by J. Pelikan, *Acts* (Grand Rapids: Brazos, 2005). Other commentary series, like the Two Horizons series from Eerdmans may also fit this agenda. It is clear that we have a similar type of move in K.J. Vanhoozer (ed.), *Dictionary for Theological Interpretation of the Bible* (Grand Rapids: Baker Academic Press, 2005).

[35] This development may help partially explain the turn to Rome on the part of a network of brilliant Protestant theologians in the last decade or so. As the aforementioned article by Rahner brings out (dated though it may now be), Rome offers a very sophisticated interaction between historical investigation and the teaching *magisterium* of the Church that will be more than enough to keep the most skilled and talented scholar hard at work for a lifetime. Contrary to first impressions,

The interesting feature of all these options is the way that they privilege epistemology. All of them depend on getting the epistemology straight, even if the epistemology is a kind of anti-epistemology, as happens in the case of the second, postmodernist option. It is precisely because of this privileging of epistemology that I refuse all of these options.[36] Having failed with the invention of biblical studies, it is now hoped that epistemology will deliver the goods. Having been hostage to the history department, theologians now sell themselves into captivity to philosophy. Trained as a philosopher, I find this solution almost comical.

The correct insight contained in this view is, of course, that we need more and not less work in the epistemology in theology. Too much theology involves halfhearted, half-baked epistemology. This is especially otiose when we are in the midst of a golden period in the history of the philosophy of religion, as represented by Basil Mitchell, Richard Swinburne, Alvin Plantinga, William Alston, Nicholas Wolterstorff, Eleonore Stump, and a host of others. We also live in a golden period of epistemology, much of it developed by robust theists.[37] So it would be silly to disparage work in epistemology just at the time when it has opened up all sorts of insights for theology.[38] The mistake is to think that epistemological considerations must be resolved first before we can begin the real work of theology.

Here theologians need to turn to the founders of their discipline. If we look, for example at such theologians as Origen, the Cappadocians, Augustine, and St Symeon the New Theologian, there is next to no agreement in epistemology; on the contrary they were all over the map in this terrain. Yet they could still do their work. Why? It was because they had an entirely different vision of what they were doing. And what were they doing? They were engaging in post-baptismal, university-level catechesis. Starting with those already converted, with folk who were initiated into the agreed faith of the Church, they sought to unpack, defend, articulate, and explore the whole New World that had been opened up in the gospel. Straining every intellectual nerve and using every tool at their disposal, they brought folk into a deeper knowledge of the God of creation and redemption. As Ellen Charry in her groundbreaking work

---

nineteenth- and twentieth-century Roman Catholicism is a massive effort to save the central tenets of Protestant doctrines of Scripture.

[36] Note that what is at stake here is not a worry about any particular school of epistemology, say, classical foundationalism, but the status of epistemological proposals in the life of the Church.

[37] I speak here only of the Anglo-American analytical tradition, but I do not mean that we limit ourselves to this strain; we need all hands on deck.

[38] For my own formal contribution to the discussion see *Crossing the Threshold of Divine Revelation* (Grand Rapids: Eerdmans, 2006).

has shown, theology fostered wisdom within the life of faith, leading the new convert into a deeper love for God and neighbor.[39] To modern and postmodern scholastics this orientation in theology looks limp and lacking in rigor; to those still caught on the epistemological merry-go-round it appears superficial and lacking in seriousness. All this, they say under their breath, is to be relegated to an extension of the Sunday school and to ascetic theology, while the real theologian gets on with deep, critical, academic theology. This is exactly the response we should expect from those who are committed to theological studies rather than to theology. It is real theology that we need: serious discourse about the living God who has truly saved us from despair and evil and who has opened up for us in the faith of the Church a strange New World that not even the most brilliant among us will fathom this side of eternity.

Theology is first-order discourse about God; it is not one more interaction with what this or learned scholar has written about God. It goal is to deepen our knowledge and love of God. So when we offer up biblical and theological studies in its stead we are cheats and imposters. This is even more so when we turn theology into grand tomes on epistemology or on this or that political change in Western culture. To return to our main theme, the invention of biblical studies by theologians was a great moment in the history of Western ideas; but it was a wrong turn in the history of theology. Theology became a slave to historical investigation; over time she dug her own grave; she entered the darkness of Good Friday, and awaits her Easter resurrection.

Ironically, this shift of perspective leaves everything as it is where historical study is concerned. Historians are free to explore biblical texts, the history of Israelite religion, the emergence of the doctrine of the Trinity, and a thousand and one issues. They can even explore whether and how they might envisage biblical theologies. They can do so without the constraints that theologians sought to impose on them in the past. Perhaps the New Testament writers were merely functional Trinitarians; perhaps Paul was really a binatarian; perhaps Mark knows nothing of the virginal conception of Jesus. So be it. The deep convictions of the soteriologically oriented theologian are not undermined by such convictions. The Church did not simply commit herself to a canon of Scripture, she also committed herself to a whole nexus of canons, that is, to a canonical heritage of Scripture, saints, teachers, liturgical practice, creed, iconography, episcopacy and the like. These were not grand norms of truth, justification and knowledge; they were truly effective means of grace that, with the guidance and energy of the Holy Spirit, enabled vulnerable, fragile people to become saints and martyrs. So the theologian can relax and be flexible in how best to respond to the results of historical investigation. She can

---

[39] E. Charry, *By the Renewing of Your Minds, The Pastoral Function of Doctrine* (New York: Oxford University Press, 1997).

let the historian loose to understand the whole life of the Church in all its maddening complexity and development.[40]

In the meantime the theologian need not wait to have a set of secure foundations; that whole topic needs to be addressed in the field of the epistemology of theology. True theologians have better and more interesting things to do. They are required before God to enable people who have entered into new life in Jesus Christ through the energy of the Holy Spirit to come to terms with the full riches of wisdom and life that have come to the world as an incomparable gift and challenge. To be sure, this will require them to play a host of roles akin to that of defense lawyer, medical doctor, inventive apologist, adept cartographer, sensitive prophet, ecclesial renewalist, and biblical exegete. Happily all this work can be done without first farming out the precious Scriptures of the Church to biblical scholars, who may, according to the erratic contingencies of the guild, operate as functional atheists or as amateur epistemologists. Scripture will, of course, have its own inimitable place in the repertoire of resources deployed by the theologian; but it will not be their only resource; and it will function first and foremost soteriologically rather than epistemologically. At that point, those who come to theology looking for fish will no longer be given a scorpion; hopefully too, we will have less use for millstones.

---

[40] It need hardly be said that any historical work will rest on all sorts of contested background beliefs, including theological and atheological beliefs, so the philosophical theologian will have plenty to say about the complex logic of historical explanation and judgment. We can be sure that many secularist historians will resist this observation, as they have done for generations, but the days of that kind of imperialism and intellectual intimidation are over.

Bibliography

Abraham, W.J., *Canon and Criterion in Christian Theology* (Oxford: Clarendon, 1998)

—, *Crossing the Threshold of Divine Revelation* (Grand Rapids: Eerdmans, 2006)

—, 'Canonical Theism and the Future of Systematic Theology' in W.J. Abraham, N.B. Van Kirk, and J.E. Vickers (eds.), *Canonical Theism* (Grand Rapids: Eerdmans, 2007)

Aichele, G., et al., *The Postmodern Bible: The Bible and Culture Collective* (New Haven: Yale University Press, 1995)

Barr, J., *The Concept of Biblical Theology* (Minneapolis: Fortress, 1999)

Berlinerblau, J., *The Secular Bible, Why Nonbelievers Must Take Religion Seriously* (Cambridge: Cambridge University Press, 2005)

Charry, E., *By the Renewing of Your Minds, The Pastoral Function of Doctrine* (New York: Oxford University Press, 1997)

Collins, J., *The Bible after Babel; Historical Criticism in a Postmodern Age* (Grand Rapids: Eerdmans, 2005)

Ehrman, B.D., *Misquoting Jesus: The Story Behind who Changed the Bible and Why* (New York: HarperSanfrancisco, 2005)

Gabler, J.P., 'An Oration on the Proper Distinction between Biblical and Dogmatic Theology and the Specific Objectives of Each' in J. Sandys-Wunsch and L. Eldredge, 'J.P. Gabler and the Distinction between Biblical and Dogmatic Theology: Translation, Commentary, and Discussion of His Originality,' *SJT* 33 (1980), 133–58

Gerrish, B.A., *Saving and Secular Faith, An Invitation to Systematic Theology* (Minneapolis: Fortress, 1999)

Harvey, V.A., *The Historian and the Believer* (Urbana: University of Illinois Press, 1996)

McGlasson, P.G., *Invitation to Dogmatic Theology, A Canonical Approach* (Grand Rapids: Brazos Press, 2006)

Neill, S., and T. Wright, *The Interpretation of the New Testament, 1861–1986* (Oxford: Oxford University Press, 1989)

Nevin, J.W., *Antichrist, or, The Spirit of Sect and Schism* (New York: J. S. Taylor, 1848)

Newman, J.H., *Apologia Pro Vita Sua* (London: Longmans, Green, Reader, and Dyer, 1875)

Pelikan, J., *Acts* (Grand Rapids: Brazos, 2005)

Rahner, K., 'Exegesis and Dogmatic Theology' in *Theological Investigations, vol. 5* (London: Dartman, Longman, and Todd, 1966), 71–72

Vanhoozer, K.J. (ed.), *Dictionary for Theological Interpretation of the Bible* (Grand Rapids: Baker Academic Press, 2005)

3

No Longer Queen

The Theological Disciplines and Their Sisters ★

Al Wolters

In the project of doing Christian scholarship, a crucial issue is the relationship of Scripture to the academic disciplines. In that connection, it is often suggested that the theological disciplines, notably biblical studies, have a privileged position, since theology and biblical studies clearly have a long history of reflection on the role of Scripture. However, although in an important sense this is undoubtedly true, it is also – and less obviously – true that there is a significant sense in which the theological and non-theological disciplines are on a par when they wrestle with the question of how the authority of Scripture should function in their respective scholarly specialties. In my opinion, the very nature of scholarship puts theological and non-theological disciplines on an equal footing with respect to how the authority of the Scriptures should be brought to bear on them.

What I mean is this. Every scholarly discipline, whether biblical studies or sociology or literary criticism, of necessity works with a number of foundational assumptions that shape its theoretical work. These may be called control beliefs, or root metaphors, or metaphysical axioms, or worldviews, but they are pervasive and inescapable. To deny that they exist, or to deny that they *necessarily* exist, is a form of positivism – a view of the academic enterprise which I take to have been thoroughly discredited in the philosophy of science in recent decades. Such a denial is also a particularly telling example of the

---

★ The following is a revised version of the keynote address to the biblical and theological subgroup at the conference on 'Scripture and the Disciplines,' held at Wheaton College, May 24–27, 2004.

modernism, which it is one of the virtues of postmodernism to have unmasked. It is impossible to do scholarship, to engage in the business of academic inquiry, without basing oneself to a significant extent on pre-theoretical commitments which cannot themselves be justified on theoretical grounds.[1] Such pre-theoretical commitments may include the belief that reality is orderly and can be known (or that it is chaotic and unknowable); that physical laws as they operate today operated in the same way thousands of years ago; that human culture is a reflex of economic conditions; that the unconscious is a significant component of the human psyche; that patriarchy is a fundamental explanatory category in understanding human society, and so on. The point is not whether these or a host of similar assumptions are true or not, but that assumptions of this kind necessarily underlie all academic work, and that their truth or falsity cannot be adjudicated on strictly academic grounds. They all involve choices of a kind that are difficult to define, but which may be called personal and existential, as well as broadly cultural. I would argue that they are, in fact, ultimately religious.

The ultimately religious character of these kinds of assumptions can be illustrated by a number of examples. To assume that reality is essentially disordered and meaningless, and that whatever order or meaning is ascribed to the world is the product of human creativity, clearly constitutes a denial of a creator who invests the world with reliable regularity and intrinsic goodness. To proceed on the assumption that all human culture, specifically including religion and its belief in a transcendent deity, is ultimately explainable in terms of the ownership of the means of production, is to challenge on a fundamental level the claims of all world religions. To argue that all human truth claims are ultimately a disguised assertion of the will to power is to undermine at its core all appeals to divine revelation.

My basic thesis is therefore the following. If it is true that all scholarly disciplines are shaped to a significant extent by foundational assumptions, and that those assumptions at bottom involve religious choices, then the normative bearing of Scripture on the academic disciplines, including the theological disciplines, is primarily a matter of letting Scripture guide our choice of foundational assumptions. In other words, in the enterprise of doing Christian scholarship the point at which the authority of Scripture is most appropriately and most effectively brought to bear on the scholarly disciplines is on the level of the pre-theoretical commitments which shape the way theories are formed in those disciplines. In making this claim I am following the lead of the Dutch

---

[1] In this essay I am using 'pre-theoretical commitment' as an occasional synonym for 'foundational assumption.' I mean 'pre-theoretical' in the sense 'preceding or underlying theory-formation in a given discipline.' A pre-theoretical commitment in this sense may well be 'theoretical' in a broader sense, as in the Kantian epistemological split between knowledge and belief.

theologian Herman Bavinck, and the tradition of Christian scholarship that he and Abraham Kuyper inaugurated in the nineteenth century.[2]

It is of particular importance for my present argument to underscore the fact that the theological disciplines are no different from their non-theological sisters in this respect. They too necessarily work with foundational assumptions in their ordinary academic work, and they too must reflect on the way these assumptions should be shaped by Scripture. Like other scholarly fields, the theological disciplines are subject to the influence of the isms and ideologies of the day, and need to be on their guard against uncritically adopting the pre-theoretical commitments made culturally plausible by such influential intellectual movements. I would argue that it is a dangerous naïveté on the part of many theologians and biblical scholars to assume that they do not need to reflect critically on their own epistemological presuppositions, or that they can borrow the foundational commitments of an influential current ideology without compromising the Christian integrity of their scholarship.

Having sketched the terrain in this way, and having posited my basic thesis with respect to the crucial bearing of Scripture on foundational assumptions, I propose in what follows to do two things. First, I will give a series of examples, drawn largely from my own work, of the ways in which basic presuppositions play a role in biblical scholarship, and how it is important to relate presuppositions, with the help of colleagues in other disciplines or sub-disciplines, to biblical authority. Second, but very briefly, I will offer a few thoughts on how Christians in the theological disciplines can most effectively be a help to their colleagues in other fields in the communal task of doing Christian scholarship. To put it another way, my paper will endeavor to illuminate the two primary epistemological relationships which I discern in the proper connection between Scripture and the disciplines: the relationship between foundational assumptions and scholarship (in this case biblical studies), and the relationship between those assumptions and Scripture.

I must ask the reader's indulgence in advance for citing so much of my own work in the presentation that follows. I recognize that it may seem like an exercise in self-advertisement. My excuse for this immodesty – apart from the convenience of referring to material that I know well, and therefore of being in little danger of misrepresenting the author! – is that I need a willing guinea pig for my analysis, a concrete example of a fallible Christian biblical scholar to illustrate some of the encyclopedic relationships which I wish to explore. In effect, I have volunteered to be my own guinea pig. As a Christian biblical scholar with a background in philosophy, I offer myself, with what I hope is

---

[2] On Bavinck, see my essay 'Herman Bavinck on Faith and Science' in *Facets of Faith and Science*, 2.23–55.

appropriate humility and vulnerability, as Exhibit A of the following discussion.

Since I myself am a biblical scholar, I will restrict my comments very largely to the academic study of Scripture. However, I would point out that the same general point can be made for any of the other theological disciplines, notably systematic theology. A cursory glance at some of the theological giants of the past will quickly confirm this. Who would deny that Augustine was heavily influenced by the basic categories of Neoplatonism, Thomas Aquinas by those of Aristotelianism, Schleiermacher by those of Romanticism, or Barth by those of existentialism? In fact, I would venture to say that the same point can be made about such a resolutely antithetical Christian philosopher as Herman Dooyeweerd and his indebtedness to Neo-Kantianism. However highly we may respect and honor each of these thinkers as being in many ways admirable champions of Christianity in their own day, we can say in all humility that it is clear with the benefit of hindsight that they all, to a greater or lesser extent, compromised their Christian witness by giving undue allegiance to foundational assumptions that were not shaped by Scripture.[3] They stand as an instructive reminder of the continual challenge to be epistemologically self-critical as we engage, with fear and trembling, in the daunting task of doing Christian scholarship, in both the theological and non-theological disciplines.

Foundational Assumptions in Biblical Scholarship

In illustrating the role of foundational assumptions in biblical scholarship I will divide them in a rough and ready way into three categories. I will call them theological, worldview, and philosophical assumptions. By theological assumptions I refer to fundamental beliefs about the nature of Scripture and its overall teaching which have long been a staple of theological discourse. They have to do with such matters as the inspiration, historicity and unity of the canonical Scriptures, and are widely recognized as being the source of considerable dissension among biblical scholars. Different assumptions about these matters not only divide Christian scholars from their non-Christian colleagues, but also provoke division among Christian scholars themselves. They are foundational assumptions because they have a decisive influence on the way biblical scholarship is done, yet they cannot be either proved or refuted on the basis of scholarly criteria alone.

---

[3] This is not to deny that the adoption of an unbiblical categorical framework may well yield valuable insight. I discuss this paradoxical state of affairs in my 'Facing the Perplexing History of Philosophy,' 1–17, esp.12–13.

Theological assumptions

As an illustration of such a foundational assumption I choose the contested belief that the narratives in the book of Daniel, specifically the story of Belshazzar's feast and the handwriting on the wall in Daniel 5, are historically reliable. Such an assumption obviously makes a considerable difference to the way a biblical scholar goes about interpreting the dramatic incident recorded in that chapter. In my own work on this passage, I have concluded that the assumption of historicity allows one to come to insights that would otherwise be obscured. For example, there are good reasons to conclude that the festival which Belshazzar was celebrating was a Babylonian *aktu* festival in honor of the moon god Sîn.[4] Furthermore, it turns out that if we take seriously the putative date of this incident, namely the night before the fall of Babylon to Cyrus the Persian (Oct. 12, 359 BC), there is an illuminating connection between the mysterious handwriting on the wall and the rise of the constellation Libra in that year.[5] My point here is not to argue that the assumption of historicity is in this case correct, but simply that it makes a decisive difference for the way biblical scholarship on this chapter is done.

Another assumption of a theological sort is the belief that the Old Testament points forward to the New Testament as its fulfillment. Among other things this means that the Old Testament priesthood is understood as foreshadowing Jesus Christ as the New Testament High Priest and Lamb of God, whose sacrifice atones once for all for human sin. This belief has ramifications for the way Christian biblical scholars interpret Zechariah 3:8–9, which reads as follows in the NIV: 'Listen, O high priest Joshua and your associates seated before you, who are men symbolic of things to come: I am going to bring my servant, the Branch. See, the stone I have set in front of Joshua!' In my own work for a commentary on Zechariah I am seriously entertaining the possibility that the Hebrew preposition *lifne*, here translated 'before' and 'in front of' in a spatial sense, should be understood to mean chronologically 'after,' even though this is not the usual meaning of this preposition. My foundational assumption about the redemptive-historical connection between the Israelite priesthood and the future Messiah, influence me in weighing this lexical possibility.[6] Again, the point is not that this would be a correct lexicographical decision, but that a foundational assumption affects the inner workings of biblical scholarship. The same point would be illustrated if someone were to assume

---

[4] Wolters, 'Belshazzar and the Cult of the Moon God Sîn,' 199–206.

[5] Wolters, 'An Allusion to Libra in Daniel 5,' 291–306; also 'The Riddle of the Scales in Daniel 5,' 155–77.

[6] Wolters, 'Confessional Criticism and the Night Visions of Zechariah,' 90–117 (here 109).

instead that theological considerations should be kept strictly separate from exegetical decisions.

A third example of the kind of foundational assumption that I am here calling 'theological' involves the belief that the Bible contains predictive prophecy. I refer in this connection to the expression *zhar hrqîaʿ* in Daniel 12:3, usually translated 'the brightness of the firmament.' However, in an article published ten years ago in *JSOT* I argued that a better translation would be 'the luminary of the firmament,' and that this expression actually refers to the remarkable appearance of Halley's Comet in 164 BC, at the time of the Maccabean Revolt.[7] Since I myself accept a sixth-century date for the prophecies of Daniel, this conclusion clearly presupposes a belief in predictive prophecy. As a matter of fact, a prediction would be involved even if we adopt the commonly accepted Maccabean dating of the book of Daniel, since this is usually fixed at 165 BC, a year before the comet's appearance.

The three examples adduced from my own work in biblical studies clearly show the influence of 'theological' foundational assumptions on my scholarship: the belief in the historicity of Daniel, in the typological significance of the Israelite priesthood, and in the reality of predictive prophecy. However, it is no secret that this kind of influence is generally looked upon with suspicion by my colleagues in the discipline. In fact, within the contemporary guild of biblical studies at large, the influence of theological assumptions on one's scholarship is generally disallowed altogether, although of course it was the norm before the rise of classical historical criticism in the late eighteenth century. We will return to this anomaly below, when we consider foundational assumptions of a philosophical kind.

If we now ask whether these assumptions are warranted in the light of Scripture as a whole, I venture to suggest that a positive answer is fairly obvious. Although we always need to be discriminating and judicious in invoking and applying basic beliefs of this kind to specific passages, there can be little doubt that the Christian Scriptures affirm the essential historicity of their narratives, the typological foreshadowing of New Testament realities in the Old, and the reality of predictive prophecy. If the authority of Scripture is to be brought to bear on biblical scholarship, then basic assumptions like these must surely inform the academic work that is done in this scholarly discipline.

At this point Scripture scholars can also be helped by their colleagues in other disciplines or sub-disciplines. It is probably not an exaggeration to say that Christian biblical scholars today who wish to honor the authority of Scripture in these foundational ways live in something resembling a state of siege within their own broader discipline. In a guild still largely dominated by classical historical criticism, any suggestion that one is 'theological' in one's

---

[7] Wolters, '*Z_har h_r_qîaʿ* (Daniel 12:3) and Halley's Comet,' 111–20.

scholarship is anathema, and is often associated with other dismissive epithets, such as 'apologetic' and 'fundamentalistic.' For biblical scholars who wish to resist the pressure to conform to the Enlightenment ideal of biblical criticism, there is welcome assistance available from their colleagues in other disciplines, both in theology and in the broader academy. Among fellow-theologians, colleagues in systematic theology can help in articulating a sophisticated contemporary understanding of organic inspiration or progressive revelation, and colleagues in church history can help with rediscovering the goldmine of pre-critical exegesis, which effectively relativizes the claims of the contemporary guild. From fellow-scholars in other disciplines there is much to learn from philosophers, historians and literary critics. A Christian philosopher who has provided helpful philosophical analysis of the 'quest for the historical Jesus' is C. Stephen Evans in his *The Historical Christ and the Jesus of Faith* (1996).[8] An Old Testament scholar who has worked very fruitfully with the insights of contemporary historiography is Iain W. Provan, most recently in his article 'Knowing and Believing: Faith in the Past.'[9] No one denies the seminal contributions that have been made to biblical studies by the Jewish literary critic Robert Alter.[10] And of course the whole shift in contemporary academia from modernism to postmodernism has at least this advantage, that it helps biblical scholars to make the case that classical historical criticism is a prime example of ideological modernism.

Worldview assumptions

I turn now to the second kind of foundational assumptions which I distinguished above, which I am calling 'worldview' assumptions. I am here using 'worldview' in a narrow sense to refer to the fundamental relationship which is assumed to exist between 'nature' and 'grace,' that is, between the created but fallen 'world' outside of redemption in Jesus Christ (including the whole range of human culture), and the new reality of life in Christ. In other words, I am using the terms 'nature' and 'grace' in the classical theological sense to stand as a shorthand for the entire range of human life as defined by creation and fall, on the one hand, and salvation or re-creation, on the other. As such, these categories correlate roughly with such perennial pairs as Christ and culture, faith and reason, church and world. In the history of Christian reflection the relationship between these two prime realities have been construed in a limited number of ways. To restrict myself to the tradition of historic Christian orthodoxy

---

[8] (New York: Oxford University Press, 1996).
[9] In *'Behind' the Text: History and Biblical Interpretation*, 229–66.
[10] See especially *The Art of Biblical Narrative*; *The Art of Biblical Poetry*; and *The World of Biblical Literature*.

(defined in terms of adherence to the ecumenical creeds of the early church), the basic paradigms for construing this relationship can be reduced to four, and these four can be conveniently labeled with contrasting Latin prepositions. The *gratia contra naturam* perspective sees grace in opposition to nature, and can be characterized by Tertullian's question 'What does Jerusalem have to do with Athens?' The *gratia supra naturam* paradigm is that of Thomas Aquinas, and is characterized by grace as the *donum superadditum* to nature. The *gratia iuxta naturam* construal is characterized by the two-realm conception of classical Lutheranism. The *gratia intra naturam* view, finally, construes the relationship as one in which grace renews and restores nature.[11]

Although 'worldview' assumptions in this specific sense could also be called 'theological,' they are here distinguished from what I have called theological foundational assumptions for two reasons. The first is that the four basic construals of the nature-grace relationship operate at a much more fundamental level than the theological beliefs we have mentioned. In the hierarchy of background beliefs, worldview assumptions are more basic and comprehensive than specific confessional commitments about inspiration and historicity. In fact, a person's understanding of the Bible's inspiration and historicity is likely to be shaped by deeper lying assumptions about nature and grace. The second reason for distinguishing worldview foundational assumptions from theological ones is related to the first. Because worldview assumptions are so basic and comprehensive, they are usually 'tacit' in the sense of not clearly entering the awareness of those who hold them. They define a cognitive stance that the individual Christian scholar may not even be able to articulate. Most Christians, even those who have had a theological education, would have difficulty defining how they construe the relationship between nature and grace.[12]

Nevertheless, divergent answers to that question do shape biblical scholarship. This can be demonstrated by observing the way commentators on the Song of the Valiant Woman, the concluding pericope of the book of

---

[11] For an elaboration of these categories, see the following essays from my hand: 'Nature and Grace in the Interpretation of Proverbs 31:10–31'; 'On the Idea of Worldview in its Relation to Philosophy'; 'Christianity and the Classics: A Typology of Attitudes.'

[12] What I have in mind here is something basic and comprehensive. I am taking it as axiomatic that on the fundamental point of the relationship between creation and redemption the Scriptures as a whole do not teach a multiplicity of perspectives. In other words, individual biblical passages or themes which on one level may seem to support different paradigms for construing the nature-grace relationship (for example, God loves the *kosmos*, yet friendship with the *kosmos* is hatred toward God) are not ultimately contradictory. For my understanding of these matters I am heavily indebted to the work of H. Bavinck. See J. Veenhof, *Nature and Grace in Herman Bavinck*.

Proverbs, have approached the question of the relationship between verse 30b, 'but a woman who fears the Lord is to be praised,' and the body of the Song, which celebrates the Valiant Woman's extraordinary, but decidedly this-worldly, exploits of estate management. The answers given to this question correlate rather precisely with the four nature-grace paradigms that we have briefly sketched. Those who see grace as essentially incompatible with nature (*gratia contra naturam*) have adopted two strategies: they either spiritualize the body of the Song by making it into an allegory for the Church or some other spiritual reality, or they secularize verse 30b by emending away the reference to the fear of the Lord. The first strategy was followed for centuries by ancient and medieval commentators, both Jewish and Christian; the second has been followed by a number of twentieth-century exegetes. Those who see grace as supplementing nature (*gratia supra naturam*) picture the Valiant Woman's 'fear of the Lord' as a kind of culmination or capstone of her secular activities. Those who see grace as flanking nature (*gratia iuxta naturam*) conceive of the woman's religious commitment as being on a par with her other activities, but without intrinsic connection. Finally, those who see grace as restoring nature (*gratia intra naturam*) understand the heroine's 'fear of the Lord' to be the animating principle which pervades and motivates all her other activities.[13]

Another example of this kind of worldview assumption making its presence felt in the details of biblical scholarship is found in the exegesis of 2 Peter 3:10, which reads as follows in the NIV: 'But the day of the Lord will come like a thief. The heavens will disappear with a roar; the elements will be destroyed by fire, and the earth and everything in it will be laid bare.' The difficulty in this verse is the verb *heurethsetai*, literally 'will be found.' The context suggests that the entire universe will be destroyed, but that doesn't seem to fit very well with the verb 'will be found.' The Textus Receptus has *katakasetai*, 'will be burned up,' which would solve the difficulty, but it is clear that *heurethsetai* is the best attested text. The NIV translation 'will be laid bare' smooths over the difficulty, but there is really no evidence that the verb *heurisk* ever means 'to lay bare' elsewhere.

In my own exegesis of this verse I challenge the assumption that the context in fact describes the end of the world in terms of absolute destruction or annihilation. Instead, I argue that the apostle is here picturing the coming Day of the Lord in terms of a smelting process by which the earth and everything in it is put in a crucible in order to be purified. The present heaven and earth will not be discarded, but will be purged through the purifying fires of judgment to emerge as 'a new heaven and a new earth, the home of righteousness' (verse 13). The initially puzzling reading *heurethsetai* fits with this, because the passive

---

[13] Wolters, 'Nature and Grace in the Interpretation of Proverbs 31:10:31.'

form of this verb refers elsewhere to the emergence of purified metal from the melting pot.[14]

The details of this argument need not detain us in the present context. I bring it up here to illustrate the point that a worldview assumption is making its presence felt. I am myself committed to the fourth of the worldview assumptions that I have sketched, the view that grace restores nature. The eschatological corollary of that view is that the new heaven and new earth of which 2 Peter 3:13 speaks are in fact the old ones renewed. The meaning of grace is that God ultimately does not discard nature (heaven and earth), but rather renews and restores it to what it was meant to be from the beginning. What we can expect at the climax of the biblical story is the purification, not the annihilation, of the created order.

How can the authority of Scripture be brought to bear on the question of the proper construal of the relationship between nature and grace? This is a difficult question to answer, since different strands of orthodox Christendom have traditionally given different answers. It is probably true that the four basic paradigms that I have outlined will continue to be hardy perennials within the world church, with some paradigms tending to be associated with certain confessional and ecclesiastical traditions. However, if we restrict our attention to evangelical Protestantism, it is possible to discern a growing consensus in the last number of decades away from the first three paradigms, which tend in various ways to be associated with a sacred-secular dualism and a pietistic world-flight mentality, toward the more integral perspective of the *gratia intra naturam* paradigm, which emphasizes an affirmation of, and engagement in, the earthly and mundane realities of created life. In my own little book *Creation Regained: Biblical Basics for a Reformational Worldview* I have argued for the biblical legitimacy of what is in effect the fourth paradigm,[15] and I am encouraged to see that a good number of other recent books promote the same overall perspective, the best-known probably being *How Now Shall We Live?* by Charles Colson and Nancy Pearcey.[16] It is also encouraging to see that there is a movement in the same direction in Roman Catholic circles, as exemplified in David L. Schindler's *Heart of the World, Center of the Church: Communio Ecclesiology, Liberalism and Liberation.*[17]

---

[14] Wolters, 'Worldview and Textual Criticism in 2 Peter 3:10,' 405–13.

[15] Wolters, *Creation Regained: Biblical Basics for a Reformational Worldview.*

[16] Other notable titles include R. Middleton and B. Walsh, *The Transforming Vision*; P. Marshall, *Heaven Is Not My Home*; D.B. Hegeman, *Plowing in Hope: Toward a Biblical Theology of Culture*; D.K. Naugle, *Worldview: The History of A Concept*; C. Plantinga, *Engaging God's World: A Christian View of Faith, Learning and Living*; M.E. Wittmer, *Heaven Is a Place On Earth*; Nancy Pearcey, *Total Truth: Liberating Christianity from its Cultural Captivity*; C. Bartholomew and M.W. Goheen, *The Drama of Scripture: Finding Our Place in the Biblical Story.*

[17] (Grand Rapids: Eerdmans, 1996).

Philosophical assumptions

I turn now to my third and final kind of foundational assumptions, which I have labeled 'philosophical.' They are like what I have called 'worldview' assumptions in that they are often not explicit in the awareness of those who hold them. Many of them are considered self-evident, things that 'everyone knows.' What I have in mind here are basic beliefs about the nature of reality and of knowledge. I will first give two examples of how such ontological or epistemological assumptions have affected the way detailed exegetical work has been done, and then speak more broadly of the effect of implicit philosophical commitments on the academic study of Scripture in general.

A curious example from the history of interpretation is the way various commentators have interpreted an obscure phrase in Zechariah 2:8 (MT 2:12). Literally rendered, the text reads as follows: 'Thus says the Lord, After glory he sent me to the nations which plundered you.' This is one of the most difficult passages in the book of Zechariah, and has given rise to a host of different interpretations and emendations.[18] In traditional Christian interpretation the speaker was taken to be the Angel of the Lord, who in turn was equated with Christ, so that the words 'he sent me' refer to the incarnation.[19] What is assumed in this interpretation is that 'after glory' should be understood in an ontological sense as referring to the Neoplatonic chain of being, with heavenly 'glory' at the top of the scale, and earthly incarnation at the bottom of the scale. This was for many centuries the standard Christian exegesis of these words, no doubt because the Neoplatonic scale of being was the shared ontological framework of orthodox Christendom until early modern times. It was not until Calvin, who understood 'after glory' in a redemptive-historical sense, that this tradition of exegesis was challenged.[20]

But the exegetical influence of an assumed Platonic ontology is not restricted to this curiosity from the history of interpretation. In my opinion it is still alive and well in the standard reading of the Greek expression Θείας κοινωνοὶ φύσεως in 2 Peter 1:4. Usually translated 'partakers of the divine nature,' it is often understood to refer to the believer's ontological participation in the being of God. All the key terms of this verse are understood in a Hellenistic philosophical sense, with the result that this text is considered by many to be something of an anomaly in the New Testament as a whole, which nowhere else speaks of salvation in terms of ontological participation. However, as I have argued in an exegetical essay on this verse, this conclusion is not necessary.

---

[18] For a sampling, see Wolters, 'Confessional Criticism,' 95–96.

[19] For references, see Wolters, 'Confessional Criticism,' 110.

[20] See J. Calvin, *Commentaries on the Twelve Minor Prophets,* vol. 5, *Zechariah and Malachi,* 69.

In fact, the canonical context supports an alternative translation of the Greek phrase, namely 'partners of the Deity.'[21] Understood in this way, the verse simply reflects the well-attested biblical concept of the believer's partnership with God in the covenant.

However, it is clear that philosophical foundational assumptions play a far greater role in Scripture studies than such incidental exegetical examples reveal. No one denies that the history of biblical interpretation is closely bound up with the history of philosophy. We need only think of the influential synthesis of Julius Wellhausen in the nineteenth century, and its close dependence on contemporary German historicism, to illustrate this point.[22] Too often, however, this dependence on currently prevalent philosophies is recognized only in retrospect, and biblical scholars are rather uncritical in the way they adopt a current philosophical model to do their own research and writing. In this connection I would refer to an excellent article by my colleague Craig Bartholomew, who argues that biblical exegetes need to become much more critically alert to the role of philosophy in their work.[23]

Among the philosophical assumptions which must be taken into account are some of the fundamental beliefs we mentioned earlier: that reality is orderly and can be known (or is chaotic and unknowable); that economic conditions are determinative of cultural values; that all claims to knowledge are a disguised assertion of power, and so on. All of these necessarily have a significant influence on the way scholarship is done in any field, including the theological disciplines.

But a philosophical assumption that has had a particularly decisive impact on the theological disciplines is the Kantian split between knowledge and belief, a version of the influential dichotomy between fact and value. According to this epistemological axiom, religious beliefs – and indeed any kind of belief not based on sense-experience – cannot count as knowledge. True knowledge is *Wissenschaft* or scientific cognition, which is empirically based and methodically established. It has to do with facts, and is objective in nature. Anything that falls outside of this kind of empirical *Wissenschaft* is subjective, and belongs to the realm of values. It may be useful and valuable in its own way, as in attributing beauty or purpose to nature, or in regulating one's behavior by a belief in a divine Lawgiver, but it cannot count as knowledge. Consequently, all religious beliefs need to be kept strictly separate from genuinely *wissenschaftlich* – that is, rigorous and objective – scholarship.

---

[21] Wolters, '"Partners of the Deity": A Covenantal Reading of 2 Pet 1:4,' 28–44. See also 'Postscript to "Partners of the Deity,"' 418–20.

[22] See C.G. Bartholomew, 'Uncharted Waters: Philosophy, Theology and the Crisis of Biblical Interpretation,' 1–39 (here 15–16).

[23] Bartholomew, 'Uncharted Waters.'

It is this Enlightenment epistemology that has undergirded the widespread adoption and enormous prestige of classical historical criticism in biblical studies. In order to qualify as a legitimate member of the academic community, the biblical scholar had to lay aside all so-called 'dogmatic' beliefs – for example the belief in the inspiration of Scripture or the reality of miracles and predictive prophecy – since such beliefs were subjective and incapable of empirical proof. Consequently, biblical studies was put on an entirely new footing, and began to call itself 'critical.' This meant that as a matter of principle the most basic claims of the Scriptures – that God exists, and speaks, and acts, that Jesus Christ is the Savior of the world – were methodologically excluded from biblical scholarship as being unscientific. In effect, all the 'theological' foundational assumptions of which we spoke earlier were declared illegitimate in the academic arena. In fact the very word 'theology' became suspect in biblical studies. In an academic revolution of enormous religious and cultural significance, continuity with previous Scripture scholarship – now rather dismissively labeled 'precritical' – was largely cut off.

Although in the contemporary academic climate postmodernism has done much to discredit mainline historical criticism as a typical product of the Enlightenment project, and thus of the modernism against which postmodernism reacts,[24] it is still true, as we noted above, that the guild of biblical studies is still largely dominated by it, and tends to marginalize those who challenge it on religious grounds. Furthermore, the influence of mainline historical criticism even in avowedly Christian circles has tended to exacerbate the already somewhat strained relations between biblical scholars and dogmatic theologians. Long gone are the days when Christian theologians were trained to be competent in both of these theological disciplines, or when specialists in these fields were mutually supportive as a matter of course. Even among evangelical biblical scholars there is often a certain suspicion of bringing 'theology' into one's professional work.

It should also be mentioned that it is possible for the Enlightenment epistemological split between knowledge and belief to be aided and abetted by the second (*supra*) and third (*iuxta*) paradigms of the nature-grace relationship. If grace is conceived as supplementing or flanking nature, it is all too easy to conflate the 'natural reason' of a religiously neutral domain of nature with the Enlightenment ideal of a religiously neutral *Wissenschaft*. In that case the worldview assumptions of the Christian tradition are in danger of reinforcing the philosophical assumption of modernism, in effect baptizing an epistemological dichotomy born of secular humanism. By contrast the first paradigm (*contra*) tends to be religiously suspicious of biblical scholarship as such, and the fourth paradigm (*intra*) seeks to engage and renew it.

---

[24] A.K.M. Adam, *What Is Postmodern Biblical Criticism?*

If we now raise the question of bringing to bear the authority of Scripture on the philosophical assumptions we have briefly mentioned, we must be aware that we are doing something highly unusual. Philosophy has a long tradition of claiming to be autonomous and religiously neutral, and even Christian philosophers have tenaciously defended that putative autonomy and neutrality.[25] However, I take it as an axiom of the entire enterprise of Christian scholarship that there is a normative relationship between Scripture and the various academic disciplines, and there is no reason to believe that philosophy is excluded from that relationship. I would myself certainly affirm that philosophy stands under the authority of Scripture, although it may be difficult to define just how that authority should function.

However, in some ways it is not difficult at all to see how the overall teaching of Scripture bears on the philosophical assumptions we have been considering. I take it that the Scriptures rule out the assumption that the world is fundamentally chaotic and unknowable. Similarly, although we can undoubtedly learn a great deal from Marx, Freud and Foucault, it seems to me that the canonical Scriptures of the Christian religion rule out the view that the ownership of the means of production is the decisive factor in explaining all human culture (including religion), or that the dynamics of the human psyche can explain why people believe in a transcendent deity, or that all claims to knowledge are some kind of self-interested power grab.

More specifically, it is clear to me that the Kantian split between knowledge and belief flies in the face of a biblical epistemology. The way the Scriptures talk about human knowing is deeply and pervasively religious. To know is to be personally engaged with someone or something before the face of God. Out of the heart are the issues of life. The fear of the Lord is the beginning of wisdom. We are to serve God with everything we have, including our minds. The attempt to read Romans 1 as teaching a kind of natural theology which abstracts from humanity's religious commitments and struggles contradicts what the chapter clearly teaches. Over and over again the prophets and apostles of the canonical Scriptures demand total allegiance and unqualified obedience to the God who is sovereign over all. To suggest that there is any kind of knowing or thinking, let alone a particularly reliable and prestigious one, which is somehow exempt from the pervasive call to serve God in Christ, and which in fact deliberately seeks to be free of all religious commitment, is nothing short of biblical nonsense. The Bible does not countenance religious neutrality. (This does not mean, of course, that academic research and writing should not strive for a kind of objectivity and judicious fair-mindedness. Christian scholars as much as anyone else should guard against undue bias, and cultivate a healthy skepticism about their own motivations and their tendency to fit the evidence

---

[25] Wolters, 'Facing the Perplexing History of Philosophy,' 1–17.

into inappropriate categories. But this very attitude of scholarly honesty and restraint is to be understood as their 'reasonable service' to God.)

But what of positive ways in which the Scriptures give guidance in the area of philosophical foundational assumptions? We are here sailing in what Bartholomew calls 'uncharted waters,' because philosophy has for so long been declared the business of 'unaided reason,' even by Christian believers. Besides, it is as true of philosophy as of the other academic disciplines that we need to proceed carefully in defining the way in which biblical authority is appropriately invoked. There are many dangers attendant upon putting forward a 'biblical philosophy,' not least that of investing a human theoretical construct with divine authority. Nevertheless, the attempt must be made, with appropriate humility and tentativeness, if the Christian community is not to be derelict in its duty. After all, there is no venture of obedience in the Christian life which is not subject to the dangers of self-righteousness and missing the mark.

Let me suggest one possible way of proceeding. This is to look to the Scriptures for a biblical 'worldview' – now taking that term in an expanded sense to refer to an overall perspective on the world and human life in general. To repeat a formulation which I have used in another context:

> Biblical faith in fact involves a worldview, at least implicitly and in principle. The central notions of creation (a *given* order of reality), fall (human mutiny at the root of all perversion of the given order) and redemption (unearned restoration of the order in Christ) are cosmic and transformational in their implications. Together with other basic elements of the biblical *doctrina* (Christ's universal kingship, for example; the eschatological labor pangs of the groaning creation, and 'world' as the perverted and enslaved creation), these central ideas... give believers the fundamental outline of a completely anti-pagan *Weltanschauung*, a worldview which provides the interpretive framework for history, society, culture, politics, and everything else that enters human experience.[26]

This biblical worldview in turn can be theoretically deepened and elaborated into the outlines of a positive Christian systematic philosophy. Such is essentially the approach of the Dutch Christian philosopher D.H.T. Vollenhoven (1892–1978), a close associate of the philosopher Herman Dooyeweerd (1894–1977). These two men (each in his own distinctive way) worked out a systematic philosophy which has proved useful to Christian scholars in many disciplines. In systematic theology their philosophy has been made fruitful in the work of the American dogmatician Gordon Spykman.[27]

But even without an elaborately worked-out system of ontological categories, the work of Christian philosophers can be invaluable to believing

---

[26] Wolters, 'Gustavo Gutiérrez (1928–),' 229–40 (esp. 237–38).
[27] See G.J. Spykman, *Reformational Theology: A New Paradigm for Doing Dogmatics.*

academics in other fields, including the theological disciplines. An impressive example of philosophical help to both biblical scholars and systematic theologians is the book *Divine Discourse* by Nicholas Wolterstorff, in which he applies the insights of speech-act theory to a sophisticated philosophical account of how the Bible can be said to be the Word of God.[28]

However, I would single out another work as a particularly fine example of philosophical help for biblical scholars. This is the essay 'Two (or More) Kinds of Scripture Scholarship' by Alvin Plantinga, which uses the arguments of so-called Reformed Epistemology to demonstrate the legitimacy of bringing confessional commitments into biblical scholarship.[29] In fact, his essay can be described as a masterful exposé of the epistemological pretensions of classical historical criticism. It should be required reading for every Christian biblical scholar who feels oppressed by the hegemony of the Kantian split in their discipline.

Now of course it is one thing to expose the epistemological weaknesses of classical historical criticism; it is quite another to propose a positive alternative. If various Christian theological assumptions – or, for that matter, worldview and philosophical assumptions – are not to be excluded from the business of doing biblical scholarship, as Enlightenment epistemology had decreed, how should they be properly integrated with the other levels of Scripture interpretation – textual criticism, for example, or synchronic literary analysis? To answer that question in the present state of the discipline is an important and daunting task for Christian biblical scholars. In an essay entitled 'Confessional Criticism and the Night Visions of Zechariah,' I have endeavored to give an initial and partial answer to that question.[30] In this essay I distinguish nine levels of biblical interpretation, running from textual criticism and lexicography to redemptive-historical analysis and confessional discernment, and explore the various kinds of relationships that obtain between them. Rather than pitting two blocks of these levels against each other, in the manner of the classical fact-value split, I argue that there is in fact an intricate interplay between all levels, such that decisions on one level may legitimately affect, or be affected by, decisions on every other level, including the explicitly 'theological' ones.

The burden of my argument so far has been to highlight the role of foundational assumptions – not only in the non-theological disciplines, but also in the theological ones, especially in biblical studies. Whether these assumptions be of

---

[28] N. Wolterstorff, *Divine Discourse: Philosophical Reflections on the Claim That God Speaks.*

[29] A. Plantinga, 'Two (or More) Kinds of Scripture Scholarship,' 243–77. Repr. in *'Behind' the Text*, 19–57. A longer version appears as ch. 12 in Al Plantinga, *Warranted Christian Belief.*

[30] Wolters, 'Confessional Criticism.'

the theological, the worldview, or the philosophical kind, they are a legitimate and indispensable component of academic Scripture study. Furthermore, I have argued that it is primarily on the level of these pre-theoretical commitments that Scriptural authority should be brought to bear in biblical studies, and that therefore the Christian biblical scholar has as much to learn from her colleagues in other disciplines as she has to teach them. Christian scholarship is a cooperative venture, and theology can no longer be said to be – if it ever was – the *regina scientiarum*, 'the queen of the sciences.' Furthermore, given the crucial role of philosophical foundational assumptions, in the theological disciplines as much as in any other, philosophy can no longer be rightly considered – if it ever was – the *ancilla theologiae*, 'the handmaid of theology.' The erstwhile queen can learn much from her sisters in the other disciplines, not least from her former handmaid.

However, she does also have things that she can *teach* her academic sisters. I turn now from a consideration of the first epistemological relationship which we set out to discuss, the relationship of foundational assumptions to the disciplines, to a brief look at the second, the relationship of Scripture to these foundational assumptions. This is a large topic, but space limitations compel us to be brief.

Bringing Scripture to Bear on Christian Scholarship

How can biblical scholars and theologians be helpful to their colleagues in the task which they all share of bringing the authority of Scripture to bear on their respective disciplines? Please note, this is not a question of the theologians telling their colleagues what the Scriptures say to the specific disciplines of those colleagues. There is a priesthood of all believers also in the Christian academy; every scholar has the responsibility to bring her own field under biblical authority, using whatever help she can get. Rather, the theologians can be helpful by facilitating the proper authoritative functioning of Scripture for their colleagues. Let me briefly suggest just two ways in which they can be helpful to that end.

The first is to emphasize the unity and coherence of Scripture as presenting a single story of salvation.[31] One of the results of mainline historical criticism has been the atomization of Scripture, an emphasis on the diversity and apparent incoherence of its several parts at the expense of seeing the overall biblical story. This has also contributed to the alienation that has crept in between biblical scholars and systematic theologians. These two disciplines must not

---

[31] See the recent essay by R.C. Van Leeuwen, 'Reading the Bible Whole in a Culture of Divided Hearts,' 1–21.

compete with each other, but must cooperate to develop a credible biblical theology that highlights continuities and unity as well as discontinuities and diversity. Unfortunately, the great mass of professional biblical scholarship is quite useless for helping non-specialists (whether academic or not) hear what the central thrust of the biblical story is. Without some sense of the overall unity of the biblical narrative, Bible readers of whatever station or specialty (including many biblical scholars) have little choice but to resort to proof-texting and moralism.

A second way in which theologians can help their colleagues is in explicating the significance of certain biblical themes or concepts, especially those that run right through the canon, like temple, or covenant, or kingdom. An explanation of the biblical institutions of jubilee, or sabbath, or of rules of warfare can also be quite illuminating to colleagues in other disciplines. On occasion it may be possible to suggest a connection between a biblical concept and a philosophical foundational assumption. I myself once launched the idea that the biblical notion of creation as separation might be fruitful as a general principle of non-reductionism in our approach to the variety of created things.[32] It is up to the philosophers to follow this up as a possible clue to a biblical way of doing ontology.

As in the body of this paper, so in these concluding remarks about facilitating the exercise of biblical authority, my concern is to stress the importance of disciplinary cooperation in the Christian academy. The development of Christian scholarship is a preeminently interdisciplinary exercise, which requires humility and a teachable spirit on the part of everyone. To repeat the image I mentioned a moment ago in another connection, the relationship between the various disciplines, like that of the various levels of interpretation, should be that of an 'intricate interplay' of each with all the others. Biblical scholars and theologians have an important role to play, but they, like all their colleagues in the academic enterprise, are called to be servants, not only of God, but also of their fellow-academics.

---

[32] Wolters, 'Creation as Separation: A Proposed Link Between Bible and Theory,' 347–52.

Bibliography

Adam, A.K.M., *What Is Postmodern Biblical Criticism?* (Minneapolis: Fortress, 1995)

Alter, R., *The Art of Biblical Narrative* (New York: Basic Books, 1981)

—, *The Art of Biblical Poetry* (New York: Basic Books, 1985)

—, *The World of Biblical Literature* (New York: Basic Books, 1991)

Bartholomew, C.G., 'Uncharted Waters: Philosophy, Theology and the Crisis of Biblical Interpretation,' in *Renewing Biblical Interpretation*, Scripture and Hermeneutics Series, vol. 1, ed. C. Bartholomew, et al. (Carlisle: Paternoster; Grand Rapids: Zondervan, 2000), 1–39

Bartholomew, C.G., and M. Goheen. *The Drama of Scripture: Finding Our Place in the Biblical Story* (Grand Rapids: Baker, 2004)

Calvin, J., *Commentaries on the Twelve Minor Prophets*, vol. 5, *Zechariah and Malachi*, trans. J. Owen (Edinburgh: Banner of Truth Trust, repr. 1986)

Colson, C., and N. Pearcey, *How Now Shall We Live?* (Wheaton: Tyndale House, 1999)

Evans, C.S., *The Historical Christ and the Jesus of Faith* (New York: Oxford University Press, 1996)

Hegeman, D.B., *Plowing in Hope: Toward a Biblical Theology of Culture* (Moscow ID: Canon Press, 1999)

Marshall, P., *Heaven Is Not My Home* (Nashville: Word, 1998)

Middleton, R., and B. Walsh, *The Transforming Vision* (Downers Grove: InterVarsity Press, 1984)

Naugle, D.K., *Worldview. The History of a Concept* (Grand Rapids: Eerdmans, 2002)

Pearcey, N., *Total Truth: Liberating Christianity from its Cultural Captivity* (Wheaton: Crossway, 2004)

Plantinga, A., 'Two (or More) Kinds of Scripture Scholarship,' *Modern Theology* 14 (1998), 243–77; reprinted in *'Behind' the Text: History and Biblical Interpretation*, ed. C. Bartholomew, et al. (Carlisle: Paternoster; Grand Rapids: Zondervan, 2003), 19–57

—, *Warranted Christian Belief* (New York: Oxford University Press, 2000)

Plantinga, C., *Engaging God's World. A Christian View of Faith, Learning and Living* (Grand Rapids: Eerdmans, 2002)

Provan, I.W., 'Knowing and Believing: Faith in the Past,' in *'Behind' the Text: History and Biblical Interpretation*, Scripture and Hermeneutics Series, vol. 4, ed. C. Bartholomew, et al. (Carlisle: Paternoster; Grand Rapids: Zondervan, 2003), 229–66

Schindler, D.L., *Heart of the World, Center of the Church: Communio Ecclesiology, Liberalism, and Liberation* (Grand Rapids: Eerdmans, 1996)

Spykman, G.J., *Reformational Theology: A New Paradigm for Doing Dogmatics* (Grand Rapids: Eerdmans, 1992)

Van Leeuwen, R.C., 'Reading the Bible Whole in a Culture of Divided Hearts,' *ExAud* 19 (2003), 1–21

Veenhof, J., *Nature and Grace in Herman Bavinck*, trans. A.M. Wolters (Sioux Centre: Dordt College Press, 2006)

Wittmer, M.E., *Heaven Is a Place on Earth* (Grand Rapids: Zondervan, 2004)

Wolters, A., 'Facing the Perplexing History of Philosophy,' *Tydskrif vir christelike wetenskap* 17 (1981), 1–17

——, 'Nature and Grace in the Interpretation of Proverbs 31:10–31,' *Calvin Theological Journal* 19 (1984), 153–66

——, 'Worldview and Textual Criticism in 2 Peter 3:10,' *WTJ* 49 (1987), 405–13

——, 'On the Idea of Worldview and Its Relation to Philosophy,' in *Stained Glass: Worldview and Social Science*, ed. P.A. Marshall, et al. (Lanham MD: University Press of America, 1989), 14–25

——, 'Christianity and the Classics: A Typology of Attitudes,' in *Christianity and the Classics: The Acceptance of a Heritage*, ed. W. Helleman (Lanham MD: University Press of America, 1990), 189–203

——, '"Partners of the Deity": A Covenantal Reading of 2 Pet 1:4,' *Calvin Theological Journal* 25 (1990), 28–44

——, 'Postscript to "Partners of the Deity,"' *Calvin Theological Journal* 26 (1991), 418–20

——, 'The Riddle of the Scales in Daniel 5,' *HUCA* 62 (1991), 155–77

——, 'Gustavo Gutiérrez (1928–),' in *Bringing into Captivity Every Thought, Capita Selecta in the History of Christian Evaluations of Non-Christian Philosophy*, ed. J. Klapwijk, et al. (Lanham MD: University Press of America, 1991), 229–40

——, 'An Allusion to Libra in Daniel 5,' in *Die Rolle der Astronomie in den Kulturen Mesopotamiens*, Grazer Morgenländische Studien 3, ed. H.D. Galter (Graz, 1993), 291–306

——, 'Zohar Hārāqîa' (Daniel 12.3) and Halley's Comet,' *JSOT* 61 (1994), 111–20

——, 'Belshazzar's Feast and the Cult of the Moon God Sin,' *Bulletin for Biblical Research* 5 (1995), 199–206

——, 'Herman Bavinck on Faith and Science,' in *Facets of Faith and Science*, 4 vols., ed. J. van der Meer (Lanham MD: Pascal Centre, University Press of America, 1996), 2.23–55

——, 'Creation as Separation: A Proposed Link Between Bible and Theory,' in *Facets of Faith and Science*, 4 vols., ed. J. van der Meer (Lanham MD: Pascal Centre, University Press of America, 1996), 4.347–52

——, 'Confessional Criticism and the Night Visions of Zechariah,' in *Renewing Biblical Interpretation*, Scripture and Hermeneutics Series, vol. 1, ed. C. Bartholomew, C. Greene, and K. Möller (Carlisle: Paternoster; Grand Rapids: Zondervan, 2000), 90–117

——, *The Song of the Valiant Woman: Studies in the Interpretation of Proverbs 31:10–31* (Carlisle: Paternoster, 2001)

—, *Creation Regained: Biblical Basics for a Reformational Worldview* (Grand Rapids: Eerdmans, 1985); second edition with M. Goheen (Grand Rapids: Eerdmans, 2005)

Wolterstorff, N., *Divine Discourse: Philosophical Reflections on the Claim That God Speaks* (Cambridge: Cambridge University Press, 1995)

4

At the School of Truth

The Ecclesial Character of Theology and Exegesis in the Thought of Benedict XVI

Scott W. Hahn

The initial public statements of a new pope are made with care and deliberation, for they signal, if not a fully developed program for leadership, at least a précis of the pontiff's pastoral and theological concerns. It is highly significant, then, that in his most symbolic inaugural statement, Pope Benedict XVI devoted considerable attention to the 'science' of biblical interpretation, the relationship between historical and critical methods of interpretation, the Church's understanding of Scripture as the Word of God, and its role as that of obedience to the divine Word.[1] He is thought to be the first pope since the earliest days of the Church to make biblical interpretation a keen concern of his leadership. Indeed, while the popes of the modern era have been closely involved in the development and progress of scientific exegesis and the historical reading of the Bible, Benedict, formerly Joseph Ratzinger, is the first pope in our times to have been an academic theologian and exegete.

As I hope to show, Benedict XVI has developed a profound vision of the freedom and responsibility of the theologian and biblical scholar. We will look first, in detail, at his understanding of the nature and mission of the academy, and of the role of the theology and exegesis in the academy. We will then consider Benedict's critique of the way exegesis is typically conducted in the academy today and his proposed alternative, what he calls a 'hermeneutic of faith.' After examining the elements of that hermeneutic, including Benedict's definition of theology and its ecclesial and liturgical locus, we will offer a sketch of

---

[1] Homily, Mass of Possession of the Chair of the Bishop of Rome, 3.

Benedict's own biblical theology, which, as I will argue, holds great promise for the future of the Bible in the academy.[2]

Truth, Freedom, and the Academy

A brief theological and ecclesial résumé

While most popes in the modern era have hailed from the Vatican's diplomatic corps, Benedict, like his immediate predecessor Pope John Paul II, was an influential scholar and university professor before being named a bishop of the Church. As John Paul continued to make important scholarly contributions to the field of philosophy throughout his career as a Church official, Benedict, in parallel fashion, has been arguably among the most seminal thinkers in theology and biblical interpretation in the last half-century.

While it is beyond the scope of this essay to provide a complete résumé of Benedict's career,[3] we should note a few highlights. He received his doctorate in theology from the University of Munich in 1953, writing his dissertation on Augustine's exegesis and ecclesiology. He lectured in fundamental theology at several German universities before assuming the chair in dogmatic theology at the University of Tübingen in 1966. He was a key theological adviser to the Second Vatican Council (1963–1965) and made important contributions to the council's document on divine revelation, *Dei Verbum*. In addition to hundreds of articles published in academic and ecclesial journals, he is the author of books of enduring importance and influence on patristic theology and exegesis,[4] ecclesiology,[5] dogmatic theology,[6] and the Christian symbol of faith.[7] He

---

[2] For the purposes of this paper, I will be considering almost exclusively the theological opinions and insights that Benedict articulated prior to his pontificate. Also, I will restrict myself to articles and addresses authored under his own name and not decisions or other writings issued in his official capacity as prefect of the Vatican's Congregation for the Doctrine of the Faith. The theological and exegetical judgments and conclusions discussed herein, while reflective of and in accord with Catholic dogma and teaching, are not considered binding on Catholics.

[3] A good introduction, especially to his early academic writings, remains Nichols, *The Thought of Benedict XVI*. For comprehensive bibliographies, see Nichols, 297–330, and Ratzinger, *Pilgrim Fellowship of Faith*, 299–379.

[4] Ratzinger, *The Theology of History in St. Bonaventure*. Unless otherwise noted, all titles noted in this paper are authored by Benedict XVI under the name Joseph Cardinal Ratzinger.

[5] *The Meaning of Christian Brotherhood*.

[6] *Eschatology*.

[7] *Introduction to Christianity*.

was the co-founder of an important theological journal, *Communio,* in collaboration with some of the last century's most important theologians, including Henri de Lubac and Hans Urs von Balthasar. As the highest ranking doctrinal official in the Catholic Church for nearly twenty-four years, he helped oversee the academic presentation of the faith in Catholic universities and seminaries throughout the world and played an important role in the work of the International Theological Commission and the Pontifical Biblical Commission. He was a decisive intellectual force in the development of the 1992 *Catechism of the Catholic Faith,* the first comprehensive statement of Catholic belief and practice to be published in more than 450 years.

'The freedom for the truth'

Throughout his career, Benedict has been keenly interested in issues related to the practice of theology and biblical interpretation in the academy. Indicative is his statement that

> The presence of theology in the university is, in my opinion, a precious patrimony which it is incumbent upon us to defend. That theology be at home in the 'house of learning' and be a partner in its discourse is crucially important both for theology and for the other sciences. That theology be able to research and speak with the seriousness and liberty which pertain to scientific endeavor is a value which everyone must have at heart.[8]

These issues are central to his larger project of establishing the true nature and mission of theology, and the fundamental principles and methods for its practice.

Perhaps surprisingly, Benedict does not take as his model the university as it developed in Catholic Europe during the medieval era. Instead, he grounds his understanding of higher education on the classical model of Plato's Academy. For Benedict, the decisive feature of the Academy was not its commitment to the search for truth, but its fundamental cultic character as a religious guild dedicated to the veneration of the Muses. The Academy, he reminds us, included a chapel for liturgical worship and a specific office responsible for the preparation of sacrificial offerings.[9] This original association of worship and truth reveals, for Benedict, the essence of the academy in all times and places, including our own. He believes the search for truth, undertaken in freedom, necessarily culminates in the encounter with the ground of being, or the divine, God.

---

[8] *The Nature and Mission of Theology,* 114.
[9] *Nature and Mission of Theology,* 40–41.

As a consequence, he thinks much contemporary debate about the academic freedom of theologians and exegetes is misguided, and rooted in a problematic concept of freedom that began in the writings of Luther and has dominated since the Enlightenment.[10] The freedom of the theologian in the academy cannot be conceived as freedom *from* the constraints of religious tradition, he argues. To define freedom in this way is to conceive it too narrowly, and in terms alien to the origin and essence of the academy, in which freedom is inseparable from truth as truth is inseparable from worship. "'Academic freedom" is freedom *for* the *truth,* and its justification is simply to exist for the sake of the truth,' according to Benedict.[11] To be free, in the context of the academy, is to be able to pursue truth unencumbered by ulterior motives, such as the desire for profit or power. And the truth, freely pursued, is the truth about God, which inevitably leads to worship:

> To think through the essence of truth is to arrive at the notion of God. In the long run, it is impossible to maintain the unique identity of the truth … without learning to perceive in it the unique identity and dignity of the living God. Ultimately, therefore, reverence for the truth is inseparable from that disposition of veneration which we call adoration. Truth and worship stand in an indissociable relationship to each other…. The freedom for the truth and the freedom of the truth cannot exist without the acknowledgment and worship of the divine.[12]

Here we see a distinctive mark of Benedict's thought – a belief in the unity of the truth. 'Truth is the whole,' he has written.[13] He sees an integral unity, a *communio*, at the heart of creation and history, a unity that likewise lies at the heart of Christian revelation and the way of thinking and living to which it gives rise.

In all of his writings, we can see a concerted effort to restore this integrity, this unity, to Christian thought, to bring back together what the modern academy has driven asunder – freedom and truth, law and liturgy, faith and reason, the old and new covenants, Scripture and tradition, the Bible and the Church, philosophy and theology. This sense of the wholeness of truth stands in sharp contrast to the dominant models of biblical scholarship in the academy today. And that, for Benedict, has serious implications, not only for academic research, but for the pastoral use and appropriation of Scripture in the Church. We turn, then, to a detailed look at Benedict's 'critique of criticism.'

---

[10] *Truth and Tolerance,* 236–45.

[11] *Nature and Mission of Theology,* 37.

[12] *Nature and Mission of Theology,* 40–41.

[13] 'Preface,' in J.H. Nicolas, O.P., *Synthèse dogmatique. De la Trinitè à la Trinitè* (Fribourg 1985), 5, quoted in Nichols, *The Thought of Benedict XVI,* 1.

The Critique of Academic Biblical Criticism

The presumptions of the historical-critical method

Benedict's theological training and career were shaped by his encounter with the historical-critical method, which by that time, in the late 1940s, had become the dominant theoretical model in the academy.[14] In autobiographical reflections, he has related how confident scholars then were that the method gave them 'the last word' on the meaning of biblical texts. He relates a story, for instance, about a leading Tübingen exegete who announced he would no longer entertain dissertation proposals because 'everything in the New Testament had already been researched.'[15]

While very well schooled in its techniques and findings, Benedict has emerged as a forceful and articulate critic of what he describes as the theoretical hubris and practical limitations of historical criticism. That said, he is far from embracing fundamentalism, a reactionary stance toward the text that he has also sharply criticized.[16] His own theological writings, as we will see, are deeply informed by historical and critical research. Indeed, his thought is marked by its appreciation for the 'historicity' of Christian revelation.[17] God has revealed himself in human history, and the vehicle for this revelation has been the Scriptures of the Christian Church. Hence, the historical context and literary form in which this revelation comes to us must be attended to in order for us to grasp its meaning for ourselves.

The insights of historical criticism, Benedict has said, are invaluable for helping us understand how biblical texts came to be written and what these texts might have meant to their original audience.[18] He demonstrates a commanding grasp of New Testament exegesis, especially scholarship on the Gospel of John, and the relationship of the Old and New Testaments. He frequently employs or assumes scholarly hypotheses concerning the dating, compositional form, and original setting of biblical texts. Often he will find insightful clues to meaning in philology, or in the text's interpretive history, especially in rabbinic and liturgical traditions. He avails himself of such contextualizations as ancient Near Eastern notions of covenant and kinship, concepts in Greek philosophy and definitions in Roman law. He has even been known to bring anthropological studies to bear on his subjects.[19] Benedict,

---

[14] *Eschatology*, 271–72.
[15] *Pilgrim Fellowship of Faith*, 27.
[16] *Biblical Interpretation in Crisis*, 3.
[17] Nichols, *Thought of Benedict XVI*, 292.
[18] *Behold the Pierced One*, 43–44.
[19] See, for instance, his discussion of the 'anthropological basis' of tradition in *Principles of Catholic Theology*, 86–88.

then, does not at all seek to invalidate the historical-critical method, only to 'purify' it through self-examination, so that it can serve its proper function in the search for the truth. He observes that, while they freely submit the biblical text to all manner of probing and analysis, biblical scholars have been remarkably unreflective about their own methods and presuppositions.[20] His own critique, meanwhile, shows him to be conversant not only with the long history of biblical interpretation, but also with the broader currents in the post-Reformation history of ideas. Specifically, he roots what he calls the 'crisis' in modern biblical interpretation in philosophical, epistemological, and historical assumptions inherited from the Enlightenment.

Benedict XVI's most basic criticism of contemporary biblical criticism is that it is far from what it purports to be – a value-neutral science akin to the natural sciences, the findings of which are objective and rendered with a high degree of certitude. Invoking the Heisenberg principle, he notes that even experiments in the natural sciences have been found to be influenced by researchers' own involvement and presuppositions. It should be no surprise, then, that in 'scientific' biblical criticism, no less than in any other area of human inquiry, researchers' subjectivity shapes the object of their study, including the questions they pose, the methods they develop to seek answers, and the eventual outcome of their study.

In the case of biblical criticism, Benedict pinpoints several deep-seated, yet unquestioned presuppositions that scholars bring to their work. The first they inherit from the natural sciences that they have been so anxious to emulate – the evolutionary model of natural development. Evolution posits that later, more complex life-forms evolve from earlier, simpler forms. Applied to Scripture study, this has led exegetes to suppose that, in Benedict's words, 'the more theologically considered and sophisticated a text is, the more recent it is, and the simpler something is, the easier it is to reckon it original.'[21]

---

[20] 'The historico-critical method is essentially a tool, and its usefulness depends on the way in which it is used, i.e., on the hermeneutical and philosophical presuppositions one adopts in applying it. In fact there is no such thing as a pure historical method; it is always carried on in a hermeneutical or philosophical context, even when people are not aware of it or expressly deny it' (*Behold the Pierced One*, 43).

[21] *Biblical Interpretation in Crisis*, 10. It is not difficult to see how this evolutionary hypothesis has influenced such articles of modern exegetical faith as the priority of Mark's shorter, narratively more skeletal gospel, or the presumed existence of a more primitive 'Q' source supposedly relied upon by Matthew and Luke's gospels. For his part, Benedict sees the evolutionary theory underlying the penchant for distinguishing between 'Jewish' elements in the gospel – which are presumably original and historical because Jesus was a Jew – and supposedly later interpolations from 'Hellenistic' or Greek thought. This latter example perhaps explains why modern

Benedict is not out to score points by identifying discarded scholarly opinions. He wants us to see something more fundamental – how the findings of modern exegesis are shaped by the prior hermeneutical and philosophical assumptions of the exegetes. He questions why modern scholarship would presume that religious and spiritual texts and ideas develop along the same lines, or according to the same rules, as organisms are observed to develop in nature. Such a development is hardly self-evident and, as Benedict points out, there are many contrary examples in the history of Christian spirituality, and more generally in the history of ideas:

> First and foremost, one must challenge that basic notion dependent upon a simplistic transferral of science's evolutionary model to spiritual history. Spiritual processes do not follow the rule of zoological genealogies.[22]

Indeed, the historical development of the *symbol*, or the Christian confession of faith, reveals a diametrically opposite process, one that might even be described as anti-evolutionary. The early Church's beliefs about the identity of Jesus started from an original multiplicity of complex names and concepts found in Scripture and the early liturgical and creedal tradition – Jesus as Prophet, Priest, Paraclete, Angel, Lord, and Son of Man. Finally, through a process of what Benedict calls 'increasing simplification and concentration,' Church authorities settled on the three titles found in the earliest creeds – Christ, Lord, and Son of God.[23] This historical footnote is intriguing on a number of levels. The modern exegete is taught to regard creeds and liturgical formulations as later 'ecclesial' additions that are 'discontinuous' with and likely to be distortions of Jesus' original witness. However, as Benedict shows, the earliest Christian witness was decidedly more complex and theologically layered, while the later work of Church authorities was in fact one of simplification and clarification. This not only calls into question the evolutionary hypothesis that underlies modern exegesis, it also raises interesting questions about the central importance of ecclesial tradition in the formation and redaction of biblical texts.

---

scholars for many years could not see clearly what centuries of earlier Church interpreters had been able to see, namely the deep Old Testament substratum to the New Testament. Elements that scholars for much of the modern period have confidently asserted to be Hellenistic imports, such as the 'Logos' theology in John's prologue, cultic and mystery language, and notions of divine sonship, are now widely recognized to reflect deep Old Testament themes.

22 *Biblical Interpretation in Crisis*, 10.
23 *Behold the Pierced One*, 15–17.

The separation of Church and Scripture

Benedict's second major critique of criticism concerns the assumed necessity of studying the biblical texts apart from their original ecclesial and liturgical context. Benedict sees the critical method laboring, perhaps unselfconsciously, under mistaken assumptions rooted in the Enlightenment's anticlerical wing, and perhaps even earlier, in the French encyclopedists' critique of organized religion.[24] Accordingly, there is more at work here than the methodological operation of isolating the texts for study. There is a prior question: Why would students of the Bible establish, as a methodological principle, the necessity of deliberately excluding reference to the texts' original and living 'habitats' in the faith communities that gave rise to these texts and still regard them to be sacred and authoritative? A natural scientist, by comparison, would never presume to study an animal or plant without considering its surrounding environment or ecosystem. Yet this is precisely the *modus operandi* of 'scientific' exegesis.

Moreover, the 'scientific' exegete adopts a hermeneutic of suspicion toward the larger ecclesial and liturgical tradition. It is presumed that we cannot trust the plain sense of the biblical texts. The Church's traditional use of texts in its dogmas, moral teachings, and liturgical rituals, comes to be seen as an impediment to a true understanding of their original meanings. While seldom stated in such stark terms, it is implicit in the basic operation of biblical 'science,' that the received biblical texts are a species of ideology, part of an ecclesiastical machinery used to legitimate and consolidate power and control by religious elites.[25]

The root of the problem is a refusal, on methodological grounds, to engage the divine nature of the religious text. Benedict traces this to the epistemological agnosticism of the German Enlightenment philosopher, Immanuel Kant, who believed it was impossible for human reason to know the truth and reality of 'things in themselves,' especially God. As Kant believed we can never know things that transcend our sensory perceptions, historical criticism starts with the presumption that it can only analyze the 'human element' in Scripture, defined as those things that conform to the evidence of our senses and our understanding of natural laws.[26] This philosophical presupposition, Benedict believes, is of 'great consequence':

---

[24] See the sources assembled in *Principles of Catholic Theology*, 92 n. 5.

[25] In fact, as Benedict notes, the earliest attempts to study the historical Jesus had an explicitly anticlerical aim, 'the aim of using history to correct dogma, setting up a purely human, historical Jesus against the Christ of faith' (*Behold the Pierced One*, 43).

[26] Again, for Benedict, the root of this suspicion of Church dogma runs deep. 'For Reimarus, the Church's faith was no longer the way to find Jesus but a mythical

It is assumed that history is fundamentally and always uniform and that therefore nothing can take place in history but what is possible as a result of causes known to us in nature and in human activity. Aberrations from that, for instance, divine interventions that go beyond the constant interaction of natural and human causes, cannot therefore be historical. ... According to this assumption, it is not possible for a man really to be God and to perform deeds that require divine power – actions that would disrupt the general complex of causes. Accordingly, words attributed to Jesus in which he makes divine claims and the corresponding deeds must be 'explained'... everything in the figure of Jesus that transcends mere humanity is ... thus not really historical.... [27]

Because of this prior assumption, the method is compelled to bracket off as pious exaggerations or legends every claim made in the texts about miracles, or about God's work in the world and in history. This puts historical critics in the position of having to explain away rather than to explicate the plain sense of many biblical texts, such as those of Christ walking on water, multiplying loaves and fishes, healing the sick, and raising persons from the dead. [28] Again, the question is why such a posture towards the texts would be considered necessary or even desirable. Why would we want to study religious texts in such a way as to exclude in advance any reference the texts make to divine or supernatural phenomena?

The hermeneutic of faith

The power of Benedict's critique lies in its insistence that he evaluate the merits of method in modern exegesis purely on 'scientific' grounds; when he does this, he finds the method seriously wanting. He does not write as a Church official concerned that historical criticism is undermining Church beliefs and doctrines. Rather, as a scholar, he invites us to consider whether the method is capable of really explaining as much as it claims to explain. At the most basic level, he suggests, to study a religious text without the ability to explain its divine meaning is to have failed, or at least to have completed only half the task:

> From a purely scientific point of view, the legitimacy of an interpretation depends on its power to explain things. In other words, the less it needs to interfere with the

---

smokescreen that concealed the historical reality. Jesus was to be sought, not *through* dogma, but *against* it, if one wanted to arrive at historical knowledge of him. Historical reason became the corrective of dogma; critical reason became the antipode of traditional faith' (*Principles of Catholic Theology*, 92).

[27] *On the Way to Jesus Christ*, trans. M. Miller (San Francisco: Ignatius, 2005 [2004]), 61–65.

[28] *A New Song for the Lord*, 30.

At the School of Truth 89

sources, the more it respects the corpus as given and is able to show it to be intelligible from within, by its own logic, the more apposite such an interpretation is. Conversely, the more it interferes with the sources, the more it feels obliged to excise and throw doubt on things found there, the more alien to the subject it is. To that extent, its explanatory power is also its ability to maintain the inner unity of the corpus in question. It involves the ability to unify, to achieve a synthesis, which is the reverse of superficial harmonization. Indeed, only faith's hermeneutic is sufficient to measure up to these criteria.[29]

We will consider the last line of this quotation momentarily. On the simple measure of its 'power to explain things,' the historical-critical method is found to be sorely deficient. The hermeneutic of suspicion vis-a-vis the Church, the search for the 'evolution' of individual texts, the excising of all reference to supernatural phenomena – all these represent a high degree of interference with the texts themselves as they have been given to us. Nor do the operations of the method preserve or identify any inner unity or inner logic in the texts.

For Benedict, another fatal defect in the method is in severing the bond that unites the Bible and the Church. Studying biblical texts in isolation, with no reference to the way these texts have been and continue to be used in the Church's liturgy, preaching and practice, makes the Bible a dead letter – like an artifact from a long extinct, exotic culture. The process of biblical exegesis becomes an exercise in 'antiquarianism' or 'archeology,' even 'necrophilia.'[30]

Benedict notes that 'the history of exegesis is a history of contradictions,' a constantly shifting succession of competing hypotheses concerning the meaning of texts. And the method, as he sees it, cannot yield much more unless yoked to a faith perspective:

By its very nature, historical interpretation can never take us beyond hypotheses. After all, none of us was there when it happened; only physical science can repeat events in the laboratory. Faith makes us Jesus' contemporaries. It can and must integrate all true historical discoveries, and it becomes richer for doing so. But faith gives us knowledge of something more than a hypothesis; it gives us the right to trust the revealed Word as such.[31]

He calls for a 'hermeneutic of faith,'[32] one in which historical and critical methods are subordinated to, and harnessed by, the living faith of the Church. In his own theological writing, we see him unfolding such a hermeneutic,

[29] Behold the Pierced One, 44–45.
[30] Nature and Mission of Theology, 65, 95; Feast of Faith, 28; New Song for the Lord, 50–51; Biblical Interpretation in Crisis, 17.
[31] Gospel, Catechesis, Catechism, 67–68; On the Way to Jesus Christ, 152.
[32] Eschatology, 272.

always making use of contemporary exegesis, but refusing to abide by the artificial limits the method imposes on inquiry. In his writing we see the full explanatory power of the hermeneutic of faith, which respects the biblical texts as they are given in the Church and shows their inner unity and logic. One thing Benedict does insist upon – that faith itself is a legitimate source of knowledge and inquiry. To reduce all human knowledge to the realm of the subjective, the empirical, as the critical method presumes to do, marks a distortion of reason:

> Faith has a contribution to make with regard to the interpretation of Scripture ... To reduce all of reality as we meet it to pure material causes, to confine the Creator Spirit to the sphere of mere subjectivity, is irreconcilable with the fundamental message of the Bible. This involves, however, a debate on the very nature of true rationality; since, if a purely materialistic explanation of reality is presented as the only possible expression of reason, then reason itself is falsely understood. ... Faith itself is a way of knowing. Wanting to set it aside does not produce pure objectivity, but comprises a point of view which excludes a particular perspective while not wanting to take into account the accompanying conditions of the chosen point of view. If one takes into account, however, that the sacred Scriptures come from God through a subject which lives continually – the pilgrim people of God – then it becomes clear rationally as well that this subject has something to say about the understanding of the book.[33]

The Ecclesial Locus of Theology and Exegesis

The 'interwoven relationship between Church and Bible'

Benedict's biblical theology and his hermeneutic of faith grow organically from the historical structure of revelation. In formulating his understanding of theology and exegesis, he appropriates an important finding of modern form and redaction criticism – namely, that Scripture is the product of the Church, and that its contents originated in this ecclesial context and were shaped over long years by the Church's proclamation, confession, catechesis and liturgical worship. Following this line of enquiry, Benedict then draws out from scholarly findings concerning the growth and development of the early Church a correlative conclusion – that there is an obvious and undeniable inner unity, an 'interwoven relationship between Church and Bible, between the People of God and the Word of God.'[34] The appreciation of this relationship determines

---

[33] 'Relationship between Magisterium and Exegetes,' 8.

[34] 'Two things have above all become clear about the nature of the biblical word in the process of critical exegesis. First of all, that the word of the Bible, at the moment it was set down in writing, already had behind it a more or less long process of shaping

his understanding of such key considerations as revelation, inspiration, canon, theology, authority, interpretation, mission and liturgy.

As Benedict describes it, the Church was born in the coming of the Word of God, called into being by Christ's gospel and the salvation-historical event of his resurrection, and ordered to the mission of witnessing to that event. The Church is the 'living, historical subject' of God's Word.[35] The Church lives by the Word it has heard, pondering and proclaiming it that others might hear and believe and enter into the fellowship or *communio* of the Church, through the power of Word and sacrament. In the Church's proclamation and liturgical celebration, the Word of salvation spoken in the past is always 'a present reality.'[36] The community's identity is defined by its liturgical remembrance in the Eucharist of the event the Word speaks of, and in this 'solemn remembrance *the means of salvation history* – the death and resurrection of the Lord – is truly present.'[37]

What is true for the Church is true for each member of the Church. To enter into this people of God is to be born of the Word. It is to hear the Word

---

by oral tradition and that it was not frozen at the moment it was written down, but entered into new processes of interpretation – 'relectures' – that further develop its hidden potential. Thus, the extent of the Word's meaning cannot be reduced to the thoughts of a single author in a specific historical moment; it is not the property of a single author at all; rather, it lives in a history that is ever moving onward and, thus, has dimensions and depths of meaning in past and future that ultimately pass into the realm of the unforeseen . . . . Certainly, Scripture carries God's thoughts within it: that makes it unique and constitutes it an 'authority.' Yet it is transmitted by a human history. It carries within it the life and thought of a historical society that we call the 'People of God,' because they are brought together, and held together, by the coming of the divine Word. There is a reciprocal relationship: This society is the essential condition for the origin and the growth of the biblical Word; and conversely, this Word gives the society its identity and continuity. Thus, the analysis of the structure of the biblical Word has brought to light an interwoven relationship between Church and Bible, between the People of God and the Word of God' (*Pilgrim Fellowship of Faith*, 32–33).

[35] *Spirit of the Liturgy*, 168. 'The faith of the Church does not exist as an ensemble of texts, rather, the texts – the words – exist because there is a corresponding subject which gives them their basis and their inner coherence. Empirically speaking, the preaching of the apostles called into existence the social organization "Church" as a kind of historical subject. One becomes a believer by joining this community of tradition, thought and life, by living personally from its continuity of life throughout history and by acquiring a share in its way of understanding, its speech and its thought' (*Nature and Mission of Theology*, 94).

[36] *Called to Communion*, 19.

[37] *Principles of Catholic Theology*, 2 [emphasis added]; *Church, Ecumenism and Politics*, 8.

and believe. Yet faith is not simply an intellectual assent to a set of principles or texts. Faith requires from each believer 'a word about the Word,' a personal profession of faith in the Word that is heard.[38] Since the Word cannot be heard unless it is heard *from* the Church, the confession of faith is an ecclesial and liturgical action, an event that takes place *in* the Church. One does not confess faith in the gospel by oneself, but in the presence of the community of those already living this faith, and this confession takes place in the ritual context or form of the sacrament.[39] The communal celebration of baptism recognizes the historical and ecclesial character of conversion, that the faith of the Church precedes every believer's faith and is the instrument by which believers come to the faith.

The confession of faith itself, the *symbol* or the creed, is an interpretive synthesis of the Word by which the Church determined 'what actually constituted Christianity.'[40] But profession of this creed, from the start, was preceded by a period of *catechumenate* or instruction in the truths of the faith.[41] The Church's catechesis, in which its doctrines and dogmas originally arose,[42] was aimed at forming the believer's life according to the Word, making that Word the deep source of new life for the believer. 'That is, the faith that comes to us as a Word must also become a word in us, a word that is simultaneously the expression of our life.'[43]

---

[38] *Gospel, Catechesis, Catechism*, 30–31.

[39] *Nature and Mission of Theology*, 52.

[40] *Principles of Catholic Theology*, 149.

[41] 'Hand in hand with the sign there was always the instruction, the word, that gave the sign its place in the history of Israel's covenant with God' (*Principles of Catholic Theology*, 29).

[42] *Principles of Catholic Theology*, 27. 'To become a Christian is to enter into this one particular creed, into the communal form of the faith. The inner bond between the community itself and this creed is expressed by the fact that the acceptance into the community has the form of a sacrament: baptism and catechesis are inseparable. . . . By its very nature, the word of faith presupposes the community that lives it, that is bound to it, and adheres to it in its very power to bind mankind' (*Principles of Catholic Theology*, 329–30).

[43] 'We do not think up faith on our own. It does not come *from* us as an idea of ours but *to* us as a word from outside. It is, as it were, a word about the Word; we are "handed over" *into* this Word . . . that precedes us through an immersion in water symbolizing death . . . We cannot receive this word as a theory in the same way that we learn, say, mathematical formulas or philosophical opinions. We can learn it only in accepting a share in Christ's destiny. But we can become sharers in Christ's destiny only where he has permanently committed himself to sharing in man's destiny: in the Church. In the language of the Church we call this event a "sacrament." The act of faith is unthinkable without the sacramental component. . . . That is, the faith that comes to

The sacrament of baptism, like the Eucharist, is also a real initiation into the salvation-historical event that is the content of the Word. The Church's sacraments, which consist of the scriptural word and material signs, are true acts of God, 'the communications of him who . . . is God's visible Word.'[44] By these acts, God establishes a covenant, family bond with each person, making them sons and daughters in 'the great family' of the Church.[45] This ontic status of divine filiation is another inward confirmation of the divine nature and efficacy of the sacramental Word and sign. One cannot declare oneself to be a child of God. This character must be received as a gift bestowed by the only One who has the power to bestow such a gift. In the sacrament, the believer is united into God's larger salvific design, 'a common history in which God brought the people together and became their way.'[46]

Canon, apostolic succession, and the 'rule of faith'

The structure of the sacramental confession of faith presupposes the institution and mission of the Church. That is, it presupposes *apostolic succession*, the means by which responsibility and authority for bearing witness to the Word is handed on in the Church; the *canon* of Scriptures determined to be authoritative written expressions of that Word; and the 'rule of faith' (*regula fidei*), established to guarantee the integrity and orthodoxy of that witness.

In his theoretical work on the nature of theology and exegesis, Benedict consistently presses for closer attention to the history of the early Church and the original inner unity of Word, sacrament, and Church order and authority. That history demonstrates that the institutions and practices of the Church are not artificial or arbitrary later constructs, but organic developments of the encounter of the people of God's with the Word of God. Put another way, the structure of revelation and the faith – how the early Church heard the Word of God and responded to it – is itself the source of the Church's sacramental worship, its teaching office, and its principles of governance. Benedict notes the interdependence of these three critical 'establishments' in the early Church – canon, apostolic succession, and the *regula*

---

us as a word must also become a word in us, a word that is simultaneously the expression of our life' (*Gospel, Catechesis, Catechism*, 30–31). See also, 'The life embraced the Word, and the Word formed the life. Indeed, it is only to one who has entered into the community of faith that the Word of faith reveals itself' (*Principles of Catholic Theology*, 26).

[44] *Principles of Catholic Theology*, 47.

[45] *Principles of Catholic Theology*, 32; *Behold the Pierced One*, 105–106; *Called to Communion*, 23.

[46] *Principles of Catholic Theology*, 29–31.

fidei.[47] For Benedict, these three establishments are actually one in the same decision, made in service of 'the presence of the Word in the world.'[48] Establishment of the canon acknowledged the 'sovereignty of the Word,' and the Church as servant of the Word. At the same time it fixed the form of that Word, establishing the New Testament and the Hebrew Scriptures as 'a single Scripture' and the 'master text.' Word and witness cannot be separated and the continuity of that witness through history is guaranteed by the establishment of apostolic succession and the episcopal ministry. Finally the truth of that witness is guaranteed by the rule of faith which becomes 'a key for interpretation.'[49]

From this 'reciprocal compenetration'[50] of Word, witness, and rule of faith, come the distinctive characteristics of Sacred Scripture. First, Scripture, as 'Scripture,' is entrusted to and enacted by the Church.[51] The Bible, the canon of texts that make up the Old and New Testaments, is the product of this integral, organic development, composed, edited and organized according to the Church's needs for preaching, catechesis and especially, liturgy. The criteria for the canon are primarily liturgical: 'A book was recognized as "canonical" if it was sanctioned by the Church for use in public worship. . . . In the ancient Church, the reading of Scripture and the confession of faith were primarily liturgical acts of the whole assembly gathered around the risen Lord.'[52] The Church is the living subject of Scripture, which is the *viva vox,* the living voice of Scripture, protecting the Word from manipulation and distortion.[53] As the confessional and sacramental life of the Church were the criteria by which the

---

[47] Address to Ecumenical Meeting at the Archbishopric of Cologne, 8–9.

[48] 'The establishment of the canon and the establishment of the early Church are one and the same process but viewed from different perspectives' (*Principles of Catholic Theology*, 148).

[49] Address to Ecumenical Meeting at the Archbishopric of Cologne; *Principles of Catholic Theology,* 148–49.

[50] Address to Ecumenical Meeting at the Archbishopric of Cologne.

[51] In this regard, Benedict quotes Heinrich Schlier, the student of Bultmann and courageous member of the Christian opposition to Hitler: 'It is unlikely that any sensible Christian would contest that the care for the Word of God among men is entrusted to the Church alone' *(Nature and Mission of Theology,* 45).

[52] *Principles of Catholic Theology,* 148, 150.

[53] 'The original sphere of existence of the Christian profession of faith, however, was the sacramental life of the Church. It is by this criterion that the canon was shaped, and that is why the Creed is the primary authority for the interpretation of the Bible. . . . Thus the authority of the Church that speaks out, the authority of apostolic succession, is written into Scripture through the Creed and is indivisible from it. The teaching office of the apostles' successors does not represent a secondary authority alongside Scripture but is inwardly a part of it. This *viva vox* is not there to restrict the

canon was formed, the Scriptures are intended to be interpreted according to the rule of faith or the creed, under the authority of the apostolic succession.[54]

Memoria Ecclesiae

The Church, then, is the living memory of God's salvation-historical acts, and the memory of these deeds gives the Church its 'common identity as God's family.'[55] Benedict speaks of 'the memoria Ecclesiae, the memory of the Church, the Church as memory.'[56] As the memory of God's saving words and actions in history, the Church brings about the unity of humankind's history with God. In the memory of the Church, the present experience of the faith is joined to the past and oriented to the future, the expectation of which is also the subject of the word of faith preserved in the Church. This memory is deepened and renewed through the Church's liturgy and theology. The central expression of the Church's identity is the eucharistic memorial, which brings about communion and 'contemporaneity with Christ.'[57]

Without the Church, the Word would be consigned to oblivion, a private memory of things past. But the Word is not a kind of static deposit of faith. Nor is the Church a museum or an archive. It guarantees that the Word continues to be heard afresh throughout time. 'Scripture alive in the living Church is also God's present power in the world today – a power which remains an inexhaustible source of hope throughout all generations.'[58] Because the Church 'preserves faith's experiences with God,' it makes a deeper integration of theology and exegesis possible. Indeed, Benedict insists on 'the essentially ecclesial identity of theology.' The Church is the living subject or 'do-er' of theology. Theology flows out of the Church's remembrance – its listening, pondering,

---

authority of Scripture or to limit it or even replace it by the existence of another – on the contrary, it is its task to ensure that Scripture is not disposable, cannot be manipulated, to preserve its proper *perspicuitas,* its clear meaning from the conflict of hypotheses. Thus, there is a secret relationship of reciprocity. Scripture sets limits and a standard for the *viva vox;* the living voice guarantees that it cannot be manipulated' (*Pilgrim Fellowship of Faith,* 35).

[54] *Pilgrim Fellowship of Faith,* 35.
[55] *Gospel, Catechesis, Catechism,* 63.
[56] 'Christian faith, by its very nature, includes the act of remembering; in this way, it brings about the unity of history and the unity of man before God, or rather: it can bring about the unity of history because God has given it memory. The seat of all faith is, then, the *memoria Ecclesiae,* the memory of the Church, the Church's memory. It exists through all ages, waxing and waning but never ceasing to be the common situs of faith' (*Principles of Catholic Theology,* 23).
[57] *Nature and Mission of Theology,* 60; *Principles of Catholic Theology,* 88, 100.
[58] *New Song for the Lord,* 52.

and explaining the Word of God. And the Church is the 'living environment' of all theological activity.

In Benedict's view, theology thus grows out of the very structure of the faith, as a consequence, even an imperative of the faith. Theology begins in the response to God's greatest gift, the divine Word that God has spoken to us in Jesus.[59] Theology is the response of the believer to the Word, who is a divine Person, and to the 'contents' of his Word – the revelation of God's love, expressed in the new covenant made in the death and resurrection of Jesus Christ. We 'do' theology in the first place because we believe in and love the God who has shown his face to us in Jesus Christ. Theology is faith seeking better understanding of the One who reveals himself as love. It is an 'imperative' because there is an inward desire to seek the truth and the most intimate knowledge possible of the One we love:

> Faith can wish to understand because it is moved by love for the One upon whom it has bestowed its consent. Love seeks understanding. It wishes to know ever better the one whom it loves. It 'seeks his face,' as Augustine never tires of repeating. Love is the desire for intimate knowledge, so that the quest for intelligence can even be an inner requirement of love. Put another way, there is a coherence of love and truth which has important consequences for theology and philosophy. Christian faith can say of itself, I have found love. Yet love for Christ and of one's neighbor for Christ's sake can enjoy stability and consistency only if its deepest motivation is love for the truth. This adds a new aspect to the missionary element: real love of neighbor also desires to give him the deepest thing man needs, namely, knowledge and truth.[60]

We see that for Benedict theology is not a private affair. The desire to know and love God better is always ordered to the Church's proclamation of the saving Word – 'to tell man who he is and . . . to disclose to him the truth about himself, that is, what he can base his life on and what he can die for.'[61] In Benedict's understanding, there is an original and inner dynamism that orients theology to proclamation and catechesis. This is not at all to reduce the work of theology to apologetics or catechetics. Instead, Benedict sees a missionary impulse issuing from the heart of the Christian faith experience. Faith, because it possesses the truth about human history and happiness, must necessarily express itself in proclamation and catechesis so that others may share in the truth.

---

[59] *Nature and Mission of Theology*, 103–104; *Pilgrim Fellowship of Faith*, 32; *Principles of Catholic Theology*, 325.

[60] *Nature and Mission of Theology*, 27.

[61] *Nature and Mission of Theology*, 63–64.

The authors of Scripture as the 'normative' theologians

If the activity of theology flows from the inner structure of Christian faith, its content and methodology in a similar way issue from the inner structure of revelation. Benedict appropriates a distinction first drawn by Aristotle and later adopted by pseudo-Dionysius and Bonaventure – between 'theology' proper, the words of God, and the study of theology, our efforts to understand the divine discourse.[62] He sees Sacred Scripture as theology in its original and pure form, because it is 'the discourse of God rendered in human words . . . it does not just speak of him but *is* his own speech. It lets God himself speak.' He accepts the traditional Catholic notion of Scripture's dual authorship, divine and human. But he notes that the human writers of Scripture are the original theologians, 'those through whom God . . . as the Word that speaks itself, enters into history.' This originary aspect of revelation has great significance for him: 'the Bible becomes the model of all theology,' and the authors of Sacred Scripture become the norm of the theologian, who accomplishes his task properly only to the extent that he makes God himself his subject.' This in turn leads to perhaps his most daring and fruitful assertion of theological principle:

> Theology is a spiritual science. The normative theologians are the authors of Holy Scripture. This statement is valid not only with reference to the objective written document they left behind but also with reference to their manner of speaking, in which it is God himself who speaks.[63]

For Benedict that means that Scripture, and the human authors of Scripture, are meant to serve as the model for how we should 'do' theology, and for what our theology should be about.

Taking the New Testament authors as normative means, in the first place, that the theologian must be a person of faith, who has heard and believed the Word, professed that faith in the Church, and committed oneself to the teachings of the Church and its sacramental life. 'Theology presupposes faith. . . . There can be no theology without conversion.'[64] Inasmuch as the authors of the New Testament were themselves men of faith, the written proclamation of these authors teaches us that to know Jesus we must follow him as his disciples.[65] Following the New Testament writers, Benedict accordingly sees theology as essentially about Christology and ecclesiology. 'All Christian theology,

---

[62] *Principles of Catholic Theology*, 320–22.
[63] *Principles of Catholic Theology*, 320–22.
[64] *Nature and Mission of Theology*, 55, 57.
[65] See the biblical citations in *On the Way to Jesus Christ*, 67. 'Just as we cannot learn to swim without water, so we cannot learn theology without the spiritual praxis in which it lives' (*Principles of Catholic Theology*, 323).

if it is to be true to its origin, must be first and foremost a theology of resurrection.'[66] Theology is 'about' Jesus Christ – who he is, the full meaning of the salvation event of his resurrection, and how his presence remains in the world in his Church.[67] The primary data for theology becomes the words and deeds of Jesus as remembered and interpreted in the New Testament.[68] This remembrance takes a definite shape in the Scriptures.

Benedict illuminates his thought on the Church as *memoria* by reflecting upon a passage in John's Gospel, a brief statement made after the cleansing of the temple: 'When therefore he was raised from the dead, his disciples remembered that he had said this; and they believed the scripture and the word which Jesus had spoken' (Jn. 2:22 [RSV]). The passage refers to Jesus' declaration that should his enemies destroy 'this shrine,' he would raise it in three days. Benedict reads this passage in light of the promise found later in John's Gospel, that Jesus would send the Holy Spirit to lead the disciples to remembrance of all that he had said (Jn. 14:26).[69] He suggests that in this passage we have all the elements for a biblical doctrine of the Church as living memory of the faith: belief in the salvation-historical event of the resurrection; belief in the unity of the Old Testament (the 'Scripture' Jesus referred them to) and the New Testament (the 'Word' spoken by Jesus); and remembrance in the Spirit, which takes place in the ecclesial context and authority established by Jesus.

One could develop Benedict's insights even further by delineating more precisely the 'content' of the disciples' remembrance. The 'word' that the Spirit brings them to remember is a spiritual or typological interpretation of the Old Testament. In light of the resurrection, and under the guidance of the Spirit, the apostles understand Jesus' words about the temple to have been referring to the 'temple' of his body. The passage gives us insight into Jesus' own preaching, which is the model for the human authors of the New Testament. It also suggests a distinctive way in which the New Testament appropriates the unity of its witness to Jesus with the Scriptures of the Old Testament: the New Testament word of Jesus, ratified by his resurrection from the dead, is the fulfillment of the Old Testament word.

---

[66] *Principles of Catholic Theology*, 184–85.

[67] *On the Way to Jesus Christ*, 76–77.

[68] 'The remembrance and retention of the words of Jesus and of the course of his life, especially his passion, were from the beginning an essential factor in the formation of Christian tradition and in the norms applied to it' (*Dogma and Preaching*, 4).

[69] 'Tradition is ultimately based on the fact that the Christ event cannot be limited to the age of the historical Jesus, but continues in the presence of the Spirit, through which the Lord who "departed" on the cross "has come again" and through which he "reminds" the Church of what happened, so that it is led as it remembers, into its inner significance and is able to assimilate and experience it as present event' ('Commentary on *Dei Verbum*,' 3:189–90; *Milestones*, 59).

Read through Benedict's eyes, we see the New Testament writers in constant dialogue with the Old Testament texts. Indeed, the New Testament is a spiritual exegesis of the Old. 'The New Testament is nothing other than an interpretation of "the Law, the prophets, and the writings" found from or contained in the story of Jesus.'[70] Jesus' preaching, which forms the narrative structure of the gospels and is reproduced in the accounts of the apostolic preaching found in Acts and in the epistles, consists largely of Old Testament interpretation. But so also for his actions: the central salvation-historical event, his resurrection, is both a mighty act of God and a vindication of Jesus' interpretation of the Old Testament, or 'God's defense of Jesus against the official interpretation of the Old Testament as given by the competent Jewish authorities.' By his resurrection, God 'proves,' so to speak, that Jesus is the suffering servant, the divine son, and the messiah from the line of David, foretold by the prophets and the psalms.[71] Of critical significance, in Benedict's mind, is the portrayal of Jesus as 'the true lamb of sacrifice, the sacrifice in which the deepest meaning of all Old Testament liturgies is fulfilled.' As we will see below, this has 'essential significance for the Christian liturgy.'[72] Jesus did not invent this way of reading the Scriptures, according to Benedict. He notes that in the prophets and psalms, we find increasing anticipation of a messianic king to be 'the fulfilled image of the true Israel.'[73]

Benedict's New Synthesis

'Theology is interpretation'

We are now in the position to sketch, if only in the broadest outlines, some of the elements of what I would describe as Benedict's biblical theology. For Benedict, 'theology is interpretation,'[74] a reflection on the Word that has been given. Exegesis, he has said, has always been 'the center of my theological work.'[75] We might characterize Benedict as a 'biblical realist.' What he says

---

[70] *Milestones*, 53.
[71] *Dogma and Preaching*, 3.
[72] *Dogma and Preaching*, 3–5.
[73] *Meaning of Christian Brotherhood*, 48.
[74] *Nature and Mission of Theology*, 93.
[75] *Milestones*, 52–53. Describing his thought to a journalist, he once said: 'Exegesis was always very important. . . . The point of departure is first of all the Word. That we believe the word of God, that we try really to get to know and understand it, and then . . . to think it together with the great masters of the faith. This gives my theology a somewhat biblical character and also bears the stamp of the Fathers, especially Augustine' (*Salt of the Earth*, 66).

about the Catechism of the Catholic Church, which he was instrumental in conceiving and editing, is true of his own thought:

> The *Catechism* trusts the biblical word. It holds the Christ of the gospels to be the real Jesus. It is also convinced that all the gospels tell us about this same Jesus and that all of them together help us, each in its own way, to know the true Jesus of history, who is no other than the Christ of faith.[76]

He has often stated that the testimony of the New Testament is far more reliable that the constantly shifting hypotheses of historical-critical scholarship.[77] He accepts the gospel testimony as 'a written record of the most ancient catechesis.'[78] The Old Testament witness, too, he likewise treats seriously as history.[79] He is quite conscious that in this stance he is at odds with the dominant model of 'scientific exegesis.' Again, he rejects the notion that faith and history are somehow in dialectical opposition, that the biblical narrative cannot be a source of true historical knowledge.

> The opinion that faith as such knows absolutely nothing of historical facts and must leave all of this to historians is Gnosticism: this opinion disembodies faith and reduces it to pure idea. The reality of events is necessary precisely because the faith is founded on the Bible. A God who cannot intervene in history and reveal himself in it is not the God of the Bible.... That Jesus – in all that is essential – was effectively who the Gospels reveal him to be to us is not mere historical conjecture, but a fact of faith. Objections which seek to convince us to the contrary are not the expression of an effective scientific knowledge, but are an arbitrary over-evaluation of the method.[80]

---

[76] *Gospel, Catechesis, Catechism*, 64.

[77] 'I credit biblical tradition with greater truthfulness than I do the attempts to reconstruct a chemically pure historical Jesus in the retort of historical reason. I trust the tradition in its entirety. And the more reconstructions I see come and go, the more I feel confirmed in my trust.... In the face of such partial authorities the vital power of the tradition carries incomparably greater weight with me.... I know that the Jesus of the gospels is the real Jesus and that I can trust myself to him with far greater security than I can to the most learned reconstructions; he will outlast all of them. The gospel tradition with its great breadth and its range of tone tells me who Jesus was and is. In it he is always present to be heard and seen anew' (*Dogma and Preaching*, 9–10).

[78] *Gospel, Catechesis, Catechism*, 61.

[79] For example, he writes of 'the whole history recounted in the books of the Judges and Kings, which is taken up afresh and given a new interpretation in Chronicles,' and uses the account of Israel's exodus and settlement of the land as an insight into the meaning of worship (*Spirit of the Liturgy*, 15–20). Likewise, he considers the history of liturgy from Genesis to the Christian era (*Spirit of the Liturgy*, 35–45), and discusses the biblical nature of wisdom in light of Isaiah's prophecy and the Davidic monarchy (*Principles of Catholic Theology*, 356–58).

[80] 'Relationship between Magisterium and Exegetes.'

Throughout this history, he sees not only a series of events in the life of a people, but also the hand of God, 'the great acts of God in history.'[81] In this, we see Benedict's hermeneutic of faith, again in sharp distinction from the supposedly 'scientific' worldview of biblical criticism. The exegete, he says,

> ... may not exclude a priori that (almighty) God could speak in human words in the world. He may not exclude that God himself could enter into and work in human history, however, improbable such a thing might at first appear. He must be ready to learn from the extraordinary. He must be ready to accept that the truly original may occur in history, something which cannot be derived from precedents but which opens up out of itself. He may not deny to humanity the ability to be responsive beyond the categories of pure reason and to reach beyond ourselves toward the open and endless truth of being.[82]

Benedict shares the view of Bonaventure, that to understand the literal, historical text is not to understand Scripture as it is given, as revelation. What is needed is to understand the 'spiritual meaning lying behind the letter.'[83] He insists that 'spiritual [interpretation] does not mean that the exegesis lacks realism or disregards history but that it brings into view the spiritual depth of the historical events.'[84]

As we have pointed out, Benedict reads biblical history using sophisticated tools of historical and literary criticism. However, in endeavoring to read the Bible with the normative theologians, the biblical authors, he does not stop with history, but reads also with the eyes of faith. Faith, informed by the teaching of the Church, especially the creed, 'gives us the right to trust the revealed Word as such.'[85] Again and again, Benedict urges us not to oppose faith and reason. Faith does not exempt us from careful literary and historical analysis of the texts. Indeed, faith is a form of special knowledge that empowers us to undertake this analysis with deeper insight and lends to our work a greater unity and coherence.

Faith's inner unity and historical structure

Following the biblical authors, Benedict's theology is built on a series of *unities* – 'the unity of the Old and New Testaments, of the New Testament and early

---

[81] *Principles of Catholic Theology*, 190.
[82] *Biblical Interpretation in Crisis*, 19.
[83] *Theology of History in St. Bonaventure*, 66–68, 78–79.
[84] *Gospel, Catechesis, Catechism*, 65, n. 24.
[85] *Gospel, Catechesis, Catechism*, 67–68. He describes this spiritual reading as 'a faith that does not set history aside but first opens its eyes so as to be able to understand it in its entirety' (*On the Way to Jesus Christ*, 59).

Church dogma, of all these elements together and the ongoing life of faith.' His goal is to 'seek the inner unity and totality of the truth in the grand historical structure of the faith.'[86]

We have seen already how the New Testament witness presumes the 'inner unity' of the Old and New Testaments.[87] This notion of the unity of the Scriptures is not a superimposed theory or hypothesis; it is suggested by the very structure of the faith. The Bible, in its final canonical form, is essentially a historical narrative. It purports to tell a single story about events that have taken place in the history of a people – from the first day of creation to the last day, which is the beginning of new heavens and a new earth. The canonical text, then, claims to be more than an account of historical facts or the memoir of a particular people. It claims that God himself was at work in the events it records, and that the words of various characters and their deeds are themselves actions of God.[88] This suggests, too, within the very structure of biblical revelation, a twofold sense of meaning – the one literal and historical, and the other the sense or senses of the text that can only be gained by faith, by belief in the claims made about God in these texts. This unity is likewise a constituent element of early Church faith and dogma, seen most clearly in the establishment of the canon.

The confession of faith also reflects this belief in the unity of Scriptures, and implies a particular way of reading the Scriptures, a spiritual reading based on the salvation-historical event of God in raising Jesus from the dead on the third day. In its simplest form, the confession is in the name, 'Jesus Christ.' In this confession, Jesus, the historical figure whose life and deeds are recorded in the New Testament is affirmed to be the 'Christ,' the anointed Messiah foretold in the Old Testament. In this, we see that 'Christian identity . . . is founded on the unity of the testaments.'[89]

Benedict, following the normative theologians, reads the Scriptures as a single story, as one book about Jesus Christ. Reading the Scriptures as a single history of salvation, Benedict detects in this history a 'pedagogy,' a long, historical tutelage or 'educational process' by which God prepared humankind for the revelation of Christ and his new covenant.[90] He sees in the 'inner continuity and coherence'[91] of the Old and New Testaments a revelation of the divine intent in salvation history. 'The totality of the Scriptures on which the

---

[86] *Nature and Mission of Theology*, 96.

[87] *Behold the Pierced One*, 44.

[88] *On the Way to Jesus Christ*, 147–48.

[89] *Many Religions, One Covenant*, 18.

[90] *Many Religions, One Covenant*, 55–56; *Pilgrim Fellowship of Faith*, 270; *Principles of Catholic Theology*, 344–45; *In the Beginning*, 9, 16.

[91] *Many Religions, One Covenant*, 36.

Christian faith rests is God's "testament" to mankind, issued in two stages, as a proclamation of his will to the world.'[92]

In 'the profound compenetration of the two testaments as the one Scripture of the Christian faith,' Benedict sees the meaning of God's plan revealed in Jesus Christ:

> The real novelty of the New Testament lies not so much in new ideas as in the figure of Christ himself, who gives flesh and blood to these concepts – an unprecedented realism. In the Old Testament, the novelty of the Bible did not consist merely in abstract notions but in God's unpredictable and in some sense unprecedented activity. This divine activity now takes on dramatic form when, in Jesus Christ, it is God himself who goes in search of the 'stray sheep,' a suffering and lost humanity. . . . His death on the cross is the culmination of that turning of God against himself in which he gives himself in order to raise man up and save him. This is love in its most radical form.[93]

Covenant, the central theme of Scripture

God's will for the world is the *covenant*, a relationship of communion in love that embraces heaven and earth, spirit and matter, the divine and the human. Benedict reads God's covenant will and desire on the first pages of Scripture, in the account of creation. He expresses the meaning of the creation account in a series of statements: 'Creation is oriented to the sabbath, which is the sign of the covenant between God and humankind. . . . Creation is designed in such a way that it is oriented to worship. It fulfills its purpose and assumes its significance when it is lived, ever new, with a view to worship. Creation exists for the sake of worship.'[94]

Fashioned in the image of God, the human person was created for relationship with God. Men and women were created for worship, which is an

---

[92] *Many Religions, One Covenant*, 47. 'The synthesis of the testaments worked out in the early Church corresponds solely to the fundamental intention of the New Testament message, and it alone can give Christianity its own historical force' (*New Song for the Lord*, 72). 'The understanding of Holy Scripture as an inner unity in which one part sustains the other, has its existence in it, so that each part can be read and understood only in terms of the whole' (*Principles of Catholic Theology*, 135–36). 'The New Testament itself wished to be no more than the complete and full understanding of the Old Testament, now made possible in Christ. The whole Old Testament is a movement of transition to Christ, a waiting for the One in whom all its words would come true, in whom the "Covenant" would attain fulfillment as the New Covenant' (*Feast of Faith*, 58).

[93] Benedict XVI, *Deus Caritas Est*, 12.

[94] *In the Beginning*, 27–28.

expression of 'the pure relationship of love'[95] of the creature with the Creator. The story of the world told in Scripture is 'the love story of God and man.'[96] For Benedict, the God who reveals himself to us, the God who creates and redeems, reveals himself in Scripture as a 'God-in-relationship.' He reveals himself in word and deed in the acts of creation and redemption, acts expressed in the making of covenant. Covenant is the way of God's self-revelation, of his entering into relationship with his creation.[97]

Benedict's biblical theology of covenant synthesizes a great deal of scholarship. He presents the covenant, not as a reciprocal partnership, but as the initiative and gift of the divine will. The covenant is a 'creative act of God's love,' Benedict says, noting that the prophets often described God's 'passionate love' for Israel in terms of a husband's love for his bride.[98] In the covenant, we see the perfect 'manifestation of his self, the "radiance of his countenance."'[99] Moreover, God's covenant is always expressed in words and sign, in law and liturgy. Beginning with the sabbath ordinances, there is a profound inner connection in the covenant structure of revelation between the 'legal and cultic' order, between the moral order and the liturgical order, between the commands and ordinances of God and the sacrificial worship of God.[100] Law and worship are two sides of the covenant relationship. Each is 'an expression of God's love, of his "yes" to the human being that he created, so that he [the human being] could both love and receive love. . . . God created the universe in order to enter into a history of love with humankind. He created it so that love could exist.'[101]

In Benedict's reading, God's testament or covenant is 'the central theme of Scripture itself, thus giving a key to the whole of it.'[102] Covenant forms the narrative structure of Scripture, and the story of Scripture unfolds in the sequence of covenants that God makes – with Noah, with Abraham, with Jacob-Israel, with Moses at Sinai, and finally, with David. The plurality and interrelatedness

---

[95] 'The true center, the power that moves and shapes from within in the rhythm of the stars and of our lives, is worship. Our life's rhythm moves in proper measure when it is caught up in this' (*In the Beginning*, 29–30).

[96] 'The sabbath is the sign of the covenant between God and man; it sums up the inward essence of the covenant. . . . Creation exists to be a place for the covenant that God wants to make with man. The goal of creation is the covenant, the love story of God and man' (*Spirit of the Liturgy*, 26).

[97] *Many Religions, One Covenant*, 75–77.

[98] 'The "covenant" is not a two-sided contract but a gift, a creative act of God's love. . . . God, the king, receives nothing from man; but in giving him his law, he gives him the path of life' (*Many Religions, One Covenant*, 50–51).

[99] *Many Religions, One Covenant*, 77.

[100] *In the Beginning*, 29; *Many Religions, One Covenant*, 68.

[101] *In the Beginning*, 29–30.

[102] *Many Religions, One Covenant*, 48.

of these covenants makes up the one old covenant. Manifest in them is the truth of God's providential plan, the truth revealed in the covenant of creation.[103] While each of these covenants is significant, the foundational covenant of salvation history is the covenant with Abraham who, by not withholding from God his only son, was blessed by God with the promise that he would become the father of many nations. This promise is fulfilled in Jesus Christ, who makes it possible for men and women of all nations to share in the spiritual destiny of Israel, as the children of Abraham.[104]

Benedict sees in Israel's prophets an insistent promise of universalism, that all the nations will come to worship the God of Israel. The work of Jesus becomes the fulfillment of the 'prophetic thrust of the Old Testament itself.'[105] Jesus' mission, then, can only be understood in light of the sacred Scriptures of Israel, which become, through his interpretation, continued in the Church, the source of salvation for all the nations. The covenantal sequence of the canonical narrative indicates an 'inner continuity' in salvation history – from Abraham and Israel to Jesus and the Church of Jews and Gentiles.[106] Benedict speaks of 'the inner continuity and coherence of law and gospel' and the 'deep unity between the good news of Jesus and the message of Sinai.'[107] In fact, Christian identity is defined by reference to the old covenant. The Christian joins himself or herself to a history that began with Abraham and culminates in the kingdom of David.[108]

> The mission of Jesus is to unite Jews and pagans into a single people of God in which the universalist promises of the Scriptures are fulfilled that speak again and again of the nations worshipping the God of Israel. . . . The mission of Jesus consists in bringing together the histories of the nations in the community of the history of Abraham, the history of Israel. . . . The history of Israel should become the history of all, Abraham's sonship is to be extended to the 'many.' . . . All nations . . . become brothers and receivers of the promises of the chosen people; they become people of God with Israel through adherence to the will of God and through acceptance of the Davidic covenant.[109]

---

[103] 'There is only *one* will of God for men, only *one* historical activity of God with and for men, though this activity employs interventions that are diverse and even contradictory – yet in truth they belong together' (*Many Religions, One Covenant,* 57).

[104] '"You will be a blessing," God had said to Abraham at the beginning of salvation history (Gen. 12:2). In Christ, the son of Abraham, these words are completely fulfilled' (*Spirit of the Liturgy,* 183).

[105] *Many Religions, One Covenant,* 28.

[106] *Many Religions, One Covenant,* 68.

[107] *Many Religions, One Covenant,* 33, 36.

[108] *Truth and Tolerance,* 97.

[109] *Many Religions, One Covenant,* 26, 27–28; *Gospel, Catechesis, Catechism,* 78–79.

Thus the old covenant is fulfilled in the new covenant made in the blood of Christ. The cross by which the new covenant is enacted can only be understood in light of the old covenant. Benedict explains the meaning of the new covenant in light of the exodus and passover of Israel, and in light of the covenant made at Sinai. Christ is the new passover.[110] Indeed, all of Israel's liturgical forms and feasts point to the new passover of Jesus Christ.[111]

Benedict sees in the covenant at Sinai parallels with ideas of treaty and cove-nant-making in the ancient Near East. In sprinkling sacrificial 'blood of the covenant' on the altar and then on the people (Ex. 24:8), Moses was evoking the idea of the covenant as forming a 'blood association' between the covenant partners, in a sense making Israel and God, 'brothers of the same blood.'[112] At the last supper, when Jesus refers to the cup as the blood of the covenant, 'the words of Sinai are heightened to a staggering realism, and at the same time we begin to see a totally unsuspected depth in them.'[113] What the sacrifices of the old covenant all pointed to, are made a 'reality' in Christ's death. 'All cultic ordinances of the Old Testament are seen to be taken up into his death and brought to their deepest meaning.'[114] In the last supper, Jesus announces the final covenant in biblical salvation history. This covenant does not abrogate the covenant at Sinai. Rather it prolongs and renews it. The blood of the covenant is Christ's, given for the sake of the world. He is the new covenant by which 'God binds himself irrevocably' to his creation.[115] Here we see the liturgical destiny of creation. As the covenant blood at Sinai symbolized the sharing of flesh and blood between God and Israel, this sharing is made real, literal, in the blood of Christ, in which all nations are made kin, flesh and blood, one body with Christ through 'sacramental blood fellowship.'[116]

The embrace of salvation

For Benedict, the sacramental liturgy of the Church, worship within the new covenant, is the goal and consummation of the biblical story. If everything in Scripture is ordered to the covenant that God wants to make with his creation,

---

[110] *Principles of Catholic Theology*, 189–90.

[111] *New Song for the Lord*, 16.

[112] Quoting G. Quell, in *Many Religions, One Covenant*, 59–60.

[113] *Many Religions, One Covenant*, 60.

[114] *Many Religions, One Covenant*, 41.

[115] *Many Religions, One Covenant*, 62–65.

[116] *Many Religions, One Covenant*, 60. 'In the last supper he recapitulates the covenant of Sinai, or rather what had there been an approximation in symbol now becomes reality: the community of blood and life between God and man' (*Church, Ecume-nism and Politics*, 8).

then everything in the Church is ordered to proclaiming that new covenant and initiating people into it through the sacramental liturgy. The mission of the Church is liturgical, its identity and actions defined by the Word revealed in history.[117] In a sense, he says, the revelation of God is not 'complete' without the response of the Church, and of the individual Christian, in the liturgy, the primary expression of the tradition.[118]

In all his writings, Benedict stresses the unity of the old and new covenant liturgies. The eucharistic liturgy 'places us in continuity with Israel and the whole of salvation history,'[119] revealing the Eucharist as the fulfillment of the liturgies of the old covenant. Israel's liturgical worship was ordered to remembrance, memorial, and 'renewal of the covenant.'[120] Christian worship, too, becomes a remembrance of God's mighty works in history. And like Israel's worship, especially the passover Haggadah, the Eucharist is both a remembrance of the past and thanksgiving for God's continued presence among his people.[121]

Christian liturgy takes up the two impulses of Old Testament covenant worship – the reading of the Word of God and the offering of sacrifice. Benedict sees the pattern of the liturgy reflected also in Jesus' Easter appearance to his disciples on road to Emmaus (Lk. 24:25-31), in which Jesus reads and interprets the Scriptures in light of his resurrection, and then reveals himself in the breaking of the bread.[122]

Benedict notes, too, the important role that Scripture plays in the eucharistic celebration. During the course of the year, the Scripture readings 'enable man to go through the whole history of salvation in step with the

---

[117] 'The Church . . . is there so that the world may become a sphere for God's presence, the sphere of the covenant between God and men . . . in order that the covenant may come to be in which God freely gives his love and receives the response of love' (*Pilgrim Fellowship of Faith*, 288–89).

[118] 'Christians know that God has spoken through man and that the human and historical factor is, therefore, part of the way God acts. That, too, is why the Word of the Bible becomes complete only in that responsive word of the Church which we call Tradition. That is why the accounts of the Last Supper in the Bible become a concrete reality only when they are appropriated by the Church in her celebration' (*Spirit of the Liturgy*, 169).

[119] Homily, Mass at Marienfeld Arena, 11–12.

[120] *Many Religions, One Covenant*, 62–65.

[121] *God Is Near Us*, 48–49.

[122] 'First we have the searching of the Scriptures, explained and made present by the Risen Lord; their minds enlightened, the disciples are moved to invite the Lord to stay with them, and he responds by breaking the bread for his disciples, giving them his presence and then withdrawing again, sending them out as his messengers' (*Feast of Faith*, 47).

rhythm of creation.'[123] Through the Word read and prayed in the liturgy, one is slowly transformed into the person that Christ intends.[124] In the liturgy, he notes, the Old Testament is read typologically, as it is in the New Testament. And the liturgy is not merely evocative, representative, or commemorative. More than that, it brings about a kind of communion with the events narrated. Writing of early Christian liturgical art, Benedict has said:

> On liturgical feasts the deeds of God in the past are made present. The feasts are a participation in God's action in time . . . . The individual events are now ordered toward the Christian sacraments and to Christ himself. Noah's ark and the crossing of the Red Sea now point to baptism. The sacrifice of Isaac and the meal of the three angels with Abraham speak of Christ's sacrifice and the Eucharist. Shining through the rescue of the three young men from the fiery furnace and of Daniel from the lions' den we see Christ's resurrection and our own. Still more than in the synagogue, the point of the images is not to tell a story about something in the past, but to incorporate the events of history into the sacrament. . . . We are taken into the events. . . . The centering of all history in Christ is both the liturgical transmission of that history and the expression of a new experience of time, in which past, present, and future make contact, because they have been inserted into the presence of the risen Lord.[125]

It follows that the liturgy is the privileged context in which the community hears the Word and the authentic interpretation of the Word. This was the pattern of Christ at Emmaus and, as we have seen, it was part of the very structure of revelation that the Scriptures were written and canonized for use in the liturgy. And it is in the liturgy that the texts are realized as Scripture, as divine communication:

> . . .the liturgy is the true, living environment for the Bible. . . . The Bible can be properly understood only in this living context within which it first emerged. The texts of the Bible, this great book of Christ, are not to be seen as the literary products of some scribes at their desks but rather as the words of Christ himself delivered in the celebration of holy Mass. The scriptural texts are thoroughly imbued with the awe of divine worship resulting from the believer's interior attentiveness to the living voice of the present Lord.[126]

---

[123] *Co-Workers of the Truth: Meditations for Every Day of the Year*, ed. I. Grass (San Francisco: Ignatius, 1992 [1990]), 2.
[124] Through the liturgy '. . . the language of our Mother becomes ours; we learn to speak it along with her, so that gradually, her words on our lips become our words. We are given an anticipatory share in the Church's perennial dialogue of love with him who desired to be one flesh with her' (*Feast of Faith*, 30).
[125] *Spirit of the Liturgy*, 117.
[126] 'Introduction,' *The Lord*, xii [emphasis added].

Benedict, drawing on exegetical and historical scholarship, traces the sacrificial form, content, and meaning of the eucharistic liturgy to the old covenant *todah* ('thanksgiving sacrifice'), by which Israelites gave thanks to God after having been delivered from suffering or some life-threatening situation.[127] In this, he shows the Eucharist to be an eloquent fulfillment of the Old Testament understanding of sacrifice, as expressed by the psalmists and prophets. In offering his life on the cross, and in establishing the Eucharist as the memorial of that self-offering, Jesus revealed that the worship God desires is 'the transformation of existence into thanksgiving,'[128] our 'giv[ing] ourselves back to him' in love and gratitude.

In the unity of the last supper and the crucifixion, Benedict sees the true depth of the Bible as the saving Word of God. For in the crucifixion, intended by Christ to be represented in the sacrificial offering of the Eucharist, we have, in effect, the death of death. By this action, which will be perpetuated in the sacramental form of the Eucharist, Christ transforms death itself into a life-giving word. The gospel of Christ is, then, the good news that love is stronger than death, and salvation history culminates in the transformation of death into the saving word of life.

> . . . the indissoluble bond between the supper and the death of Jesus is . . . plain: his dying words fuse with his words at the supper, the reality of his death fuses with the reality of the supper. For the event of the supper consists in Jesus sharing his body and his blood, i.e., his earthly existence; he gives and communicates himself. In other words, the event of the supper is an anticipation of death, the transformation of death into an act of love. Only in this context can we understand what John means by calling Jesus' death the glorification of God and the glorification of the Son (John 12:28; 17:21). Death, which by its very nature, is the end, the destruction of every communication, is changed by him into an act of self-communication; and this is man's redemption, for it signifies the triumph of love over death. We can put the same thing another way: death, which puts an end to words and to meaning, itself becomes a word, becomes the place where meaning communicates itself.[129]

The sacred Word heard delivered in the Mass, and the sacrificial offering of that Word on the cross, come together in the canon or Eucharistic Prayer of the Church. Here, too, Benedict explains the Christian beliefs in terms of Old Testament belief in the creative power of the Word of God as both speech and deed.[130] As God's Word was held to create the heavens and the earth, and as

---

[127] *Feast of Faith,* 51–60.
[128] *God Is Near Us,* 48, 51.
[129] *Behold the Pierced One,* 24–25.
[130] 'God reveals himself in history. He speaks to humankind, and the word he speaks has creative power. The Hebrew concept *"dabar,"* usually translated as "word," really conveys both the meaning of *word* and *act.* God says what he does and does what he says' (Benedict XVI, Message to the Youth of the World.)

Jesus' word was held to heal the sick and raise the dead, the divine Word spoken in the liturgy also possesses transformative powers.[131]

Notice in the following long passage, how Benedict integrates modern rhetorical insights, especially speech-act theories, with the perspectives of liturgical theology and metaphysics in order to articulate a compelling and thoroughly up-to-date, biblically grounded understanding of what happens in the liturgy, especially the Eucharist:

> This *oratio* – the Eucharistic Prayer, the 'Canon' – is really more than speech; it is *actio* in the highest sense of the word. For what happens in it is that the human *actio*.. . steps back and makes way for the *actio divina*, the action of God. In this *oratio* the priest speaks with the I of the Lord – 'This is my body,' 'This is my blood.' He knows that he is not now speaking from his own resources but in virtue of the sacrament that he has received, he has become the voice of someone else, who is now speaking and acting. This action of God, which takes place through human speech, is the real 'action' for which all of creation is an expectation. The elements of the earth are transubstantiated, pulled, so to speak, from their creaturely anchorage, grasped at the deepest ground of their being, and changed in the body and blood of the Lord. The new heaven and new earth are anticipated.
>
> The real 'action' in the liturgy in which we are all supposed to participate is the action of God himself. This is what is new and distinctive about the Christian liturgy: God himself acts and does what is essential. He inaugurates the new creation, makes himself accessible to us, so that, through the things of the earth, through our gifts, we can communicate with him in a personal way. . . . The whole event of the incarnation, cross, resurrection, and second coming is present as the way by which God draws man into cooperation with himself. . . . True, the sacrifice of the Logos is accepted already and forever. But we must still pray for it to become our sacrifice, that we ourselves . . . may be transformed into the Logos, conformed to the Logos, and so made the true body of Christ. . . . The uniqueness of the Eucharistic liturgy lies precisely in the fact that God himself is acting and that we are drawn into that action of God.[132]

Here we have reached the summit of the liturgy and the summit of Benedict's biblical theology. In the liturgy, we are drawn into contact with the very means of salvation history, the saving act of Christ on the cross. In the liturgy, the desire of God's condescension meets the desire of humankind for transcendence. Benedict suggests this might even be a kind of definition for liturgy, namely that it brings about 'an embrace of salvation between God and man.'[133]

---

[131]   In the liturgy, the scriptural word is truly 'the Word of transformation, enabling us to participate in the "hour" of Christ. . . . It is the Word of power which transforms the gifts of the earth in an entirely new way into God's gift of himself, and it draws us into this process of transformation' (Homily, Mass at Marienfeld Arena).

[132]   *Spirit of the Liturgy*, 172–74.

[133]   Pope Benedict XVI, General Audience (September 28, 2005).

In Benedict's biblical theology, liturgy is the proper end of creation and of the human person. And in the liturgy, the purposes of salvation history are realized – heaven and earth are filled with God's glory, each participant is swept up into the embrace of salvation, into the communion of God's eternal love. The communion that God desires between heaven and earth, divine and human, towards which all of salvation history has tended, is revealed and effected in the liturgy. Every celebration of the Eucharist on the earth becomes 'a cosmic liturgy . . . an entry into the liturgy of heaven.'[134] In the liturgy, the eschatological orientation of Scripture is actualized. 'In the celebration of the liturgy, the Church moves toward the Lord; liturgy is virtually this act of approaching his coming. In the liturgy the Lord is already anticipating his promised coming. Liturgy is *anticipated Parousia . . .*'[135]

A significant failing of modern exegesis, as Benedict sees it, has been exegetes' general confusion and misunderstanding regarding the eschatological expectation expressed in the Gospels. For much of the last century, it has been an exegetical commonplace that the oldest New Testament writings are shot through with expectation of the imminent end of the world. Without rehearsing Benedict's critique of this exegetical assumption, we note that, in their preoccupation with historical reconstruction, exegetes have ignored or downplayed the fact that eschatological expressions like parousia and maranatha 'belong in the context of early Christian eucharistic celebration.'[136]

Certainly, the first Christians, the normative theologians who authored the New Testament, expected a second coming or 'parousia' of Christ. But they anticipated that second coming in every celebration of the coming of Christ in the Eucharist. 'The parousia is the highest intensification and fulfillment of the liturgy. And the liturgy is parousia, a parousia-like event taking place in our midst. . . . Every Eucharist is parousia, the Lord's coming, and yet the Eucharist is even more truly the tensed yearning that he would reveal his hidden glory.'[137]

---

[134] *Spirit of the Liturgy*, 70.

[135] *New Song for the Lord*, 129 [emphasis added]. 'Christian liturgy is never just an event organized by a particular group or set of people or even by a particular local Church. Mankind's movement toward Christ meets Christ's movement toward men. He wants to unite mankind and bring about the one Church, the one divine assembly, of all men . . . the communion of all who worship in spirit and in truth . . . . Christian liturgy is a liturgy of promise fulfilled, of a quest, the religious quest of human history, reaching its goal. But it remains a liturgy of hope . . . . Christian liturgy is liturgy on the way, a liturgy of pilgrimage toward the transfiguration of the world, which will only take place when God is "all in all"' (*Spirit of the Liturgy*, 49–50).

[136] *Eschatology*, 6; 202–203.; For Benedict's critique, see *Eschatology*, 35–45; 271–72.

[137] *Eschatology*, 202–3.

The beauty and necessity of the theological and exegetical task

The liturgy, then, is the ultimate ecclesial locus in which, of necessity, the work of the theologian and exegete must always be grounded, according to Benedict. Again, by way of conclusion, it must be stressed that this is not a confessional argument, but an academic and scholarly one. The goal of scientific research, as we pointed out in considering Benedict's critique of criticism, is to understand and explain things. If the academic study of Scripture ever is to seriously approach its oft-stated goal of being 'scientific' in its methodology and in its conclusions, then it must be able to understand and explain the texts of the Scriptures. The encounter with Benedict's critique of criticism and his new synthesis for biblical theology demonstrates that any 'scientific' explanation that does not account for the ecclesial content and context of Scripture is bound to be arbitrary and partial, and wholly inadequate by any scientific measure.

Benedict's critique of criticism and his own biblical theology open up new possibilities for the study of Scripture in the academy. Basing his conclusion on sound historical and critical research, he has demonstrated that we cannot claim to be reading the Bible *as* the Bible unless we are reading it in continuity with the ecclesial tradition in which it was composed and handed on. And his findings, in effect, 'authorize' a way of reading that promises the greatest 'explanatory power' because it reads Scripture as it was written – as a divine Word spoken in history to the Church, a Word whose meaning is understood within the broad unity of the Church's experience of the faith, an experience that includes liturgy and dogma, and is not limited to the expectations and contexts of a text's original audience. And he promises to the theologian and exegete in the academy that reading in continuity with this ecclesial tradition 'increases the excitement and fecundity of inquiry.'[138]

> How exciting exegesis becomes when it dares to read the Bible as a unified whole. If the Bible originates from the one subject formed by the people of God and, through it, from the divine subject himself, then it speaks of the present. If this is so, moreover, even what we know about the diversity of its underlying historical constellations yields its harvest; there is a unity to be discovered in this diversity, and diversity appears as the wealth of unity. This opens up a wide field of action both to historical research and to its hypotheses, with the sole limit that it may not destroy the unity of the whole, which is situated on another plan that what can be called the 'nuts and bolts' of the various texts. Unity is found on another plane, yet it belongs to the literary reality of the Bible itself. For the theologian and exegete of faith, this is truly an exciting vision. The work of theology and exegesis assumes a place within the grand

---

[138] *Nature and Mission of Theology*, 97.

unity of God's plan as it is revealed in Scripture – that of bringing about the divinization of creation in the liturgical offering of the sacrifice of praise.[139]

The unity of the person of Jesus, embracing man and God, prefigures that synthesis of man and world to which theology is meant to minister. It is my belief that the beauty and necessity of the theologian's task could be made visible at this point. . . . But [the theologian] can only do this provided he himself enters that 'laboratory' of unity and freedom . . . where his own will is refashioned, where he allows himself to be expropriated and inserted into the divine will, where he advances toward that God-likeness through which the kingdom of God can come.[140]

Indeed, if we take Benedict's thought seriously and consider the New Testament authors to be the normative theologians, then the academic study of theology and Scripture brings us into the heart of what might be called the sacerdotal nature of the biblical texts.

We will close with a particularly fertile passage, one that indicates the beauty and necessity of the theological and exegetical task, as well as the excitement and fecundity of Benedict's own research. Through a close reading of the text, he notes the curious preponderance of cultic and priestly language in Romans 15:16, where Paul describes his purpose in writing his letter as part of his mission 'to be a minister of Christ Jesus in the priestly service of the gospel of God, so that the offering of the Gentiles may be acceptable.'

The Letter to the Romans, this word that has been written that it may then be proclaimed, is an apostolic action; more, it is a liturgical – even a cultic – event. This it is because it helps the world of the pagans to change so as to be a renewal of mankind and, as such, a cosmic liturgy in which mankind shall become adoration, become the radiance of the glory of God. If the apostle is handing on the gospel by means of this letter . . . this is a priestly sacrificial action, an eschatological service of ministry . . . Now it is the specifically apostolic service of preaching the faith that appears as a priestly activity, as actually performing the new liturgy, open to all the world and likewise worldwide, which has been founded by Christ.[141]

Here Benedict opens for students of Sacred Scripture an exhilarating new window into the New Testament texts, one in which we see the unity of the Old and New Testaments, of Church and Scripture, Scripture and sacrament, the Bible and liturgy, all in the service of the divine plan.

---

[139] *Spirit of the Liturgy*, 28.
[140] *Behold the Pierced One*, 45–46.
[141] *Pilgrim Fellowship of Faith*, 118–19.

Bibliography

Benedict XVI, Pope, Address to Ecumenical Meeting at the Archbishopric of Cologne (August 19, 2005) in *L'Osservatore Romano,* Weekly Edition in English (August 24, 2005), 8–9

—, *Deus Caritas Est,* Encyclical Letter on Christian Love (December 25, 2005) in *L'Osservatore Romano,* Weekly Edition in English (February 1, 2006), 12

—, General Audience (September 28, 2005) in *L'Osservatore Romano,* Weekly Edition in English (October 5, 2005), 8

—, Homily, Mass at Marienfeld Arena (August 21, 2005) in *L'Osservatore Romano,* Weekly Edition in English (August 24, 2005), 11–12

—, Homily, Mass of Possession of the Chair of the Bishop of Rome (May 7, 2005) in *L'Osservatore Romano,* Weekly Edition in English (May 11, 2005), 3

—, Message to the Youth of the World on the Occasion of the 21st World Youth Day (April 9, 2006) in *L'Osservatore Romano,* Weekly Edition in English (March 1, 2006), 3

Nichols, A., *The Thought of Benedict XVI: An Introduction to the Theology of Joseph Ratzinger* (London: Burns & Oates, 2005)

Ratzinger, Joseph Cardinal, *Behold the Pierced One: An Approach to a Spiritual Christology,* trans. G. Harrison (San Francisco: Ignatius, 1986 [1984])

—, *Biblical Interpretation in Crisis: The Ratzinger Conference on Bible and Church,* ed. R.J. Neuhaus (Grand Rapids: Eerdmans, 1989)

—, *Called to Communion: Understanding the Church Today,* trans. A. Walker (San Francisco: Ignatius, 1996 [1991]

—, *Church, Ecumenism and Politics: New Essays in Ecclesiology* (New York: Crossroad, 1988)

—, 'Commentary on *Dei Verbum*' in *Commentary on the Documents of Vatican II,* ed. H. Vorgrimler (New York: Herder and Herder, 1967), 3:189–90

—, *Co-Workers of the Truth: Meditations for Every Day of the Year,* ed. I. Grass (San Francisco: Ignatius, 1992 [1990])

—, *Dogma and Preaching,* trans. M.J. O'Connell (Chicago: Franciscan Herald, 1985)

—, *Eschatology: Death and Eternal Life,* trans. M. Waldstein (Washington: Catholic University of America, 1988 [1977])

—, *Feast of Faith: Approaches to a Theology of the Liturgy,* trans. G. Harrison (San Francisco: Ignatius, 1986 [1981])

—, *God Is Near Us: The Eucharist, the Heart of Life,* ed. S.O. Horn and V. Pfnur, trans. H. Taylor (San Francisco: Ignatius, 2003 [2001])

—, *Gospel, Catechesis, Catechism: Sidelights on* The Catechism of the Catholic Church (San Francisco: Ignatius, 1997 [1995]), 75

—, *In the Beginning: A Catholic Understanding of the Story of Creation and the Fall,* trans. B. Ramsey, O.P. (Grand Rapids: Eerdmans, 1995 [1986])

— , 'Introduction' in Romano Guardini, *The Lord* (Washington, DC: Regnery, 1996 [1954]), xi–xiv

— , *Introduction to Christianity*, trans. J.R. Foster (San Francisco: Ignatius, 1990 [1968])

— , *Many Religions, One Covenant: Israel, the Church and the World*, trans. G. Harrison (San Francisco: Ignatius, 1999 [1998])

— , *The Meaning of Christian Brotherhood* (San Francisco: Ignatius, 1993 [1960])

— , *Milestones: Memoirs, 1927-1977*, trans. E. Leivas-Merikakis (San Francisco: Ignatius, 1998)

— , *The Nature and Mission of Theology: Approaches to Understanding its Role in the Light of Present Controversy*, trans. A. Walker (San Francisco: Ignatius, 1995 [1993])

— , *A New Song for the Lord: Faith in Christ and Liturgy Today*, trans. M.M. Matesich (New York: Crossroad Herder, 1997 [1995])

— , *On the Way to Jesus Christ*, trans. M. Miller (San Francisco: Ignatius, 2005 [2004])

— , *Pilgrim Fellowship of Faith: The Church as Communion*, ed. S.O. Horn and V. Pfnür, trans. H. Taylor (San Francisco: Ignatius, 2005 [2002]), 299–379

— , *Principles of Catholic Theology: Building Stones for a Fundamental Theology*, trans. M.F. McCarthy, S.N.D. (San Francisco: Ignatius, 1987 [1982])

— , *The Ratzinger Report: An Exclusive Interview on the State of the Church*, with V. Messori, trans. S. Attanasio and G. Harrison (San Francisco: Ignatius, 1985)

— , 'Relationship between Magisterium and Exegetes,' Address to the Pontifical Biblical Commission, in *L'Osservatore Romano*, Weekly Edition in English (July 23, 2003)

— , *Salt of the Earth: Christianity and the Catholic Church at the End of the Millennium*, with Peter Seewald, trans. Adrian Walker (San Francisco: Ignatius, 1997)

— , *The Spirit of the Liturgy*, trans. John Saward (San Francisco: Ignatius, 2000)

— , *The Theology of History in St. Bonaventure*, trans. Zachary Hayes (Chicago: Franciscan Herald, 1971)

— , *Truth and Tolerance: Christian Belief and World Religions*, trans. Henry Taylor (San Francisco: Ignatius, 2004 [2003]), 236–45

5

The Spiritual Sense(s) Today

Glenn W. Olsen

Even if I shall not have been able to understand everything, if I am, nevertheless, busily engaged in the divine Scriptures and 'I meditate on the Law of God day and night' and at no time at all do I desist inquiring, discussing, investigating, and certainly, what is greatest, praying God and asking for understanding from him who 'teaches man knowledge,' I shall appear to dwell 'at the well of vision' (Gen 25:11).[1]

Recovering the Spiritual Sense(s)

The writings of Henri de Lubac (1896–1991) on the spiritual sense(s) of scripture, especially his studies of Origen and of medieval exegesis, were path-breaking in their day and continue to provide the point of departure for study of the spiritual senses of Scripture today.[2] The four volumes on medieval exegesis have been considered to be of such enduring value that, almost forty years after their original publication, they began to be published in English translation.[3] De Lubac belonged to a generation with many luminaries interested in the spiritual

---

[1] Origen, *Homilies on Genesis and Exodus* 11.3, trans. R.E. Heine, 173–74. The 'well of vision' is 'Scripture as an endless well of God's revelations': E.A. Dively Lauro, *Soul and Spirit*, 96–103, at 96.

[2] *Histoire et Esprit; Exégèse médiévale.* Also *Scripture in the Tradition*, trans. L. O'Neill, a selection from the earlier books. Dively Lauro, *Soul and Spirit*, 13–14,16–19, explains and defends the views of those like de Lubac, who insist on the continuing importance of Patristic exegesis, and that Origen and others not be judged by an anachronistic standard but by how well they achieve their purpose of using allegory to promote spiritual growth and salvation. Against many earlier scholarly analyses (including, at points, de Lubac's), she argues that Origen clearly defines three senses of Scripture, including the middle psychic or moral sense, the relationship of which to the pneumatic or spiritual sense constitutes the core of his attempt to transform the reader.

[3] *Medieval Exegesis*, vol. 1, trans. M. Sebanc; vol. 2, trans. E.M. Macierowski. See S.K. Wood, *Spiritual Exegesis and the Church in the Theology of Henry de Lubac.*

sense, none greater than his companion in the Society of Jesus, Jean Cardinal Daniélou, who examined biblical typology in many of his writings, especially *Sacramentum futuri*, which had a wide readership in its English translation, *From Shadows to Reality: Studies in the Biblical Typology of the Fathers.*[4] Though the two great Jesuits did not always agree in their understanding or evaluation of the spiritual sense(s), or always use the same terminology or system of classification, it is probably fair to say that after their generation many institutionalized misapprehensions about how Scripture had been read historically were viewed by scholars of virtually all confessional backgrounds as no longer tenable.

Before de Lubac, as an extension of the idea that there is only one sense of Scripture, called literal or historical, it had been common to hold that allegorical or typological or spiritual readings of Scripture – that is, readings which found in Scripture second- or third- or fourth-level meanings – had not been a part of original Christianity. On this view, primarily among Protestants, spiritual interpretation was thought to be an alien imposition, perhaps something akin to Greek philosophy itself, which had entered Christianity at some later time, perhaps through the exegesis of Origen in the third century.[5] All modern discussion was muddied by the fact that the Fathers did not mean precisely the same thing by the 'literal' sense that modern critical scholarship has come to associate with the term: a fine book on Origen, for instance, notes erroneously that he understood 'literal' to be 'an antonym for figurative or metaphorical.'[6] If, with many moderns, one insists that the literal sense must be the sense a (human) author intended, one has little choice but to dismiss much of the exegesis of an early authority such as Origen, which seeks first the authorial intent of the Holy Spirit, and then is willing to read Scripture allegorically without necessarily considering any human author's intent.[7]

Everyone recognized that multi-level interpretation had flourished in the pre-Reformation Church, but this was taken by some as yet another evidence of how Christianity had lost its way, one more reason why the Reformation was needed to restore and simplify biblical interpretation so that a purified

---

[4]   *Sacramentum futuri*, trans. W. Hibberd, *From Shadows to Reality*. For the differences between de Lubac and Daniélou, see Dively Lauro, *Soul and Spirit*, 21–24; see also 25–26, on Henri Crouzel.

[5]   See, e.g., Eugéne de Faye as treated by Dively Lauro, *Soul and Spirit*, 15–16. J.D. Dawson, *Christian Figural Reading*, esp. 13–16, 141–206, gives a very instructive treatment of Hans Frei's admission that figural reading is 'a kind of allegorical reading. . . governed by allegiance to the gospel's literal sense' (13).

[6]   Dively Lauro, *Soul and Spirit*, 3, n. 9. An unpublished study by P.S. Williamson, 'Defining the Spiritual Sense,' which Prof. Williamson kindly made available to me, considers such questions as the different understandings of the 'literal sense. See also Williamson's *Catholic Principles for Interpreting Scripture*, esp. chs. 12–14.

[7]   Dively Lauro, *Soul and Spirit*, 13.

Christian message, comprehensible to all, might stand forth.[8] Such sentiments were particularly strong in forms of Christianity that descended from Calvin. In more recent centuries, the confidence of many in modern critical methods, and academic consensus that these are the only methods suitable to understanding the biblical text, have led to a widespread dismissal of all 'allegorical' exegesis.[9] Through the work of scholars like de Lubac, however (and here, especially Daniélou), it has been established that various forms of spiritual exegesis were already present in Judaism, from which they were inherited by Christianity; that the very relation of Christianity to Judaism as understood by early Christians was Christological, Christ being the key by which the Old Testament was finally to be understood; and that therefore the relation between the two Testaments is finally that between, if not exactly shadow and reality, between shadow and Image – the coming of the Light.

Rethinking the 'Apostolic' Exegetical Tradition

Since de Lubac's mid-twentieth-century work, the study of early Christian biblical interpretation has acquired new energy. The current state of scholarship for earliest Christianity is helpfully summarized in three subsections that Richard N. Longenecker has added to the Preface of his second edition of *Biblical Exegesis in the Apostolic Period*.[10] The first, on 'The Fulfillment Theme in the New Testament,' restates the established fact that 'Jewish exegetes of the first century viewed their task as primarily that of adapting, reinterpreting, extending, and so reapplying sacred Scripture to the present circumstances of God's people.'[11] As I put it in my own earlier studies of the spiritual sense, Jewish interpretation was involved in a constant process of updating or contemporizing, in which the biblical text was applied to or extended to new circumstances and problems.[12] This was in effect a form of spiritual exegesis, for the exegete was taking what he understood to be the original sense of the text, and showing how it might have relevance to other than its original subject. (Of

---

[8] A. Jacobs, 'Robert Alter's Fidelity,' gives a brief, judicious, statement of the problem of 'Gospel simplicity.'

[9] R.P.C. Hanson, *Allegory and Event*, considered throughout Dively Lauro, *Soul and Spirit*, as at 19–21. See for the issues, J.J. O'Keefe and R.R. Reno, *Sanctified Vision*, 107–08.

[10] Cf. the more popular treatment found in J.L. Kugel and R.A. Greer, *Early Biblical Interpretation*, Part 1, on Jewish history and exegesis, and Part 2, esp. ch. 2, on the early Christian centuries.

[11] R.N. Longenecker, *Biblical Exegesis in the Apostolic Period*, xxvi–xxvii. The Christian idea that one may interpret difficult passages by the light of clearer passages of Scripture seems a form of 'inner-biblical' exegesis.

[12] G.W. Olsen, 'Allegory, Typology and Symbol,' Parts 1 and 2.

course this could be described under other terminology than that of spiritual interpretation; especially if the subject in view was a moral question, it might even be viewed by contemporary scholars as an early form of casuistry.)

Thus, while in a fully developed late Roman or medieval version of the idea that there are four senses of Scripture we find the anagogical sense designating an expansion of a biblical text to consider eschatological matters, Longenecker notes something similar already existed in the 'mantological' stance of the Qumran covenanters, which tried to open up biblical texts to show their significance in what they assumed to be the last days.[13] Other scholars have shown that though the rabbis thought of themselves as practicing an inner-biblical exegesis, we can find non-rabbinic (that is, Greek) as well as rabbinic interpretive methods in their exegesis: the main point is that Christianity was born into a world which regularly practiced some form of contemporizing interpretation.[14] In this context, one might be tempted to say, we may account for the Gospel of Matthew's reading of Jewish Scripture. But of course the goal in Matthew's gospel was the theme of fulfillment, and Longenecker emphasizes that for the most part the New Testament writers used the (Jewish) Scriptures for a different purpose than did Jewish exegetes. The Christians' first interest was this theme of fulfillment, which Longenecker argues was different from simply contemporizing.[15] Whereas the Jewish exegete began with a biblical text and then attempted to contemporize, the Christian biblical author began with a stance outside the (Jewish) Bible itself, a stance that we might call Christological, in which existing biblical texts were used to illustrate an understanding of fulfillment that had been received in Christ.[16] This requires Longenecker's emphasis in a second subsection of his new preface on 'The Christocentric Nature and Pneumatic Quality of New Testament Exegesis.'[17]

More than a half-century ago Raymond Brown took up the question of whether there is a *sensus plenior* in 'the New Testament's use of the Old,' and

---

[13] Longenecker, *Biblical Exegesis*, xxvi. I, not Longenecker, am making the parallels specific. Longenecker goes on to note similar practices among the Pharisees and Tannaitic rabbis, noting that they viewed 'exegesis as a contemporizing enterprise' (xxvi).

[14] Longenecker, *Biblical Exegesis*, xxvi.

[15] Longenecker, *Biblical Exegesis*, xxvii.

[16] Longenecker, *Biblical Exegesis*, xxvii–xxx. This is a distinction I did not make in 'Allegory, Typology and Symbol,' though in a sense one is comparing apples (the updating of a tradition from within), and oranges (the updating of a tradition from without). The first involves a contemporizing exegesis within a tradition, the second is a more radical form of contemporizing in which the whole earlier tradition is seen as fulfilled or superseded in something more.

[17] Longenecker, *Biblical Exegesis*, xxx–xxxi.

Longenecker's third subsection considers the adequacy of Brown's answer in the affirmative.[18] For once, I find Longenecker's discussion less than clear. He begins by saying that if we define the literal sense as Brown defines it, as 'that meaning which by the rules of historico-critical exegesis we can determine as the author's message for his time,' and we define a *sensus plenior* as 'that meaning of his text which by the normal rules of exegesis would not have been within his clear awareness or intention but which by other criteria we can determine as having been intended by God,' there seems to be much in favor of Brown's claim, at least in so far as the New Testament's reading of the Old is involved.[19] Let me explain this qualification. Protestants such as Longenecker who hold for *sola Scriptura* are often willing to admit that in the New Testament there are quite a few passages that seem best described as discovering a *sensus plenior* in an Old Testament text. Again, Matthew frequently quotes (Jewish) Scripture in a way that sees in it a meaning that its original human author did not likely see, that is, that goes beyond its Jewish literal sense. While Longenecker is willing to go along with Brown and acknowledge a *sensus plenior* in these texts, he is not willing to accept Brown's further understanding that the 'other criteria' that might be introduced to determine the presence of a *sensus plenior* could be the writing of a Church Father or a later ecclesiastical pronouncement. That is, as a Protestant Longenecker holds that there can be no criteria later than the New Testament for finding a *sensus plenior* in an Old Testament text, while the Catholic Brown is open to an authoritative reading of the Old Testament by a Church Father or ecclesiastical authority. Obviously we have in this a classical clash between a view that founds all doctrine on the Scripture alone, and one that sees Scripture as itself the product of a believing community.

Longenecker is quite candid that his reluctance to accept criteria beyond the New Testament text by which to interpret a *sensus plenior* is a result of his Protestantism, and not of any further evidence or argument. Obviously I cannot resolve a central conflict between the forms of Christianity here, but I do note a certain incongruity in what Longenecker says. Whereas he strongly emphasizes 'the christocentric nature and pneumatic quality of New Testament exegesis,' and I suppose also recognizes that, as Hans Urs von Balthasar has so strongly emphasized, the exegesis of the Fathers continues to be both a 'praying exegesis' (a prayer rooted in ascetic discipline) and a 'spirit-filled' exegesis in which it is assumed that the same Spirit who is the Author of Scripture still speaks (or may speak), Longenecker wants to deny to ecclesiastical authority (perhaps as epitomized by later conciliar or magisterial interpretation of Scripture) any authority in post-biblical interpretation. That is, he resists the idea that a similar sharing in the Spirit could authoritatively draw out a *sensus*

---

[18] Longenecker, *Biblical Exegesis*, xxxi–xxxiv, at xxxi.
[19] Longenecker, *Biblical Exegesis*, xxxii.

plenior – for instance finding a Trinitarian reference in an Old Testament passage – when no New Testament passage has already done this.[20]

I also note that Longenecker does not here consider the slip into 'apostolic' categories we arguably find in some New Testament passages and then in first- and second-century writers. His stance seems quite opposed to that of perhaps the most important of the second-century exegetes, Irenaeus, who insisted that the Scripture be read communally, that is, in fidelity to apostolic witness as found both in the canonical books and as preserved by the bishops as the successors of the apostles.[21] Of course later writers such as Augustine (*On Christian Doctrine*, 3.2) held a similar view. One would have thought all this relevant to the question of whether there are other than biblical criteria by which one can discover a *sensus plenior*.

The doctrine of apostolic succession is first of all the claim that some living person has the authority to interpret the original 'deposit of faith,' but also implicitly carries the idea that the bishops may discover a *sensus plenior* in Scripture. Since I cannot resolve this issue by the authority of scholarship, my observation here is that everything I have thus far said involves the same question. If a Jewish or Christian writer can contemporize his tradition; if a Gospel author can find more in an Old Testament passage than the original human author could reasonably be assumed to have intended; if a council can find at least an anticipation of, say, purgatory in certain biblical texts; or if, more generally, one can develop a spiritual sense of Scripture, always some idea similar to Brown's *sensus plenior* must be present. If a *sensus plenior* is itself a form of spiritual exegesis in which we move beyond the original literal sense of a text to something fuller which nevertheless is held not to betray the literal sense of that

---

[20] Longenecker, *Biblical Exegesis*, xxxii–xxxiii. I reluctantly pass over consideration of Longenecker's discussion, xxxiv–xxxix, of whether the exegetical methods found in the New Testament remain normative today. A new journal, *Letter and Spirit* (2006), is regularly to contain articles on allegory and related subjects, and see in the same project, E. Sri, *Queen Mother: A Biblical Theology of Mary's Queenship*. The question of magisterial authority remains of course a debated question: see my 'Theologian and the *Magisterium*.' On prayer as the source of understanding in scriptural exegesis, see the quotation from Origen at the beginning of this essay. J.P. Bequette, 'Illumination, Incarnation, and Reintegration,' explains why in Catholic tradition, 'revelation is not simply equated with Scripture,' and how this is related to the spiritual senses of Scripture (70).

[21] O'Keefe and Reno, *Sanctified Vision*, 23, noting too that the development of creeds was an exercise in 'interpretive control.' See further on Irenaeus, 28, 33–44, 120, 124–26. The Pontifical Biblical Commission's '*The Interpretation of the Bible in the Church*' (II.B.3.c), discussed by Williamson, 'Defining the Spiritual Sense,' gives examples of conciliar teaching defining a *sensus plenior*. See also Williamson's 'The Place of History in Catholic Exegesis.'

text (obviously a Jewish exegete would not agree), the importance of a correct understanding of the *sensus plenior* bears on the larger question of the existence and nature of spiritual exegesis.

Much still needs sorting out. What, for instance, is to be said about the way in which post-biblical Christian writers like Eusebius, in the *Praeparatio Evangelica,* extended the same pattern of foreshadowing and fulfillment found in the New Testament reading of the Old to Church history, seeing things said in the New Testament as in turn pointing to or fulfilled in events in the life of the Church? Implicitly Eusebius was claiming an authority to pursue such an interpretation, though I doubt that he was aware of what he was doing, or of the problems it raised. Such a habit of reading as we find in Eusebius subsequently took the form of all the providential histories, from Eusebius's own *Ecclesiastical History* to Boussuet to, I suppose, the latest evangelical declaration as to how God's eschatological judgments are working out today.[22] Famously such a view fell under Leo Tolstoy's censure in *War and Peace,* especially his Second Epilogue. The claim in such cases is to be able to tell where the Great Deeds of God, begun in the Old Testament, stand today. The Christian historian is thought to have some privileged access by which he can tell how God continues to act in time. The Christian belief that God is always present in time is turned by such methods into a claim that his purposes can be read, that the Christian historian has some method or access by which he can trace God's will. Now I assume that in his own rejection of the idea that there are any post-biblical criteria for finding a *sensus plenior,* Longenecker has excused himself from having to deal with such questions of latter-day interpretation. But what is a Catholic like the present writer to say?

I myself have formerly argued that Augustine had it right when he denied that the interpretation of God's ways with man that we find in the Two Testaments can be extended later in time than the apostolic period, if by that we mean that a Christian can chart, by the means of comparative biblical exegesis, the course of history to and into his own times with any reliability or certitude.[23] I have nothing against – indeed I would encourage – a meditation on one's life or times in the light of Scripture; to be opposed to this would indeed render much of patristic spiritual exegesis a dead

---

[22] I really should say 'to Warren Carroll,' since the late Prof. Carroll continued to practice a form of what I would call 'Eusebian history' into our own day: see his *A History of Christendom.*

[23] 'Christian philosophy.' D.L. Jeffrey, *Houses of the Interpreter,* 32–37, makes complementary points, though the suggestion, 33 and 35, that for Augustine the earthly city might be identified with some historical entity is unfortunate. K. Pollmann and M. Vessey (eds.), *Augustine and the Disciplines,* considers Augustine's views on biblical interpretation.

letter. But such 'discernment' or reflection on providence does not mean that we do not continue to walk 'by faith.' We may reflect with Alexis de Toqueville on the significance of the seemingly irresistible spread of democracy, or with Tolstoy on the ways in which war overrides all human plans, but such exercises should result in a sense of our own limitations in understanding anything, let alone something so intractable as 'the times' in which we live. When the Scriptures tell us that God did such-and-such a thing we may believe them, and on the basis of that belief we may presume that God continues to be at work in our world, but since the Scriptures, except arguably in a few eschatological matters, do not give us a 'reading' of post-biblical history (and even here the reading is notoriously figurative and hence to some degree unclear), we can guess but never speak with certainty about how a post-biblical event is to be understood. This was apparently already Irenaeus's sense of the matter in the second century, for in treating the divine economy he seems simultaneously to hold that the Scriptures reveal a divine purpose, but that that purpose is unclear.[24] In like spirit, though I do not see that in principle we can rule out the possibility that some post-biblical criteria might find in Church history a *sensus plenior* of either an Old or New Testament text, I also do not see how the Christian historian *qua* historian could authenticate such an interpretation. It certainly is possible that, just as the last word was not said in an Old Testament text (that is, understood by the human author to have been said), it was also not said in a New Testament text. If so, is there a way by which we can discern the completion or proper development of something said in a New Testament text? If we deny such discernment to the Christian historian, even on his knees, what of all those patristic bishops and theologians, similarly on their knees, or, for that matter (in each case the magisterial question is different), all those contemporary charismatics who speak with burning tongue? And what are we to say of Balthasar's idea that each age receives its appropriate saints, each a response to, or with a reading of, the age's needs?

I remember when a young Balthasarian theologian told me that the saints articulate God's will and judgment. My response was to ask whether that meant that we can know via Joan of Arc that God approves French nationalism. My friend's answer was, 'He did in 1440.' I, a fellow traveler of Radical Orthodoxy with what I consider a healthy suspicion of all nationalisms, cringed. But the point is clear. The most obvious brake on such partiality in reading is the *magisterium*.[25] The scholars may have their say, along with the charismatics and saints – and for that matter the liberation theologians, with their 'spiritual

---

[24] O'Keefe and Reno, *Sanctified Vision*, 38.

[25] Of course, in the case of the anecdote just given, I would have either to say that the magisterium did not in fact sanction everything Joan had said or done, even

exegesis' of Exodus – but ultimately the *magisterium* is to judge.[26] One of the reasons I converted to Catholicism was because it seemed to me that some such logic had to be followed, or literally as the years passed the Bible became increasingly either a dead letter or a letter of always-uncertain significance. It is not clear to me that in holding that there are no 'other criteria' beyond the New Testament text by which a *sensus plenior* can be found in Scripture, that Longenecker can have a living Church: or maybe I should say that he is reduced to the caricature, 'every man his own pope.' Here again we come back to a classical division between the Christianities.

Reconsidering Terminology: 'Allegory' and 'Typology'

Study of spiritual exegesis in the post-apostolic period has flourished in the last half-century as much as has study of the apostolic period itself.[27] De Lubac and others of his generation had made it clear that there was no common or settled terminology in early Christianity with which to label spiritual interpretation. These scholars continued a Protestant habit of using the word 'typology,' obviously a word derived from the Greek τύπος but used only in the modern period, to designate a form of interpretation which, though in some sense figurative, was legitimate, because it was rooted in the literal sense of Scripture.[28] The words τύπος and *figura* had been frequently used in the ancient period, but

---

something central to her mission, in declaring her a saint; or I would have to give up a central tenet of Radical Orthodoxy. The situation in the 1430s (pace my friend, Joan actually died in 1431) involved much more than nationalism: see S.J. Dudash, 'Eustache Deschamps,' on the misery of the French countryside in the wake of the Hundred Years' War. J. Coakley, *Women, Men, and Spiritual Power*, is replete (as at 12–13, 15, 73–74) with examples of late medieval prophesies, some involving the interpretation of Scripture, and how contemporaries dealt with them. Particularly interesting is Hildegard of Bingen's explication of her calling, in which she insists, as Coakley puts it (63), that 'her words are God's own words.'

[26] O'Keefe and Reno, *Sanctified Vision* , offer Martin Luther King's 'I have been to the mountaintop' speech as an example of typological exegesis, 'associating the civil rights movement with the divinely guided deliverance of the Israelites out of their slavery to Egypt' (70). In this King explicitly placed himself within the divine economy (71). O'Keefe's and Reno's understanding of typology is more rhetorical than theological, involving simply a shared type which needs no explanation (72), which differs somewhat from that of de Lubac's generation.

[27] O'Keefe and Reno, *Sanctified Vision*.

[28] O'Keefe and Reno, *Sanctified Vision*, 19–20. Dively Lauro, *Soul and Spirit*, 43, n. 28, observes that the rivalry between Antiochene and Alexandrian exegesis expresses a difference in the evaluation of allegory and typology; only typology

'typology' was coined to designate an acceptable form of exegesis in contrast to 'allegory' (ironically a word that the Bible and Fathers *had* used), so far as Protestant scholars were concerned, to develop a willful and arbitrary exegesis.[29]

In the ancient period there often had been a certain instability of terminology within the writings of a single author. Neither 'allegory' nor 'type' had a fixed meaning. Therefore to make theological issues clear, many modern writers, including de Lubac and myself, followed the early Protestants in distinguishing between 'allegory' – as an interpretation, implicitly not useful for normative theology, which completely abandons the literal sense of the text from which it begins, to pursue some other meaning – and 'typology' – as an interpretation that moves from an Old Testament 'type' to a New Testament 'antitype,' somehow fulfilling or expanding the meaning of the original type without abandoning or destroying it.[30] Some modern scholars have gone further, and call typological any interpretation that remains within the sweep of salvation history. But such usage is not found as such in the Fathers, and such distinctions are implicitly theological before they are historical, for they are used to distinguish acceptable from unacceptable forms of symbolism for the development of normative theology.[31]

A related classificatory schema – namely a division of exegesis into three strategies, literal (or 'intensive'), typological and allegorical – is used by John J. O'Keefe and R. R. Reno in their recent introduction to early Christian biblical interpretation. These authors sometimes introduce rather new questions into the study of the history of the interpretation of the Bible.[32] They remind us that the Fathers did not normally hold that 'typology' proved anything in a

---

was accepted by the Antiochenes because they understood it to be dependent on the literal sense.

[29] Cf. F.M. Young, *Biblical Exegesis and the Formation of Christian Culture*, 152–57, 161–85, 248–64.

[30] Again, see my 'Allegory, Typology and Symbolism.' O'Keefe and Reno, *Sanctified Vision*, as at 20, also defend retention of the word 'typology' to designate figural exegesis as distinct from allegory.

[31] J.D. Dawson, 'Figure, Allegory,' argues that no sharp distinction between typology and allegory can be applied to any of the Fathers.

[32] *Sanctified Vision*, 19, on the three strategies of textual analysis, with ch. 3 on intensive reading, ch. 4 on typological interpretation, and ch. 5, on allegorical interpretation. O'Keefe and Reno, 81, coin the term 'postfiguration' to label the application of typology to something postdating Christ. Some of their examples (see for instance 83–84) seem to me to be forms of *mimesis, imitatio Christi.* Jeffrey, *Houses of the Interpreter*, 22–23, using different language, draws a distinction similar to that of O'Keefe and Reno between the modern concern to establish data and a traditional concern to work from an authoritative text.

strict sense. That is, for the Fathers typological arguments were cumulative. One type did not establish Jesus as fulfilling the Scriptures, but many pointing in the same direction tended to.[33] Further, though typological exegesis could be used to interpret salvation history as it extended into the present, such exegesis seems generally to have lacked the claim of absolute certainty.[34]

In the light of his famous doctrine of recapitulation, one might have thought that a second-century writer such as Irenaeus would have used a simple typological interpretive method, but he illustrates the cacophony of the period in his use of a traditional typology both to designate the divine instruction taking place in history, and to describe the relationship between earthly and heavenly reality. His understanding of typology in this latter sense as describing a relationship between earthly and heavenly realities was not unlike a good deal of the literary allegory of his day, and we are not surprised to find him also interpreting parables of Jesus as allegorical.[35] Origen in the following century more or less retains this position, not as someone who introduced a foreign and unbiblical method of interpretation into Christianity, but as 'the first, if not the only one, of the fathers to argue in detail for a method by which to interpret Scripture.'[36] Like other Alexandrian allegorists, Jewish and Christian, he used Scripture more to revise than to maintain the cultural norms of his day.[37]

Since caricatures of Origen continue to abound, in spite of the fact that good work on his exegesis has continued apace, let me state what seems to me the central point.[38] It is quite correct to say that 'if we are inclined to think that Christ is the incarnate Word of God who fulfills the scriptures [that is, if we are

---

[33] O'Keefe and Reno, *Sanctified Vision*, 76.

[34] O'Keefe and Reno, *Sanctified Vision*, 82. Thus I am assuming it was more or less compatible with Augustine, but not with my Balthasarian friend.

[35] Kugel and Greer, *Early Biblical Interpretation*, 172–73. For Irenaeus's use of traditional typology, see my *Beginning at Jerusalem*, 24–27, and also 201–06. Of the valuable essays reprinted in *Bible in the Early Church*, ed. E. Ferguson, see D. Farkasfalvy, 'Theology of Scripture in St. Irenaeus,' 47–61.

[36] Kugel and Greer, *Early Biblical Interpretation*, 178–79, at 179. Whether 'method,' with its post-Cartesian associations, is the right word can be doubted. Orientation to Origen's exegesis is provided by M. Harl in her introduction to Origen, *Philocalie*, and by Dawson, *Christian Figural Reading*, but there are useful remarks also in O'Keefe and Reno, *Sanctified Vision*, 129–39. Origen has long been suspected, from a later Catholic point of view, of having an inadequate sacramental theory. I regret that space does not allow consideration of the issue, raised by Dawson, of whether his figural reading supersedes the sacraments.

[37] J.D. Dawson, *Allegorical Readers and Cultural Revision in Ancient Alexandria*, with Dively Lauro, *Soul and Spirit*, 35, n. 110, 44.

[38] Dively Lauro, *Soul and Spirit*, is particularly well informed bibliographically.

inclined to think that there is an assumed economy of salvation underlying the Scriptures], then we will not think Origen's reading "doctrinal" [an ideology read into the Scriptures]. We assume that the very idioms and images of the Song of Songs do *in fact* have a Christological shape. Origen, then, is not inventing his allegorical interpretation. He is uncovering the true, redemptive meaning encoded into the Song of Songs by the divine intention that structures all of scripture (and all creation and history).'[39] This is the heart of the matter. If one accepts the patristic assumption that what unifies the Bible is an economy of salvation, Origen, though often foreign to modern ways of thought, makes sense; otherwise he does not.

Origen must be seen not just as Jean Daniélou's 'man of the Church,' but as an integrated soul, uniting thought and practice.[40] Far from avoiding the literal sense (what he called the somatic sense) of Scripture, as an earlier caricature would have it, Origen's first intent, as well as that generally of a whole subsequent tradition of ancient and medieval interpretation, was to establish the 'historical sense' of the biblical text. That meant resorting to all the existing critical tools of his day. The literal sense established, he believed that he must completely submit himself to what this historical sense demanded of him, even if it involved the giving up of property and family, praying without ceasing, or castration. He pursued the spiritual sense(s) not normally as an alternative to this historical sense (in some instances, he could not find a somatic sense), but as a deepening of what he already knew through that sense, as a way of applying it further to such realities as the life of his soul and of the Church. For him 'to penetrate the deeper meaning of the sacred text is to participate so far as possible in the ultimate realities that mark the Christian's destiny.'[41]

On many issues Origen provoked opposition, and one of these was his exegetical approach. Sometimes the issues have been reduced to a neat opposition between a more allegorical Alexandrian and a more historical Antiochene exegesis, with Theodore of Mopsuestia a chief exponent of the latter. We must pass over the details of this important discussion here except to say that already de Lubac did not see things so simply: over time the consensus has grown that, though there were differences, Theodore's position, which did threaten to de-link Old and New Testament, nevertheless preserved a sense of 'type'

---

[39] O'Keefe and Reno, *Sanctified Vision*, 111. Cf. F.M. Young, *Biblical Exegesis*, Part 1, 'Exegesis and the Unity of the Scriptures.' Again, on 'the transcendence of revelation beyond the letter of Scripture' see Bequette, 'Illumination,' 71, 73–74, and *Dei Verbum*, I.2.

[40] J. Daniélou, *Origen*.

[41] Kugel and Greer, *Early Biblical Interpretation*, 180. K.J. Torjesen, *Hermeneutical Procedure*, concentrates on exegesis as, for Origen, personal transformation, and lies behind much in Dively Lauro.

that allowed a Christian reading of the Hebrew Scriptures.[42] The important point is that, using whatever terminology, the Fathers tended to distinguish between a use of the Scripture to articulate doctrine; a use of it to determine how Christians are to live, that is, a moral use; and a use of it to articulate a path of spiritual progress. That is, the Scriptures could be seen as aiming at various things. Especially from the time of Origen, there was a tendency to associate doctrine with the literal sense, and morals and spiritual growth with the spiritual senses.[43] This does not mean that the Fathers did not think that all three – doctrine, morals, and the spiritual life – could be found in the literal sense, but that they tended to think of the spiritual senses as ways of particularly pursuing something more personal than doctrine, such as spiritual development. *Contra de Lubac,* Dively Lauro has argued at length, for instance, that Origen's psychic sense is not just a Philonic notion of natural virtue, but is specifically Christian, that is, aims at a specifically Christian form of the moral life.[44]

By the end of the ancient world some pursued three senses of Scripture, some four, and eventually in the early Middle Ages we will find some speaking of more than four senses. But pretty obviously, as with, say, the developing idea that there are seven deadly sins, these were conventions that the more literal-minded might think definitive, but which the more sophisticated could understand as a provisional schema for arranging their thought on various matters. If I may put it this way, just as we can not conclude from the fact that Thomas Aquinas later offered five proofs for the existence of God that he thought there are only five ways of proving God's existence, we can not conclude that there are a fixed number of spiritual senses. A spiritual sense was a way of asking, in fidelity to the corporeal sense of Scripture, what its implication might be for some such subject as the life of one's soul or the life of the Church. Since there was no such thing as an 'academic theology' which could be separated from daily living, all the senses of Scripture were seen as intertwined. Theory or theology was to lead to practice.[45]

Reclaiming the 'Historical' Sense

All this said, in the last generation, primarily through the study of such scholars as Frances M. Young, John David Dawson, John J. O'Keefe, and R. R. Reno,

---

[42] Kugel and Greer, *Early Biblical Interpretation,* 182–83. O'Keefe and Reno, *Sanctified Vision,* as at 29, worry about the adequacy of the traditional contrast of Antioch and Alexandria; see also Young, *Biblical Exegesis,* 161–85.

[43] Kugel and Greer, *Early Biblical Interpretation,* 190–95.

[44] *Soul and Spirit of Scripture,* 192–93, 195.

[45] Kugel and Greer, *Early Biblical Interpretation,* 190–91.

considerations of which de Lubac's generation was only partially aware have come to center stage.[46] Taken as a group, these newer scholars have tended to undermine things long thought settled in suggesting that the Fathers' sense of what reading and interpretation involve is so different from modern academic practice that it is not just the Fathers' idea of a spiritual sense that is foreign to the modern reader, but also their understanding of the historical sense itself. The more pugnacious of recent scholars, such as O'Keefe and Reno, to whom I pay special attention in what follows because they are so 'up-front' about theoretical issues, go so far as to call into question a dominant understanding of the modern academy, which assumes that reading is (must be) an exercise in 'referential theory.' 'Most modern readers hold a referential theory of meaning, which assumes that our words and sentences are meaningful insofar as they successfully refer or point.... A referential theory of meaning encourages us to read out of the text and toward the true subject matter to which it seeks to refer.'[47] Modern academic biblical study, in this analysis, has been largely just one more exercise in a referential theory of meaning. In such study a good interpretation is understood to shift attention from the signs and words of the text to some subject to which they refer. When pursued, one quickly discovers a distance between what the text says, and what likely occurred. Discovery of this distance in turn has lead to the proposition that the Bible is not about historical information but about theological truths or religious meaning. But whether it is claimed that the Bible is about historical facts or theological principles, the theory of reading is the same: the Bible refers to a subject matter beyond itself.

O'Keefe's and Reno's goal is not to reject modern scholarly analysis, but to suggest that this analysis has led to a way of reading Scripture which is very different from that of pre-modern people. It is not that the ancients were not concerned with 'what really happened' – the most casual acquaintance with Origen suggests that this cannot be true – but that for moderns biblical scholarship is much more narrowly defined by its concern for historical reference. According to O'Keefe and Reno, this was not so with ancient or medieval readers, who presumed the actual occurrence of the things described in the Bible but whose first interest was not to pass beyond the text, but to see the text itself as what had been revealed and therefore as the glowing object of interest. The Fathers' goal was to luxuriate in the text, to wander around in it, to discover connections between one biblical passage and another, to contemplate all the Scriptures had to say by intra-textual comparison.

In my opinion O'Keefe and Reno sometimes over-generalize and sometimes speak without sufficient qualification, particularly in the matter of

---

[46] See the overview in Young, *Biblical Exegesis*.
[47] O'Keefe and Reno, *Sanctified Vision*, 8–10.

contrast between ancient and modern. For instance, toward the end of their book they draw an analogy between patristic exegesis and modern science, in that both, they say, are attached to their subject matter – the Scriptures on the one hand, or the natural world on the other – in such a way that that subject matter is considered the proper object of study, without there being something 'more real' standing behind it.[48] These two things are taken as real in themselves, and there is no need to probe beyond them for something more real that they merely represent. Indeed, their argument goes, modern science was born in the overthrow of the idea that there might be something more real 'behind' the natural order, namely God, finality, metaphysics, etc.

Such an argument raises serious problems. Let us accept the idea that the Fathers' first interest in biblical interpretation was the text itself, and not something more real than it. And let us accept the idea that something similar is true of the modern natural scientist, namely that he takes the natural world, and not something behind it, as his proper object of study. An obvious question is how either of these views are related to their own age, or to the ages that separate them. O'Keefe and Reno seem to take the Fathers' way of reading Scripture as symptomatic of a larger approach to reality found in the pre-modern world. But how could this world be simultaneously the world that modern science rebelled against? Where had the notion come from that the views of scholasticism – resting as they did on a very expansive idea that much behind the order of nature was more important than its own views of nature – need to be overthrown? That is, the 'pre-modern' world, or at least some in it, seems, after all, to have had a very modern idea of referentiality, against which modern science rebelled in the name of a very antique idea of interpretation, in which the 'surface' is all there is. Further, to go back to the ancient world, what was exactly the relationship between the Fathers' neo-Platonism and their alleged idea that Scriptural exegesis is only of the text itself?[49] I won't belabor the point, but there is much that needs clarification in O'Keefe's and Reno's comparison of modern and pre-modern.

That said, they do seem to me to be on to something important here, perhaps not least because what they call modern has existed in some degree – as they seem fitfully to realize –across the arc of church history. A casual acquaintance with Origen's *De principiis* or Augustine's various commentaries on Genesis will serve to confirm this point.[50] Origen specifically disputed the historical

---

[48] O'Keefe and Reno, *Sanctified Vision*, 116–18.

[49] O'Keefe and Reno, in *Sanctified Vision*, are aware of this problem. 'The philosophy of science is a rich and varied discipline because the interaction of scientific theory and experimental data is no clearer than the relationship between Origen's speculative theology and the text of scripture' (117).

[50] O'Keefe and Reno, *Sanctified Vision*, 95–96, describe both men, but with a crabbed reference, 95, n. 5. For Augustine see *On Genesis*, and the translation (selections with

veracity of various biblical narratives in ways recognizable to a modern critical historian, claiming that the events narrated in them could not have happened as described, and Augustine clearly worried about what the literal sense of Genesis might be, or how the Gospels might be harmonized. Much later the twelfth-century Victorines are witness to a simultaneous interest in 'literality' or 'intensive reading' (both O'Keefe's and Reno's terms) and in 'referentiality.'[51] But O'Keefe's and Reno's larger point seems right, that for the Fathers Scripture was true not because it successfully represented either historical facts or eternal realities, but because it itself was true, it told the truth about 'the order and pattern of all things.'[52] 'Literality,' in O'Keefe's and Reno's terminology, is central for the Fathers, not 'reference.' Scripture does not have meaning because of connection to something beyond it, but 'because it is divine revelation.'[53] The pre-critical presumption (as O'Keefe and Reno would call it – I bridle at such terminology) is 'that the meaning of scripture is in the words and not behind them. . . the text is the subject matter.'[54]

What this means is that, though the Fathers were aware of, and sometimes concerned themselves with, the questions that we find in modern 'referential' scholarship, for them such questions reached beyond the literality of the text, the center of their interest. 'Literality' as thus used can easily be misunderstood. What O'Keefe and Reno mean is that the words of Scripture are themselves the focus in such a form of reading, they are what the Word and the Spirit spoke. O'Keefe and Reno make the important point, neglected in earlier scholarship, that typological and allegorical readings of Scripture do not necessarily 'move away' from literality or the text, but sometimes are brought to bear

---

additions) of the important series *Bible de Tous les Temps*, vol. 3, *Augustine and the Bible*, ed. and trans. Bright, esp. M. Cameron, 'The Christological Substructure of Augustine's Figurative Exegesis,' with a list of recent bibliography on 'allegory' (321).

[51] B. Smalley, *The Study of the Bible in the Middle Ages*. I have expressed reservations about the basic interpretive framework of this book (of which limitations this edition shows Smalley became partly aware), in my 'From Bede to the Anglo-Saxon Presence,' 330–32. There is an essay by R.W. Southern, 'Beryl Smalley and the Place of the Bible in Medieval Studies; Smalley is considered especially in Part 2 (239–67 are on Victorine exegesis) of G. Cremascoli and C. Leonardi (eds.), *La Bibbia nel Medio Evo*. See also F. Ohly, *Sensus Spiritualis*. A. Sylwan, *Petri Comestoris Scolastica Historia*, begins a new edition of one of the first (Peter relied on Andrew of St. Victor) great medieval works (*ca.* 1170) to concentrate on the historical sense of Scripture in treating biblical history. There is a useful online review of Sylwan by D. Hobbins at *Medieval Review*.

[52] O'Keefe and Reno, *Sanctified Vision*, 11.

[53] O'Keefe and Reno, *Sanctified Vision*, 12.

[54] O'Keefe and Reno, *Sanctified Vision*, 13.

on the 'literal sense' as if useful in explicating it or seeing what the text has to say more fully: such readings may be ways of tying to the text spiritual insights an author thinks important. 'The patristic tradition of interpretation is best understood as a continuous effort to understand how a faith in Jesus Christ brings order and coherence to the disparate data of scripture.'[55] It has been easier for modern Christians to accept some form of typology than it has been to accept allegory. The understanding of this last term varies considerably from writer to writer, but at least some, seeing allegory too as exploring the density of scriptural meanings, wish a definition that does not utterly oppose it to typology.[56] Thus John David Dawson writes of 'figural reading' as a spiritually enriched form of loyalty to the literal sense.[57] As Dawson has presented Origen, all his reading practices were integrated into a vision of salvation.[58]

Restoring the Analogical Imagination

Recently Robert Bellah has applied David Tracy's distinction between a Catholic analogical imagination and a Protestant dialectical imagination to suggest what he considers grave consequences that have resulted from our culture having followed the latter in recent centuries.[59] To rather different purpose, O'Keefe and Reno have used the historical-Jesus scholar, Marcus Borg, to show that the most recent non-Catholic exegesis still employs type and fulfillment: O'Keefe and Reno argue that this is unavoidable.[60] This would suggest that though there may be a line to be drawn between Catholic and Protestant

---

[55] O'Keefe and Reno, *Sanctified Vision*, 22; also 24–44.

[56] O'Keefe and Reno, *Sanctified Vision*, for instance, write 'Allegories are basically interpretations that claim that the plain or obvious sense of a given text is not the true meaning, or at least not the full meaning' (89). O'Keefe and Reno see the difference between allegory and typology as one of degree: both assume the divine economy, but the former involves more interpretive work because less obvious (90). They view some allegories which have usually been taken as abandoning the literal sense – such as some of the Fathers' interpretations of the opening chapters of Genesis – as turning away from the literal meaning of the text, but not from the literal structure, 'the order and sequence of the words' (99).

[57] *Christian Figural Reading.* Also O'Keefe and Reno, *Sanctified Vision*, 89.

[58] *Christian Figural Reading.*

[59] See R. Bellah's essay, 'On Being Catholic and American,' esp. 32–33. Also D. Tracy, *The Analogical Imagination.* Bellah gives as an example of the 'one-sidedness' of Protestantism emphasis on the Word at the expense of Sacrament (33).

[60] *Sanctified Vision*, 85–87, at 87: '…modern exegetical projects, no less than their ancient counterparts, need this technique to bring the disparate data of the scriptures into a coherent economy.'

imagination, such a line would not necessarily place spiritual exegesis only in the former camp. However this may be, I would observe by way of conclusion that in many ways what we see in the new scholarship on the spiritual sense is an attempt, after a long period in which the dialectical imagination has tended to dominate biblical scholarship in the academy, to return to appreciation of the analogical imagination in a way that crosses confessional lines.[61] By understanding the contrast between a (modern) exegesis which tends to explain the diversity of Scripture by reference to historical context and development, and an (ancient/medieval) exegesis which tends to invoke such theological distinctions as that between the divine essence and the divine economy to explain the apparently irreconcilable things said of God in different passages of Scripture, we come to appreciate what is at stake in any attempt to discover a *hypothesis* (to use the ancient word) or general argument in the biblical text.[62] This need not make us say that one approach, the ancient or the modern, is as good as the other; but it may lead to a larger view in which we say that though, having discovered modern critical tools we cannot abandon them, these tools need to be in service to some overarching theological idea, such as the unity of Scripture, this latter being of course the driving idea behind ancient exegesis. I take it that such a view, in a specifically ecclesiological form, is found in Raymond Brown or Luke Timothy Johnson.[63]

All this can be illustrated by returning to Origen. It can and has been argued that Origen draws his exegetical method from Scripture itself. According to him the Holy Spirit gave Scripture a structure that reflects tripartite human nature. Further, just as in the well-ordered person body and soul submit to spirit, so in Scripture the psychic and somatic senses both point to and are ordered by the spiritual sense, 'Scripture's full story,' Jesus the Christ.[64] The interpretation of Scripture is nothing other than the spiritual life; 'the "dialectic" between contemplation and moral action' in understanding Scripture is the spiritual life, the process of becoming conformed to Christ.[65] Rowan Greer argues this much for Origen, more generally for the Fathers. Scripture itself embodies this same dialectic in the interaction found within it between figurative moral and spiritual meanings. In turn Dively Lauro, having established against some earlier scholarship that Origen defends three clearly distinguished

---

[61] Cf. O'Keefe and Reno, *Sanctified Vision*, 84–88. I have been unable to see W.M. Werbylo, *Living Waters: Integrating Patristic and Modern Interpretations of Scripture*.

[62] O'Keefe and Reno, *Sanctified Vision*, 63.

[63] L.T. Johnson and W.S. Kurz, *The Future of Catholic Biblical Scholarship*, discusses various ways in which a patristic approach to Scripture remains useful.

[64] Dively Lauro, *Soul and Spirit*, 129.

[65] Dively Lauro, *Soul and Spirit*, 32, also presenting Origen's argument that Paul already practiced the three senses of Scripture in regard to Jewish Scripture (41).

senses of Scripture, argues that the relationship between Origen's 'two separate moral (psychic) and spiritual (pneumatic) senses embodies this dialectic [between contemplation and action]. Through their practical interrelationship, led by the pneumatic sense in telling the salvation story, with each sense building on the last and at the end all enriching each, the senses lead Scripture's hearers through a transformation toward the spiritual life that signifies salvation.'[66] To reject such an approach would be not just to reject the most expert advice from an advanced spiritual guide (Origen), but a precious model of how to read the Scripture, not just so as to find whether it corresponds to some historical reality beyond it, but as itself the living Word of God.

Dively Lauro holds that the distinction and relation between the moral and spiritual senses is the key to Origen's exegetical goal of transforming the reader. In order to be perfected, the believer must become internally ordered in imitation of Christ, a specific goal of the psychic sense, but such order can only be obtained communally, within the Church, and thus is the aim of the pneumatic sense.[67] While the moral sense may be viewed in relation to the spiritual or mystical sense, it has its own message about the general nature of virtue. Each of these spiritual senses reinforces the message of the other.[68] But it is the spiritual sense which is focused on incarnation, Church, and salvation: 'the pneumatic sense focuses on the Incarnation, the age of the church that emerges from it, and the eschatological hope of salvation, all unified by the central, connecting theme of Christ and his saving power.'[69] While the somatic sense may edify by moral instruction, and the psychic sense may consider growth in virtue more generally, it is the pneumatic sense which 'centers on Christ, conveying insights about the Incarnation, Church and Eschaton. While all three senses contribute to Scripture's salvation story, the pneumatic sense *completes* or *fulfills* this story.'[70]

Of course far from everyone writing on the spiritual sense has been an advocate of it; some have simply wanted to make clear how different are the dominant ways of reading Scripture in the modern academy and in the ancient Church. But clearly there is a larger impulse at work here, evident for instance

---

[66] Dively Lauro, *Soul and Spirit*, 33, building on Greer's analysis; also 36, 50–51, 84, 90–91, 94–130.

[67] Dively Lauro, *Soul and Spirit*, 231–40, offers the speculative suggestion that 'Origen may understand Scripture's somatic, psychic and pneumatic senses to be equivalent to Christ's human body, soul and spirit,' and that for Origen the encounter with Scripture is 'a sacramental consumption of Christ' (240).

[68] Dively Lauro, *Soul and Spirit*; and see 104–09, 121–22, 124, 130, for the third as the mystical sense.

[69] Dively Lauro, *Soul and Spirit*, 76.

[70] Dively Lauro, *Soul and Spirit*, 76.

in Eamon Duffy's *The Stripping of the Altars* and other of his writings.[71] Against a long-established view of the Reformation that Duffy takes to be little more than propaganda, the view of the victor, he has argued not only that Catholicism in England was something healthy and flourishing at the time of Henry VIII, something viciously attacked by the crown for reasons of state, but he has expanded this argument into a kind of personal war on all those who want an essentially didactic (dialectical) liturgy, the pared down liturgy of much of Protestantism, and since Vatican II of much of Catholicism.[72] For Duffy the liturgy does not exist essentially to teach but to glorify God, to worship. Participating in it is not essentially a didactic but a contemplative/analogical exercise. He wants, if you will, to foster a pre-Reformation liturgical imagination, which like the exegesis of the Fathers or of the Middle Ages views Scripture as a vast garden. This desire is not completely dissimilar from that of, on the Anglican side, Catherine Pickstock.[73] Although we cannot pursue this here, clearly the study of the exegesis of the Fathers and of the spiritual sense is linked to many other issues.

---

[71] Needless to say, this and Duffy's subsequent *Voices of Morebath*, have generated extensive discussion. An entrance into Duffy's larger views is provided by my *Beginning at Jerusalem*, ch. 2, esp. 59–63.

[72] A recent contribution here is his *Faith of Our Fathers*.

[73] *After Writing*. S. Hahn, *Letter and Spirit*, explores the relationship between Scripture and liturgy.

Bibliography

Augustine of Hippo, *On Genesis: Two books on Genesis against the Manichees*; and, *On the Literal Interpretation of Genesis*, an unfinished book, trans. R.J. Teske (Washington, D. C.: Catholic University of America Press, 1991)

Bellah, R., 'On Being Catholic and American,' in *Fire and Ice: Imagination and Intellect in the Catholic Tradition*, ed. M.K. McCullough (Scranton, PA: University of Scranton Press, 2003), 29–47

Bequette, J.P., 'Illumination, Incarnation, and Reintegration: Christian Humanism in Bonaventure's *De Reductione Artium ad Theologiam*' in *Fides Quaerens Intellectum* 2 (2003), 63–85

Bible de Tous les Temps, vol. 3 (Paris: Beauchesne, 1986), partially translated and added to as *Augustine and the Bible*, ed. and trans. P. Bright (Notre Dame: University of Notre Dame Press, 1999)

Cameron, M., 'The Christological Substructure of Augustine's Figurative Exegesis,' in *Augustine and the Bible*, ed. and trans. P. Bright (Notre Dame: University of Notre Dame Press, 1999), 74–103

Carroll, W., *A History of Christendom*, 4 vols. (Front Royal, VA: Christendom College Press, 1985–2000)

Coakley, J., *Women, Men and Spiritual Power: Female Saints and Their Male Collaborators* (New York: Columbia University Press, 2006)

Cremascoli, G., and C. Leonardi (eds.), *La Bibbia nel Medio Evo* (Bologna: Edizioni Dehoniane, 1996)

Daniélou, J., *Origen*, trans. W. Mitchell (New York: Sheed and Ward, 1955)

—, *Sacramentum futuri: études sur les origines de la typologie biblique* (Paris: Beauchesne, 1950), trans. W. Hibberd, *From Shadows to Reality: Studies in the Biblical Typology of the Fathers* (London: Burns & Oates, 1960)

Dawson, J. D., *Allegorical Readers and Cultural Revision in Ancient Alexandria* (Berkeley: University of California Press, 1992)

—, *Christian Figural Reading and the Fashioning of Identity* (Berkeley: University of California Press, 2002)

—, 'Figure, Allegory,' in *Augustine Through the Ages: An Encyclopedia*, ed. A.D. Fitzgerald (Grand Rapids: Eerdmans, 1999)

De Lubac, H., *Exégèse médiévale: les quatre sens de l'écriture*, 4 vols. (Paris: Aubier, 1959–64), trans. as *Medieval Exegesis: The Four Senses of Scripture*, 2 vols. to date: vol. 1, trans. M. Sebanc, vol. 2, trans. E.M. Macierowski (Grand Rapids: Eerdmans, 1998–2000)

—, *Histoire et Esprit: l'intelligence de l'Écriture d'après Origène* (Paris: Aubier, 1950)

—, *Scripture in the Tradition*, trans. L. O'Neill (New York: Crossroad, 2000)

Dively Lauro, E.A., *The Soul and Spirit of Scripture within Origen's Exegesis*, vol. 3 of *The Bible in Ancient Christianity*, ed. D.J. Bingham (Boston: Brill, 2005)

Dudash, S.J., 'Eustache Deschamps: poète et commentateur politique' in *Les* '*dictez vertueulx*' *d'Eustache Deschamps: Forme poétique et discours engagé à la fin du Moyen Âge*, ed. M. Lacassagne and T. Lassabatère (Paris: Presses de l'Université Paris-Sorbonne, 2005), 147–62

Duffy, E., *Faith of Our Fathers: Reflections on Catholic Tradition* (London: Continuum, 2004)

—, *The Stripping of the Altars: Traditional Religion in England, 1400–1580* (New Haven: Yale University Press, 1992)

—, *The Voices of Morebath: Reformation and Rebellion in an English Village* (New Haven: Yale University Press, 2001)

Farkasfalvy, D., 'Theology of Scripture in St. Irenaeus' in *The Bible in the Early Church*, ed. E. Ferguson (New York: Garland, 1993), 47–61

Hahn, S., *Letter and Spirit: From Written Text to Living Word in the Liturgy* (New York: Doubleday, 2005)

Hanson, R.P.C., *Allegory and Event*, repr. edn. (Louisville: Westminster John Knox, 2002)

Harl, M., 'Introduction' to Origen, *Philocalie: sur les écritures*, 1–20, Sources Chrétiennes 302 (Paris: Cerf, 1983)

Hobbins, D., online review of A. Sylwan, ed., Peter Comestor, *Scolastica Historia*, *The Medieval Review* (2006)

Jacobs, A., 'Robert Alter's Fidelity,' *First Things* 155 (2005), 22–26

Longenecker, R.N., *Biblical Exegesis in the Apostolic Period* (Grand Rapids: Eerdmans, 1999)

Jeffrey, D.L., *Houses of the Interpreter: Reading Scripture, Reading Culture* (Waco, TX: Baylor University Press, 2003)

Johnson, L.T., and W.S. Kurz, *The Future of Catholic Biblical Scholarship: A Constructive Conversation* (Grand Rapids: Eerdmans, 2002)

Kugel, J.L., and R.A. Greer, *Early Biblical Interpretation*, ed. W.A. Meeks (Philadelphia: Westminster, 1986)

Ohly, F., *Sensus Spiritualis: Studies in Significs and Philology of Culture*, ed. S.P. Jaffe, trans. K.J. Northcott (Chicago: University of Chicago Press, 2005)

O'Keefe, J.J., and R.R. Reno, *Sanctified Vision: An Introduction to Early Christian Interpretation of the Bible* (Baltimore: Johns Hopkins University Press, 2005)

Olsen, G.W., 'Allegory, Typology and Symbol: The Sensus Spiritualis, Part I: Definitions and Earliest History,' *Communio: International Catholic Review* 4 (1977), 161–79, 'Part II: Early Church through Origen,' 257–84

—, *Beginning at Jerusalem: Five Reflections on the History of the Church* (San Francisco: Ignatius, 2004)

—, 'Christian Philosophy, Christian History: Parallel Ideas?' in *Eternity in Time: Christopher Dawson and the Catholic Idea of History*, ed. S. Caldecott and J. Morrill (Edinburgh: T & T Clark, 1997), 131–50, to be republished in *The Catholic as Historian*, ed. D. D'Elia and P. Foley

—, 'From Bede to the Anglo-Saxon Presence in the Carolingian Empire,' *Angli e Sassoni al di qua e al di là del Mare*, 2 vols., Settimane di studio del Centro italiano di studi sull'alto medioevo, 32 (Spoleto: Centro italiano di studi sull'alto Medioevo, 1986), 1.305–82

—, 'The Theologian and the *Magisterium*: The Ancient and Medieval Background of a Contemporary Controversy,' *Communio* 7 (1980), 292–319

Origen, *Homilies on Genesis and Exodus*, trans. R.E. Heine, in Fathers of the Church, vol. 71 (Washington, D. C.: Catholic University of America Press, 1982)

Pickstock, C., *After Writing: On the Liturgical Consummation of Philosophy* (Oxford: Blackwell, 1998)

Pollmann, K., and M. Vessey (eds.), *Augustine and the Disciplines: From Cassiciacum to Confessions* (Oxford: Oxford University Press, 2005)

Smalley, B., *The Study of the Bible in the Middle Ages*, 3rd ed. (Oxford: Blackwell, 1983)

Southern, R.W., 'Beryl Smalley and the Place of the Bible in Medieval Studies, 1927–84' in *The Bible in the Medieval World: Essays in Memory of Beryl Smalley*, ed. K. Walsh and D. Wood, *Studies in Church History, Subsidia* 4 (Oxford: Basil Blackwell, 1985), 1–16

Sri, E., *Queen Mother: A Biblical Theology of Mary's Queenship* (Steubenville, OH: Emmaus Road, 2005)

Sylvan, A., *Petri Comestoris Scolastica Historia Liber Genesis*, Corpus Christianorum Continuatio Mediaevals 191 (Turnhout: Brepols, 2005)

Torjesen, K.J., *Hermeneutical Procedure and Theological Method in Origen's Exegesis* (Berlin: De Gruyter, 1986)

Tracy, D., *The Analogical Imagination: Christian Theology and the Culture of Pluralism* (New York: Crossroad, 1981)

Werbylo, W.M., *Living Waters: Integrating Patristic and Modern Interpretations of Scripture* (Front Royal, VA: Christendom Press, 2005)

Williamson, P.S., *Catholic Principles for Interpreting Scripture: A Study of the Pontifical Biblical Commission's 'The Interpretation of the Bible in the Church,'* Subsidia Biblica, vol. 22, ed. James Swetnam (Rome: Pontifical Biblical Institute, 2001)

—, 'Defining the Spiritual Sense for Catholic Exegesis Today,' unpublished paper given for the Continuing Seminar on Historical Criticism and the Spiritual Sense of the Catholic Biblical Association

—, 'The Place of History in Catholic Exegesis: An Examination of the Pontifical Biblical Commission's The Interpretation of the Bible in the Church' in *'Behind' the Text: History and Biblical Interpretation*, ed. C. Bartholomew, C.S. Evans, M. Healy and M. Rae (Grand Rapids: Zondervan, 2003)

Wood, S.K., *Spiritual Exegesis and the Church in the Theology of Henri de Lubac* (Grand Rapids: Eerdmans, 1998)

Young, F.M., *Biblical Exegesis and the Formation of Christian Culture* (Cambridge: Cambridge University Press, 1997)

6

Situationism and the New Testament Psychology of the Heart[1]

Robert C. Roberts

Introduction

I want to explore the concept of heart (*kardia*) in the New Testament, as one of several possible points of entry for a study of the psychology of the New Testament. The concept is rich and multi-faceted, perhaps the most encompassing psychological concept in the New Testament – a crucial locus of its understanding of human personality.

Personality theory is a major subfield within contemporary academic and experimental psychology, so we may hope that the concept of heart might articulate a Christian perspective from which to put the New Testament in conversation with contemporary psychology. I want to see what the concept of heart might say to a particular school or trend in personality theory known as 'situationism,' and also to see how situationism and the findings it is based on might help us understand the concept of heart. Situationism's main thesis is to the effect that the whole idea of personality or character – in the sense of a relatively fixed and integrated set of personality traits that explain the behavior of the people who possess the traits – is misconceived. According to this view, the personality-oriented way of thinking about persons and explaining what they do vastly over-rates the role of traits and underrates the role of situational variables, the behavior-triggering features of the situations in which the behavior arises.[2] I shall begin by reviewing observations that have led some personality theorists to embrace situationism.

---

[1] I am grateful to Elizabeth Roberts for helpful comments on an earlier draft of this paper.

[2] It is perhaps interesting, just as an aside, that at the end of the twentieth century another movement in personality theory emerged and is currently gaining strength, the so-called positive psychology movement. This movement gives traits – indeed,

Situationism[3]

A study[4] investigating helping behavior[5] placed a stooge outside a phone booth. The stooge would drop a bunch of papers from a folder just as the caller emerged from the booth, and the question was, Would the caller stop to help? The situation varied, for two groups of callers, in one small detail: some found a dime in the coin-return and others didn't. As it turns out, of the fifteen who stopped to help, fourteen had just found a dime; of the twenty-six who didn't stop to help, only two had found a dime.[6] On the assumption that the average personality of the dime-finders didn't differ in any systematically relevant way from that of their less fortunate brethren, it looks as though the dime made a surprisingly big difference in their helping behavior. The investigators speculate that finding the dime elevates mood in the moments before encountering the distressed paper-dropper, and the difference in mood accounts for the difference in behavior. Cheerful people are more helpful than others, and a fortuitous dime is all it takes!

---

virtues in a fairly traditional sense of the word – a central role in the explanation of people's behavior and psychological wellbeing, and seems hardly to be fazed by the situationist findings (for a brief discussion, see C. Peterson and M. Seligman, *Character Strengths and Virtues*, 55–59). Positive psychology boldly asserts some of the propositions that situationism tends to deny, for example, the trait-relative consistency of people's behavior and the integration of the various traits in the most mature personalities. Positive psychology testifies to the tenaciousness of the concept of a trait in explaining people's behavior. P. Goldie, *On Personality*, points out the indispensability of the concept of a trait, and J. Annas, 'Virtue Ethics and Social Psychology,' argues that situationism is based on a thoroughly non-classical understanding of character traits, especially virtues.

[3] I am indebted to J. Doris, *Lack of Character: Personality and Moral Behavior*, for collecting highlights of the situationist findings and providing considerable philosophical reflection about them. My conclusions about situationism and its findings, oriented by the New Testament psychology of the heart, differ somewhat from Doris's.

[4] A.M. Isen and P.F. Levin, 'Effect of Feeling Good on Helping.'

[5] Ordinarily, I would distinguish pretty strictly between behavior and action. Behavior is any kind of external movement (say, blinking in response to a bright flash; but blood flow is not behavior), while action is purposive on the part of the agent. Thus, if a person blinks as a signal, the blink is an action and not just behavior. Actions typically have a behavioral side (though purely mental actions, like silent deliberation, do not), but actions are more than behavior. Roughly, then, action is behavior with a purpose, where the purpose is the agent's. However, in the present paper I will use 'behavior' in the way psychologists often use it, namely, as encompassing actions. I do insist on the distinction, in a way, later in the paper.

[6] Other researchers have failed to replicate this result. See G. Blevins and T. Murphy, 'Feeling Good and Helping,' and J. Weyant and R. Clark, 'Dimes and Helping.'

In another study,[7] undergraduates were filling out forms when smoke was directed into the room through a vent – enough to impede vision and breathing. If the subject was alone in the room, he or she reported the smoke within four minutes 75 percent of the time, while with three subjects in the room, one of them reported within four minutes only 38 percent of the time. Another experiment[8] had undergraduates participating in a 'market research study.' The 'market research representative' would provide questionnaires and then retire behind a curtain. Then, from that direction would come a loud crash and a woman's cries of pain (tape recording). Fully 70 percent of subjects offered help if alone in the room, while only 7 percent did so if accompanied by an unresponsive confederate. If two unacquainted subjects were together, one of them intervened 40 percent of the time. It seems that we see dangers and crises, and our own responsibility to act, differently as we read the reactions of others. The general phenomenon here is called 'group effect,' and again, it shows the importance of situational variables in the production of behavior.

Princeton Seminary students participated in a study[9] supposedly about religious education and vocations. They filled out questionnaires in one building, after which they were sent to another part of campus to make a short presentation on the Parable of the Good Samaritan. Some were told they were running late, some that they were right on time, and some that they were a little early. On the walk across campus they encountered an experimental confederate slumped in a doorway, apparently in some kind of distress. Of those who were told they had plenty of time 63 percent stopped to help; of those who were told they were right on time 43 percent stopped; only 10 percent of those who were told they had to hurry stopped to render aid. Again, it looks as though a situational factor that is rather unimportant as compared to the apparent need of a person in distress has a disproportional effect on human behavior.

The studies summarized so far focus on helping behavior or the lack of it. The Stanford prison experiment[10] examined active cruelty that seems largely attributable to situational factors. From a pool of 75 male college student applicants, investigators chose the most stable and mature and placed them in the basement of a Stanford University building, a simulated prison outfitted with barred cells and a small closet for solitary confinement. Twenty-one subjects were randomly assigned the roles of 'prisoner' and 'guard,' and the 'prisoners' were confined 24 hours per day. The experiment was to last two weeks, but had to be aborted after six days because of the decline in the condition and

---

[7] B. Latané and J.M. Darley, *The Unresponsive Bystander: Why Doesn't He Help?*
[8] B. Latané and J. Rodin, 'A Lady in Distress.'
[9] J.M. Darley and C.D. Batson, 'From Jerusalem to Jericho.'
[10] C. Haney, W. Banks, and P. Zimbardo, 'Interpersonal Dynamics of a Simulated Prison'; C. Haney and P. Zimbardo, 'The Socialization into Criminality.'

behavior of just about everybody. The guards were prohibited from corporal punishment but responded to the misbehavior of the prisoners by hosing them down with fire extinguishers, locking them in solitary confinement, making them clean out toilets with their bare hands, and force-feeding.

The obedience studies of Stanley Milgram[11] are the most famous of all the cruelty studies to which situationists appeal. Milgram recruited subjects from various walks of life for what posed as a study of the effects of punishment on learning. The experimenter welcomed the 'recruits' (one of whom was a stooge) to the study, and assigned them (supposedly randomly) to the roles of learner and teacher. The real subject was always assigned to be teacher. The learner was then constrained in a chair and fitted with an electrode on his wrist, and the teacher sat in front of a supposed shock generator with levers and labels of voltages ranging from 15 to 450. Various voltages also carried descriptors: 'slight shock,' 'strong shock,' 'very strong shock,' etc., up to 'XXX' for 435 volts and above. The learner had to select proper pairs from sets of four words, and for every wrong answer the teacher was to administer a shock, starting with the lowest voltage and increasing to the highest until a correct answer was produced. At 75 volts the learner vocalized distress, and at 150 he screamed 'Ugh! Experimenter! That's all. Get me out of here. I told you I had heart trouble. My heart's starting to bother me now. Get me out of here, please. My heart's starting to bother me. I refuse to go on. Let me out.' If the teacher hesitated to administer a shock, the experimenter urged him or her to continue with increasing firmness: 'Please continue,' 'The experiment requires that you continue,' 'It is absolutely essential that you continue,' and 'You have no other choice, you *must* go on.' In one typical version of this experiment with forty subjects, one stopped the procedure at 90 volts, six at 150, and 26 continued shocking the learner (who at 345 volts fell silent, apparently unconscious or dead) all the way to 450 volts! Many of the subjects who continued to the bitter end were mightily conflicted, being observed in many cases to 'sweat, tremble, stutter, bite their lips, groan, and dig their fingernails into their flesh.'[12] But their record of obedience to these outrageous directives was perfect.

To these more or less controlled experiments, we can add historical examples that seem to illustrate the same thing. In 1963, Kitty Genovese was attacked three times over a period of 35 minutes and finally killed, while 37 out of 38 neighbors in Queens, New York, witnessed her screams for help. Only one person even called the police, and this one did so only after calling a friend for advice, and after Genovese was mortally wounded. A group effect appears to have worked against even minimally virtuous action. But such cases of neglect of duty pale in comparison with the willing murder, by citizens of otherwise ordinary moral uprightness, in such situations as Rwanda in 1994,

---

[11] S. Milgram, 'Behavioral Study of Obedience.'
[12] S. Milgram, 'Behavioral Study of Obedience,' 375.

where eight hundred thousand people were hacked to death by their neighbors, their teachers, and their priests in a period of 100 days, or Nazi Germany,
where ordinarily virtuous citizens took part, over a period of many months, in
the brutalization and murder of their fellows.

Situationists take all of this evidence to tell in favor of denying that character
traits are all they're cracked up to be. Some deny the existence of such traits at
all, while others merely hold that they are extremely rare, and that in most
people traits are so unintegrated that the greatest consistency we can reasonably
expect of people is that they will behave consistently with a trait concept in a
very narrow range of types of situations. Such consistency can be said to imply
traits of a sort, but not what could properly be called virtues. What will the
Christian psychologist say about situationism and the evidence that is its point
of departure? To begin to give a partial answer to this question, I will expound
the New Testament psychology of the heart in the next section of this paper,
and then, in the following section, turn to an application of that psychology to
the findings and theorizing of the situationists.

Traits and Situations

But before I do that, let me make some purely philosophical remarks about the
relations between personal traits and situations. In the explanation of behavior,
traits and situations are always correlates. If the explanation is to explain why
this agent emitted *this* behavior (or performed this action), it must always refer,
at least implicitly, both to some trait of the subject and to some feature of the
situation to which the behavior is a response. Thus if we are to explain why the
frog jumped into the water at a given moment, we say both that a raccoon was
approaching and that the frog is neurologically structured to respond with
fright to the approach of a raccoon. Here I use both 'trait' and 'situation' in very
broad senses.

A 'trait' in this sense is any ongoing structural feature of the organism whose
behavior is to be explained, the feature being such that, given a situation of the
appropriate type, behavior of a given type will occur with a high degree of
probability. A trait in this sense can be any disposition from the disposition to
blink in response to a sudden loud noise, to a full-fledged human virtue like
justice or courage. Adult human beings have a large repertoire of traits on both
ends of this continuum, and thus a fairly large repertoire of behaviors.

'Situation' can refer to such things as a sudden loud noise (what some psychologists call a 'stimulus'), but it can also refer to an indefinitely complex,
narratively-mediated situation, as understood by an intelligent human being.
On this latter end of the range, situations are not just actual states of affairs. The
'state of affairs' to which the agent responds behaviorally may be mentally

endogenous, that is, concocted within his or her imagination (think of the person who wakes up screaming from a nightmare), or a conclusion or tentative hypothesis resulting from fairly elaborate reasoning (think of the 'situation' that explains the behavior of a detective in a complex investigation). The situation may be characterized by factors that conflict in the sense that one factor would, by itself, elicit one behavior, while another aspect of the situation would, by itself, elicit a contrasting or even incompatible behavior. And the situation as interpreted by the subject (this is the situation that will have to figure in the explanation of the behavior) may involve a delicate and uncertain and shifting balance of these competing factors. Given that many of the situations that figure in the explanation of the behavior of adult human beings have this deeply hermeneutical character, appealing to a complexity of traits in the agent, it should be obvious that a simple behaviorist model of action-explanation is not up to the explanatory task. As we will see, the New Testament psychology of the heart encourages us to think in this hermeneutical way about the situations that are involved in the explanation of human behavior.

So there is *something* in the subjects of the situationist experiments that is responding to the situational variables. The surprise, in these experiments, is that they seem to show that the subjects do not have the *particular* dispositions that, prior to the experiments, we would have thought they had; or that they did have dispositions that, prior to the experiments, we would not have thought them to have. We would have expected compassion to be more evident than it was in the Milgram experiments; we would have expected sensitivity to a small award to be less productive of behavior than the dime-in-the-pay-phone experiment seems to show it to be. So what, on the whole, these experiments show is not that people lack character, but that they lack some of the character we thought they had. They are less reliably kind, compassionate, etc. than we thought, and the special circumstances in which the experiments place the subjects bring this out. The scenario in Nazi Germany suggests the same conclusion.

My next task is to give a brief accounting of the psychology of the heart in the New Testament. I will do so under five headings: The heart as a locus; the heart as moral and spiritual; the heart as knower; the heart as changeable; and the heart as hidden and revealed. Then I will make some remarks, oriented by the psychology of the heart, about situationism and the data from which it derives.

The Psychology of the Heart

The heart as locus

The human heart is a container, a site, a scene, a 'place' where things can be found. A rather dizzying variety of things can be 'in' the heart, among which are thoughts (Lk. 24:38), beliefs (Rom. 6:10), laws (Rom. 2:15), desires (Mt. 6:21), concerns (2 Cor. 8:16), intentions (Jn. 13:2), imaginings (διανοίᾳ, Luke 1:51), decisions (1 Cor. 7:37, 2 Cor. 9:7), God's love (Rom. 5:5), songs (Eph. 5:19–20), emotions (Jn. 16:16, 22; Rom. 9:2, 2 Cor. 2:4), the word of God (Mt. 13:19), Jesus Christ or the spirit of Jesus Christ (Gal. 4:6, Eph. 3:17), and fellow human beings (2 Cor. 7:3, Phil. 1:7). Character traits are in (or characterize) the heart (Mt. 11:29).

The heart as moral and spiritual

The psychology of the heart is strongly evaluative, not just in the sense that the heart's contents can be healthy or unhealthy for the individual, but also in a moral sense. That is, the thoughts, emotions, desires, etc. of the heart can be good or evil; the heart can be pure or polluted (Mt. 12:33–35), its traits virtues or vices. God can put good words in one's heart (Heb. 8:10–12; Jer. 31:31–34), and the Devil can plant evil ones (Jn. 13:2). The pollution of the heart is the pollution of the whole person; the righteousness of the heart is that of the whole person. Adulterous or murderous thoughts, feelings, imaginings, intentions or proto-intentions, at least to the extent that they are engaged and endorsed by the subject, have the same moral quality as the corresponding actions (perhaps they are a kind of actions; Mt. 5:28). In fact, it appears that the moral quality of behavior, verbal or otherwise, is a function of the moral quality of the heart from which the behavior issues (Mt. 15:8; Is. 29:13); forgiving only outwardly (say, in words or gestures) differs from forgiving 'from one's heart ,' which alone is real forgiveness (Mt. 18:35). Thus the behavior of saying 'I forgive you' might not be the action of forgiving; it could in fact be the action of accusing.

The heart is the seat of moral and spiritual character; it is what has character. And character is a state, a way of being.

> Make a tree good and its fruit will be good, or make a tree bad and its fruit will be bad, for a tree is recognized by its fruit. You brood of vipers, how can you who are evil say anything good? For out of the overflow of the heart the mouth speaks. The good man brings good things out of the good stored up in him, and the evil man brings evil things out of the evil that is stored up in him (Mt. 12:33–35).

A crabapple tree produces small, sour apples because it *is* a crabapple tree; another kind of tree produces large, sweet apples because of the kind *it* is. Similarly, a person acts and speaks well because he is a good person, while from the bad person come bad actions, presumably because of the good and evil thoughts, desires, intentions, and the like, characteristic of him as a person, from which his actions spring. In a similar vein Paul says,

> A man is not a Jew if he is only one outwardly, nor is circumcision merely outward and physical. No, a man is a Jew if he is one inwardly; and circumcision is circumcision of the heart, by the Spirit, not by the written code. Such a man's praise is not from men, but from God (Rom. 2:28–29).

'Circumcision' is a mark, an impression, a character. The idea seems to be that a person is a spiritual Jew if he has a certain character, if he characteristically thinks in certain ways, desires certain things, feels certain feelings, and behaves in certain ways 'from the heart.' When his 'heart' is thus attuned to the ways of God, he lives 'by the Spirit,' and is thus a real Jew.

Character is constituted of dispositions, not of actual mental events (thoughts, emotions, intentions, etc.). So behavior, according to the psychology of the heart, would be doubly mediated: the mental events arise out of the dispositions constituting character, and the behavior arises out of the mental events. It seems to me that we need to think of the dispositions constituting character in more than one way. Something like habit seems to characterize some of them, while others (or aspects of others) are constituted by hierarchical depth. For example, patterns of thought and perception, thought of in abstraction from concerns and desires, seem to be 'ingrained' by practice; one falls into certain patterns of inference, or ways of seeing situations, by repeatedly practicing inference in that pattern, or seeing situations in that characteristic way. But desires and concerns seem to be hierarchically ordered: a person's desire to succeed at a certain task may be traceable to his desire to do well in a profession, and this desire may stem from a desire for prestige and social importance. On this reading, when Jesus says, 'Where your treasure is, there will your heart be also' (Mt. 6:21), 'treasure' would mean 'what you most *fundamentally* desire.' The actual events of the heart are not subject to the foregoing abstraction: 'thoughts' of the heart are virtually always laden with desire, and desires are infused with patterns of perception and inference.

The heart as knower

Moral orientation is impossible without a kind of knowledge of the good that is at the same time an appreciation and proper perception. Thus, according to the Bible, the heart is also an epistemic faculty, a personal power mediating knowledge. What can be known by way of the heart are various things of great positive value. 'Blessed are the pure in heart, for they will see God' (Mt. 5:8). Paul prays for the Ephesians, that the eyes of their heart may be enlightened 'so that you may know the hope to which he has called you, the riches of his glorious inheritance in the saints' (Eph. 1:18). The properly disposed heart knows, not just anything about such wonderful objects as God and our glorious inheritance, but precisely their 'glory,' the wonderfulness and high value of these things. 'For God who said, "Let light shine out of darkness," made his light shine in our hearts to give us the light of the knowledge of the glory of God in the face of Christ' (2 Cor. 4:6). If the heart is 'hardened,' then it ceases to have its proper epistemic function: 'Aware of their discussion, Jesus asked them: "Why are you talking about having no bread? Do you still not see or understand? Are your hearts hardened?"' (Mk. 8:17). 'He has blinded their eyes and hardened (epôrôsen) their hearts, so they can neither see with their eyes nor understand with their hearts, nor turn – and I would heal them' (Is. 6:10 / Jn. 12:40). 'For although they knew God, they neither glorified him as God nor gave thanks to him, but their thinking became futile and their foolish hearts were darkened' (Rom. 1:21). And this darkening fundamentally undermines proper practice: 'They are darkened in their understanding and separated from the life of God because of the ignorance that is in them due to the hardening of their hearts' (Eph. 4:18).

The heart as changeable

On the New Testament understanding of the heart, hearts can change: they can degenerate morally, and they can improve, and this depends in part on a property that the New Testament language describes variously in metaphors of the impressionability (Mk. 6:51b–52), openness (2 Cor. 6:11–13), direction (Lk. 1:17), and translucency (2 Cor. 3:15) of the heart. Hearts can be hard, open, turned toward God, and accessible to light. God can change hearts; words can change hearts. But whether this occurs depends partly on the receptivity of the heart itself, as described in these metaphors.

Exploiting the metaphor of hardness, we can note that a stone, as compared with a hunk of wet clay, is comparatively difficult to make an impression on. The clay is impressionable. It readily adopts the shape and character that the potter wishes to impress on it. God is trying to leave an impression of himself on the heart. Or, exploiting the metaphor of openness, we might think of the heart as having a shell like that of an oyster. The shell can open, and only if it does so can nutrients be brought into the heart from outside. Or we might think of the heart as mounted on a neck, so that it can turn toward God or away from him, thus putting him in its view or not. Or we might think of the heart as surrounded by something like a shade or veil, perhaps like a Venetian style blind that can be adjusted to prevent or permit the incursion of light.

On the New Testament understanding of the matter, it appears that the condition of the heart as impressionable (or hard), open (or closed), turned toward God (or away from him), accessible to the light (or not), is partly subject to the will of the person whose heart is in question, and partly a matter of outside influences. Mysteriously, God is said sometimes to harden hearts (Is. 6:10 / Jn. 12:40), and sometimes people are said to harden their hearts against him (Heb. 3:7–11; Ps. 95:7–11), though most passages assign no agent of the hardening (Mk. 6: 51b–52; Mk. 8:17).

We can make all of this psychologically plausible by applying it to a specific case. In 2 Sam. 12 the prophet Nathan comes to king David with the word of God concerning David's adultery with Bathsheba and his murder of her husband Uriah. In one sense, David is not in the dark about God's commandments about adultery and murder, and yet he commits these sins with remarkable aplomb and equanimity. It is as though, in this case at least, the word of God is not making much of an impression on his heart; or that something like a veil is keeping the light of the word from shining into his heart; or that his attention is turned away from the word; or that he has shut the entrance through which the word might go into his heart. Then comes Nathan, an external factor bearing the word of God, but bearing it in a manner that has extraordinary rhetorical power. With this help, the word makes an impression on the hard heart, shining right through the veil, forcing open the passage, getting David's attention. Now at this point David could have hardened his heart further against the word; he could have tightened the blinds, refused to look. He could have treated Nathan as some of the other kings of Israel treated their prophets, ignoring him or perhaps having him killed. He doesn't do this; instead he opens his heart, lets the light shine in, and repents, taking responsibility for his sin. His receptivity is a function of the condition of his heart, and its condition is to some extent within the power of his will. But the condition of a heart has a certain inertia, a certain habitual or dispositional character, that is to some extent reversed or forwarded by the free responses of the heart. One who *refuses* to 'listen' thereby contributes to a *disposition* in himself of not-hearing, and thus contributes to a real epistemic defect that will probably have ramifications throughout the personality. *Unwillingness* to see gradually degrades the *ability* to see, and inability to see in matters of moral and spiritual moment has disastrous moral and spiritual consequences.

The heart can be trained in good and evil, according to the New Testament: 'Their eyes are full of adultery, insatiable with sinning; they seduce the unstable, having hearts *trained* in greed (καρδίαν γεγυμνασμένην πλεονεξίας)...' (2 Pet. 2:14, italics added). Behavioral expression is one of the ways in which the heart can be trained, either for good or for evil. Jesus comments on personality development in Matthew 15:17–20.

'Don't you see that whatever enters the mouth goes into the stomach and then out of the body? But the things that come out of the mouth come from the heart, and these make a person "unclean." For out of the heart come evil thoughts, murder, adultery, sexual immorality, theft, false testimony, slander. These are what make a person "unclean" (*koinoun*); but eating with unwashed hands does not make him "unclean."'

Is it the *coming out* of these things that makes the person unclean, or their *being in* him? I think the answer is, Both, but in different senses of 'make.' The presence of the evil thoughts in him makes him unclean in the sense of constituting him as unclean, not in the sense of causal agency. Expression, Jesus seems to be saying, has a causal power, a developmental influence on personality. The man who has adulterous thoughts is already adulterous by virtue of the thoughts, but the man who expresses his adulterous thoughts by engaging in adultery typically adulterates himself further; that is, he confirms himself in adulterous ways (of thought *and* behavior), predisposes himself further to rationalization, and puts himself in situations that make further adulterous action easier. Perhaps he habituates himself to thought-patterns characteristic of an adulterer. (But I think this is not the only possible psychological trajectory. An episode of adulterous expression can be a wake-up call to clean up one's act, and one's heart. Expression can be polluting, but it can also become part of a cleansing process.) In the same way, acts of compassion, of forgiveness, of generous contribution to the life of the church, originating in good impulses of the heart, can further confirm the heart in these excellent habits of thought and desire.

The heart as hidden and revealed

The heart is the scene of hidden thoughts and desires and dispositions to action, that may be revealed *in* the corresponding actions or revealed *to* persons (in the New Testament context, God, Jesus, apostles, and others) who are able to discern them.

The contents of a heart can be hidden in at least two senses. 1) *Occurrent* thoughts can be hidden from observers in the sense that the observers cannot tell with certainty what is motivating the person to say something or other, or to do something. More discerning people are better at telling what is in a person's heart in this occurrent sense than less discerning people. 'Jesus, knowing the thoughts of their hearts, took a little child and had him stand beside him' (Lk. 9:47). The apostles are sometimes said to have unusual insights into people's hearts (Acts 8:21–23). Because of self-deception (successful rationalization) or lack of self-awareness stemming from immaturity, people often do not know their own motives. 2) In a *dispositional* sense, what is in a heart can be very deeply hidden and, in many lives, never revealed in action, because the circumstances to which that disposition is indexed as a spring of response have not obtained and may never obtain. When I speak of a disposition being indexed to a situation, I mean that the disposition is such that a situation of that type elicits the type of episodes that express the disposition – its thoughts, desires, actions, intentions. I will have more to say about situation-indexicality and its complement, situation-breadth, in the next section. I devote the remainder of this sub-section to the hiddenness and revelation of dispositions of the heart, because these are especially important to the New Testament's conversation with situationism.

The thoughts of hearts can be 'revealed' by extraordinary circumstances, and concealed by ordinary ones. In the New Testament, the overwhelmingly important example of this principle is the coming of Messiah. In the Temple shortly after Jesus' birth, the prophet Simeon blessed the family and said, 'This child is destined to cause the falling and rising of many in Israel, and to be a sign that will be spoken against, so that the thoughts (διαλογισμοί) of many hearts will be revealed. And a sword will pierce your own soul too' (Lk. 2:34b–35). The dispositional thoughts (including desires) that were hidden in hearts, no doubt even from the owners of the hearts, will be brought to light in the new *situations* that will be created by Jesus' actions and words – say, by his teaching about the law, his consorting with tax-collectors and prostitutes, his works of mercy, his criticisms of members of the religious establishment, and his death on the cross and anticipatory teaching about this. The new circumstance created by his presence, his teaching, and his actions, brings out surprising behavior in just about everybody. A prostitute becomes bold and walks in on a dinner party at a Pharisee's house; tax collectors repent of their exploitative behavior and become self-sacrificing evangelists; Peter, by all accounts the leading disciple, engages in satanic behavior and betrays his master in his final hour, but later shows extraordinary courage; the upstanding citizens who are the chief exponents and defenders of the law of God become slanderers, liars, and plot the murder of the innocent.

The Apostle Paul looks forward to a similar revelation of the hearts when Christ comes again: 'Therefore judge nothing before the appointed time; wait till the Lord comes. He will bring to light what is hidden in darkness and will expose the motives of men's hearts. At that time each will receive his praise from God' (1 Cor. 4:5). Indeed, even the Spirit-filled worship of Christ by ordinary Christians may have this revelatory effect: 'But if an unbeliever or someone who does not understand comes in while everybody is prophesying, he will be convinced by all that he is a sinner and will be judged by all, and the secrets of his heart will be laid bare. So he will fall down and worship God, exclaiming, "God is really among you!'" (1 Cor. 14:24–25).

The chief New Testament example is an *example*, because the psychological point behind Simeon's prophecy about Jesus is a general one: the contents of a person's heart may surprise that person as much they surprise those who know him; they come out only when special *circumstances* bring them out. Iago puts Othello in circumstances that are calculated to bring out, if possible, jealousy and murder. Neither Iago nor Othello knows, beforehand, whether these things are in Othello's heart, but afterwards we all know that Othello had it in him to be murderously jealous. Jim (in Joseph Conrad's *Lord Jim*), who prides himself on his courage, surprises himself to his enduring shame by his cowardly behavior when the *Patna* seems to be sinking with 800 Muslim pilgrims aboard. Sydney Carton (in Charles Dickens's *A Tale of Two Cities*), an aimless drunk, ends up sacrificing his life in a highly calculated act of courage and love, in response to the unprecedented horrors of the French Revolution.

Application of the Psychology of the Heart to Situationism

I turn now to the question of what the psychology of the heart has to say to situationism, and situationism to the psychology of the heart. The first response to situationism is that it trades on too simple a notion of behavior (action); or, what amounts to the same thing, it does not adequately integrate into its notion of behavior the events, actions, and dispositions of the heart.

The psychology of the heart stresses thought in both the identification and the explanation of behavior. Behavior expresses (often somewhat ambiguously) what is in the heart and is important in its own right (see Mt. 25:31–46), but the New Testament psychology stresses what is in the heart, and ultimately the behavior or action is what it is by reference to the thoughts and motives that give rise to it. I have noted that the action of saying 'I forgive you' is not forgiveness unless it comes from the heart; giving to the poor is not an act of generosity unless it is done with good will to the poor. This is a strongly evaluative psychology and the evaluations apply primarily to the motives, thoughts, plans, and intentions of the individual, and derivatively to behavior.

By contrast, situationism is a theory based on behavioral statistics. Some studies, such as the Stanford prison simulation and the Milgram obedience experiments, include interviews of the subjects, and what the interviews reveal about their hearts will interest the New Testament psychologist. The behavioral statistics of the Milgram experiments tell us that about 65 percent of the subjects shocked their learners all the way to 450 volts, but in the interviews we come to appreciate how widely the dispositions of the hearts of these subjects differed from one another. Some of the subjects were morally distressed, both at the time of the experiment and in retrospect, by their behavior (ashamed, guilty, anxious for the 'learner' and anxious about their own complicity in his suffering); others seemed quite content with their behavior and blamed the 'authoritative' experimenter for any harm they might have done. Through these interviews we come to appreciate the significance that the actions had for the subjects, and the variation in moral value, from subject to subject, that the same behavior could have. Subjects who did not differ on the behavioral measure of lever pulling differed, according to the New Testament psychology, on the heart-measures of compassion and sense of responsibility.

We have good philosophical reasons for insisting on a heart-oriented understanding of the identification and explanation of behavior. An approach that attempts to examine cross-situational trait consistency by collecting behavioral statistics is faced with identifying behavioral markers of the trait under examination. For example, someone who examines cross-situational consistency for the trait of conscientiousness has to decide what is to count as conscientious behavior. But what makes a behavior – simply *as behavior* – conscientious? Consider the following short list of behaviors that could, on a psychology of the heart, count as conscientious. 1) Giving a billfold to a building superintendent (one has just found the billfold on the building grounds, and supposes it belongs to someone who lives in or frequents the building); 2) Withholding a billfold from a building superintendent (same scenario as above, but one doesn't trust the superintendent to pass the billfold intact to its owner); 3) Telling what one knows about the late-night habits of the girl next door (one suspects that her safety is being compromised); 4) Not telling what one knows about the late-night habits of the girl next door (one suspects that one's urge to do so is salacious or invidious). One suspects that virtually any behavior – and its complement – can count as conscientious. The psychologist who looks for consistency of behavior among these instances will not find much, and yet the person under examination may be consistently conscientious, by the standards of a psychology of the heart. Situationism indexes behaviors to situations, and does well in this; but the situation *as relevant to the trait under examination* is not the state of affairs in which the agent acts, but the state of affairs as understood by the agent. Walter Mischel, whose book *Personality and Assessment* summarized the proto-situationist research in 1968 as part of a call for a more adequate psychology of cross-situational trait consistency than behavior-oriented research could provide, has worked out a model that is in some ways like the New Testament psychology of the heart.[13] It seeks to discern cross-situational consistency in behavior by taking into consideration

---

[13] Mischel, 'Personality Coherence and Dispositions.'

individual dispositional differences in ways of construing situations, in the individual's goals (long-term desires) and the interactions among these often competing goals, in the individual's emotional sensitivities, both conscious and unconscious, and the interactions among these. His approach conceptualizes 'the "situation" not just as a setting but in psychological terms.'[14] We see here an instance of a trend that characterized much twentieth-century psychology: a steady retreat from early efforts to simplify and mechanize human action into 'behavior,' and to reduce the situation to a 'stimulus'; and a corresponding evolution toward a more classical Aristotelian and Christian psychology.[15]

The second response to situationism is that it combines too high a standard for virtue with an assumption that if virtue exists, it must be fairly common. The situationists look at studies like the Stanford prison simulation or Milgram's obedience experiments, or at historical situations like Germany in 1942 or Rwanda in 1994, and argue that since so many good people behave 'uncharacteristically' in such situations, the concept of virtue must be a null class and 'virtuous' behavior attributable entirely to situational vicissitudes.[16] The New Testament psychologist is as impressed as anybody with these studies and historical situations, but has his own paradigm case of a behaviorally disruptive situation, deriving from the same document that is full of virtue-language and references to several paradigm individuals. He can also point to the fact that a few of Milgram's subjects passed the test pretty well, and that Nazi Germany gave rise not only to Mengele and his ilk but also to Bonhoeffer and his. We do not see studies in which people of really well attested virtue are made the subject of the kind of experiments that situationists appeal to. One wonders how Mother Teresa would fare as a guard in the Stanford prison simulation, or how Nelson Mandela or Pope John Paul II would do in a Milgram

---

[14] Mischel, 'Personality Coherence and Dispositions,' 46.

[15] For a short history of this retreat, see E. Johnson, 'Human Agency and Its Social Formation.'

[16] Again, I alert the reader that situationism comes in several versions, come of which are more radical than others. The version that says that virtue is a null class is rather radical. G. Harman strongly suggests this view in 'Moral Philosophy Meets Social Psychology.' Although Doris often sounds like a 'no virtue' theorist, he actually does not deny that some people possess virtues as 'robust' and integrated character traits. '...Even if rescuers [in World War II] exhibit a consistency of behavior suggesting highly robust dispositions to compassion, this is something I can grant, because situationism does not preclude the existence of a few saints, just as it does not preclude the existence of a few monsters. But these "tails of the bell curve," the situationism claims, are the exceptions that prove the rule: "Altruistic personalities" with consistent behavioural implications, if they exist, are remarkable precisely because they are rare' (*Lack of Character*, 60).

experiment. The situationist assumption is that the decent citizens and well-behaved college students who get recruited for the studies can pretty well be assumed to be virtuous, if anybody is.

But maybe our conclusion should be, rather, that virtue and vice come in a variety of depths of ingression. This suggestion, inspired by a New Testament psychology, might go as follows: People in whom virtue or vice is most deeply ingressed show the greatest independence of situation-variability. In some people, nastiness is so deeply ingrained that you can place them in the most nurturing and benign situations, and they will, with a high probability, behave badly. In some people, goodness is so deeply engrained that you can put them in Nazi Germany in the midst of the worst conditions and they will shine like lights in the darkness. But these are the extreme and thinly populated ends of the character-continuum. Most of us are more 'characterless' than either of these groups, which is to say, the virtuousness of our behavior is more subject to situation-variability. If we find ourselves in a well-ordered situational context to which we have been habituated, one that supports and encourages good behavior in people like ourselves, our behavior is morally acceptable, but compared to the deeply virtuous people, we are rather easily disoriented as soon as we get into a situation that does not offer the supports and cues to which we have been habituated, or one that contains features that speak to hidden parts of our personality – parts, that is, that the encouraging, 'normal' situation keeps under wraps. Since I am proposing a continuum, I am positing considerable variability also within the large middle of the continuum. People who fall closer to one or other of the extremes will be more like people on the extremes. That is, people with *more* character will be *less* subject to situation-variability than people with less character – for good or for ill. People with more virtue, for example, will be able to behave virtuously in situations that deviate more from the maximally supportive for their habituation. Similarly, people with more deeply confirmed vice will be more resistant, behaviorally, to the benign influence of virtue-encouraging situations, and will require less inciting from ones that encourage vice.[17]

Some situationists seem to think that virtues can exist only at the extreme end of the continuum, but this seems to be wrong. We can distinguish two

---

[17] In his *Life of Richard Savage*, Samuel Johnson wrote, '[Savage] was now again abandoned to fortune without any other friend than Mr. Wilks, a man who, whatever were his abilities or skill as an actor, deserves at least to be remembered for his virtues, which are not often to be found in the world, and perhaps less often in his profession than in others. To be humane, generous, and candid is a very high degree of merit in any case, but those qualities deserve still greater praises when they are found in that condition which makes almost every other man, for whatever reason, contemptuous, insolent, petulant, selfish, and brutal' (paragraph 38).

senses in which something has character. In one sense, character is distinctive form: an 'a' is a different character – has a different character – from an 'e' even if the two are written in the sand. But if they are written in the sand, the characters don't have much character in a second sense, that of durability and resistance to environmental degradation. In this sense, an 'a' etched on granite has a lot more character than one etched in sand. Both of these senses are important to virtues, and so for a disposition to be a virtue it has to have *both* a distinctive cognitive-emotional-behavioral output and some situational resistance. But its cross-situational durability need only be moderate – falling somewhere to the right or left of the middle of the continuum. A wax figurine has some character, even though it will lose it at (say) temperatures above 125°F. A fired clay figurine may have the same character in the first sense (distinctive form), while having quite a lot more in the second sense, since it will retain its character up to (say) temperatures of 2000°F. But even for the clay figurine there will be *some* temperature at which it loses its character.

Not all 'virtuous' behavior maintained by environmental constraints is compatible with virtue. A child who is kept in line by constant threats of time-out and continuous surveillance does not count as virtuous. He falls more or less in the middle of the continuum, the one place where no character at all exists. The emperor Nero is by all accounts one of the outstanding human disasters in history. Tacitus (*Annals* XIII.2. 4–5) credits the Stoic philosopher Seneca, and Burrus, an upright prefect of the praetorian guard, for the decency and effectiveness of Nero's government in the early years of his reign. But it appears that Nero's reason for submitting to Seneca and Burrus was to avoid submitting to his mother Agrippina, and after Agrippina's death Nero's behavior declined sharply. No one would argue that Nero was exhibiting virtue, with the help of his advisers, during his early reign, for at least two reasons. First, if we look at his motives, we can see quite clearly that they were not virtuous. For the less than saintly person with some virtue, the supportive situation encourages not just good behavior, but good behavior mediated by a good heart. The fact that other, less worthy things are hidden below the surface of such a heart is what prevents it from being virtuous in an eminent sense. Second, to be accounted virtuous (despite being to the left of the right end of the continuum) a person needs to exhibit fairly consistent virtuous behavior within the boundaries of the supportive environment. But prior to the death of Agrippina, Nero had his step-brother Britannicus murdered, and Agrippina's death was at Nero's orders as well. Even in the most encouraging environment, he had a pretty bad record.

Situationists typically appeal to extreme contexts in which situational *evil* tends to provoke evil behavior from the large right and left segments of the character-continuum (e.g. the Stanford 'prison' study, Milgram's 'shock' study, and the experience of Rwanda or Nazi Germany). The New Testament offers a paradigm case of a strikingly different kind. Here it is the coming of the kingdom of God, the presence of an individual of consummate moral good- ness, and the performance of acts of mercy, healing, restoration and forgive- ness, that occasion in some upright citizens the emission of very bad behavior and, among the supposed dregs of society, moral reform. Some of the mecha- nisms that mediate the bad behavior are fairly easy to see, or at least to guess at. Envy is a significant factor (Mk. 15:10): those in positions of moral leadership are being shown a better way and a more perfect leader, so that unless they pos- sess a pretty potent fund of humility, honesty, and love of the good, they are likely to feel threatened and behave badly. Daily satisfaction of the desire for dominance can encourage such a civilized pattern of expressing it that it is hardly noticed; so the desire comes out only when it begins to be frustrated. Habits of legal interpretation are well established, and obedience to the law as interpreted has achieved a comfortable equilibrium in a significant portion of the upper classes of the population, so that people who are not very open- minded and assiduous in their reading of the law, or personally in touch with the Spirit of God, are likely to see the good, such as healing on the Sabbath, as evil (Lk. 6:1–11). Fear of what outsiders may do if Jesus' program prevails is a third factor: 'If we let him go on like this, everyone will believe in him, and then the Romans will come and take away both our place and our nation' (Jn. 11:48). Not only an extraordinary love of God, as well as humility and honesty, are needed to face this situation of unprecedented good, but also courage.

We have seen that the Apostle Paul looks forward to a similar revealing of the hearts by the second coming of Christ (1 Cor. 4:5). But such exposure is prompted even by the faithful activities of disciples (1 Cor. 14:24–25). This is evident in the book of Acts (for example, chapters 5 and 7), and in the Gospel of John Jesus tells his disciples that the world will hate them as it hated their Lord (Jn. 15:18–20). In all these cases it is not just notoriously bad people whose hearts are revealed in very bad responsive behavior, but ordinarily 'vir- tuous' leading members of society. Even relatively mild expressions of Chris- tian discipleship, such as an effort to make a Christian university more faithful to its Lord and thus more rigorous in its teaching and scholarship, is capable of revealing rotten spots in the hearts of many. People who for years have done their job in a respectable way, serving students and leading a life of decent civil- ity to their colleagues, suddenly turn up as liars and slanderers, plotters of evil, unjust in their treatment of younger colleagues, full of bitterness and hatred. The mechanisms that mediate such behavior seem, in large part, to recapitulate the ones that operate in the New Testament story: envy, conservatism, fear of what the world will think. And it is not difficult to see how a fuller measure of virtues like humility, truthfulness, open-mindedness, and love of the good could have headed off the production of the nasty behavior.

Aristotle holds that virtue requires a social context that supports it. Thus his *Nicomachean Ethics* and his *Politics* are complementary volumes about the same topic: how to live a human life well. The first is about the character of the person who is fit to live a good life (a psychology of human excellence), and the second is about the society in which a person of good character will function well (a sociology of human excellence). In the *Politics* he distinguishes 'unqualified human virtue' from human virtue relative to a social constitution. Unqualified human virtue is the kind of virtue that fits a person to live in the best possible city-state (3.18), but this may not be exactly the virtue a person needs if he lives in a sub-optimal city-state. There is a character-formation that fits one to live in a democracy, and a somewhat different one that fits one to live in an oligarchy (5.9). So it is possible that a better person (in the absolute sense) would actually function less well than a less excellent person, if the two are living in a less than optimal social setting. Applying this principle in a Christian way, we might say that unqualified human virtue would fit a person to live well in the kingdom of God, but that something less than complete human virtue will fit one to live without conflict in a fallen social order. This would explain why, in a certain sense, the Pharisees function better in the social order of first-century Judaism than the Apostles do, and why, in general, really well formed Christians tend to be in conflict with their social settings. It would also explain why 'good' people can show extraordinary nastiness when extraordinary good is introduced into their social order.

The writers of the New Testament, but especially Paul, are aware that rank-and-file Christians are not usually moral heroes, not usually positioned at the extreme end of the continuum of situation-independence and depth of virtue ingression. Most of us need quite a lot of support from the community to behave as we ought. We need to be accountable to others and we need to be encouraged by others and constantly reminded of our Christian duties. We need to listen to the Word on a regular basis and receive wise counsel about how to interpret it in our life-context.[18] If in Aristotle's view the virtuous citizen needed a city that would afford both scope for virtuous action and continuing support in it, the Christian view is surely that the actual, behaviorally viable maintenance and expression of Christian virtue presupposes church life.

A third response to situationist data would be to take them as suggesting strategies of moral education. If we see consistent patterns of moral failure, such as group effects, we can train our people to be on the lookout for them and to resist them. Presumably, many of the people who witnessed Kitty Genovese's murder were disturbed by her screams, felt upset and wondered what to do. If we know that group effects are likely to play a role in situations of this sort, we

---

[18] I am grateful to Robert Merrihew Adams for stressing this point in recent years.

can give people instructions like: When you think that other people may be calling the police, don't trust it. Call them yourself anyway, because you may be the only one. And don't think that, because other people are doing nothing about what appears to be a bad situation, it must therefore be harmless; check it out. Think for yourself. This is presumably the way leaders in communities think: they take personal responsibility for the community; and this is not a bad disposition for everybody in the community to have, so we ought to educate for it. Christian psychologists ought to be able to figure out how to nurture people in a virtue of autonomy. Similarly, if we know that mood often affects human helping behavior inordinately, it is not as though we are helpless in face of this fact of human nature. We can learn from studies like the dime-in-the-payphone to train people to transcend their moods. Traditionally, the virtue by which we do this is the sense of duty: the ability and disposition to act well even when we don't feel like it.

My fourth and final point is a sort of amalgam of the previous two, namely that according to the psychology of the heart, the heart can be trained, educated, formed, improved, and that a major factor in this education is the church. It is largely through the church that the Holy Spirit works in the heart, sanctifying it. The church is a setting, a 'situation,' if you will, that guides the individual's behavior in such activities as worship, service, and loving fellowship. An important aspect of this 'situation' is that in it, the Word of God rings in the ears as these behaviors are performed, in a manner that feeds and shapes the heart.

Conclusion

Doris misreads Aristotle as holding that virtues equip a person to behave well pretty much regardless of the situation he finds himself in. No doubt he would level a similar critique against Christianity. And it may be that without the harsh reminder of the experiments and historical episodes to which the situationists appeal, we *would* think too heroically about virtues. These examples may be an important reminder for the church. But the New Testament psychology of the heart is itself a kind of situationism. It is generally skeptical about what often parades itself as virtue; given its own paradigm case, it is not surprised by the Milgram experiments or the Stanford prison simulation. And it has a healthy awareness of everybody's need for situational support, even if we are members of the very small circle of strongly virtuous Christians – of Paul, Bonhoeffer, and Mother Teresa. But I have been arguing that if the psychology of the heart is a situationism, it is one that strongly affirms the concept of a virtue.

Bibliography

Annas, J., 'Virtue Ethics and Social Psychology,' *A Priori* 2 (2003), 20–34

Aristotle, *Politics*, trans. C.D.C. Reeve (Indianapolis: Hackett, 1998)

Blevins, G., and T. Murphy, 'Feeling Good and Helping: Further Phone Booth Findings,' *Psychological Reports* 34 (1974), 326

Darley, J.M., and Batson, C.D., 'From Jerusalem to Jericho: A Study of Situational and Dispositional Variables in Helping Behavior,' *Journal of Personality and Social Psychology* 27 (1973), 100–108

Doris, J., *Lack of Character: Personality and Moral Behavior* (Cambridge: Cambridge University Press, 2002)

Goldie, P., *On Personality* (London and New York: Routledge, 2004)

Haney, C., and P. Zimbardo, 'The Socialization into Criminality: On Becoming a Prisoner and a Guard ' in *Law, Justice, and the Individual in Society: Psychological and Legal Issues*, ed. J. Tapp and F. Levine (New York: Holt, Rinehart and Winston, 1977)

Haney, C., W. Banks, and P. Zimbardo, 'Interpersonal Dynamics of a Simulated Prison,' *International Journal of Criminology and Penology* 1 (1973), 69–97

Harman, G., 'Moral Philosophy Meets Social Psychology: Virtue Ethics and the Fundamental Attribution Error,' *Proceedings of the Aristotelian Society* 99 (1999), 315–31

Isen, A.M., and P.F. Levin, 'Effect of Feeling Good on Helping: Cookies and Kindness,' *Journal of Personality and Social Psychology* 21 (1972), 384–88

Johnson, E., 'Human Agency and Its Social Formation' in *Limning the Psyche: Explorations in Christian Psychology*, ed. R. Roberts and M. Talbot (Grand Rapids: Eerdmans, 1997)

Johnson, S., *The Life of Richard Savage* (Brooklyn: AMS Press, 1992)

Latané, B., and J.M. Darley, *The Unresponsive Bystander: Why Doesn't He Help?* (New York: Appleton-Century-Crofts, 1970)

Latané, B., and J. Rodin, 'A Lady in Distress: Inhibiting Effects of Friends and Strangers on Bystander Intervention,' *Journal of Experimental Social Psychology* 5 (1969), 189–202

Milgram, S., 'Behavioral Study of Obedience,' *Journal of Abnormal and Social Psychology* 67 (1963), 371–78

—, *Obedience to Authority* (New York: Harper and Row, 1974)

Mischel, W., *Personality and Assessment* (New York: John J. Wiley and Sons, 1968)

—, 'Personality Coherence and Dispositions in a Cognitive-Affective Personality System (CAPS) Approach' in *The Coherence of Personality: Social Cognitive Bases of Consistency, Variability, and Organization*, ed. D. Cervone and Y. Shoda (New York and London: Guilford Press, 1999)

Peterson, C., and M. Seligman (eds.), *Character Strengths and Virtues: A Handbook and Classification* (New York: Oxford University Press, 2004)

Tacitus, *The Annals of Imperial Rome* (London: Penguin, 1956)

Weyant, J., and R. Clark, 'Dimes and Helping: The Other Side of the Coin,' *Personality and Social Psychology Bulletin* 3 (1977), 107–10

7

The Bible, Positive Law, and the Legal Academy

Robert F. Cochran, Jr.

Like the other authors in this collection, I as a Christian professor must deal with Tertullian's question, 'What has Jerusalem to do with Athens?' But as David Smolin has noted, as a Christian law professor I am also obliged to deal with the question, 'What has Jerusalem to do with Rome?'[1] That is, I must wrestle not only with questions of faith's relationship to reason but also with its relationship to legal power.

This study comes at a time of great confusion in the legal academy, when very different schools of legal thought struggle for control of the discipline. Liberalism controlled the legal academy through much of the twentieth century and is still with us, but its 'rights talk' is increasingly being seen as a construct that in practice often leaves individuals isolated and alone. Law and economics scholars have emphasized the importance of efficiency in law, but have provided no basis for the protection of human dignity (at least for the 'have nots'). Critical legal studies and its interest group progeny (feminism, critical race theory, etc.) have deconstructed law and concluded that law is merely power, but have failed to provide an adequate basis for reconstruction. Many law students are thus left wondering whether they enter a profession worthy of their efforts. In my view, the legal academy is to some degree now recognizing the limitations of its existing schools of thought and is more open to the possibility of religious insights than it has been in a century.

But this opportunity arises at a time when Christians themselves are greatly divided about the nature of the positive law. (By 'positive law,' I mean the commands of the sovereign – the type of law that most concerns lawyers and law schools.) Questions about legal power are difficult for Christians because the Bible, our foremost guide, speaks of and to political situations that are radically different from our own. In most of the Scriptures, the people of God are either in

---

[1] D.M. Smolin, 'A House Divided?'

control of the government (ancient Israel) or under the yoke of a pagan ruler (e.g., Egypt, Babylon, or Rome). In the West today, Christians are in a very different situation. We live in pluralistic democracies. We have varying levels of influence on, but not control of, the law. Some believers, holding theocratic Israel as their model, long for a 'Christian nation,' in which law requires that citizens comply with Christian morality. Others see 'Israel in captivity' or 'the early church in the catacombs' as their model, and believe that Christians should focus solely on faithfulness within the Christian community. Most Christians in the West, however, without a clear biblical role model for our contemporary situation, muddle along, uncertain of the proper relationship between their faith and the law.

In this essay, I will briefly survey what several sections of the Bible say about the positive law, take a more in-depth look at what Jesus says, and then consider what these passages might say to citizens, legislators, judges, and the contemporary legal academy in the West today.

The Bible and Positive Law

Creation and Fall

Like so many aspects of human life, consideration of the positive law begins with the creation and the fall. 'In the beginning, God created the heavens and the earth.'[2] He created 'man, in our image, in our likeness' and appointed 'them' to rule over creation.[3] This assignment probably implies the need for organization and, assuming God envisioned a growth in population in the Garden, of the need for a positive law to coordinate our rule over creation. From the very beginning, it appears that God envisioned man creating positive law.

The creation story tells us that humans were created in God's image. Two lessons (at least) for legislators, judges, and law professors flow from this traditional presupposition. The first concerns those who are ruled: both the highest and the lowest are created in God's image. As C.S. Lewis says, there is no such thing as an ordinary human being. All must be treated with respect and dignity. Law is to be concerned with the welfare of all; no one is to be regarded merely as an instrument for the pleasure of the others. The second lesson concerns those who rule. The creation story dramatically illustrates one aspect of God's image – his creativity. Humans are to be creative as well. Those who draft and analyze statutes, opinions, and legal instruments imitate God in his creativity.

---

[2] Gen. 1:1 (all biblical passages quoted herein are from the New International Version).

[3] Gen. 1:26.

At creation, we also see what might be called the first (and at that time, the only) positive law. God – the sovereign – commanded that Adam 'not eat from the tree of the knowledge of good and evil,' though God specifically noted that Adam was free to eat of any other tree.[4] There was law, but also great freedom. Law was designed to be a blessing; it was designed to protect Adam and Eve from death. God, the original legislator, might serve as a model for us, both in allowing great freedom and seeking to protect citizens.

But, essential to this account, man fell, providing both the need for more law – evil men must be restrained – and the need for restraints on law and those creating it – evil men may misuse law.

Captivity: Law as Curse

The Egyptian captivity is the first of many stories of the Jewish people in subjection to pagan rulers. In general, these are stories of pagan rulers using law for evil. But they also include examples of the Jewish people working for the pagan rulers in some positive ways. Joseph in Egypt (and later Daniel, Shadrach, Meshach, and Abednego in Babylon) may serve as a model for Christians in law in a non-Christian culture. Neither purely ruler nor purely subject, Joseph earned his way to a position of great power in Egypt through his effective administration in the preparation for the famine. His administration of this program, of course, required the issuance of positive law. Joseph's use of law protected not only the people in Egypt, but many other peoples of the Middle East, from starvation.[5] Even Joseph's story, however, illustrates that positive law can be used as an instrument of enslavement. In fact, Joseph may have laid the groundwork for the enslavement of the Hebrews, for Joseph used the stored food to bargain with the people and 'reduced the people to servitude, from one end of Egypt to the other.'[6] Later, Joseph's descendents were in trouble when a new Pharaoh arose 'who did not know about Joseph.'[7]

When the new Pharaoh arose, law served not only as the means of enslaving the people of Israel, but as the means for laying additional burdens on them. When the Jews grew in population, Pharaoh ordered the Egyptian midwives to kill their newborn male babies; when Moses sought to take the Jews from Egypt, Pharaoh ordered the slave drivers to deprive the Hebrew slaves of straw with which to make bricks.[8] Ultimately, of course, Moses was able to lead the people out of Egypt. The exodus of the Hebrews from Egypt is referenced

---

[4] Gen. 2:16–17.
[5] Gen. 41:41–57.
[6] Gen. 47:21.
[7] Ex. 1:8.
[8] Ex. 1:16; 5:7.

throughout the Bible as a reminder of God's protection for his people.[9] In leading the Hebrews out from Egypt, Moses became a model for Jewish and Christian leaders since that time who have led the fight – at times in revolution, at times in flight – against the strictures of unjust law.

The Mosaic Law: Law as Blessing

Our tendency in the modern West is to view law as a curse. We hear little discussion of law as a blessing. But as Oliver O'Donovan notes, 'It is a Western conceit to imagine that all political problems arise from the abuse or over-concentration of power; and that is why we are so bad at understanding political difficulties which have arisen from a lack of power, or from its excessive diffusion.'[10] One would think that reflection on the experience of countries that have been without the effective rule of law in recent decades – Somalia, Bosnia, Iraq – should correct that oversight.

Hebrew literature is full of songs in praise of law. The blessed man's 'delight is in the law of the Lord, and on his law he meditates day and night.'[11] 'The law of the Lord is perfect, reviving the soul.'[12] (Reports from American law schools today suggest that the study of law is more likely to crush the soul.[13]) What is the nature of this law that is so praiseworthy?

The first suggestion that the Hebrews should have codified law came from Moses' father-in-law Jethro. Following the departure from Egypt, Moses himself served as the judge of all disputes. Jethro noticed that Moses spent all day adjudicating conflicts, and pulled him aside.

> I will give you some advice and may God be with you… Teach [the people] the decrees and laws, and show them the way to live and the duties they are to perform. But select capable men [to serve as judges].[14]

---

[9] Ex. 19:4; 20:2; Deut. 24:17.

[10] O. O'Donovan, *The Desire of the Nations*, 94.

[11] Ps. 1:2.

[12] Ps. 19:7. Law professors W. Stuntz and D. Skeel argue that the songs in praise of the law refer to the moral law, especially the Ten Commandments, and not the more mundane positive law that regulates the affairs of daily life ('Christianity and the [Modest] Rule of Law'). But the text of the songs provides no basis for this distinction. If anything, given the high percentage of the Mosaic code that is positive law, it seems clear that the positive law is part of the law that the poets praise. Indeed, the wide range of terms that the poets use for the law that they praise (see, e.g., Ps. 119, extolling God's 'statutes,' 'precepts,' 'decrees,' 'commands' and 'laws') suggests that they are praising all of the Mosaic law. Anyone who has lived in a country where the mundane aspects of the positive law are in disarray knows of their importance and that the full range of good law is worthy of praise.

[13] See, e.g., A. Kronman, *The Lost Lawyer*, 114–15.

[14] Ex. 18:15ff.

Moses wisely followed his father-in-law's advice, creating Israel's first legislation and its first judicial system. Jethro's suggestion that Moses teach the law to the people is especially important. Positive law should be public so that people can know and conform to it.

Immediately following the report of Moses' encounter with Jethro, the text records the Israelites coming to Mount Sinai. There, amidst thunder and lightening, God gave them the Ten Commandments. The Ten Commandments are not positive law in the modern sense. They create no government enforcement mechanism nor do they identify a punishment for a violation. The Ten Commandments stand as moral guides. They are followed by the Mosaic law, an enormous number of commands, filling most of four books of the Bible. Scripture identifies God as the source of the Mosaic laws (God told Moses: 'These are the laws you are to set before them...'[15]) but they come without as much divine pomp and circumstance as the Ten Commandments. As Moses says: '[God] declared to you his covenant, the Ten Commandments, which he commanded you to follow and then wrote them on two stone tablets. And the Lord directed me at that time to teach you the decrees and laws you are to follow in the land that you are crossing the Jordan to possess.'[16]

The Mosaic law was designed to enable the Israelites to be both good ('a kingdom of priests and a holy nation'[17]) and successful (to 'live and prosper and prolong your days in the land that you will possess'[18]). As the wisdom literature makes clear, the law was also designed to teach prudence and wisdom: 'The statutes of the Lord are trustworthy, making wise the simple.'[19]

John Calvin categorized the Mosaic law under three headings: ceremonial, moral and judicial laws.[20] But the Hebrew text itself suggests no such division – they are mingled together throughout. My concern in this essay is, of course, the positive law, what Calvin called the judicial law. In the Mosaic law, as with almost all law, it is incorrect to suggest that there is a clear line between positive and moral law. Most positive law commands compliance with some portion of the moral law and is best seen as a subcategory of the moral law. Some of the Mosaic law is clearly moral law only, being by its nature unenforceable, e.g., 'Do not seek revenge or bear a grudge against one of your people, but love your neighbor as yourself.'[21] Other portions are clearly positive law, identifying a punishment and a means of enforcement. Still other portions appear to be

---

[15] Ex. 21:1; See also Ex. 24:12; Deut. 4:5.
[16] Deut. 4:13ff.
[17] Ex. 19:6.
[18] Deut. 5:33.
[19] Ps. 19:7.
[20] Calvin, *Institutes*, 4.20.15, in J. Dillenberger (ed.), *Selections*, 489–90.
[21] Lev. 19:18.

positive law, being in their nature enforceable, but appear to leave the means of enforcement to future determination.

There are striking contrasts between the Mosaic law and that of the countries that surrounded ancient Israel. As Gordon Wenham has noted, when compared with the cuneiform laws, the Mosaic law dealt harshly with offenders who took human life or interfered with the family, and leniently with offenders who committed property crimes.[22] We might draw the same contrasts when comparing Mosaic law with Western law. The Mosaic law handed out the death penalty not only to murderers, but to disobedient children, adulterers, and active homosexuals.[23] On the other hand, it merely required restitution and a penalty from property offenders.[24]

It is impossible to fit the Mosaic legal and economic system into current Western 'conservative' or 'liberal' definitions. In places, the economic system seems quite harsh. For example, the law regulates (and thus appears to sanction) slavery.[25] At other points, the law seems quite humane, especially given its setting in the ancient Middle Eastern culture. It includes what may have been the first 'equal protection' clause: 'The alien living with you must be treated as one of your native-born. Love him as yourself, for you were aliens in Egypt.'[26] Under the Mosaic law, there was private ownership of property, but property owners had social obligations. Farmers could not reap the crops at the edges of their fields and the poor were allowed to pick the remainder.[27] Capitalism reigned for limited periods of time. Land could be bought and sold, but at the end of fifty years it was returned to the family that originally owned it.[28] Loans had to be forgiven every seven years.[29]

What are Christians to do with the Mosaic law? Christians opinion ranges from that of dispensationalists, who believe that the Mosaic law applied only to ancient Israel and has no relevance for Christians today, to theonomist postmillennialists, who believe that the Mosaic law is the ideal toward which our law will evolve as the Kingdom of God emerges. I will consider the question of what to do with the Mosaic law in a later section, when I discuss Jesus' view of the positive law.

---

[22] G. Wenham, 'Law and the Legal System in the Old Testament,' 39.

[23] Ex. 22:21.

[24] Num. 5:6–7 (full restitution plus one-fifth).

[25] Ex. 21:2–11; Lev. 25:44–46.

[26] Lev. 19:34.

[27] Lev. 19: 9–10, 23–22; Deut. 24:19–22.

[28] Lev. 25:8–17.

[29] Deut. 15:1–5.

The Prophets

Though the prophets of Israel generally receive attention for their ability to foretell the future, their primary role was to speak to the nation on behalf of God. Often, what they talked about was the positive law. Their message generally was not positive. They often focused on the unjust use of law. They called for law to be just and to provide for the care of the alien, the poor, the widow and the orphan.

At times, the prophets spoke specifically of the way that law was misused in the courts. 'You hate the one who reproves in court and despise him who tells the truth. . . . You deprive the poor of justice in the courts.... Hate evil, love good; maintain justice in the courts. . . . Let justice roll on like a river, righteousness like a never-failing stream!'[30] But legislators also came under the prophets' wrath:

> Woe to those who make unjust laws,
> to those who issue oppressive decrees,
> to deprive the poor of their rights
> and withhold justice from the oppressed of my people,
> making widows their prey
> and robbing the fatherless.[31]

It is noteworthy that Isaiah here assumes that lawmaking did not end with the Mosaic code.

The prophets' constant attention to the way that the poor were being treated suggests that the primary concern of justice was care for those in need. In both Hebrew and Greek, the words for 'justice' (*tsedheq* and *dikaiosune*, respectively) imply both a prohibitive and compulsory obligation. For the prophets, then, one could be guilty of injustice for either actively abusing members of the community (oppression) or for ignoring situations in which their needs are going unmet, thereby preventing them from full participation. Prophetic condemnation was directed to individuals, as well as to the institutions responsible for creating and enacting the positive law governing the relations among those individuals.[32]

The Early Church and Paul

In this sub-section, I consider the early church's experience with and Paul's teaching on the positive law. I reserve my consideration of Jesus and the law to

---

[30] Amos 5:10, 12, 15, 24.
[31] Is. 10:1–2.
[32] S.C. Mott, 'Justice.'

the next section. The primary experience of both Jesus and the early church with the positive law was from the perspective of the victim. They came under the judgment of Jewish and Roman law – Jesus for claiming to be God, and the early church for preaching the gospel. Jesus was crucified for his violation. Many in the early church were killed or imprisoned. This has been the experience of many Christians with law since that time. And many have responded like Peter and the other apostles, who 'rejoic[ed] because they had been counted worthy of suffering disgrace for the Name.'[33]

The most influential figure in the early church was Paul. He was an expert on the law, having studied under Gamaliel, the foremost Jewish teacher of his day.[34] When the Scriptures introduce Paul to us, he is a persecutor. He obtains authority from the high priest to imprison Christians, but while on the road to Damascus, Jesus appears to him; Paul becomes a Christian and an object of the very persecution he had perpetrated.[35]

Most of Paul's writings on the law concerned law in its broadest sense – the moral law. According to Paul, this moral law is taught in the Mosaic law, but is also 'written on [the Gentiles'] hearts, their consciences also bearing witness.'[36] Paul here recognized the existence of natural law – moral law that can be known outside of written revelation.[37] Though Paul's major topic was the role of the moral law in bringing one under conviction of sin and therefore ready to receive the Gospel message that salvation is by faith in Christ,[38] Paul's reference to the moral law written on the heart has important implications for the positive law, especially in a democracy. Since the moral law is written on the hearts of non-believers, it can provide a common moral basis for positive law among those who accept and those who do not accept God's written moral code.

A community subject to persecution at the hands of the law might be expected to respond with resistance, but Paul's apostolic message was just the opposite. He called on the Christian to 'submit himself to the governing authorities, for there is no authority except that which God has established.'[39] The thought that God established the Roman and Jewish authorities who persecuted the Christians must have seemed at least as strange to the early Christians as it does to us.

Some biblical passages suggest qualifications to Paul's injunction that we are to submit to the state. He and the other apostles disobeyed the authorities when

---

[33] Acts 5:41.

[34] Acts 22:3.

[35] Acts 9:1–25.

[36] Rom. 2:15.

[37] See Aquinas, *Summa Theologica*, Q. 91, a. 2.

[38] Rom. 1–3.

[39] Rom. 13:1.

commanded to cease sharing the gospel. In the words of Peter, when human commands come into conflict with God's command, 'we must obey God, rather than man!'[40] And although Paul's message that we are to submit to the governing authorities would appear to forbid Christians from engaging in rebellion, John Calvin, citing the example of Moses, argued that God in exceptional cases raises up 'magistrates of the people' to lead in rebellion.[41]

Some of Paul's teaching, reflecting Jesus' Sermon on the Mount, would seem to call into question the morality of coercion and violence that is a necessary part of enforcing the positive law. In the words of Jesus: 'Do not resist an evil person. If someone strikes you on the right cheek, turn to him the other also. And if someone wants to sue you and take your tunic, let him have your cloak as well.'[42] Likewise Paul: 'Do not take revenge, my friends, but leave room for God's wrath, for it is written: "It is mine to avenge; I will repay," says the Lord.'[43] In light of such admonitions, is it proper for Christians to play a role in the development or enforcement of positive law?

In Romans 13, however, only a few verses after admonishing Christians not to take revenge, but to 'leave room for God's wrath,' Paul says that the magistrate is 'God's servant, an agent of wrath to bring punishment on the wrongdoer.'[44] The Christian is to leave room for God's wrath, but the civil magistrate, in bringing punishment, appears to be the agent of God's wrath. According to Calvin, 'The magistrate in administering punishments does nothing by himself, but carries out the very judgments of God.'[45]

Anabaptists have argued that the role of the magistrate was created by God, but that it is not a role approved for Christians.[46] The early church was not, of course, in a position where Christians were likely to attain roles of leadership in the state, but the Old Testament is full of stories of Hebrews assuming roles of government leadership. It seems best to see Jesus' and Paul's prohibitions of coercion as commands to Christians in their personal lives, but not a teaching that would preclude Christians from using violence in a governmental role. On the contrary, Romans 13 and the Old Testament stories of Hebrew government leaders suggest that a government role can be an important Christian calling. Calvin went so far as to argue that 'civil authority' is 'the most sacred and by far the most honorable of all callings in the whole life of mortal men.'[47]

---

[40] Acts 5:28.
[41] Calvin, *Institutes,* 4.20.30–31, in Dillenberger, *Selections,* 503–505.
[42] Mt. 5:39–40.
[43] Rom. 12:19, quoting Deut. 32:35
[44] Rom. 13.
[45] Calvin, *Institutes,* 4.20.10, in Dillenberger, *Selections,* 483.
[46] See 'The Schleitheim Articles,' 631–37.
[47] Calvin, *Institutes,* 4.20.4, in Dillenberger, *Selections,* 477.

Jesus and the Positive Law

As noted previously, the prophets both foretold the future and spoke about justice. These two roles merged in their prophesies of the coming Messiah. In one of the best-known of all prophetic passages, Isaiah said:

> Here is my servant, whom I uphold,
> my chosen one in whom I delight;
> I will put my Spirit on him
> and he will bring justice to the nations . . .
>
> In faithfulness he will bring forth justice;
>
> he will not falter or be discouraged
> till he establishes justice on earth.
> In his law the islands will put their hope.[48]

During his ministry, there was substantial controversy about Jesus' relationship to the Mosaic law. At times Jesus showed great flexibility as to the law. When the Pharisees condemned his disciples for picking and eating grain on the Sabbath in violation of the Mosaic law, he responded: 'The Sabbath was made for man, not man for the Sabbath.'[49] In apparent violation of the Mosaic code, Jesus healed on the Sabbath.[50] He condemned a group that was about to stone a woman to death under the Mosaic code for committing adultery: 'Let him who is without sin cast the first stone.'[51] He rejected the Mosaic laws concerning clean and unclean food.[52] In his Sermon on the Mount, Jesus contrasted his teachings, which dealt with the attitude of one's heart (don't be angry, don't lust), with the external strictures of the Mosaic law (don't murder, don't commit adultery). Nevertheless, at times, Jesus affirmed his commitment to the law, saying that he came to 'fulfill' (literally 'fill up') the law.[53] It is probably best to see Jesus' role as one of pointing to the true purpose of the moral law, which was to transform hearts to the point where we will want to obey the moral law scrupulously.[54]

---

[48] Isaiah 42:1–4.

[49] Mk. 2: 27.

[50] See, e.g., Mt. 12:9–13.

[51] Jn. 8:3–11.

[52] Mk. 7:1–23.

[53] Augustine understood this statement to mean both that Jesus obeyed all of the law's requirements and added to the law what it lacked. *De sermone Domini* 1.8, cited in O'Donovan, *Desire of the Nations,* 108.

[54] At the beginning of the Sermon on the Mount, Jesus addressed the question of his relationship to the law: 'Do not think that I have come to abolish the Law or the

Jesus and the Role of the Legislator

In what may be Jesus' most helpful teaching regarding positive law, he addressed the only section of the Mosaic law that discusses divorce. Here is the section of the Mosaic law:

> If a man marries a woman who becomes displeasing to him because he finds some-thing indecent about her, and he writes her a certificate of divorce, gives it to her and sends her from his house, and if after she leaves his house she becomes the wife of another man, and her second husband dislikes her and writes her a certificate of divorce, gives it to her and sends her from his house, or if he dies, then her first hus-band, who divorced her, is not allowed to marry her again after she has been defiled. That would be detestable in the eyes of the LORD. Do not bring sin upon the land the LORD your God is giving you as an inheritance.[55]

As numerous commentators have noted, the meaning of this section was hotly disputed in Jesus' time among Jewish legal scholars. Though the only explicit regulation is the prohibition of a man remarrying his ex-wife following her second divorce, the provision appears to accept divorce where the wife 'has become displeasing to [the husband] because he finds something indecent about her, and he writes her a certificate of divorce.' Shammai argued that under the Mosaic code, adultery was the only basis for divorce. Hillel argued that the code permitted divorce for almost anything.[56]

Here is the account of Jesus' discussion of the matter:

> Some Pharisees came to [Jesus] to test him. They asked, 'Is it lawful for a man to divorce his wife for any and every reason?'

Prophets; I have not come to abolish them but to fulfill them. I tell you the truth, until heaven and earth disappear, not the smallest letter, not the least stroke of a pen, will by any means disappear from the Law until everything is accomplished. Anyone who breaks one of the least of these commandments and teaches others to do the same will be called least in the kingdom of heaven, but whoever practices and teaches these commands will be called great in the kingdom of heaven. For I tell you that unless your righteousness surpasses that of the Pharisees and the teachers of the law, you will certainly not enter the kingdom of heaven' (Mt. 5:17–20). Initially, this seems to be inconsistent with the remainder of the Sermon on the Mount, which emphasizes following the spirit, rather than the letter of the law. In my view, much of this section is best understood as irony, possibly making a play on phrases that were used by the strictest of the Pharisees. Jesus may have been saying, with calculated sar-casm, 'I am more legalistic than the legalists (my irony), for I teach the deeper mean-ing of the "smallest letter" and the "least stroke of the pen."'

[55] Deut. 24:1–4.

[56] See, e.g., W.C. Allen, *A Cultural and Exegetical Commentary on … St. Matthew*, 201; also G.A. Buttrick, 'The Gospel According to St. Matthew,' 299.

'Haven't you read,' he replied, 'that at the beginning the Creator "made them male and female," and said, "For this reason a man will leave his father and mother and be united to his wife, and the two will become one flesh?" So they are no longer two, but one. Therefore what God has joined together, let man not separate.'

'Why then,' they asked, 'did Moses command that a man give his wife a certificate of divorce and send her away?'

Jesus replied, 'Moses permitted you to divorce your wives because your hearts were hard. But it was not this way from the beginning. I tell you that anyone who divorces his wife, except for marital unfaithfulness, and marries another woman commits adultery.'[57]

Jesus pushed the Pharisees beyond the controversy, back to God's original purpose that marriage be permanent, quoting two sections of Genesis. Nevertheless, he concluded by appearing to accept the Mosaic rule, basically adopting Shammai's interpretation that 'marital unfaithfulness' is the only basis for divorce.

For our purposes, the important part of the exchange is Jesus' reference to the Mosaic law: 'Moses permitted you to divorce your wives because your hearts were hard. But it was not this way from the beginning.' A couple of things are worthy of note. First, Jesus attributed this legislation to Moses, whereas many places in the Old Testament identified God as the source of the Mosaic law.[58] Does the law come from Moses or from God? But this is a false dichotomy. God does much of what he does on earth through human agents. As Luther says, 'God milks the cows with the hands of the milk maid.'[59] God supplied the law through Moses. By attributing to Moses what Scripture elsewhere attributes to God, Jesus affirmed the ordinary work of lawyers, judges, and legislators as an important and godly vocation. God supplies law with the hands of lawyers and judges.

Second, in this passage Jesus did not question the validity of the Mosaic law, but he noted that its rules deviated from the moral ideal. Only a few verses previously, Jesus identified the ideal as the permanent union of husband and wife and noted that Moses allowed divorce 'because your hearts were hard.'

---

[57] Mt. 19.

[58] See, e.g., Deut. 5:30 (God told Moses to send the people to their tents, 'but you stay here with me so that I may give you all the commands, decrees and laws you are to teach them to follow in the land I am giving them to possess.'); 6:1 ('These are the commands, decrees and laws the Lord your God directed me to teach you…'); Ex. 20:22—21:1 ('Then the Lord said to Moses. . . "These are the laws you are to set before them. . ."').

[59] Luther, *Werke*, vol. 6, 44. Cited in L. Hardy, 'A Larger Calling Still.'

Knowing all too well our fallen human nature and consequent inability to conform to the ideal, he approved of positive law that did not impose the ideal. It is likely that Moses envisioned the harmful consequences that would arise if no divorce was allowed: husbands would abandon wives and take other women without benefit of divorce; husbands would father illegitimate children; it would be unclear whether abandoned women were free to re-marry; prospective husbands would risk being accused of adultery if they married abandoned wives; abandoned wives and children would be destitute; inheritance rights would be unclear and inheritance disputes would generate conflict; children of new relationships would not be provided for at death; and hostile couples might remain together, causing harm to each other and their children. In light of these consequences, Moses allowed divorce.

Many commentators speak of the Mosaic divorce legislation as a grudging acceptance of divorce, as if it is an unusual deviation in the positive law from the moral ideal:

> Hebrew law does not institute divorce, but tolerates it, in view of the imperfections of human nature . . .[60]

> Divorce is a bad custom which has grown up amongst a degenerate people, and the Mosaic law tolerated it as an accommodation to a low level of moral concern.[61]

> Moses had only *suffered* (emphasis in the original), as an unwilling concession, because people were too hard of heart to obey God's law and intent.[62]

> [The Mosaic law permitted divorce] not because it was lawful, but because God was dealing with a stubborn and intractable people.[63]

> [Moses] did not give a law about divorce and approve of it by his consent, but when men's wickedness could be restrained by no other means, he applied the most tolerable remedy, so that a man might at least bear witness to his wife's chastity.[64]

Though I do not disagree with these statements, I think that they are wrong to imply that the Mosaic divorce legislation is somehow unusual. It is not the exception. Many elements of the Mosaic code should be understood as positive law drafted in light of human hardheartedness. Irenaeus and Justin Martyr went so far as to argue that much if not all of the Mosaic law should be seen merely as a concession to the hardness of human hearts.[65]

---

[60] Driver, *Deuteronomy*, 272.
[61] Allen, *St. Matthew*, 204.
[62] Buttrick, 'Gospel According to St. Matthew,' 480.
[63] Calvin, *New Testament Commentaries*, 2.243.
[64] Calvin, *New Testament Commentaries*, 2.245.
[65] See, e.g., Justin Martyr, *Dialogue With Trypho;* Irenaeus, *Adversus haereses.*

Positive law (including much of the Mosaic law) establishes minimum standards rather than the moral ideal, because not everyone is capable of abiding by the ideal. As Thomas Aquinas says:

> Now human law is framed for a number of human beings, the majority of whom are not perfect in virtue. Wherefore human laws do not forbid all vices, from which the virtuous abstain, but only the more grievous vices, from which it is possible for the majority to abstain; and chiefly those that are to the hurt of others, without the prohibition of which human society could not be maintained.

> The purpose of human [positive] law is to lead men to virtue, not suddenly, but gradually. Wherefore it does not lay upon the multitude of imperfect men the burdens of those who are virtuous, viz., that they should abstain from all evil. Otherwise these imperfect ones, being unable to bear such precepts, would break out into yet greater evils.[66]

Some might disagree with the argument that law might lead one to virtue, but Aquinas has the Mosaic law itself on his side. God gave the law to Israel that Israel might become 'a kingdom of priests and a holy nation.'[67] But as he notes, there is a danger that if the law imposes too heavy a burden on the population, people will give up on compliance. Such open resistance to the law would create a risk of the law falling into disrespect. It is best that we have a 'modest' positive law,[68] one that prohibits only the greatest of evils.

This view, that Jesus affirmed Moses' creation of best-practical-alternative laws, may provide a basis for understanding some of the troubling aspects of the Mosaic code. For example, the Mosaic code need not be taken to have approved of slavery, any more than to have approved of divorce. Jesus' reaction to slavery provisions in the Mosaic code might well have been similar to his reaction to divorce: 'Moses permitted slavery because your hearts were hard. But it was not this way from the beginning – it is not the ideal.' Augustine argued that in the beginning, it was not God's intention that people be under the authority of one another. According to Augustine, man was appointed to rule over the rest of God's creation (citing Gen. 1:26) but not one another. 'God wanted rational man, made to His image, to have no dominion except over irrational nature. He meant no man, therefore, to have dominion over man, but only man over beast.'[69] Augustine appears to have accepted the reality

---

[66] Aquinas, *Summa Theologica*, Q. 96, a. 2.

[67] Ex. 19:6.

[68] Skeel and Stuntz have argued for modest laws on the grounds that expansive laws give prosecutors too much power to decide whom to prosecute ('Modest Rule'). There is, however, the danger that the positive law will be the only restraint for some people.

[69] Augustine, *The City of God*, 5.19.15, 461.

of man ruling over man as a result of the fall, but Jesus' comments on divorce suggest that it is appropriate for legislation to seek to get back to God's ideal. Under this view, if the social circumstances are such that people would accept a rule that is closer to the divine ideal (on divorce or slavery), the wise legislator should pursue it.

Jesus might also have said similar things about some of the harsh punishments of the Mosaic code, possibly including capital punishment. Such punishment was a prudential response to the situation of the time – a nomadic people for whom the possibility of life imprisonment was impossible – but in a different situation the law might more closely approach the ideal; the death penalty might be abolished or reserved only for the worst of crimes. This is consistent with the recent Catholic position on the death penalty.[70]

Jesus' comments on the Mosaic divorce law suggest an enormous opportunity (and responsibility) for judges and legislators. They must prudently and creatively craft laws with eyes fixed on both God's ideal and on the practical reality. The task of the Christian legislator or judge is to identify God's ideals and to determine how to advance those ideals in light of the current social situation.

Biblical scholarship suggests that Moses' work in developing the Mosaic law was in fact very similar to the task modern lawyers face in two respects. Though, as noted above, the Mosaic code substantially differed from the law of the surrounding countries, especially in the level of punishment for different types of crimes, it appears that some of the Mosaic code was drawn from Mesopotamian law.[71] The process of considering the law of other jurisdictions, accepting that which seems sensible and rejecting those parts that conflict with local values, is part of the ordinary work of lawyers and judges today. In addition, it appears that the Mosaic divorce regulation discussed above was 'derived from [an old] courtroom decision.'[72] This is the way that much of the law is developed in modern common law countries (such as England and the United States). Unlike legislation, the common law develops as judges resolve individual cases, and their decisions establish a basis for determining subsequent cases.

Some might argue that these observations afford an insufficiently miraculous explanation for the creation of the Mosaic law. But in the Bible this is the

---

[70] According to the Catechism of the Catholic Church: 'Assuming that the guilty party's identity and responsibility have been fully determined, the traditional teaching of the church does not exclude recourse to the death penalty, if this is the only possible way of effectively defending human lives against the unjust aggressor. If, however, non-lethal means are sufficient to defend and protect people's safety from the aggressor, authority will limit itself to such means, as these are more in keeping with the concrete conditions of the common good and more in conformity with the dignity of the human person' *(Catechism of the Catholic Church, Second Edition, 2267).*

[71] G. Wenham, 'Law and the Legal System,' 24.

[72] G.E. Wright, 'The Book of Deuteronomy,' 473.

pattern by which God accomplishes many of his purposes. At times he works miracles, but generally he relies on human beings doing ordinary things through ordinary means. For example, whereas God gave John the words of the book of Revelation through an angel,[73] Luke composed his gospel through a careful investigation of all the facts, including eyewitness interviews.[74] Both were 'God breathed.'[75] We see that pattern in the giving of the law to Israel as well. God gave Israel the Ten Commandments with his own voice amidst thunder and lighting and wrote them on stone tablets with his own hand. It appears that he gave them the Mosaic positive law through many human means. It came in response to Moses' over-crowded court docket, at the suggestion of his father-in-law. It was God breathed, as Moses wrestled with the practical problem of how to pursue God's ideal in a fallen world, drawing from neighboring sources of law and particular cases.

Some have criticized modern lawmakers for failing to enact ideal biblical standards or even the less stringent (but also biblical) Mosaic standards into contemporary law. On the issue of divorce, one commentator has said: 'Brethren and fellow-citizens, I believe that our lawmakers are to blame for allowing [no-fault divorce] laws to exist as they do, and not bringing the law of divorce in these United States to the scriptural standard.'[76] But if my understanding of Jesus' teaching on the law of divorce is correct, the positive law should not necessarily adopt the moral law. The law should seek the ideal, but should do so in light of its practical impact.

Modern divorce law is an area where Jesus' model could be applied. The ideal – permanent union – has not changed, nor has the hardness of people's hearts or the danger that a rule prohibiting divorce would yield worse results than a rule allowing it. In the 1960s and 70s in the United States, legislatures in almost all jurisdictions moved from a fault-based divorce system to a no-fault divorce system. The law now provides little or no deterrence to divorce. Divorce can be obtained easily by either party based on any or no reason. As several studies have shown, the victims of easy divorce are most often women and children, who have become modern analogues to the Old Testament's widows and orphans. The hardness of human hearts may warrant laws that discourage divorce without demanding the ideal of permanent marriage. Thoughtful lawyers, legislators and law professors wrestle with alternatives to easy no-fault divorce, proposing longer waiting periods (especially for parents of young children), counseling requirements and covenant marriage

---

[73] Rev. 1:1.
[74] Lk. 1:1–4.
[75] 2 Tim. 3:16.
[76] A. Cressey, as cited in J.S. Exell, 'Matthew,' 418.

legislation, which allows couples to agree at marriage to certain impediments to divorce.[77]

Jesus' comments regarding the Mosaic divorce law suggest that lawyers, legislators, judges, and citizens have a high calling. They do God's work as they prudently seek to identify laws that will move us toward God's ideals in light of the practical problems of human sin in the current situation.

Love of Neighbor

At one point, 'an expert in the law' 'tested' Jesus with another question, 'Teacher, which is the greatest commandment in the Law?' Jesus answered that the first is love of God and added, quoting the Mosaic law, 'the second is like it: "Love your neighbor as yourself." All the Law and the Prophets hang on these two commandments.'[78] Later, another lawyer, seeking to 'justify himself,' asked concerning this second commandment, 'Who is my neighbor?'[79] Jesus responded with the story of the Good Samaritan, in which the hated Samaritan serves as the role model, caring for the needs of a man who has been beaten and robbed.

To many, the command that we love our neighbors seems odd. Nowadays, love is generally thought of purely as an emotion, something beyond our control, but the Greek word translated as 'love' is *agape*, an act of the will, a matter that is subject to the control of the individual. We are to treat our neighbors as we would want to be treated.

There are two messages here for the Christian in the field of law. The first concerns the purposes of the law. Jesus identified one of the ideals toward which the law should reach, suggesting that the Mosaic law expressed what it means to love our neighbors. The Mosaic positive law *required* the Jews to show love toward their neighbors in some respects. Just as parents teach their children to love each other by requiring them to go through the motions of forgiving, sharing, etc., it may be that requiring citizens to behave well toward one another will serve to teach them to love. Requiring farmers to make the crops at the edges of their fields available to the poor may teach them to love the poor and to be generous to them. Calvin notes that the purpose of the Mosaic positive law was 'to preserve that very love which is enjoined by God's eternal law.' In Calvin's view, 'every nation is left free to make such laws as it foresees to be profitable to itself. Yet these must be in conformity to that perpetual rule of love.'[80]

---

[77] For several additional proposals aimed at encouraging marriage stability, see Institute for American Values, *Marriage and the Law*.
[78] Mt. 22:35–40, quoting Lev. 19:18.
[79] Lk. 10:26.
[80] Calvin, *Institutes*, 4.20.15, in Dillenberger (ed.), *Selections*, 490.

A second message is that lawmaking itself should be an act of love toward the neighbor. Jack Sammons implies this possibility in his discussion of the story of the Good Samaritan. Without diminishing the importance of the Samaritan's individual acts of care – saving the injured man, binding his wounds, and taking him to an inn – we should recognize that those who develop laws can also serve their fellowman through legislation. Legislation might deal 'with the underlying problems of the dangerousness of passage to Jericho, or the need for medical care to travelers in distress, or, for that matter, the hardhearted financial shrewdness of innkeepers.'[81] The development and enforcement of wise laws can be among the most loving acts in which a person can engage.

The Legal Academy

As noted previously, the Bible has had limited influence in the modern legal academy, in part because of the difficulties in determining a biblical view of law. Obviously the Bible addressed the people of God in very different situations from those confronted by Western Christians in the twenty-first century. But even the clearest scriptural teaching concerning law encounters resistance in today's legal academy. Some of this resistance comes from secularists who oppose religiously-grounded values in any setting. Additional resistance arises from a misunderstanding of the doctrine of the separation of church and state. An anecdote will illustrate the depth of the opposition to religious perspectives on law.

At a law professors' conference a few years ago, when I complained about the anti-religious nature of most law schools, a member of the faculty at a top-tier state university pulled me aside and confessed the following. Her law school had a volunteer faculty reading group that read and discussed a book each year. One faculty member proposed that they read Yale law professor Stephen Carter's *The Culture of Disbelief*, a book that favors allowing religious values into the public square – he argues that religion should be more than just a hobby. One professor objected that for the faculty at a state university to study Carter's book would be a violation of the separation of church and state. Most of the faculty did not take that objection seriously, but a survey of the faculty revealed that not a single member of the faculty of over fifty members agreed with the position in Carter's book. Their very reaction demonstrated the thesis of his book– that elites in America are aggressively secular. The American legal academy is a place where scripturally-grounded arguments cannot readily get a

---

[81] J.L. Sammons, 'Parables and Pedagogy,' 46.

hearing. The academy, in fact, does not even want to *hear the argument* that scripturally-grounded arguments deserve a hearing.

The notion that the separation of church and state precludes the law from being based on religiously-grounded values is wrong-headed at many levels. All law is grounded on moral values and most of those moral values (including the values that many secularists use to justify their legal positions) have their source in religious teaching. The separation of church and state is itself rooted in the religious understanding of many of the founders that genuine religious faith cannot be coerced and that religion will do better if the state does not mandate or meddle with it. The separation of church and state is an institutional separation; it was never designed to keep religious values from influencing the law. To keep religiously-grounded values out of the public square is directly contrary to the goal of liberal democracy of creating a conversation in which all citizens, including religious citizens, can participate.[82]

In the legal academy, as in other corners of the university, Christians face resistance from both Enlightenment liberal and multicultural groups. Those groups may battle each other for power, but many within them are in agreement that views based on Christian faith should not have a place at the table. Liberals argue that there should be no place for religious influences because reason, not faith, should be the basis of decisions in the public square. Multiculturalists want only those at the table who agree with them that there is no meta-narrative (thereby seeking to exclude both liberals and Christians). But it may be that both liberalism and multiculturalism have run their course. Each appears to be intellectually spent and thus unable to present answers to many of the legal challenges of our day. In my view, biblical insights provide a helpful critique of the current reigning schools of legal thought. In the remainder of this essay, I consider those schools of thought.

Liberalism: 'The Ordinary Religion of the Law School Classroom'

Within most modern law schools there is little consideration of philosophy, much less theology. Professors teach law students the technical skills of legal analysis and advocacy, but give scant attention to larger issues. But whether law schools recognize it or not, they convey a philosophy to their students. If law professors do not critically evaluate their legal philosophy, they are likely to convey what Roger Cramton has called 'the ordinary religion of the law school classroom'[83]: the instrumentalism, individualism, skepticism, rationalism, and pragmatism that are the hallmarks of both liberalism and the modern legal profession.

---

[82] See M.W. McConnell, 'Five Reasons to Reject the Claim that Religious Arguments Should be Excluded,' 639.
[83] R.C. Cramton, 'The Ordinary Religion of the Law School Classroom,' 247.

Liberalism teaches that human beings are individuals, whose rights are supreme, and who have little claim on one another. At the heart of liberalism is what Oliver O'Donovan has called 'the notion of the abstract will, exercising choice prior to all reason and order, from whose *fiat lux* spring society, morality and rationality itself.' (The theological analogue is 'creation *ex nihilo*, the absolute summoning of reason, order and beauty out of chaos and emptiness.') Such a view, of course, competes with faith in the creator and leads to a refusal to accept his created order and goodness.[84] Liberalism therefore finds it difficult to critique selfishness in everything from corporate to personal relations.

Law schools and the legal profession promote a liberal ideal that Thomas Shaffer refers to as 'radical individualism': in the ideal lawyer's world, every individual would have his own lawyer, protecting his rights every step of the way.[85] Discourse in law schools is marked by what Mary Ann Glendon has called 'rights talk,' under which the default position for any controversial issue is deference to individual choice. It is for the individual to create himself. This view is reflected in the now-famous/infamous statement in *Planned Parenthood v. Casey* (a case re-affirming the right to abortion), 'At the heart of liberty is the right to define one's own concept of existence, of the meaning of the universe, and of the mystery of human life.'[86] Liberalism has influenced both the political right, which holds that individual property rights are sacred, and the political left, which holds that individual sexual freedom is sacred.

Scripture affirms many aspects of liberalism. As Jonathan Chaplin has noted, four features of liberal society are in part results of the Christian gospel: freedom, merciful judgment, natural right, and openness to speech.[87] Freedom and equality are important aspects of human dignity, grounded in our identity as persons created in God's image. But there is more to human functioning than freedom. By itself, in the words of Kris Kristofferson, 'freedom's just another word for nothing left to lose.' Many have found that our rights-based society leaves them alone and empty. Both wings of liberalism should be challenged by the Bible's message that we are *members* of a broad range of communities – including families, religious congregations, local communities, national communities, and the whole human family – and we have responsibilities as members, to the other members, of each. The law should work to protect intermediate institutions and should encourage individuals in society to care for one another. Property rights are not absolute; rather, we are trustees for God, and property laws should balance the interests of individuals and the

---

[84] O'Donovan, *Desire of the Nations*, 274.
[85] T.L. Shaffer, 'The Legal Ethics of Radical Individualism,' 963.
[86] *Planned Parenthood v. Casey*, 505 U.S. 833, 851 (1992) (plurality opinion).
[87] J. Chaplin, 'Political Eschatology and Responsible Government,' 272–75.

broader community. Individual sexual freedom should not be allowed to damage the youngest and most vulnerable members of our community or to damage the community as a whole.

'Law and Economics' and its Progeny

The law and economics school of legal thought developed great influence among law schools in the 1970s.[88] It brought to law the tools of economic analysis. For some, law and economics is merely descriptive – it identifies the economic costs and benefits of various rules of law. But for others, the discipline is normative – it holds that courts *should* always adopt the most efficient rule; law *should be* utilitarian, providing greater goods for all to enjoy. Some law and economics scholars have applied efficiency theories to matters not normally associated with economics – to the allocation of adopted children and human organs and to the efficiency of criminal punishment and suicide. Public choice theory, a child of law and economics theory, discounts the possibility that legislative solutions to social problems will be fair, arguing that legislators will always act in response to interest group pressures rather than for the broader good. Public choice theory argues for a greatly limited state, since legislative solutions, by the nature of the legislative process, will not respond to the needs of the broader community.

The Scriptures value efficiency – we are stewards of all that God gives us and should not waste it – but they also hold up other primary values, especially justice and mercy. Some rules and means of analysis advocated by law and economics scholars are inconsistent with human dignity. Humans are more than producers and consumers. Efficiency can enable us to have more goods for all to enjoy, but under the rules that law and economics scholars favor, it is generally those who already have who get to do the enjoying. Throughout the Bible, the poor, the widow, and the orphan are valued, not because of what they produce, but because they are created in God's image. A central message of the prophets is that God judges a nation by how it treats its poor.

'Critical Legal Studies' and its Progeny

On the other end of the political spectrum are Critical Legal Studies (CLS) theorists. They brought the tools of postmodern literary criticism and neo-Marxist

---

[88] Important law and economics texts include R. Coase, 'The Problem of Social Cost,' 1; R. Posner, 'The Economic Approach to Law,' 757; G. Calabresi, *The Cost of Accidents*; R. Epstein, 'Unconscionability: A Critical Reappraisal,' 18. For essays critiquing law and economics theory from a Christian perspective, see McConnell, at. al., *Christian Perspectives on Legal Thought*, 207–40.

social thought to the legal academy in the 1970s and 80s.[89] CLS advocates and their progeny of more recent decades – critical race theory, feminism, and 'queer' theory – argue that law is merely power; the legal system denies power to the poor, racial and other minorities, and women generally, and these groups should seize it. CLS criticism is also aimed at those involved in the teaching of law. Legal analysis in the legal academy is, in Roberto Unger's terms, merely 'one more variant of the perennial effort to restate power and preconception as right.'[90] While CLS advocates seek to tear down the existing legal structures, it is not clear what they would erect in their place.

The biblical message is that there is such a thing as justice and that it should be the goal of law, regardless of who is in power. CLS advocates are correct that law is too often just a matter of the exercise of power, wielded at the expense of the poor and powerless. At their best, CLS advocates are modern-day prophets, pointing to injustice in our society. However, they then proceed to disclaim the very value – justice – that would give meaning to their words and provide the basis for building a society that does more than reinforce the power of the powerful. If law is merely a tool of power, it will continue to benefit the powerful. Those who are disenfranchised should not merely seek to appropriate power. Both those in power and the disenfranchised should seek justice.

In the end, the problem with liberalism, law and economics, and CLS, is not that they are completely wrong, but that each conveys a limited understanding of law. Each is reductionistic. There is more to human functioning than merely freedom, efficiency, or power. These three schools of legal thought have failed to provide a satisfactory basis for law. I believe that there is presently a desire within law schools for a firmer basis for law, rights and justice than is afforded by current bodies of legal theory. It may be that the time is right for the academy to consider biblical accounts in a fresh way.

Natural Law

A fourth school of legal thought, especially strong at a few Catholic law schools, is natural law. Natural law theory was shunned through much of the

---

[89] For background to the CLS movement, see R. Unger, *The Critical Legal Studies Movement* ; also his *Knowledge and Politics*; M. Tushnet, 'Critical Legal Studies: A Political History,' 1515–44; A.C. Hutchinson and P.J. Monahan, 'Law, Politics, and the Critical Legal Scholars,'199–245; Kennedy, 'Form and Substance in Private Land Adjudication, 1685–1778'; and the works included in J. Boyle (ed.), *Critical Legal Studies*. For essays critiquing CLS and related schools of thought from a Christian perspective, see *Christian Perspectives*, 107–205.

[90] Unger, *Critical Legal Studies Movement*, 8.

twentieth century – Oliver Wendell Holmes called it 'that brooding omnipresence' – but it rebounded in the legal academy during the later part of the twentieth century, primarily through the influence of Oxford and Notre Dame law professor/philosopher John Finnis.[91]

'Natural law' is one of the most important concepts ever developed, but it carries a most unfortunate label. 'Natural Law' is neither natural nor law, as those terms are commonly used. Most people think of something as natural if it exists in a state of nature (for example, Scripture speaks of our sinful nature), but 'natural law' is that set of moral rules that best fits with our created nature (a far cry from merely what seems natural). Its focus is on what Abraham Lincoln called 'the better angels of our nature' (recognizing implicitly that there are also worse angels). Most of the 'law' of natural law is a best understood as the moral law, only some of which, natural law theorists argue,[92] should be incorporated in the positive law.

Natural law theorists teach that humans were created with a *telos* or purpose and that through reason we can discern moral values as well as laws that will conform to our nature and enable us to live the fullest lives. There are 'goods' – things that humans universally value, such as life, knowledge, recreation, beauty, and friendship – and with the virtue of practical reason, legislators and judges can discern what sorts of laws will maximize those goods. Natural law can be expressed and justified on a basis that is accessible to all. In a pluralistic culture, it can serve as a common basis for law.

Natural law is the current school of legal thought that is probably most compatible with a biblical view of law. Though many natural law theorists, including John Finnis, claim to rely solely on reason, the legal rules they advocate are generally very similar to the rules that might be drawn from Scripture. However, the biblical view is that reason alone will only carry us so far. Our ability to reason is itself compromised by our fallen nature and needs the light of Scripture to guide it.[93] Positive law that is most compatible with our nature will thus draw from both reason and Scripture. Blackstone, a great advocate of natural law, argued that:

> Undoubtedly the revealed law is (humanly speaking) of infinitely more authority than what we generally call the natural law. Because one [the revealed law] is the law of nature, expressly declared so to be by God himself; the other is only what, by the assistance of human reason, we imagine to be that law. If we could be as certain of the

---

[91]　For background to natural law theory, see J. Finnis, *Natural Law and Natural Rights*; R. Hittinger, *The First Grace: Rediscovering Natural Law in a Post Christian World*; and G.V. Bradley, 'Natural Law,' 277–92.

[92]　Aquinas, *Summa*, Q. 96, a. 2.

[93]　On the way human 'blindness' and 'self-love' corrupt moral judgment, see, e.g., Calvin, *Institutes*, 2.7.6.

latter as we are of the former, both would have an equal authority; but, till then, they can never be put in any competition together.[94]

As this essay has argued, determining what God's revealed law requires of the positive law is not always easy. Scriptural analysis of what law should be involves a very similar inquiry to natural law analysis. Both entail the exercise of prudence and discernment: they require us to ask, in light of the hardness of human hearts, what positive law would best enable us to approach the demands of the moral law.

If, as Christians believe, the Scripture contains what J.N.D. Anderson has called 'the maker's instructions,'[95] it should lead to the same legal positions as the natural law, and these views should ultimately be convincing to all who wrestle honestly with the issues. But we will always struggle with our fallen nature, which makes it difficult to discern the meaning of the revealed law as well the natural law. For the legal scholar, this is a challenging, humbling, engaging, and rewarding aspect of our vocation.

---

[94] Blackstone, 'Of the Nature of Laws in General,' 1.2.41–43. The context is as follows: 'And if our reason were always, as in our first ancestor before his transgression, clear and perfect, unruffled by passions, unclouded by prejudice, unimpaired by disease or intemperance, the task [of determining the law] would be pleasant and easy; we should need no other guide but this. But every man now finds the contrary in his own experience; that his reason is corrupt, and his understanding full of ignorance and error.

THIS has given manifold occasion for the benign interposition of divine providence; which, in compassion to the frailty, the imperfection, and the blindness of human reason, hath been pleased, at sundry times and in divers manners, to discover and enforce it's laws by an immediate and direct revelation. The doctrines thus delivered we call the revealed or divine law, and they are to be found only in the holy scriptures. These precepts, when revealed, are found upon comparison to be really a part of the original law of nature, as they tend in all their consequences to man's felicity. But we are not from thence to conclude that the knowledge of these truths was attainable by reason, in its present corrupted state; since we find that, until they were revealed, they were hid from the wisdom of ages. As then the moral precepts of this law are indeed of the same original with those of the law of nature, so their intrinsic obligation is of equal strength and perpetuity. Yet undoubtedly the revealed law is (humanly speaking) of infinitely more authority than what we generally call the natural law. Because one is the law of nature, expressly declared so to be by God himself; the other is only what, by the assistance of human reason, we imagine to be that law. If we could be as certain of the latter as we are of the former, both would have an equal authority; but, till then, they can never be put in any competition together.'

[95] J.N.D. Anderson, 'Public Law and Legislation,' 235.

Bibliography

Allen, W.C., *A Cultural and Exegetical Commentary on the Gospel According to St. Matthew* (New York: Charles Scribner's Sons, 1907)

Anderson, J.N.D., 'Public Law and Legislation' in *Law, Morality, and the Bible*, ed. B. Kaye and G. Wenham (Downers Grove: InterVarsity Press, 1978), 230–46

Aquinas, T., *Summa Theologica*, trans. Fathers of the English Dominican Province (New York: Benzinger, 1947)

Augustine, *The City of God*, trans. G.G. Walsh, et al. (New York: Image, 1958)

Blackstone, W., *Commentaries on the Laws of England* (Oxford: Clarendon, 1765–1769), available at www.yale.edu/lawweb/avalon/blackstone/blacksto.htm

Boyle, J. (ed.), *Critical Legal Studies* (New York: Dartmouth/New York University, 1993)

Bradley, G.V., 'Natural Law,' in *Christian Perspectives on Legal Thought*, ed. M.W. McConnell, R.F. Cochran, Jr., and A.C. Carmella (New Haven: Yale University Press, 2001), 277–290

Buttrick, G.A, 'The Gospel According to St. Matthew,' in *The Interpreter's Bible*, vol. 7 (New York: Abingdon, 1951), 250–625

Calabresi, G., *The Cost of Accidents* (Chicago: Chicago University Press, 1970)

Calvin, J., *Institutes of the Christian Religion*, from W.G. Hards, 'A Critical Translation and Evaluation of the Nucleus of the 1536 edition of Calvin's Institutes,' in J. Dillenberger (ed.), *John Calvin: Selections from His Writings* (Garden City, NY: Doubleday, 1971)

—, *Institutes of the Christian Religion (1559/60)*, trans. F.L. Battles in J. Dillenberger (ed.), *John Calvin: Selections from His Writings* (Garden City, NY: Doubleday, 1971)

—, *New Testament Commentaries, A Harmony of the Gospels Matthew, Mark and Luke*, vol. 2, ed. D.W. Torrance and T.F. Torrance, trans. T.H.L. Parker (Grand Rapids: Eerdmans, 1972)

Chaplin, J., 'Political Eschatology and Responsible Government: Oliver O'Donovan's "Christian Liberalism"' in C. Bartholomew, et al. (eds.), *A Royal Priesthood? The Use of the Bible Ethically and Politically: A Dialogue with Oliver O'Donovan*, Scripture and Hermeneutics Series, vol. 3 (Carlyle: Paternoster; Grand Rapids: Zondervan, 2002), 265–308

Coase, R., 'The Problem of Social Cost,' *Journal of Law and Economics* 3 (1960), 1–44

Cramton, R.C., 'The Ordinary Religion of the Law School Classroom,' *Journal of Legal Education* 29 (1978), 247–63

Driver, S.R., *A Critical and Exegetical Commentary on Deuteronomy* (New York: Charles Scribner's Sons, 1895)

Epstein, R., 'Unconscionability: A Critical Reappraisal,' *Journal of Law and Economics* 18 (1975), 293–315

Finnis, J., *Natural Law and Natural Rights* (Oxford: Oxford University Press, 1980)

Hittinger, R., *The First Grace: Rediscovering the Natural Law in a Post-Christian World* (Wilmington, DE: Intercollegiate Studies Institute, 2003)

Hutchinson, A.C., and P.J. Monahan, 'Law, Politics, and the Critical Legal Scholars: The Unfolding Drama of American Legal Thought,' *Stanford Law Review* 36 (1984), 199–245

Institute for American Values, Marriage and the Law: A Statement of Principles (New York: Institute for American Values, 2006)

Irenaeus, *Adversus haereses* (The Detection and Overthrow of the False Knowledge), available at www.earlychristianwritings.com/irenaeus.html

Justin Martyr, *Dialogue With Trypho*, trans. A. Roberts and J. Donaldson, available at www.earlychristianwritings.com/text/justinmartyr-dialoguetrypho.html

Kennedy, D., 'Form and Substance in Private Law Adjudication,' *Harvard Law Review* 89 (1976), 1685–1778

Kronman, A., *The Lost Lawyer: Failing Ideals of the Legal Profession* (Cambridge: Belknap, Harvard University Press, 1993)

Luther, M., *Werke: Kritische Gesamtausgabe*, vol. 6 (Weimar: Hermann Bohlaus, 1883), quoted in L. Hardy, 'A Larger Calling Still,' in Pepperdine Law Review 32 (2005), 383–93

McConnell, M.W., 'Five Reasons to Reject the Claim that Religious Arguments Should be Excluded From Democratic Deliberation,' in *Utah Law Review* (1999), 639–57

—, R.F. Cochran, Jr., and A.C. Carmella (eds.), *Christian Perspectives on Legal Thought* (New Haven: Yale University Press, 2001)

Mott, S.C., 'Justice' in T.C. Butler (ed.), *Holman Bible Dictionary* (Nashville, TN: Holman Bible Publishers, 1991)

O'Donovan, O., *The Desire of the Nations* (Cambridge: Cambridge University Press, 1996)

Planned Parenthood v. Casey, 505 U.S. 833, 851 (1992) (plurality opinion)

Posner, R., 'The Economic Approach to Law,' in *Texas Law Review* 53 (1975), 757–82

Sammons, J.L., 'Parables and Pedagogy' in *Gladly Learn, Gladly Teach: Living Out One's Calling in the 21st Century Academy*, ed. J. Dunaway (Macon, GA: Mercer University Press, 2005), 46

Schleitheim Articles, 'The Schleitheim Articles: The Brotherly Agreement of Some Children of God Concerning Seven Articles' (1527), trans. M.G. Baylor (Cambridge: Cambridge University Press, 1991), repr. in O. O'Donovan and J. Lockwood O'Donovan (eds.), *From Irenaeus to Grotius: A Sourcebook in Christian Political Thought 100–1625* (Grand Rapids: Eerdmans 1999), 631–37

Shaffer, T.L., 'The Legal Ethics of Radical Individualism,' *Texas Law Review* 65 (1987), 963–91

Skeel, D.A., Jr., and W.J. Stuntz, 'Christianity and the (Modest) Rule of Law,' *University of Pennsylvania Journal of Constitutional Law* 8 (publication pending)

Smolin, D.M., 'A House Divided? Anabaptist and Lutheran Perspectives on the Sword,' *Journal of Legal Education* 47 (1997), 28–38

Tushnet, M., 'Critical Legal Studies: A Political History,' *Yale Law Journal* 100 (1991), 1515–44

Unger, R., *The Critical Legal Studies Movement* (Cambridge: Harvard University Press, 1986)

—, Knowledge and Politics (New York: The Free Press, Macmillan, 1975)

Wenham, G., 'Law and the Legal System in the Old Testament' in *Law, Morality, and the Bible*, ed. B. Kaye and G. Wenham (Downers Grove: InterVarsity Press, 1978), 24–52

Wright, G.E., 'The Book of Deuteronomy' in *The Interpreter's Bible*, vol. 2 (New York: Abingdon, 1953), 311–537

8

Biblical Imagery and Educational Imagination

Comenius and the Garden of Delight

David I. Smith

The main aim of this chapter is to explore how a particular image from the early chapters of the Bible influenced a particular understanding of education that has in turn significantly influenced modern Western educational thought and practice. The image in question is the 'garden of delight' of Genesis 2, and the educational thinker in question is the great seventeenth-century Moravian, John Amos Comenius, sometimes referred to as the father of modern education. Comenius's reflections on the classroom, the teacher, and the learner as 'gardens of delight' offer a rich case study of a biblically informed imagination at work. They also, as I will suggest in the closing sections of the chapter, have relevance to current educational debates. Before turning directly to the garden of delight, however, I will first briefly sketch a further reason for taking an interest in Comenius's musings, one having to do with how the connection between faith and learning is pursued.

Faith, Learning and Metaphor

Some accounts of the integration of faith and learning have regarded it as basically a matter of rightly understanding relationships between propositions: on the one hand, a set of propositions forming the content of Christian belief; on the other hand, the actual or potential propositions that provide the substance of the disciplines. Christian scholarship, then, involves tracing and stating the logical connections or discontinuities between the two sets of propositions. Alvin Plantinga, for instance, once defined the task of the Christian scholar in terms of identifying 'a large number of propositions, each explicating the bearing of the faith on some part of the discipline in question.'[1] Given this starting point, further debate focuses upon the kinds of relationships – deduction, induction, permission, requirement, commendation, comportment and the like.[2] This emphasis supports the desire to distinguish intellectually defensible points of contact between Christian theology and other disciplines from 'pseudointegration,' where biblical references and images are used for the purposes of illustration or analogy but have little logical bearing on the scholarly topic under discussion.[3] Careful Christian scholars understandably wish to avoid propagating imagined connections between Scripture and scholarship grounded in rhetorical flights of fancy rather than theoretical sophistication.

One factor that greatly complicates this picture is the renewed recognition over the past several decades of the constructive role of imagination in framing inquiry, and in particular the renewed recognition that metaphors can be theory-constitutive rather than merely decorative, and that a great deal of our theorizing is in fact rooted in and organized by imagery that both guides and obscures our reflections.[4] To understand the world is in many cases to see it *as* fundamentally *this* kind of thing rather then *that* kind – to see, for instance, the mind as a kind of computer, or knowledge as a house with foundations, or schools as marketplaces. In many areas of discussion, especially those dealing with basic questions of orientation, a significant part of what we do as scholars is to propose imagery to one another, imagery that invites shifts of viewpoint and bids to guide our collective perception of the matter at hand. This is very broadly the case, but perhaps most evident in our attempts to understand invisible, intangible and normative matters such as love, knowing, spirit, mind, teaching, responsibility, virtue, and so on – matters that we can often be helped to 'see' or 'grasp' in terms of analogy or metaphor.

Not surprisingly, educational (like theological) discussion has partaken richly of metaphorical practice. Groups of metaphors drawn, for instance, from the economic sphere (schools as factories or marketplaces, teachers as managers, learners as consumers, the curriculum as a delivered product), from the

---

[1] A. Plantinga, *The Twin Pillars of Christian Scholarship*, 60.

[2] R.T. Allen, 'Christian Thinking About Education'; J.A. Keller, 'Accepting the Authority of the Bible: Is It Rationally Justified?; D.I. Smith, 'Christian Thinking in Education Reconsidered.'

[3] D.L. Wolfe, 'The Line of Demarcation between Integration and Pseudointegration.'

[4] M. Black, 'More About Metaphor'; G. Lakoff and M. Johnson, *Metaphors We Live By*; A. Ortony, *Metaphor and Thought*; S. Sacks (ed.), *On Metaphor*; J.M. Soskice, *Metaphor and Religious Language*.

domestic sphere (teachers as parents, schools as families) or from the horticultural sphere (teachers as gardeners, learners as plants, learning as natural growth) have given rise to and sustained distinct patterns of educational theory and practice. In education, as in other disciplines, the idea that metaphors are not merely decoration, but rather help to constitute and direct our thinking, has been widely noted.[5]

Given ongoing discussion from various points on the theological map of the role of metaphor and imagination in theological reflection,[6] an obvious question arises in the present context: what happens if imagery drawn from a biblical context migrates into educational discussion and begins to organize ideas there? What if theological imagination and educational imagination become intertwined? That this has happened at various points in educational history seems quite clearly the case: consider, for instance, the tendency in British educational circles to speak of extra-curricular concern for the emotional and moral wellbeing of students as 'pastoral care' (there is even a journal titled *Pastoral Care in Education* which has nothing directly to do with ecclesiological concerns, still less with sheep and hillsides). But 'has happened' does not necessarily entail 'should happen'; is such use of spiritual or theological metaphors merely 'pseudointegration' or perhaps something more substantial?

I would freely grant that such appropriation of biblical metaphors may very often, if not most of the time, be dubious. It is possible to borrow images more or less at random from the Bible and use them in educational contexts, but this practice may have little, if any, theological or educational legitimacy, for several reasons. The Bible takes its images and metaphors from human experience, and there seems to be no reason to suppose that the images found in the Bible are, themselves, specially authorized *as images*, apart from their particular discursive role in the thought-world of Scripture. In the Bible God is described as a fortress – but one would hardly suppose that thinking of the school teacher or the math worksheet as a fortress would be an especially 'biblical' thing to do. The particular force of a metaphor is, furthermore, conditioned by its textual context. An image may be used in a particular educational discourse, and may also happen to occur in the Bible – but the educational use in context may express meanings quite foreign to those of the biblical text. It should also be noted that harvesting imagery at will from the Bible may not be automatically

---

[5] D. Aspin, 'Metaphor and Meaning in Educational Discourse'; K. Egan, *Teaching as Storytelling*; R.K. Elliott, 'Metaphor, Imagination and Conceptions of Education'; M. Harris, *Teaching and Religious Imagination*; D. Huebner, 'Religious Metaphors in the Language of Education'; C. Ormell, 'Eight Metaphors of Education'; W. Taylor (ed.), *Metaphors of Education*.

[6] E.g., J.M. Soskice, *Metaphor*; G. Green, *Imagining God: Theology and the Religious Imagination*; S. McFague, *Metaphorical Theology: Models of God in Religious Language*.

helpful. The fruitfulness of a metaphor in one context is no guarantee that it will be illuminating in a different context. Even if a metaphor works powerfully in communicating a sense of how we should view some aspect of salvation, it may turn out to stimulate no particularly helpful lines of thought if we try to use it as a way of seeing, say, a school timetable. Taken together with the unfortunate tendency in certain kinds of Christian school textbooks to leap cheerfully from, say, the mechanics of short division to the need to flee worldly concerns because the time is short (an actual example from a middle-school math text), under the apparent impression that some meaningful connection exists by virtue of mere word association, careless or cavalier use of biblical imagery warrants circumspection.[7]

Granting all of this, there do seem nevertheless to be instances where the metaphorical rope connecting biblical and educational discourse is woven of tougher strands. It is commonly noted that metaphors do not simply make single feature comparisons, but open up broader webs of meaning that become transferred to new areas of perception.[8] It is also often the case that these webs of meaning depend not only on our personal experiences of the world, but on our experiences of other texts. For most modern, Western readers, for instance, the field of meaning opened up by 'The Lord is my shepherd' is not rooted in direct experience of shepherds and sheep but is mediated by commentary, preaching, the wider biblical context and various forms of general knowledge; ideas and images from these other texts heighten the resonances to which this metaphor gives rise when we encounter it. Sometimes biblical metaphors come to be used in an education context in ways that continue to evoke webs of meaning associated with them in biblical interpretation, thereby causing at least some of the normative concerns of the biblical text and its commentators to become active in the educational imagination. This, I shall argue, is what happened with the 'garden of delight.'

The Garden of Delight as a School

Comenius embraced his own equivalent of current notions of theory-constitutive metaphor, arguing for the necessity of three forms of inquiry: analysis, synthesis and syncrisis. The last of the three involved the making of apt comparisons in order to gain insight into the interconnectedness of reality.[9] A central cluster of imagery in his writings on education has to do with gardens

---

[7] On the limits of theological metaphor in education, see further D.I. Smith, 'Incarnation, Education and the Boundaries of Metaphor.'
[8] M. Black, 'More About Metaphor'; D. Davidson, 'What Metaphors Mean.'
[9] J. Janko, 'Comenius' Syncrisis as the Means of Man and World Knowledge.'

and the processes of gardening. He sees both the school and the learner as a garden, the teacher as one who waters, cultivates and prunes, the learners as grafts and saplings, and suggests that school textbooks should be named after parts of a garden. I have discussed Comenius's appropriation of garden imagery in more general terms elsewhere;[10] in what follows I would like to consider in more detail how the trail led from the biblical text to early modern educational theory.

The Great Didactic, one of Comenius's most influential texts, is prefaced by a dedicatory letter that opens with extended and overtly theological commentary on the garden of delight[11]:

> God, having created man out of dust, placed him in a Paradise of desire, which he had planted in the East, not only that man might tend it and care for it, but also that he might be a garden of delight for his God.
>
> For as Paradise was the pleasantest part of the world, so also was man the most perfect of things created. In Paradise each tree was delightful to look at, and more pleasant to enjoy than those which grew throughout the earth. In man the whole material of the world, all the forms and the varieties of forms were, as it were, brought together into one in order to display the whole skill and wisdom of God. Paradise contained the tree of the knowledge of good and evil; man had the intellect to distinguish, and the will to choose between the good and the bad. In Paradise was the tree of life. In man was the tree of Immortality itself; that is to say, the wisdom of God, which had planted its eternal roots in man.
>
> And so each man is, in truth, a Garden of Delights for his God, as long as he remains in the spot where he has been placed. The Church too, which is a collection of men devoted to God, is often in Holy Writ likened to a Paradise, to a garden, to a vineyard of God. But alas for our misfortune! We have at the same time lost the Paradise of bodily delight in which we were, and that of spiritual delight, which we were ourselves. We have been cast out into the deserts of the earth, and have ourselves become wild and horrible wildernesses.[12]

This passage prefaces an extended (and historically important) treatise on education in which the image of the garden of delight is regularly used to frame ideas about teaching and learning. In keeping with this passage, in which human beings are seen both as placed *in* a garden of delight and as themselves *being* a garden of delight, Comenius goes on to figure both the learner and the

---

[10] J. Shortt, D. Smith and T. Cooling, 'Metaphor, Scripture and Education'; D.I. Smith and J. Shortt, *The Bible and the Task of Teaching*.

[11] The extant English translation cited here both abridges this letter and omits the biblical cross-references included in the Latin text.

[12] Comenius, *The Great Didactic of John Amos Comenius*, ed. M.W. Keatinge, 11–12.

educational institution as called to be 'gardens of delight.' The learner, like the first humans in paradise, is not only to *inhabit* a garden of delight in the guise of the justly ordered classroom, but also to *be* a garden of delight insofar as he or she grows in erudition, virtue and piety through learning.

We might easily leap to the conclusion that we have here a variant of the familiar Romantic appeal to nature in opposition to civilization – learners as little plants that will blossom on their own if exposed to the air and sun. We would be wrong; such a picture does not reflect Comenius's thought. Although his own experiential delight in gardens does play a role,[13] the image is first and foremost intertextual. Tracing its sources illuminates its particular shape, and indicates the *way* Scripture influences Comenius's educational imagination.

Creation and Fall

Comenius's first and most obvious source for the 'garden of delight' is the description of the Garden of Eden in the opening chapters of the Hebrew Scriptures. According to Genesis 2:15, here rendered in modern English translation, 'The LORD God took the man and put him in the Garden of Eden to work it and take care of it.'[14] The word 'Eden' is, however, also a Hebrew noun for delight, and the phrase 'Garden of Eden' can therefore be translated instead as 'garden of delight.' This phrase in Genesis 2:15 is in fact rendered in Latin translations as *paradisum voluptatis*, or 'paradise of delight' – an expression that appears repeatedly in the Latin of Comenius's *Great Didactic*. The 'garden of delight' is thus a direct biblical allusion, reflecting Comenius's extensive first-hand immersion in Scripture as a bishop and theologian.

This does not explain, however, how we get from the image of being placed *in* a garden to the idea that each of us *is* a garden. This shift can already be found early in Christian interpretation of Genesis 2. St Augustine's literal commentary on Genesis provides a striking example, where discussion of Eden transitions smoothly from the image of Adam cultivating the garden to that of God cultivating Adam. Commenting on Genesis 2:15, our key verse, Augustine offers the following translation: '*The Lord God took the man whom he had*

---

[13] Comenius, *Panorthosia or Universal Reform, Chapters 19-26*, trans. A.M.O. Dobbie, 116–17.

[14] Genesis 2:15 is explicitly cited in the opening sentence of the Latin edition – the reference is omitted in the English translation – and the invocation of Eden is extended in the Latin original with description of the four rivers flowing from the garden and a parallel drawn between these and the living waters of the Holy Spirit giving spiritual gifts to humans. See K. Schaller (ed.), *Johann Amos Comenius: Ausgewählte Werke*, 1.19. All biblical quotations in this chapter are taken from the New International Version.

made and placed him in Paradise to cultivate him (that is, to work in him) and to guard him.[15] This is (at least in linguistic terms) a legitimate translation from Augustine's sources – the Greek and Latin pronouns can point to the person or the garden, 'to guard it' or 'to guard him.' The garden thus ends up functioning both as an environment that the human creature cultivates and as a figure for the human creature being (in Augustine's words) 'made just' as he is cultivated by God: Adam is *in* a garden and he *is* a garden.

It seems likely that the choice of 'him' over 'it' was in this instance aided by the allegorical approach to the early chapters of Genesis adopted by Augustine's teacher Ambrose, and found also in other church Fathers and in Philo. Ambrose maintained that 'by Paradise is meant the soul of man,' that the serpent represents the pleasures of the body, the woman is the senses or emotions, the man is the mind; the beasts are the irrational senses; the birds are idle thoughts; the fruits on the trees are the virtues, and so on.[16] The allegorical meaning of Genesis 2:15, with its talk of Adam cultivating the garden, is thus roughly that we are charged with cultivating our souls by exercising mastery over the body and the emotions in order that virtue might grow. The common use of imagery of trees, gardens and irrigation to portray the spiritual growth and general wellbeing of persons in biblical wisdom literature (see, e.g., Job 8:16, Ps. 1, Song 4:14–16, among other passages), no doubt did much to support this line of thinking, both for Ambrose and for Comenius. The conjunction of literal and allegorical readings together with the presence of ambiguous pronouns gives us the image of the human creature both *being in* a garden and *being* a garden, both *cultivating* and *being cultivated*.

The specific connection of Eden with teaching, or a school, also owes to patristic commentary. Ambrose, along with other early commentators, notes that Eve was not present when the original command not to eat of the tree of the knowledge of good and evil was given by God, and infers that the command must have been taught to her by Adam. Since Eve's recollection of the command when questioned by the serpent appears faulty (she adds a detail about not touching the tree, Genesis 3:3), something may have gone wrong with the teaching and learning process, with disastrous results. The association of the serpent with false teachers, as in 2 Corinthians 11:2–3, where Paul worries that false preachers and apostles will deceive the Corinthian Christians 'as the serpent deceived Eve by his cunning,' and in 1 Timothy 2:12–14, where Paul says that women are not to teach since 'the woman was deceived,' was also seized upon by patristic commentators. Jager points out further the strong patristic resistance to the Gnostic version of the story's 'educational' import,

---

[15] Augustine, *The Literal Meaning of Genesis*, trans. J.H. Taylor, 52 (emphasis in the original).

[16] Ambrose, *Hexameron, Paradise, and Cain and Abel*, ed. J.J. Savage, 329, 351.

according to which the serpent was the source of secret wisdom transmitted to Adam by Eve, resulting in the gain of God-like knowledge by both. On this heretical view, Eve represented a higher spiritual principle that first awakened Adam ('the soul') to awareness of its spiritual nature; the serpent was commonly referred to as her 'Instructor.'[17] Patristic authors felt it necessary in response to emphasize the opposite teaching hierarchy, in which the male bishop is the source and guardian of correct teaching and there is no place for female teachers.[18] In connection with this interpretation of Eden in terms of the legitimation of clerical teaching, paradise came to figure the church as well as the individual soul.[19]

If we add as final garnishes the tendency to see various details of Eden, whether the river or the tree of life, as representing Wisdom, and the influence of the classical idea of the garden as a place of philosophical dialogue, then we have a recipe formed from a potent mix of exegesis, allegory, heresy and history for thinking of the Garden of Eden as a school, and seeing learners as both *inhabiting* gardens and *being* gardens. The story of the paradise of delight and the Fall into sin comes to include an *educational* drama occurring in a morally and religiously charged site of instruction. The use of imagery of the garden to figure the spiritual growth of the believer continues to appear in later Christian writers (as, for instance, in Bernard of Clairvaux's discussions of the 'garden of the heart' in his sermons on the Song of Solomon[20]), and continues to be associated with instruction, as in the twelfth century quasi-encyclopedia authored by the Abbess Herrad of Hohenbourg for the instruction of her nuns, titled *Hortus Deliciarium,* or *Garden of Delights.*[21]

In *The Great Didactic,* Comenius comments: 'It is evident. . . that even before the Fall, a school in which he might make gradual progress was opened for man in Paradise';[22] here he explicitly works out of the tradition just sketched and transfers the imagery from the church to the day school classroom. In keeping with his wider turn to the world of experience in his pedagogy, he does not reproduce the patristic focus on correct transmission of doctrine, but instead draws from the Eden narrative the point that humans must learn from experience. With more experience, Eve would have known that snakes do not talk and would have suspected deception.[23] Although the emphasis has shifted,

---

[17] E. Jager, *The Tempter's Voice: Language and the Fall in Medieval Literature,* 26.
[18] E. Jager, *Tempter's Voice,* 26.
[19] E. Jager, *Tempter's Voice,* 27.
[20] Bernard of Clairvaux, *On the Song of Songs,* trans. K. Walsh.
[21] Herrad of Hohenbourg, *Hortus Deliciarium,* ed. R. Green, M. Evans, and C. Bischoff.
[22] Comenius, *Great Didactic,* 53–54.
[23] Comenius, *Great Didactic,* 53–54.

however, Comenius does invoke here both the tradition of paradise as a school and the connection between the Fall and failed learning. Careful education is, he goes on to argue, even more necessary after the Fall, now that corruption has taken hold and impedes growth. Recall the emphases of the passage already cited from the dedicatory letter: since the Fall both the school classroom and the individuals in it fail to exist naturally as gardens of delight and are always caught up in the tension between garden and wilderness. This imagery and its biblical context frame key aspects of Comenius's educational theory. His insistence, for instance, that erudition, virtue and piety cannot be separated, and that teaching and learning have to be conceived as always essentially moral and spiritual as well as cognitive enterprises, comports well with the tradition of the school as an echo of Eden.[24]

Shalom

Before going further into Comenius's ideas, however, there is more to be said about the biblical origins of his use of the garden of delight, and about ways in which it goes beyond the account sketched thus far. There is another strand of interpretation of Eden within the Bible, in the writings of the Hebrew prophets, in which the garden functions as an image not of pre-social innocence, conservative hierarchy or the individual soul growing in virtue, but of society ordered by peaceful relationships and characterized by flourishing. In the book of Joel, for instance, a metaphorical account of military invasion says of the incoming armies 'the land is as the garden of Eden before them, and behind them a desolate wilderness' (Joel 2:3), offering a basic opposition of garden and wilderness that is so characteristic of Comenius's rhetoric. In Ezekiel, prophecies of restoration echo this opposition, in reverse:

> On the day I cleanse you from all your sins, I will resettle your towns, and the ruins will be rebuilt. The desolate land will be cultivated instead of lying desolate in the sight of all who pass through it. They will say, 'This land that was laid waste has become like the garden of Eden; the cities that were lying in ruins, desolate and destroyed, are now fortified and inhabited (36:35).

These passages do not use the garden as an image of unspoiled nature; they refer to land that is cultivated to sustain human community. As suggested by the emphasis on human cultivation in Genesis 2:15, intentional, formative human activity has a key role in shaping the community of peace, or making it desolate. While God sends judgement, it is soldiers who will ravage the fields. While God promises to resettle, rebuild and cultivate it will be human hands

---

[24] D. Smith, 'Gates Unlocked and Gardens of Delight: Comenius on Faith, Persons and Language Learning.'

that dig the furrows and lay the bricks. When the fields are diligently cared for and produce good food, when people live together without fear of violence, when cities prosper, the land is like the garden of Eden. This state of communal wellbeing, in which relationships are well ordered and can produce delight, is brought about in significant measure by the care and diligence of people.

A related echo of Eden occurs in the fifth chapter of Isaiah, where Israel is pictured as a vineyard planted by an owner who hoped for a plentiful harvest but who returned at harvest time and found only bad fruit. In response the vineyard owner declares:

> I will take away its hedge,
> and it will be destroyed;
> I will break down its wall,
> and it will be trampled.
> I will make it a wasteland,
> neither pruned nor cultivated,
> and briers and thorns will grow there. (5:5–6)

Here we see the same contrast as in the other passages: a garden, carefully pruned and fenced and cultivated, will because of hardness of heart turn into a wilderness, a place without shape or comfort or fruit. The passage continues:

> The vineyard of the Lord Almighty
> is the house of Israel,
> and the men of Judah
> are the garden of his delight.
> And he looked for justice,
> but saw bloodshed;
> for righteousness,
> but heard cries of distress. (5:7)

This is a tantalizing passage for present purposes, since the phrase rendered in English as 'garden of . . . delight' is in Latin versions not *paradisum voluptatis* but *germen delectabile*, and so it is difficult to be fully certain whether Comenius had this passage specifically in mind alongside Genesis 2 as he wrote the preface to his *Great Didactic*. I suspect, however, that it played a role in his thinking, largely because of the close similarity between its ideas and images and those of the preface (the sought-for garden of delight become a wasteland); it is a clear candidate for being one of the passages he was referring to when he noted in the preface (expanding his own terminology) that 'the Church too, which is a collection of men devoted to God, is often in Holy Writ likened to a Paradise, to a garden, to a vineyard of God.'[25]

---

[25] Comenius, *Great Didactic*, 11.

Two features of this Isaiah passage are particularly interesting. First, it is allegorical, with the garden of delight used as a metaphor for the men of Judah; here we have an antecedent within Scripture for at least some aspects of the patristic tendency to see the garden of delight both as the context within which people are placed by God and as an image of people themselves being cultivated by God. This does not necessarily justify the patristic exegesis of Genesis 2:15; it does suggest, however, that whatever the status of that specific piece of exegesis they were on to something that is part of the larger biblical tapestry. Second, however, the central point at issue in the contrast between the garden of delight and the unfruitful vineyard is not whether the individual soul is growing in virtue or whether there is spiritual growth in the inner life, but whether there is justice or violence in social relationships. This chapter of Isaiah continues with examples of the 'wild grapes' that are leading to judgement; the first example in the list is a unscrupulous land distribution, in particular the marginalization of the poor as wealthy landowners buy up increasingly large tracts of land: 'Woe to you who add house to house and join field to field till no space is left and you live alone in the land' (Is. 5:8). The focus here is more on economics than spirituality, or perhaps it would be more accurate to say that economics and spirituality are not regarded as separate or separable concerns. The garden of delight is a society of shalom, and that means a just society marked by ethical attentiveness and care for the distressed rather than by selfish acquisition and the flourishing of the powerful. This strand too is present in Comenius's appropriation of the garden of delight for educational purposes, as we shall see presently.

The School as a Garden of Delight

All of the preceding is by way of unpacking the point that Comenius's use of the garden of delight image is shaped by prior texts, and in particular by the Bible. It remains only a sketchy account in historical terms, and is far from exhaustive, but it will suffice for present purposes. When Comenius framed his thoughts on education with meditations on the garden of delight this was not because he happened to look out of the window and enjoy the roses, still less because he was a proto-Romantic who thought that learners are little flowers that should be left to blossom in their own fashion. He was invoking a complex tradition of interpretation of Genesis 2:15, both within and subsequent to the biblical canon, and establishing it as a lens through which to view schools, a lens that focuses attention on spiritual and moral growth and the establishment of a just community. This was one of the central ways in which Christian theology influenced his understanding of teaching and learning. I will now give some substance to this claim by briefly illustrating how the garden of delight image becomes active in Comenius's educational reflections.

For Comenius, the 'garden of delight' connects the inner state of the individual, the social setting of the classroom, and the wider social realities of the world at large. The preface to *The Great Didactic*, cited above, lamented that 'We have at the same time lost the Paradise of bodily delight in which we were, and that of spiritual delight, which we were ourselves. We have been cast out into the deserts of the earth, and have ourselves become wild and horrible wildernesses.'[26] The restoration of the self as a garden of delight is to take place through simultaneous and interdependent growth in erudition, virtue and piety; immediately after quoting Genesis 1:26 in connection with the aims of education, Comenius says:

> It is plain that man is situated among visible creatures so as to be (i.) a rational creature. (ii.) The Lord of all creatures. (iii.) A creature which is the image and joy of its Creator. These three aspects are so joined together that they cannot be separated.... From this it follows that man is naturally required to be: (1) acquainted with all things; (2) endowed with power over all things and over himself; (3) to refer himself and all things to God, the source of all. Now if we wish to express these three things by three well-known words, these will be (i.) Erudition. (ii.) Virtue and seemly morals. (iii.) Religion or piety.[27]

Note the inseparability of these three aspects for Comenius. In brief, Comenius's view was that as soon as understanding becomes linked to the power to affect other creatures, then reason and ethics are necessarily connected; once thinking affects behavior and behavior affects those around us and the creation we inhabit, then reason and virtue cannot be isolated from one another. Both of these lack the context that would give them point and direction without the further addition of piety – and Comenius defined piety in terms of delight, with explicit reference to garden imagery. He explains that while piety is the gift of God, the Holy Spirit works through human agencies, including parents and teachers who 'plant and water the grafts of Paradise.'[28] Piety means 'that (after we have thoroughly grasped the conceptions of faith and of religion) our hearts should learn to seek God everywhere. . . and that when we have found Him we should follow Him, and when we have attained him [we] should enjoy Him.'[29] While the seeking and the following correspond loosely to the exercise of reason and will in Comenius's schema, the element most distinctive of piety is to 'enjoy God by so acquiescing in His love and favour that nothing on earth appears to us more to be desired than God himself.'[30] Piety is thus closely tied both to paradise and to delight, and provides

[26] Comenius, *Great Didactic*, 12.
[27] Comenius, *Great Didactic*, 36–38; D. Smith, 'Gates Unlocked.'
[28] Comenius, *Great Didactic*, 218.
[29] Comenius, *Great Didactic*, 218.
[30] Comenius, *Great Didactic*, 218.

the ultimate reference point for erudition and virtue. The garden of delight thus frames the aims of learning.

Noting the injunctions in Scripture to raise godly children, Comenius reasons that with the participation of God's Spirit it must be possible for educational agencies to become a means of restoring the garden of the self in place of the personal wilderness. In the *Pampaedia*, a later systematic treatise on education, he poses the question of how we can further human development so that people come to recognize and enjoy the good life. His answer is that 'we require an imitation of the School of Paradise, where God revealed the whole choir of His creatures for man to behold.'[31] The ultimate aim of this school of paradise is that the human learner should be led through all of creation to God as its pinnacle and 'consent to be captivated, carried away and absorbed by Him (with God's help).'[32] The original garden of delight forms the point of reference, piety as the expression of delight informs the ultimate purpose.

There are practical consequences: if schooling is to lead to the creation of gardens of delight, Comenius argues, then the school itself must change. 'Schools,' he writes, 'will then be planned to such pleasant effect that they all become gardens of delight.'[33] The school is consequently to be a place that fosters pleasure. It could not serve as a garden of delight without playfulness, and accordingly play comes to take on an important (and historically innovative) role in Comenius's approach to learning. He is careful to distinguish his use of the term from what he calls 'mere amusement,'[34] but gives specific attention to the role of enjoyment in learning in his advocacy of attractive, illustrated learning materials for the classroom, of humane teaching methods, including dialogues and plays, and of literal gardens with animals where young students can take refreshment during the day. It is noteworthy that the prayer that prefaces the *Pampaedia* is couched in terms of God's play with us and us learning to play with God and with each other:

> Do thou, everlasting wisdom, who dost play in this world and whose delight is with the sons of men, ensure that we in turn may now find delight in thee. Discover more fully unto us ways and means to better understanding of thy play with us and to more eager pursuance of it with one another, until we ourselves finally play in thy company more effectively to give increasing pleasure unto thee, who art our everlasting delight! Amen![35]

---

[31] Comenius, *Comenius' Pampaedia or Universal Education*, 29.
[32] Comenius, *Pampaedia*, 29.
[33] Comenius, *Pampaedia*, 56.
[34] Comenius, *Great Didactic*, 251.
[35] Comenius, *Pampaedia*, 16.

In *The Great Didactic*, Comenius goes so far as to describes the purpose of human existence as being 'that we may serve God, his creatures and ourselves, and that we may enjoy the pleasure to be derived from God, from his creatures and from ourselves.'[36] Schooling, accordingly, is to pursue this threefold service and delight as its goal, fostering, for instance, a sense of the attractions of disciplined absorption in the intricacies of creation. Pleasure in self is defined as 'that very sweet delight which arises when a man, who is given over to virtue, rejoices in his own honest disposition, since he sees himself prompt to all things which the order of justice requires.'[37] In the midst of this meditation on the relationships between delight, learning and justice we again find explicit reference to paradise as the framing image – a chief reason for focusing on delight, the same passage notes, is that God prepared for the first humans a 'paradise of delights.'[38]

The connection between piety, pleasure and 'the order of justice' points us outward beyond the individual to social relationships. Delight must not become narcissistic; since spiritual, rational and ethical growth are not to be separated and are all bound up with our human responsibility for our neighbour and for creation, the restoration of the garden of delight in the individual has to be reflected in the way in which the neighbour and the rest of creation are attended to and treated. The basic aims of education include for Comenius learning 'how far our neighbour's interests should be consulted.'[39] Youth must be taught from the beginning, he urges, 'that we are born not for ourselves alone, but for God and for our neighbour, that is to say, for the human race.'[40] This concern, based as it is in creation, extends specifically to members of other cultures. Comenius writes in his *Panegersia*:

> Bias towards persons, nations, languages and religious sects must be totally eliminated if we are to prevent love or hatred, envy or contempt, or any other emotion from interfering with our plans for happiness…How utterly thoughtless…to hate your neighbour because he was born in another country or speaks a different language.[41]

Not only other people, Comenius notes, but also the rest of creation has suffered from human misuse and longs for deliverance. 'It is desirable,' he urges, 'that this hope and longing of creatures should be fulfilled, and that everything everywhere should advance correctly, and that all creatures should have cause

---

[36] Comenius, *Great Didactic*, 72.
[37] Comenius, *Great Didactic,* 73.
[38] Comenius, *Great Didactic*, 73.
[39] Comenius, *Great Didactic*, 37.
[40] Comenius, *Great Didactic*, 214.
[41] Comenius, *Panegersia, or Universal Awakening*, trans. A.M.O. Dobbie, 70.

to join us in praising God.'[42] In other words, an ecologically rooted and distributed delight will not come into being without learning that focuses on ethically motivated and informed service and on the maintenance of just relationships. This conjoining of individual, social and creational wellbeing is summed up, again using the ubiquitous garden image, in Comenius's statement that the ultimate aim of the school being reformed in imitation of the school of Paradise is that 'the entire world will be a garden of delight for God, for people and for things.'[43] All are called to realize their humanity in such a way that they not only become gardens of delight themselves, but in doing so contribute to the realization of the garden of delight as a wider social and ecological reality. Individual piety and social justice are regarded as part of the same larger whole.[44] As education comes to make its contribution to the redemptive process of restoration, there should be a co-dependence between holiness within us and justice among us, peace in our hearts and peace in our own and other societies.

Finally, Comenius argues, with explicit reference to the common creation of all humans in the image of God, that education must be provided in common to both rich and poor, to those of both greater and lesser intellectual ability, and to both boys and girls, lest false distinctions of worth between these groups should lead to pride.[45] One of his hallmark commitments is to universal education; this commitment underlies the title and fills the opening chapter of his *Pampaedia*, where he declares:

> *Firstly,* the expressed wish is for full power of development into full humanity not of one particular person, but of *every single individual,* young and old, rich and poor, noble and ignoble, men and women – in a word, every being born on earth, with the ultimate aim of providing education to the entire human race regardless of age, class, sex and nationality.[46]

He goes on to explain that this is necessary because 'they are all human beings with the prospect of the same future life in the way appointed by heaven yet beset with snares and obstructed by diverse pitfalls.'[47] The chapter culminates with the characteristic appeal to garden imagery to frame the point:

> I had this consideration in mind when I put the symbol of the art of the tree pruner in the frontispiece to this Deliberation, showing gardeners grafting freshly-plucked

---

[42] Comenius, *Pampaedia,* 26.

[43] Comenius, *Pampaedia,* 29.

[44] For recent discussion of this matter in relation to education, see D.I. Smith, J. Shortt, and J. Sullivan (eds.), *Spirituality, Justice and Pedagogy.*

[45] Comenius, *Great Didactic,* 61–69.

[46] Comenius, *Pampaedia,* 19.

[47] Comenius, *Pampaedia,* 20.

shoots from the tree of Pansophia into rooted layers in the hope of filling God's whole garden, which is the human race, with saplings of a similar nature.[48]

Much more could be said about Comenius's educational vision and practice, including its limitations;[49] I have restricted my focus here to key points at which the basic image of the garden of delight, informed by a long tradition of reflection on particular passages from the Bible, frames his educational deliberations and tethers them to biblical interpretation. Comenius habitually thinks against a scriptural backdrop, and the way that this backdrop enters his educational thinking is through both doctrinal reasoning (such as appeal to the creation of all in God's image or the nature of the future life) and an imaginative indwelling of biblical metaphor. Innovations for which Comenius is justly famous – the focus on play, the reform of learning materials, the establishment of approaches to teaching and learning suited to children's capabilities and interests, the turn to the exploration of the empirical world, and so on – are rooted in and nurtured by this imaginative indwelling of the garden of delight. A biblical metaphor comes to be used as an educational metaphor in such a way that a cluster of emphases associated with the image in the context of biblical interpretation inform his educational reflections and their consequences.

The Garden of Delight Today

As an admirer of Comenius I find all of this inherently interesting; I would like to conclude, however, by suggesting two broader reasons why this exploration of Comenius's mental habits might be appropriate material for reflection today. These have to do, first, with the enduring nature of questions of basic educational vision and, second, with the bearing of Comenian imagery on present day educational research.

Pedagogy and Vision

Many aspects of Comenius's writings retain considerable relevance to discussions of how we should view the purposes and central emphases of teaching and learning, especially in relation to faith. I have been struck by the degree of similarity between Comenius's account and that offered more recently by Nicholas Wolterstorff. Wolterstorff seeks to ground our vision of education in the Hebrew conception of *shalom*. While no direct debt is indicated,

---

[48] Comenius, *Pampaedia*, 21.
[49] See further, D. Murphy, *Comenius: A Critical Reassessment of His Life and Work*; also D. Smith, 'Gates Unlocked.'

the following summary by Wolterstorff could, allowing for a shift in idiom, equally well have been written by Comenius:

> There can be no shalom without justice.... In shalom each person enjoys justice.... Shalom goes beyond justice, however. Shalom incorporates right relationships in general, whether or not those are required by justice: right relationships to God, to one's fellow human beings, to nature, and to oneself. The shalom community is not merely the *just* community but is the *responsible* community, in which God's laws for our multifaceted existence are obeyed. It is more even than that. We may all have acted justly and responsibly, and yet shalom may be missing: for the community may be lacking delight...shalom incorporates *delight* in one's relationships. To dwell in shalom is to find delight in living rightly before God, to find delight in living rightly in one's physical surroundings, to find delight in living rightly with one's fellow human beings, to find delight even in living rightly with oneself.[50]

I think it is fairly clear from the passages considered above that Comenius would have heartily agreed with all of this, and I suspect that the chief reason for this agreement is a common debt to the Hebrew prophets. We need to labour, both authors counsel, for the restoration of relationships with God and with others, within ourselves and with the world, that are characterized by justice, responsibility and delight: this is what it means for the wilderness to become a garden. Such metaphorical talk (e.g., 'shalom community' or 'garden of delight') might serve some purposes less directly served by epistemological argument. What I have particularly in mind is the firing and shaping of teacherly imagination and pedagogical practice. To my mind's eye, while neither 'renewing the garden of delight' nor 'educating for shalom' comes close to telling me exactly what to do, both nevertheless point compellingly to a pedagogical journey informed by the ethical and spiritual horizons of the Scriptures.

This draws us back to a consideration of the role of educational imagination and its relationship to biblical metaphor. What Comenius's and Wolterstorff's accounts share is a focus on the normative horizon that is to guide the shape of teaching and learning practices. This may both clarify and complicate the role of biblical metaphor in thinking about teaching and learning. Nothing in this essay is intended to suggest that images from the Bible will provide Christian educators with automatically correct theories about education, or function as esoteric data regarding learning processes. It would, moreover, be rash to suggest that the garden image was the sole or sufficient cause of Comenius's various educational innovations, or that the Bible was the only influence on his thinking. Much educational debate, however, whether of the academic or popular varieties, is debate about how we *should* educate, and is ineluctably tied to wider conceptions of the good life and of how we might best promote some conception of

---

[50] N. Wolterstorff, *Educating for Shalom: Essays on Christian Higher Education*.

human flourishing. It does seem that the garden image played a significant role in pointing Comenius's imagination in certain directions, in making certain issues attractive for him because of their connection with his passionately held vision of human flourishing, and in linking that vision to Scripture.

The need for basic orienting metaphors has not gone away in the intervening centuries. Bill Johnston, writing outside of any Christian discussion, has recently summarized some of the reasons that broad questions of moral and spiritual orientation remain basic to the discussion of teaching. Teaching, he writes, is

> value-laden, in at least three crucial ways. First, teaching is rooted in relation, above all the relation between teacher and student; and relation in turn – the nature of our interactions with our fellow humans – is essentially moral in character....Second, all teaching aims to change people; any attempt to change another person has to be done with the assumption, usually implicit, that the change will be for the better.... Third, although 'science' in the form of research in various disciplines (second language acquisition, education, sociology, etc.) can give us some pointers, in the overwhelming majority of cases it cannot tell us exactly how to run our class. Thus, the decisions we make as teachers ... ultimately also have to be based on moral rather than on objective or scientific principles: That is, they have to be based on what we believe is right and good..... We recognize that our deepest and best instincts as teachers arise from belief or faith rather than from pure logic.[51]

Our basic individual, communal and cultural metaphors for educational wellbeing speak to this need more than to our need for, say, empirical data on how people acquire conversational fluency. David Purpel notes this in his critique of the trivialization of talk about teaching, arguing that in discussions of schooling 'the primary language is the technical and bureaucratic one of control, task, and engineering,' and that there is an urgent need to recapture an engagement with vision and wisdom. He suggests that 'the language of this vision belongs to the moral and religious family of language, for it is the function of moral and religious language to provide the essential dimension of education – a language of meaning.'[52] Insofar as biblical imagery continues to address our visions of what it means to flourish, it remains relevant to the essential question of how we can prepare people in classrooms for the good life.

Vision and Scholarship

Put this way, however, the distinction is too sharp, for our basic metaphors also play a significant role in guiding the kind of data that we look for when engaged

---

[51] B. Johnston, *Values in English Language Teaching*, 4–5, 9.
[52] D.E. Purpel and W.M. McLaurin, *Reflections on the Moral and Spiritual Crisis in Education*, 39–41.

in more empirically-oriented kinds of investigation. One of my reasons for becoming particularly interested in Comenius's garden metaphors is a shift from technical to ecological metaphors going on within my primary discipline of second language pedagogy – a discipline of which Comenius, alongside his influence on education more generally, is considered a very significant early modern instigator.[53] I will briefly describe this shift as a more specific example of possible connections between the imagery that I have been exploring and current research in education.

For most of the twentieth century, mainstream discussion of modern language education relied heavily on an underlying metaphor of teaching as a form of *technology*. Discussions of how to teach were couched in terms of the quest for the most efficient teaching *method*, and the best method was to be established by empirical experiment. This implied a view of teaching as a collection of 'routines of efficiency'[54] that could be applied to students universally, regardless of local contingencies such as time, place, beliefs, gender or culture and would, if applied correctly, lead to reliable and repeatable outcomes. This is, of course, what a technology is supposed to do – you do not expect to find, for instance, that your new battery shaver does not work for people with southern accents. Learners' minds have commonly been pictured as computers – influential sectors of the literature have analyzed language learning processes as consisting of the reception and processing of input and the generation of output. Ellis describes this brain-as-computer approach as the 'dominant metaphor' of second language acquisition research.[55] This view of teaching as ideally consisting of an efficient technology practiced on machine-like learners with universally reliable outcomes reflects wider twentieth-century cultural commitments to empirical science and technology as core sources of truth and effective practice.

Consistent with growing concern in the wider culture about the negative effects and epistemological limits of modern science and technology, there has been widespread criticism of 'method' talk in scholarly discussions of language education since the early 1990s.[56] As a result, there has been an increased

---

[53] J. Caravolas, *Le Gutenberg de la didacographie, ou, Coménius et l'enseignement des langues*; J.-A. Caravolas, 'Comenius (Komensky) and the Theory of Language Teaching.'

[54] W.J. Ong, *Ramus, Method and the Decay of Dialogue*, 225.

[55] R. Ellis, *Second Language Acquisition*, 89.

[56] C. Brumfit, 'Problems in Defining Instructional Methodologies'; B. Kumaravadivelu, 'The Postmethod Condition: (E)Merging Strategies for Second/Foreign Language Teaching'; see also his 'Toward a Postmethod Pedagogy,' and *Beyond Methods: Macrostrategies for Language Teaching*; also D. Larsen-Freeman, 'Research on Language Teaching Methodologies: A Review of the Past and an Agenda for the Future'; A. Pennycook, 'The Concept of Method, Interested Knowledge, and the Politics of Language Teaching.'

openness in recent years to alternative metaphors that promise a more adequate map of the pedagogic landscape. A prominent emerging candidate pictures the language classroom as an *ecology*, that is, a complex environment in which a very wide range of factors interact with one another to bring about particular local patterns.[57] This image implies that effects may not be traceable to single, linear causes: since factors interact, it may be very difficult to say in any clearcut or empirically valid fashion that teaching technique *A* led to learning increment *B*. It also implies that there may be significant variations rooted in the peculiarities of local contexts, and that this is normal rather than something to be overcome.

It might help to picture the difference if we think of a medical analogy. Consider on the one hand the kind of modern medicine that has relied on universally and objectively applicable chemical and surgical procedures to produce health: the medical problem is isolated, the appropriate drug or incision is applied, and if everything is handled correctly then recovery should follow. This has commonly happened in abstraction from other aspects of the patient's experience – we have a specific technology targeted at a specific condition in isolation, and it is assumed that the problem has a single cause and will therefore be removed if that cause is dealt with. Compare this to the more recent emphasis on wellness, on taking into account the patient's lifestyle, the patient's beliefs and cultural preferences, the patient's relational context and so on as factors affecting health. Once one begins to take such contextual factors into account as possible causes of failure in medical care, the list of potential factors becomes long and unpredictable; the doctor's bedside manner, for instance, becomes a potential medical factor rather than an incidental quirk. Current newspaper articles regularly provide examples. In one recent case, the cause of a woman's distress upon being admitted to hospital was discovered to be that the bed assigned to her was pointing toward the door – in her culture this was considered a sign that she would die in hospital. Another report described recent research suggesting that a person suffering a verbal attack is three times more likely to become ill during the following two weeks, since verbal abuse causes similar rises in stress hormones to those caused by physical abuse. Some time back I read of a study showing that increasing natural light and the number of plants in doctors' waiting rooms led to a decrease in the number of symptoms reported by patients. Even physical illness, it seems, is firmly embedded in a much larger complex of interacting factors. How much more the various

---

[57] C. Kramsch (ed.), *Language Acquisition and Language Socialization: Ecological Perspectives*; D. Larsen-Freeman, 'Chaos/Complexity Science and Second Language Acquisition'; I. Tudor, 'Learning to Live with Complexity: Towards an Ecological Perspective on Language Teaching'; A. Pennycook, 'Language Policy and the Ecological Turn'; J. Leather and J. Van Dam (eds.), *Ecology of Language Acquisition*.

interpersonal learning processes that take place among groups of teachers and learners in schools?

In a broadly similar fashion, much past research on language learning has sought to isolate particular (linguistic and psychological) facets of learning, test interventions under controlled conditions, and establish causal relationships between particular teaching procedures and particular outcomes: if the teacher does X, then learning increment Y will follow. Once the classroom is viewed as an ecology, in which an open-ended range of contextual factors may interact to affect outcomes, this becomes problematic. Perhaps a certain technique only works in a certain way if the weather is good and the students trust the teacher. There are clear signs in ecological studies of language classrooms of a desire to increase the range of factors taken into account. Van Dam, for instance, in a recent book on the topic, stresses the need for 'minimal *a priori* assumptions about what can be ignored.'[58]

Placing this development (in which there have actually been occasional discussions of the classroom as a garden[59]) in relation to Comenius's use of garden imagery both reveals convergences and suggests under-explored avenues in the contemporary debate. Comenius also understands the classroom as an environment in which multiple factors are inseparably at work and processes beyond the narrowly cognitive are an important part of the overall picture. He is himself very fond of method talk (in this respect he is every bit a child of the seventeenth century) and willing to use technological metaphors for the learning process (albeit with an import rather different from that typical in more recent times[60]). The focus on the garden of delight, however, helps to underscore the inseparability of erudition, virtue and piety and of self and society. To understand classrooms, he would say, we need more than study of technique and cognitive processes; we would have to keep track of what is going on spiritually and ethically both within and between individuals, and in relation to the wider world. It is precisely at this point that Comenius's writings present a challenge to the present discussion of classroom ecology. If little can be ignored in terms of potential factors interacting to influence classroom realities, then not only the already traditional categories of power, race, gender and socioeconomic

---

[58] J. van Dam, 'Ritual, Face, and Play in a First English Lesson: Bootstrapping a Classroom Culture.'

[59] M.P. Breen, 'The Social Context for Language Learning: A Neglected Situation'; M. de Courcy, 'Australian Teachers' Experiences of Language Learning and Their Effect on Practice'; D.I. Smith, 'Coral Gardens and Classroom Ecology.'

[60] When Comenius uses technological images such as the clock or the printing press to describe learning, they are closely associated for him with harmony and wonder; the significance of these images is not for him soulless mechanism, but the amazing working together of diverse parts in harmony. The technological and horticultural metaphors are therefore not at odds, as they might at first seem.

factors need to be consulted, but also matters of faith, spirituality and commit-ment as they influence both individual and institutional identity. There is little sign as yet of systematic attention to these matters as they affect language learn-ing, although there are some scattered signs of a relevant mainstream literature emerging.[61] One recent study, for example, suggested a connection between a conservative Muslim student's religiously informed attitude towards the inter-pretation of written language and her behaviours during a pair work activity during language learning (Platt). My own involvement in seeking to develop this line of discussion is indebted to, among other things, my longstanding interaction with Comenius.[62]

Coda: Of Math, Grammar and Reconciliation

I have sought in this paper to show some interconnections between what may at first appear to be rather disparate concerns – neither Ambrose nor the Bible are commonly referenced in current academic debates about language peda-gogy, and discussions of biblical hermeneutics do not frequently enter into educational theory. Perhaps this represents a failure of imagination. The rela-tionship between faith and learning, I have suggested, can work by no means exclusively but nevertheless legitimately through imagery that is rooted in bib-lical interpretation. Although incidental use of biblical metaphor may be little more than decorative, there are occasions when metaphors more deeply expressive of aspects of the worldview of Scripture enter discourse outside the-ology in such a way as to make that worldview fruitfully active within disci-plinary reflection. I have described Comenius's use of the garden of delight image and some of its sources in order to illustrate this process at work. In Comenius we find an example of biblical imagery shaping an important Chris-tian view of teaching and learning. Finally, I have suggested that Comenius's project can still speak to us, both because of the enduring nature of the ques-tions regarding human flourishing that must undergird any thoughtful peda-gogy and because of the complex relationships between these basic questions of orientation and even the more technical forms of present day scholarship on learning processes. I wish to close with two stories, one told to me recently by a colleague, the other from my own classroom, that ground in a still more practi-cal way the continued relevance of Comenius's contention that the classroom is a place where the biblical wilderness and garden are in tension.

A colleague of mine, Jim Bradley, teaches mathematics. Recently a student enrolled in a compulsory college statistics class approached him with concerns

---

[61] For a survey, see D.I. Smith and T.A. Osborn (eds.), *Spirituality, Social Justice and Language Learning*.

[62] D.I. Smith, *The Spirit of the Foreign Language Classroom*; also 'Coral Gardens.'

about whether he could pass the class. He had the student take a diagnostic test, designed to show what mathematical concepts the student had internalized. The results astounded him – they suggested that the student did not have even the most basic mathematical concepts. At a loss to understand how a student who was this far off the scale had even made it to college, Jim sat the student down for a conversation about his past learning experiences. What emerged was that years earlier the student's mathematics teacher had held his homework up before the rest of the class as an example of how not to go about mathematics homework. The student had been so angry that he had vowed to himself that he would never learn mathematics. He spent the rest of his schooling learning enough to pass necessary tests and then deliberately forgetting the material. Jim advised the student that the first thing he needed to do was consider forgiving his former teacher. He asked the student about this the next day; the student's surprised reaction suggested that he had not taken the suggestion seriously. A few days later, however, the student came and told him that he had been thinking and praying about what he had said and had forgiven his teacher. He scored 69 percent on his first test, 95 percent on the next, and 99 percent on the third.[63]

I suspect that no amount of carefully applied technique could have brought about significant progress with Jim's student in the absence of forgiveness and reconciliation. I also wonder whether Jim's solution would have occurred to anyone but a Christian teacher, or at least one for whom forgiveness and reconciliation were of conscious significance. The success of the solution, moreover, depended on the exercise of certain beliefs and dispositions in the student that had nothing to do with mathematical aptitude or processing. What Jim ran into was a broken relationship rooted in a past injustice that continued to poison present learning in an area as apparently technical as the learning of statistical procedures. What he set out to do was to restore wholesome relationships, to restore a little of the garden of delight, and learning flourished as a result.

My second story comes from my own experience a few years ago. In an intermediate German class, I had my students read in German the passage from Deuteronomy that begins 'Hear, O Israel' (Deuteronomy 6:4). I commented briefly that this kind of hearing is the opposite of autonomy and basic to Israel's identity, and that one of my aims for my German students was that they should learn to *hear* others who do not speak their language. There has been a big emphasis on speaking and getting your message across, I told my students, in recent language education, but you are not in my class just so that you can bless more of the world with your opinions. You are here to learn to hear what others want and need to say to you. I said this, moved on, and forgot all about it. Over a year later I received a phone call from Matthew, a student who had

---

[63] D.I. Smith, J. Shortt, and J. Bradley, 'Reconciliation in the Classroom.'

been in that class and was now bursting with excitement. He was in Germany, studying for a semester in Marburg. That morning he had boarded a bus, sat down next to a German man, and noticed that he seemed dejected. He started a conversation and discovered that the man had just lost his job. 'I remembered what you said in class,' Matthew said (what did I say in class, I wondered?), 'about hearing people instead of just speaking, and I just listened to him talk. By the end he seemed really relieved to have been able to talk to someone about it. I offered some words of encouragement and he thanked me for listening. I just got home and I had to call you.'

Again, this is not a case of repeatable technique – I don't know of any teaching trick that will consistently cause American students to go to Germany and choose to listen to and console unemployed Germans. The result did, however, follow from a conscious choice of text, carefully chosen words to my class, and indirectly from long reflection on the spiritual and moral dimensions of language learning. Observation of classroom behaviour would have offered few clues to what was going on in Matthew, as he took a particular teacher utterance to heart and made it part of his own discipleship. Matthew's response is another small example, I think, of the kind of thing Comenius had in mind, where learning German grammar takes place in the context of spiritual and ethical concern and leads to moments of shalom in a world of broken relationships, budding signs of the garden of delight. I submit that if we were to let Comenius's biblically rooted images play in our teacherly imaginations we might increase the chances of such moments multiplying.

Bibliography

Allen, R.T., 'Christian Thinking in Education,' *Spectrum* 25 (1993), 17–24

Ambrose, *Hexameron, Paradise, and Cain and Abel*, ed. J.J. Savage, Fathers of the Church, Vol. 42 (Washington, DC: Catholic University of America Press, 1961)

Aspin, D., 'Metaphor and Meaning in Educational Discourse,' *Metaphors of Education*, ed. W. Taylor, Studies in Education (London: Heinemann, 1984), 21–37

Augustine, *The Literal Meaning of Genesis*, ed. and trans. J.H. Taylor, Ancient Christian Writers, Vol. 2 (New York: Newman Press, 1982)

Bernard of Clairvaux, *On the Song of Songs*, trans. K. Walsh, Cistercian Fathers (Spencer, MA: Cistercian Publications, 1971)

Black, M., 'More About Metaphor,' *Metaphor and Thought*, ed. A. Ortony, 2nd edn. (Cambridge: Cambridge University Press, 1993), 19–41

Breen, M.P., 'The Social Context for Language Learning: A Neglected Situation,' *Studies in Second Language Acquisition* 7 (1985), 135–58

Brumfit, C., 'Problems in Defining Instructional Methodologies,' *Foreign Language Research in Cross-Cultural Perspective*, ed. K. de Bot, R.P. Ginsberg and C. Kramsch (Amsterdam/Philadelphia: John Benjamins, 1991), 133–44

Caravolas, J.-A., 'Comenius (Komensky) and the Theory of Language Teaching,' *Acta Comeniana* 10 (1993), 141–70

Caravolas, J., *Le Gutenberg de la didacographie ou Coménius et l'enseignement des langues* (Montréal: Guérin, 1984)

Comenius, J.A., *Panegersia, or Universal Awakening*, trans. A.M.O. Dobbie (Shipston-on-Stour: Peter I. Drinkwater, 1990)

—, *Comenius' Pampaedia or Universal Education*, trans. A.M.O. Dobbie (Dover: Buckland, 1986)

—, *The Great Didactic of John Amos Comenius*, ed. M.W. Keatinge, 2nd edn. (New York: Russell and Russell, 1967)

—, *Johann Amos Comenius: Ausgewählte Werke*, ed. K. Schaller and D. Tschizewskij, Vol. 1 (Hildesheim/New York: Georg Olms Verlag, 1973)

—, *Panorthosia or Universal Reform, Chapters 19–26*, trans. A.M.O. Dobbie (Sheffield: Sheffield Academic Press, 1993)

Davidson, D., 'What Metaphors Mean' in *On Metaphor*, ed. S. Sacks (Chicago: University of Chicago Press, 1979), 29–46

de Courcy, M., 'Australian Teachers' Experiences of Language Learning and Their Effect on Practice,' *Third International Conference on Language Teacher Education* (Minneapolis: Center for Advanced Research on Language Acquisition 2003)

Egan, K., *Teaching as Storytelling* (London: Routledge, 1988)

Elliott, R. K., 'Metaphor, Imagination and Conceptions of Education' in *Metaphors of Education*, ed. W. Taylor (London: Heinemann, 1984)

Ellis, R., *Second Language Acquisition* (Oxford: Oxford University Press, 1997)

Green, G., *Imagining God: Theology and the Religious Imagination* (Grand Rapids: Eerdmans, 1998)

Harris, M., *Teaching and Religious Imagination* (San Francisco: Harper and Row, 1987)

Herrad of Hohenbourg, Hortus Deliciarium, ed. R. Green, M. Evans, and C. Bischoff, 2 vols. (London: Publication of the Warburg Institute, 1979)

Huebner, D., 'Religious Metaphors in the Language of Education,' *Religious Education* 80 (1985), 460–72

Jager, E., *The Tempter's Voice: Language and the Fall in Medieval Literature* (Ithaca: Cornell University Press, 1993)

Janko, J., 'Comenius' Syncrisis as the Means of Man and World Knowledge,' *Acta Comeniana* 9 (1991), 43–55

Johnston, B., *Values in English Language Teaching* (Mahwah, NJ: Lawrence Erlbaum, 2003)

Keller, J. A., 'Accepting the Authority of the Bible: Is It Rationally Justified?' *Faith and Philosophy* 6 (1989), 378–97

Kramsch, C., ed., *Language Acquisition and Language Socialization: Ecological Perspectives* (New York: Continuum, 2003)

Kumaravadivelu, B., *Beyond Methods: Macrostrategies for Language Teaching* (New Haven, CT: Yale University Press, 2003)

—, 'The Postmethod Condition: (E)Merging Strategies for Second/Foreign Language Teaching,' *TESOL Quarterly* 28 (1994), 27–48

—, 'Toward a Postmethod Pedagogy,' *TESOL Quarterly* 35 (2001), 537–60

Lakoff, G., and M. Johnson, *Metaphors We Live By* (Chicago: University of Chicago Press, 1980)

Larsen-Freeman, D., 'Chaos/Complexity Science and Second Language Acquisition,' *Applied Linguistics* 18 (1997), 141–65

—, 'Research on Language Teaching Methodologies: A Review of the Past and an Agenda for the Future,' *Foreign Language Research in Cross-Cultural Perspective*, ed. K. de Bot, R. P. Ginsberg, and C. Kramsch (Amsterdam/Philadelphia: John Benjamins, 1991), 119–32

Leather, J., and J. Van Dam (eds.), *Ecology of Language Acquisition* (Dordrecht: Kluwer, 2002)

McFague, S., *Metaphorical Theology: Models of God in Religious Language* (Minneapolis: Augsburg Fortress, 1997)

Murphy, D., *Comenius: A Critical Reassessment of His Life and Work* (Dublin: Irish Academic Press, 1995)

Ong, W.J., *Ramus, Method and the Decay of Dialogue* (Cambridge, MA: Harvard University Press, 1958)

Ormell, C., 'Eight Metaphors of Education,' *Educational Research* 38 (1996), 67–75

Ortony, A., *Metaphor and Thought*, 2nd edn. (Cambridge: Cambridge University Press, 1993)

Pennycook, A., 'The Concept of Method, Interested Knowledge, and the Politics of Language Teaching,' *TESOL Quarterly* 23 (1989), 589–618

—, 'Language Policy and the Ecological Turn,' *Language Policy* 3 (2004), 213–39

Plantinga, A., *The Twin Pillars of Christian Scholarship* (Grand Rapids: Calvin College and Seminary, 1990)

Platt, E., '"Uh Uh No" 'Hapana': Intersubjectivity, Meaning and the Self,' *Dialogue with Bakhtin on Second and Foreign Language Learning: New Perspectives*, ed. J.K. Hall, G. Vitanova, and L. Marchenkova (Mahwah, NJ: Lawrence Erlbaum, 2005), 119–47

Purpel, D.E., and W.M. McLaurin. *Reflections on the Moral and Spiritual Crisis in Education* (New York: Peter Lang, 2004)

Sacks, S. (ed.), *On Metaphor* (Chicago: University of Chicago Press, 1979)

Shortt, J., D. Smith, and T. Cooling, 'Metaphor, Scripture and Education,' *Journal of Christian Education* 43 (2000), 22–28

Smith, D.I., 'Gates Unlocked and Gardens of Delight: Comenius on Faith, Persons and Language Learning,' *Christian Scholar's Review* 30 (2000), 207–32

—, 'Christian Thinking in Education Reconsidered,' *Spectrum* 25 (1995), 9–24

—, 'Coral Gardens and Classroom Ecology,' *Journal of Christianity and Foreign Languages* 7 (2006), 87–90

—, 'Incarnation, Education and the Boundaries of Metaphor,' *Journal of Christian Education* 45 (2002), 7–18

—, *The Spirit of the Foreign Language Classroom* (Nottingham: The Stapleford Centre, 2001)

—, and T.A. Osborn (eds.), *Spirituality, Social Justice and Language Learning* (Greenwich, CT: Information Age Publishing, forthcoming)

—, and J. Shortt, *The Bible and the Task of Teaching* (Nottingham: The Stapleford Centre, 2002)

—, J. Shortt, and J. Bradley, 'Reconciliation in the Classroom,' *Journal of Education and Christian Belief* 10 (2006), 3–5

—, J. Shortt, and J. Sullivan (eds.), *Spirituality, Justice and Pedagogy* (Nottingham: The Stapleford Centre, 2006)

Soskice, J.M., *Metaphor and Religious Language* (Oxford: Clarendon, 1985)

Taylor, W. (ed.), *Metaphors of Education* (London: Heinemann, 1984)

Tudor, I., 'Learning to Live with Complexity: Towards an Ecological Perspective on Language Teaching,' *System* 31 (2003), 1–12

van Dam, J., 'Ritual, Face, and Play in a First English Lesson: Bootstrapping a Classroom Culture,' *Language Acquisition and Language Socialization: Ecological Perspectives*, ed. C. Kramsch (New York: Continuum, 2002), 237–65

Wolfe, D.L., 'The Line of Demarcation between Integration and Pseudointegration,' *The Reality of Christian Learning*, ed. H. Heie and D.L. Wolfe (Grand Rapids: Eerdmans, 1987), 3–11

Wolterstorff, N., *Educating for Shalom: Essays on Christian Higher Education*, ed. C.W. Joldersma and G.G. Stronks (Grand Rapids: Eerdmans, 2004)

9

Reading Habits, Scripture and the University

John Sullivan

Is the practice of reading in the university in decline? I think it is. Many factors play a part in this decline. First there is the shift towards mass higher education, so that the university experience is not restricted to a relatively prosperous and leisured elite. The effort to widen participation and thus become more inclusive, a highly worthy and welcome endeavour, nevertheless exists in some tension with a commitment to preserving academic standards. Second, many students nowadays need paid employment alongside their studies, leaving much less time available for study. Third, in some countries increasing intrusion by government into university affairs diverts attention and energy away from traditional priorities, relationships and patterns of behaviour. As a result, faculty members face more students, have less time for each one, have to cover their tracks with multiple forms of accountability and audit, are pressured to secure higher levels of income for their university (and themselves) through grants and consultancies, and are expected to be highly productive in their publication rate. Fourth, although it is still too soon for the effects of new technologies to be adequately mapped and evaluated, it seems clear to me that, along with the massive increase in access to information on any subject under the sun that the internet makes possible, students are drawn into its 'nets' in a different sense; they are as ready to mistake the information it offers for reliable knowledge as are many of their teachers to assume that the use of Powerpoint is coterminous with effective teaching.

Of course, there are many other factors at work that contribute cumulatively to a decline in reading. One might consider, for example, reduced stability in the home, with frequent marriage breakdown, both parents working, and separation from extended family networks of support. Then there is the intrusive role played from a very early stage in a child's life by exciting new technology and media. The sheer pace at which knowledge becomes superseded is another factor, one that leads to the traditional case for investment in learning to read being downgraded. Also playing a part, I believe, is much less trust in or respect for authority and therefore less willingness to engage with authorities as identified in recommended literature. The sheer idea of spending much of one's time 'reaching up to' the thought of a master in a field might be considered an unwarranted restriction on personal autonomy, inhibitive of creativity and threatening authenticity and self-expression.

However, the decline of reading in the university, whether or not the evidence supports my assertion about this, and whether the factors that I have suggested contribute to this phenomenon, is not the main focus of this paper. I am not going to consider how texts are decoded, how clues on the page are indwelt or deployed by readers, nor will I comment on particular techniques used by teachers to engage students in learning how to read, or even on the range of reading practices that have been used in the past or that are current now, in schools or universities. I am using the term 'reading' in a very broad way, avoiding some of the distinctions that would be required if my focus were to be on the range of practical activities that constitute particular occasions of reading. I am more interested in how readers relate their reading to what is most important in their lives. In particular, my constructive purpose is to consider how Scripture might exercise a role in the university today. How might its voice be heard? How might a scriptural vision influence university priorities and practices, mentalities and modes of relating? I am not seeking to draw out from Scripture a particular set of insights, comprising a coherent programme, so as to apply this to university. Neither am I am seeking to overturn historical developments and restore some idealised past. Nevertheless, I do believe that we can learn valuable lessons from appreciating how some pre-modern patterns of relating Scripture and scholarship cast light on deficient features of our contemporary university education.

One of these lessons is about the match between the character of readers and what they are capable of understanding. Readiness for reading, in this light, is intimately connected to moral and spiritual development. In considerations of how best to teach reading in general and, more particularly, how to promote academic literacy in the university, it would seem counter-cultural as well as counter-intuitive to ask if the practice of religious reading has anything to teach secular readers. Yet, 'we have forgotten how central religious reading is to our notions of reading in general. It is in religious contexts that reading has been practiced by a large part of the population over the years. Church reading was the first introduction to reading for countless generations, and for many it is so still.'[1] Furthermore, 'For the greater part of its history, literacy as a practice has derived its nature from being an extension of the activity of scripture.'[2]

At the heart of my reflection is a desire to suggest that readers of Scripture can influence the way other types of reading are carried out in the university

---

[1] A. Purves, *The Web of Text and the Web of God*, 62.
[2] A. Purves, *Web of Text*, 71.

and to indicate briefly how they might expect to do so. In the section that follows I offer a (very sketchy) historical perspective on how the world and self have been read in the light of Scripture. I indicate some of the factors that influence reading and how the quality of reading is linked to moral and spiritual development. I show how different habits of reading and a different institutional habitat for reading have displayed assumptions about and treatment of Scripture that contrast sharply with much contemporary practice. In the second section I bring out some features of the cultural and university environment that make each of them inhospitable to Christian faith, suggesting that a dismembering of religious reading has taken place, partly because of the influence of a series of alien worldviews or 'isms.' Three particular challenging features of cultural change are identified: the emergence of a hermeneutics of suspicion; the growth of historical consciousness; and sensitivity to the way ideology functions. In analysing recent worrying trends in the university, I draw heavily on the contribution of Ronald Barnett, showing how new language, priorities and structures have operated largely in service of the malign influence of the market and been instrumental in the distortions brought about by a deficient approach to teaching, learning and leadership, the competency approach. These developments have led to a gain in technical control but a loss of personal depth. In the final section of this essay I argue that religious reading requires personal transformation and that there is scope for Christian influence in all universities, but most especially in Christian universities. However, I advocate a deliberate policy of self-limitation on the part of Christians as an integral feature of the way they make their contribution, suggesting that they work according to an alternative set of verbs to those commonly privileged in the university. With the right reading habits, guided by Scripture, the university can once again become a place where it is possible to move from knowledge to wisdom.

Scripture and Scholarship

Permit me to make a further distinction: Christians have always read their Scriptures in the light of other types of knowledge. Over the centuries these other types of knowledge and the scholarly techniques associated with them have massively increased and diversified. These changes are not my concern here. When universities were first founded it was accepted without contradiction that one should learn to read the world and oneself in the light of reading the Scriptures. Closely connected to this expectation was the assumption that understanding a text requires the right sort of reader. These two points, the necessity of viewing the world in general and my life in particular in the light of

Scripture, and the concomitant demands this makes of readers if they are to read rightly, are my concern here. Let me take them each in turn.

Reading the world and oneself in the light of Scripture requires both exegesis and interpretation. Exegesis has the text and its author as its focus, while interpretation has meaning for us as its focus. The first looks back and requires some historical reconstruction. Its purpose, however, is not antiquarianism; it is, rather, to provide a sound foundation for, to feed into, to cast light on and to secure a reliable guide for the second, the practice of interpretation. This second order of practice regards our present context and the questions this poses for us and seeks to relate the findings of exegesis to this present context and to imminently pressing questions. For a Christian worldview to emerge, certain foundations must be in place; without these, whatever is built will be precarious, uncertain, flawed and thus unreliable. Christians cannot 'float free' of these foundations, without loss of identity. However, there is scope for creativity and variety in the types of dwelling we construct on the basis of these foundations, since Christian faith does not entail conformity in the way it is articulated, expressed, practised and celebrated.

One interesting description of the difference between exegesis and interpretation is quoted by the historian Robert Markus.

> Exegesis is the incessant commentary that a culture makes on its symbolism, its gestures, its practices, on all that constitutes it as a system in action. Exegesis proliferates from inside; it is a speech which nourishes the tradition of which it is a part, whereas interpretation emerges the moment there is an outside perspective, when some in society begin to question, to criticize the tradition, to distance themselves with regard to the histories of the tribe.[3]

This description of the difference between exegesis and interpretation applies more broadly than simply to the study of Scripture. Certainly, when applied to Scripture, despite having some value, it exaggerates, in my view, the difference between these two modes of investigation. Some of what is described here as exegesis has often, in Christian tradition, fallen under the label of interpretation, although this might also be called 'spiritual' reading. The value of the description quoted by Markus, as a clarification, lies in the tension that it suggests arises between a received tradition and a critical interrogation of that tradition prompted by its adherents as they encounter external perspectives. Such critical questioning may lead to reiteration of the tradition, in the light of better marshalled defence, apologetics or explanation; it may well lead to a modified understanding of the tradition; it may lead to it being (in some respects at least) radically altered or even dropped. At its best, I believe, Christian use of

---

[3] R. Markus, *Signs and Meanings*, 38, quoting a 1982 essay by M. Detienne, 'Rethinking Mythology.'

Scripture has always recognized, appreciated and incorporated this tension into its mode of operation. God's ways are not the ways of the world. In the light of our appreciation of God's ways, as revealed in Scripture, we expose the defects of the ways of the world; in the face of feeling the attraction of the ways of the world, we also fear God's ways are a kind of constraint upon worldly appetites.

Let me now consider the reader. Many factors influence what the reader is equipped to take in through what he or she reads: what s/he already knows; what s/he remembers; what s/he is committed to; what s/he enjoys; what s/he desires, fears, and regrets. As individuals, our reading is intimately related to our life story, the company we keep and our lifestyle. It is also deeply affected by the kinds of training and discipline we have undergone, the degree of struggle and effort we put into it, the quality of our ethical life and whatever level of self-knowledge we have been able to develop. This is where traditional under-standings of the relationship between Scripture and scholarship present inter-esting challenges and resources for the university today.

A neglected aspect of the tradition (actually predating Christianity, for example, in Aristotle) is the emphasis it placed on the axiom, 'as we are, so shall we know.' This is a recurrent theme, apparently unquestioned as recently as Samuel Taylor Coleridge's *Aids to Reflection* (1825).[4] According to the tradi-tional view, the state of my spirit will enhance or inhibit the reach of my mind. When a person who is under-developed spiritually tries to understand the things of the spirit, this, Coleridge says, parallels 'those who would try to judge Titian or Raphael by Canons of Criticism deduced from the Sense of Smell.'[5] In other words, it is to try to judge what is higher from what is lower, to pene-trate the supernatural with the limited tools of the natural. Before this is possi-ble, the Christian tradition has constantly implied, we require purification of character and a purging of the soul. Origen, for example, deployed 1 Corinthi-ans chapter 2 to develop a taxonomy of spiritual growth, contrasting human wisdom with divine truth, so that the capacity to know spiritual things is linked to conversion and spiritual growth. Thus, 'a man who is unspiritual refuses what belongs to the Spirit of God; it is folly to him; he cannot grasp it. ... A man gifted with the Spirit can judge the worth of everything' (1 Cor. 2:14–15). For Origen, Scripture is addressed to everyone, despite the great differences there are between us, especially in the level of spiritual growth we have reached. It has the depth and a capacity to communicate to us, at whatever level we are currently.[6] As the Pontifical Biblical Commission put this in 1993,

---

[4] See D. Hedley, *Coleridge, Philosophy and Religion*.
[5] Hedley, *Coleridge*, 21.
[6] D. Williams, *Receiving the Bible in Faith*, 16, 23.

The meaning of a text can be fully grasped only as it is actualized in the lives of readers who appropriate it. . . . Access to a proper understanding of biblical texts is only granted to the person who has an affinity with what the text is saying on the basis of life experience. . . . As the reader matures in the life of the Spirit, so there grows also his or her capacity to understand the realities of which the Bible speaks.[7]

I shall say more below about how an advocacy of the kind of qualities required of the reader as suggested here sits uneasily in the context of a modern university, but first I attend more generally to the links between Scripture and scholarship.

Scripture has in the past enjoyed a very different status and role in the university than pertains today. It was once interpreted in the context of significantly different governing assumptions, for example, about its over-riding authority; the agencies mandated to speak on behalf of Scripture had a special position. At the birth of the university the church was the dominant social agency. Theology, heavily based on Scripture and set in the context of community worship, was considered both a study of the Holy and a path to a life of holiness, sharing God's life, enjoying the vision of God, in preparation for enjoying God's company for ever; it was about being shaped by and inducted into a way of life, so that discipleship was integral to theology, rather than separated from it. The cloister, sacred liturgy, prayer, participation in a religious way of life – all these were integral to the practice of theology and to its central activity, the meditative reading of Scripture. Study and prayer were intimately linked. No sharp separation was expected between different kinds of reading – reading the Scriptures, reading the 'book of nature' or reading the lives of those who studied – since reading was to be considered not simply an accumulation of data, but embarkation upon a journey that inevitably transforms what we desire, conditions who it is we are becoming and informs us concerning how we are to be oriented towards God.[8]

Thus, several key features of the relationship between Scripture and scholarship can be identified as pertaining during the early years of the university. Knowledge was sought within an overall context where the student was a person who acknowledged and practised the duty of worship. Study – whatever other earthly (and lesser) goals it might serve – was carried out essentially in service of discipleship; knowing and loving God was widely held to be the primary aim; learning pursued as an element in, and a way of accessing, salvation. Reading, in this view, is letting oneself be inserted into a text, rather than standing over it in judgement. 'The pious reader desires to be possessed by the word, not to manipulate it';[9] he wanted his life to be incorporated into the story

---

[7] *The Interpretation of the Bible in the Church*, 75–77.
[8] P. Candler, *Theology, Rhetoric, Manuduction*.
[9] I. Illich, *In the Vineyard of the Text*, 43.

told in the text, rather than to impose his perspective and priorities on the story.[10] Students belonged to a believing community, were formed by this community and prepared to contribute further to this faith community by helping to form others. Formation is something much more all-enveloping than training: it involves simultaneously a way of believing, a way of behaving, a way of belonging and a way of worshipping.[11] These four dimensions of formation echo the primary grammar of Christian faith, which employs the languages of proclamation, of service, of community and of prayer, each nourishing, expressing, applying, amplifying, qualifying, guiding and renewing the others. From the security of belonging to a faith community, there was much greater openness to explore questions and a remarkable freedom to express disagreement than is often realized today. Criticisms about interpretations were made from a position of commitment.

Pre-critical spiritual readings of Scripture were not, as is well known, lacking sophistication, nuance, creativity or critical discernment. Augustine, for example, was steeped in the scholarship of his culture and, as a highly sophisticated teacher of rhetoric, he pondered long and hard on the nature of reading and its intellectual requirements. Brian Stock, in a magisterial study, *Augustine the Reader*, says , 'it is his writings that provide Western reflection on reading, inwardness and transcendence with their earliest synthetic statement.'[12] Reading, for Augustine, involved a step away from being totally immersed within and consumed by external things and a journey inwards, a pilgrimage towards transcendence, undertaken in order to rise above oneself (or, perhaps better put, entered into so that we can be lifted up to a level beyond the reach of our own powers). Augustine drew on the ancient world's understanding of philosophy as a spiritual discipline,[13] and shared to some degree its view of reading as a form of ascesis, as well as a form of aesthetic appreciation. In *Confessions* 10.1–35 he unites study, remembering, and self-examination as part of a general approach to disciplining himself, bodily and spiritually. The kind of reading he has in mind is one whereby we contemplate the text with a view to the light it casts on our ultimate end, an end that requires self-improvement. The difference between reading for pleasure only – which has its place in life – and reading for ascetic purposes, with a higher self as goal, is that 'in the one, ethical considerations are subordinated to enjoyment; in the other, enjoyment is postponed until ethical imperatives are met.'[14]

---

[10] Illich, *Vineyard of the Text*, 31.
[11] J. Sullivan, 'From Formation to the Frontiers: the Dialectic of Christian Education.'
[12] B. Stock, *Augustine the Reader*, 2.
[13] See P. Hadot, *Philosophy as a Way of Life*.
[14] B. Stock, *Augustine the Reader*, 29.

A much invoked formula for traditional modes of biblical interpretation involves four levels or aspects, all intimately linked. These were the literal (or historical), allegorical, tropological (or moral) and anagogical senses of Scripture. The first teaches us what took place in the original setting of the text. The second alerts us to what we ought to believe about how the text casts light on our understanding of Christ and the church. The third advises us on what we personally ought to do in the light of the first two senses and the fourth shows us what we should hope and strive for, in view of our eternal destiny, giving the eschatological meaning of the text.[15] The three senses added onto yet always drawn from the literal or historical sense of Scripture can all be said to fall under the heading of spiritual exegesis.

The prolific and immensely influential French theologian Henri de Lubac (1896–1991) wrote more about spiritual exegesis than anything else, in one period of his life devoting twenty years to this topic, producing five books and numerous articles. For de Lubac, historical criticism sought to understand past persons, events, ideas and texts in their original contexts. Critical study meant disciplined, discriminating interrogation of the sources. This is both valuable and necessary, if personal faith and ecclesial life is to be built on sound foundations, rather than mere wishes. However, critical methods are insufficient on their own, for such work is methodologically limited and tends to be vulnerable to questionable assumptions.

De Lubac wanted to overcome the separation between exegesis, systematic theology and spirituality that he, along with many others, acknowledged had occurred during and since the later Middle Ages. Before then these disciplines had been much closer. For a while it had been assumed that the beginnings of this separation stemmed from the inception of scholasticism in the thirteenth century. A common view has been that

> *lectio divina* in monasteries was oriented toward *meditatio* (reflection, reminiscing, and ruminating) and *oratio* (prayerfulness) while the *lectio* in scholastic schools came from *question* (question) proposed to the *pagina* (text) and was oriented toward the *disputatio* (debate).[16]

Recent scholarship[17] has established that the differences, originally identified by Leclercq, between monastic and scholastic theologians (many, though not all of whom, were either Dominican or Franciscan friars) were much less sharp in reality. Their respective intended audiences, homiletical subjects, pastoral orientation, desire for church reform, sources used, intellectual methods and

---

[15] S. Wood, *Spiritual Exegesis and the Church in the Theology of Henri de Lubac*, 25, 27.
[16] J. Elias, *A History of Christian Education*, 55.
[17] E.g., L. Smith, 'The Use of Scripture in Teaching at the Medieval University.'

modes of expression, were very close in many ways, despite differences of emphasis. If monastic books were 'few, fat, and fixed, whilst friars' books were many, mobile, and minute,' for both they were 'tools to be used as much as treasures to be pondered over.'[18] For the vast majority of medieval scholars, wherever their place of study, the knowledge and love of God was top priority and care of souls was a major aim. In this task nothing was more important than Scripture. Smith points out that

> The exegesis of scripture was the highest pinnacle of the highest faculty of the higher learning.... The exegesis of scripture pervaded all other parts of theology.... Scriptural expression had seeped into their bones. Beyond the faculty, medieval people had a biblical imagination.[19]

Common medieval metaphors for Scripture in relation to the life of faith referred to it as foundation, walls and roof, constructed around us to ensure a safe space for eating and drinking the stuff of eternal life and protecting us from temptations and threats.[20] Hearers and readers of Scripture were expected to have not only their ears but their hearts attuned to its music, to have their souls, as well as their minds, regenerated. Texts were not only to be read but to be performed and lived, to become so internalised that they became rooms in their souls, exuding energy, light and grace, constantly available to be drawn upon in guiding, reforming and renewing one's life. Truth was expected to touch and transform, not simply to be entertained on a temporary basis before we pass onto something else for our use. Charles Dumont compares Bernard of Clairvaux's approach to this kind of knowledge with Heidegger's distinction between meditative and calculative thinking: 'The kind of knowledge which contributes to the transformation of the deepest part of our being in the perspective of our destiny, and another kind which seeks only to acquire tools for action in this world.'[21]

Inhospitable Environments

The cultural environment of modernity, and of the university in particular, presents formidable obstacles to such an encounter with Scripture. I believe that a dismembering of religious reading has taken place in the two different, but related, contexts of the wider culture and of the university. Such dismembering within the wider culture results from the interaction of many factors.

---

[18] L. Smith, 'Use of Scripture,' 234.
[19] L. Smith, 'Use of Scripture,' 230.
[20] L. Smith, 'Use of Scripture,' 239.
[21] C. Dumont, *Pathway of Peace,* 72.

Scripture is obscured as a principal source from which the majority of people draw their worldview, values, metaphors and imagination. Far from being the staple diet from which people learn to read, then to read themselves and their world, Scripture has become for most people simply a foreign land, one that is populated by those who hold assumptions that now no longer deserve allegiance. Mentalities and moralities that are alien to a scriptural perspective have become widespread. I am referring here to the many 'isms' that infect our thinking, for example, materialism, individualism, utilitarianism and relativism. These have led to ways of thinking that sit uncomfortably with the perspectives and habits of behaviour prescribed by Scripture. For example, if truth is unattainable, elusive or merely subjective, concern for truth cannot be a supreme value, worthy of self-sacrifice; or if sin is a concept that is unfashionable because it sounds judgemental, then salvation too seems no longer necessary. There has been an erosion of confidence and an increase in suspicion of tradition, accompanied by hostility to the notion of authority. Distorted understandings of freedom and an excessive reliance on the value of autonomy have contributed to resentment of all ties that bind, a retreat from commitment and fragmentation of community. Without defending these assertions about the wider culture, I merely comment briefly here on three elements that have to be taken into account when one tries to appreciate key challenges to the reception of Scripture (within and beyond the university). These are the rise of the hermeneutics of suspicion, historical consciousness and awareness of the functioning of ideology.

In a sense, there is bound to be some ongoing tension between academic eros, the desire to pursue knowledge without constraint, and the obedience called for by religion. On the one hand, there is the intellectual drive endlessly to question, criticise, dispute, consider alternative explanations, to hold suspicions about the credibility of authorities, to note shortcomings and to withhold trust. On the other hand, discipleship entails a high degree of obedience, self-sacrifice, trust, docility and fidelity. As historian John O'Malley puts it, 'If the prophetic culture is founded on "I-say-unto-you" . . . [the academy] replies "Why should I accept your 'I-say-unto-you? On what basis do you know what you say you know?"'[22] While for much of church history it has been possible to hold together religious faith and the intellectual life in an unstable but creative synthesis, from the nineteenth century onwards it has become increasingly difficult to sustain this synthesis. Various forms of the hermeneutics of suspicion have permeated the academy and sidelined religious faith. The theories of Feuerbach, Marx, Darwin, Nietzsche, Freud have all taken their toll. However, in my view another challenge has turned out to be even more disconcerting for religious believers, namely the development of a new form of historical consciousness.

---

[22] J. O'Malley, *Four Cultures of the West*, 77.

The development of history as a serious academic discipline in the nineteenth century undermined belief in permanence and stability, casting doubt on many treasured beliefs and customs thought to have been more or less handed down by God. Naturalistic analysis showed that ecclesial understandings and practices had changed over time because of human choices and thus that they could do so again, exposing the many shortcomings of those in authority in times past, and uncovering in detail the messy and frequently unsavoury politics involved in doctrinal and disciplinary decisions. In brief, the human dimension of religion was exposed to a degree that belief in the divine dimension became difficult to sustain. The very way that history, as a post-Enlightenment scholarly activity, came to be conducted seemed at odds with faithful commitment and affiliation. 'The ideals of historical scholarship as formulated in the nineteenth century were objectivity, disinterest, and detachment,'[23] as distinct from a prior approach that used history to provide moral examples for improving behaviour.

One theologian in the early part of the twentieth century who deployed history in the new way was Ernst Troeltsch (1865–1923). Troeltsch embraced history as a master key for understanding the biblical text.[24] In him, the credibility of scriptural accounts becomes sifted by our sense of what is normally acceptable and likely; this is to impose our standards on the Bible. Earlier uses of Scripture had tended to stress its unity, intended for our instruction and edification in view of salvation, and thereby slid too easily over the diverse historical situations out of which the text emerged, in the process sometimes obscuring or distorting the actual texts. In contrast,

the modern way of reading lays almost all its stress upon scripture as the product of history. The Bible is seen as an assemblage of diverse texts from diverse historical circumstances that convey the concerns and thoughts of their authors from within their own particular situations.[25]

If we get a better sense of 'what was going on' then, we can lose sight of the way this approach might speak to us now. For the historicist, 'we are no more the intended audience of the Bible than we are of Herodotus.'[26]

If the historical-critical method considers the text as a window into the past, Christian use has always been to treat Scripture also as a mirror bringing home to us aspects of our own lives now, in order to change them for the better.[27] Not only is there a need to tell the story of salvation in an informative way,

---

[23] D. Williams, *Receiving the Bible in Faith*, 3.
[24] D. Williams, *Receiving the Bible*, 50.
[25] D. Williams, *Receiving the Bible*, 53.
[26] D. Williams, *Receiving the Bible*, 53.
[27] Pontifical Biblical Commission, *Interpretation of the Bible*, 45–6.

which benefits from historical accuracy and insight, there is also a need to tell the story 'in view of salvation (the "performative" aspect).'[28] Furthermore, although a Christian use of Scripture in liturgy (for me the primary context for appreciation, internalisation and appropriation of Scripture) may begin with '"the letter of Paul to the Galatians," for example,' it closes 'by recognising what has been read as "the word of the Lord."'[29] This is to acknowledge dual authorship, the human and the divine. Christians believe that God may have had in mind for us more than the biblical writers understood even in their inspired state.

Apart from the challenge posed by historical consciousness, a more recent challenge has been an appreciation of the functioning of ideology in the communication (and rejection) of ideas and practices, perhaps with Michel Foucault (1926–84) as one the leading thinkers alerting us to the use and misuse of power by social institutions, not least the Church. As a result we are more sensitive about how the exercise of power – often in aid of perpetuating oppression – inextricably accompanies pronouncements within any community and that the exercise of power does not leave untouched the way Christians use Scripture. However, such an awareness about the insidious links with power can actually be assimilated by Christians in service of their faith. For example, theologian Juan Luis Segundo's approach to Scripture treats it 'as teacher of liberative practice rather than a depository of theological data.'[30]

In the university context, we should consider among the influences on dismembering religious reading some of the modern university's own governing assumptions: the centrality of the market and associated emphases on entrepreneurialism, targeted research, and the neglect of personal transformation in education. New priorities, the employment of new language that subtly and surreptitiously colonises perceptions of the purpose and essential nature of university life, together with the development of new structures and roles in service of these priorities and perceptions, cumulatively create an environment that is at least inhospitable, if not quite alien, to a Christian worldview that is informed, inspired and guided by Scripture. I concur with the following judgement about higher education which links some of these developments to the rise of the 'isms' I have mentioned above:

> Learning environments have become inhospitable to religiously informed perspectives for a number of reasons: professionalization of the academic vocation, divestiture of clerical control of colleges, increasing influence and funding by government and business. Changing views of the mission of universities as well as the widespread

---

[28] Pontifical Biblical Commission, *Interpretation of the Bible,* 46.
[29] D. Williams, *Receiving the Bible,* 187.
[30] D. Williams, *Receiving the Bible,* 107.

appeal of agnosticism, relativism, scientific empiricism, and social constructivism have created classroom conditions in which religious ideals are questioned suspiciously or antagonistically.[31]

One of the most perceptive commentators on higher education in the UK over the past fifteen years has been Ronald Barnett, a professor at London University's Institute of Education. He writes without any reference to religion, but throughout his work there is an evident ethical concern. He shares penetrating insights, shows a nuanced appreciation of the ideological implications of recent developments, and he is fair and balanced in his judgements. Here I draw heavily on two of his many books. *Beyond All Reason* brings out clearly the nature and functioning of ideologies at work in the university that undermine these institutions. An earlier work, *The Limits of Competence*, exposes the shortcomings of a particular recent emphasis in educational policy, the skills-based approach to education and educational leadership, a development I have written about at length elsewhere.[32] Barnett has valuable things to say in each of these books about the deleterious effects in the university of the metaphor of the market and the emphasis on competence, entrepreneurialism, vocationalism, research, instrumental thinking and the growth of administration that purports to operate in a value-neutral manner. Cumulatively, he sees these emphases as deeply damaging. 'We are seeing a profound shift in the value-base of academic life and, with it, a withering away of the virtues which the university has supplied in and to society.'[33]

The metaphor of the market brings into the university the notion of knowledge as a commodity, something that can be 'delivered' in discrete packages internally and externally as required. It treats the student as a consumer, with rights to direct the composition and selection of what is purchased. It suggests that the customer is always right and therefore that the university should adjust what it offers to that which is acceptable to the market. There is, of course, quite a difference between being market-informed and being market-driven. Too often the difference between these two is insufficiently appreciated. Barnett suggests that, under market conditions, students 'recede from a sense of themselves as contributors to a pedagogical transaction. . . . Learning is reduced to assimilation rather than being a personally authored learning that helps to form the student's identity.'[34] Once the market metaphor achieves dominance, then marketing as a function receives high priority. 'Image, badging, branding

---

[31] M. Buley-Meissner, et al., *The Academy and the Possibility of Belief*, 5.

[32] J. Sullivan, 'Skills-based Models of Leadership'; also 'Wrestling with Managerialism.'

[33] R. Barnett, *The Limits of Competence*, 152.

[34] R. Barnett, *Beyond All Reason*, 44.

and positioning: this is the new vocabulary of this form of university life.'[35] Imagine the alarm bells that a good teacher, at any level of education, would feel if told that it was her or his principal task, above all, to be popular; such a stance would be likely to lead to all kinds of compromises that would undermine the healthy dynamic of educational relationships at individual and institutional level. Where the market rules, this is a danger, including in the university, for 'those who live by the market will see the world through the market.'[36] As Barnett puts it, 'In living others' agendas – as the entrepreneur must do – the university is surrendering its integrity. . . . its inner callings are emptied out to be replaced by the callings of others.'[37]

In 'selling' (I shall leave in the quotation marks for now) the university to the highest bidder, the funds attracted by research are especially important. Inexorably academics are expected to spend more and more energy securing grants for research and their performance is judged against this criterion. Although Barnett does not make the link that I am making here between the dominance of the market metaphor and the emergence of research as the dominant project in university life, he rightly sees research as a major priority functioning ideologically, relying on interests, promoting causes other than intellectual discovery, becoming entangled in power structures, directed against alternative priorities and interests and, in the process, in turn helping to provoke competing falsely dichotomous ideological priorities such as learning and teaching. Instead of being intimately linked, increasingly these two endeavours, teaching and research, have become separated, 'with entirely different structures, forces and interests.'[38]

I find it sad that recent emphases on learning and teaching (as well as discussions about leadership) have become unduly dominated by the language of competence, skills, outcomes, and transferability. Knowledge is reduced to being a commodity, with a view to its operational promise, its instrumental pay-off, with presentation, rather than understanding, coming to be highly prized. ' Performativity' becomes all-important. That is, what you do with knowledge, for purposes that are other than central to the life of the mind, is what matters. This is in contrast to a concern for the effect of learning on the student as a person, with the wisdom that helps him or her to become a better person, ready to make sense of life in its wholeness. As Barnett puts it, 'understanding is replaced by competence; insight is replaced by effectiveness; and rigour of interactive argument is replaced by communication skills.'[39] Learning

---

[35] R. Barnett, *Beyond All Reason*, 70.
[36] R. Barnett, *Beyond All Reason*, 70.
[37] R. Barnett, *Beyond All Reason*, 71.
[38] R. Barnett, *Beyond All Reason*, 149.
[39] R. Barnett, *Limits of Competence*, 37.

objectives and competencies are described without reference to the perspectives and passions of the people involved. A false sense of certainty and the dangerous illusion of control are hinted at as the desired outcomes if the relevant competencies are developed. In my experience, there are so many variables involved in education that, no matter how confident a teacher is in employing a range of techniques, they can never claim predictive powers for their classroom efforts. Most worthwhile responses from learners require a degree of freedom, without which they cannot be responsible. Educational exchanges in classrooms and lecture theatres are, in their very particular dynamics, inherently ambiguous, complex, unpredictable and open-ended. This is part of the attraction teaching has for teachers. The emphasis on what might be called the 'software' of competencies that can be deployed on demand but which make no permanent or deep-seated demands for transformation on their users is of limited value while it continues to ignore the 'habitus' or 'hardware' of character in the person in whom these competencies reside. I think Barnett is right to view the recent emphasis on competencies at the heart of learning as being essentially reductive. I think he is also right in drawing our attention to the way that market-related qualities exert too great an influence, leading to loss of attention to other necessary qualities.

> Those human capacities that are picked out are intended to improve economic competitiveness; other possible human capabilities and virtues which might promote different kinds of human society – friendship, altruism, ethical concern, carefulness, generosity – are entirely neglected.[40]

In all this Barnett is not naïvely idealistic about how universities have operated in the past. As he says,

> the academic life has *always* been characterized by unreason, by inequalities of power, by micro-politics: back-stabbing, the undue presence of gender, manipulation and authoritarianism have been the order of the day. Modern managerialism is only a past Machiavellianism on campus, now become explicitly on show.[41]

Sin has always flourished as much in the university as anywhere else; this has never been a privileged or safe zone, free from human shortcomings and thus the misuse of the very qualities the university is supposed to develop. However, recent developments, as described above, exacerbate this inescapable feature of all human institutions by having the effect of replacing the very ideals to be striven for, first, by the importing of 'foreign' language, then by setting up systems to implement what is entailed by this new language. Although he does

---

[40] R. Barnett, *Limits of Competence*, 45.
[41] R. Barnett, *Beyond All Reason*, 60.

not make the contrast that I would wish to make between contemplative and instrumental reason, Barnett has insightfully shown how there has been a marked shift towards instrumental reason in the university, with more attention being paid to systems, structures and resources – which he calls the 'hardwiring of the university' – than to ideas and understanding – what he calls its 'conceptual tissue.'

> Hard-wiring complexity is connected primarily to *instrumental reason* whereas ideological complexity is connected to *communicative reason*. . . . *Management* becomes a matter of producing positive effects amid hard-wiring complexity whereas *leadership* becomes a matter of making progress amid soft-tissue or ideological complexity.[42]

Barnett also refers to the creation of new types of administrative posts that embed the new language and priorities in university life. He claims, with some justice I believe, that these administrators 'wear the icon of value freedom,' where 'issues are presented as technical issues (how to generate more investment for higher education, how to generate more participants from lower socio-economic classes, how to ensure that the intellectual products of universities are contributing to the "knowledge economy."'[43] He links internal apparent value-neutrality, equidistant from any particular worldview, and thus supposedly favouring pluralism, to similar external aspirations to value-neutrality: 'The work of the state's agencies, too, is presented as if their activities – in allocating state monies, in determining initiatives, in conducting quality evaluations – are also purely technical matters.'[44]

The use of technical or instrumental language assumes that ends or ultimate purposes and values are either already agreed upon and can be taken for granted or that they cannot be agreed upon and are best left out of consideration. With performance and competence, it is means that forms the focus of study, how to do things, not addressing why they deserve our efforts. The end product or outcome is what matters, not the prior process that has to be gone through, the dynamic educational relationship and associated human encounter and personal adjustments, disciplines and transformations. Mastery of, and the capacity to manipulate, the material – 'overstanding' rather than understanding – is the goal. One might say that, too often, *scientia* had been reduced to *techne* and *sapientia* ruled out-of-bounds, relegated to the private zone, inappropriate for public consideration in the university. As a recent critic of the same trends identified by Barnett has said, 'if the basis of one's anthropology is essentially materialistic and rationalistic then the dimension of the spiritual will be

---

[42] R. Barnett, *Beyond All Reason*, 165–66 (his emphasis).
[43] R. Barnett, *Beyond All Reason*, 122.
[44] R. Barnett, *Beyond All Reason*, 122.

excluded or reduced to these categories....' Accordingly, insufficient attention will be paid to 'actual practices of the faith communities as providing a form of knowledge for authentic action' or to the possibility that 'certain knowledge and understanding can be gained through prayer and meditation that could not possibly be gained in any other way.'[45]

Moving Forward in Hope

The conditions that pertained earlier historically, the close connection between church and academy, no longer exist generally, and even in the case of Christian universities and colleges, do not exist in the same form as before. Christianity is not the default position. There are various constraints on the exercise of Christian influence in the academy. The climate in which much academic work is conducted is inhospitable to religious ways of reading texts and the world in general. As Gavin D'Costa puts it, theology has become 'separated from the practices that are required for its proper understanding: prayer, sacraments and virtue.'[46] He even goes so far as to suggest that 'students take prayer as seriously as their reading lists.'[47] If theology becomes disembodied from spiritual practice and ecclesial accountability, it becomes dismembered and loses much of its potential to illuminate other disciplines. I have written elsewhere about how religious ways of reading contrast sharply with ways of reading encouraged within the contemporary university (and I draw heavily for the rest of this paragraph from those earlier comments).[48] Religious reading depends on a relationship with the text that allows the text to address, to question and to challenge the reader, and at the same time it adopts an attitude of reverence and obedience towards the text. Rather than standing in authority over it, interrogating it with critical tools, deferring commitment, questioning its authenticity, the religious reader stands under or in the light of the text. A religious reading is willing to be vulnerable to the message contained in a text, to submit to its power, to trust its source, to inhabit its ambience, to carry out its instructions, to belong to the community which treasures it. If the university treats the individual reader as the basic unit, religious readers give priority to the religious community. If the university adopts a detached and distanced perspective, religious readers expect engagement, participation and commitment. The personal qualities of the seeker cannot be expected to be irrelevant to what the search turns up with. Conversion and transformation of life is the

---

[45] M. Cartledge, 'Christian Theology for Ministry,' 34, 36, 39.
[46] G. D'Costa, *Theology in the Public Square*, 19.
[47] G. D'Costa, *Theology in the Public Square*, 114.
[48] J. Sullivan, 'Scholarship and Spirituality,' 131–32.

price for – and the key to – unlocking the doors to the riches made available through the tradition. An effort at alignment between the subject who studies and the object being studied is required.

The whole point of biblical reading is to lead to transformation of the reader in order for us to access God's offer of new life. Such reading – indeed, any serious reading – cannot rely only on passive observation and spectatorship; it needs the reinforcement provided by practice and engagement. The French religious philosopher Maurice Blondel (1861–1949) published in 1893 a celebrated (and notorious) book, *l'Action*. This had a chapter that had to be omitted from his doctoral thesis, submitted earlier that same year, a chapter considered unacceptable in the highly secular university atmosphere dominant even then, on the value of religious practice as a condition for knowledge.[49] Without in any way determining access to God, which would not be possible merely as a result of human initiative, Blondel's focus on the role of action was intended to uncover the conditions on our side that help to make us actively receptive to what God has to communicate to us. Without practice, for Blondel, we could not properly access the truth, claim it for ourselves, appreciate its profundity or allow it to penetrate our being. We have to do the truth if we wish to understand truth.

This was – and remains – an uncomfortable counter-cultural message. There remain spaces, even within secular universities, for alternative, indeed, counter-cultural values to be upheld and healthier ways of being to be promoted, if the appropriate will, imagination, courage and political wisdom are deployed. Despite the difficulties presented by the inhospitable climate pervading many universities, I believe that there is scope for Christians to contribute – drawing from their understanding of, appreciation for and application of Scripture as central in the life of faith and as guide to discipleship – to dialogue in the university, for example, dialogue about institutional priorities, curriculum, pedagogy, community life, marketing, external relationships and partnerships. The tone and style of that contribution and the qualities required to carry this off effectively will include a spirit of hope, humility, self-emptying, sensitivity, respect, gentleness, resilience and trust – all from a position of relative weakness, relying on the power of the Gospel and the workings of grace.

In a Christian university, these same qualities will still be required, but at least we can expect more deliberate and consistent support by institutional leaders for religious ways of reading and for alternative and richer ways to encounter truth to be offered. Building on a biblical foundation will not necessarily lead to uniform approaches by Christian universities, for the course that each one takes 'will always depend on its view of truth, the common good, the

---

[49] M. Blondel, *l'Action*, 405–23.

needs of its students, and its ability to accommodate the interests of its student body, faculty, and sponsoring religious institution.'[50]

I am arguing here for a disciplined display of self-limitation on the part of Christians in the academy, no matter whether their university is secular or affiliated with a faith community. If they are to be true witnesses to Scripture, Christians must beware deploying instrumental means to promote contemplative ends. They should not slip into the contradiction of using power to defend the virtue of self-emptying vulnerability. They should take great pains to avoid buttressing a strong establishment position within a university by stifling the risk-taking entailed by following the Gospel. They must not allow Christian orthodoxy to function as an ideology. Their convictions cannot be protected from being questioned and criticized. For all its sacredness, centrality and authority in the life of Christians, the Bible cannot be promoted with all the accoutrements of institutional levers of influence without gravely compromising the very wisdom it makes available for lighting our path if only we trust in the way, truth and the life it offers. Christians should come across, not as seeking to capture or dominate people with the truth they stand for, but instead, through their generous and inspirational example, their self-denying avoidance of power-games, their joyful trust in their own good news, to attract people to a life bathed in God's grace.

One upshot of this is that, even in a Christian university, there should be room for doubters, dissenters, disbelievers, and critics of religion. There will be a confident and warm hospitality, welcoming dialogue and difference. Although promoting the mission must be a central concern in faculty appointments, this does not rule out appointing good teachers, researchers and administrators who can constructively contribute a dissenting voice on religious matters. Christians have a duty to speak; they must not abdicate their responsibility. But they also have a duty to listen, to take seriously those who disagree, to value their insights and contributions, to enter into dialogue, to learn from them, as well as from those 'inside the tent.'

The kind of self-limiting behaviour for Christians in the academy, I have suggested in the last few paragraphs, is on my view more likely to elicit a less suspicious reading of their endeavours by non-Christians and to invite a more willing engagement with a vision of Christian education that is based upon a worldview illuminated by Scripture. What I envisage here harmonizes with university President Duane Litfin's description of an 'umbrella' model of a Christian university. 'Umbrella institutions seek to provide a Christian "umbrella" or canopy under which a variety of voices can thrive.' It 'seeks to house a variety of perspectives without sacrificing its sponsoring perspective.' It

---

[50] E. Bramhall and R. Ahrens, 'Academic Freedom and the Status of the Religiously Affiliated University,' 331.

aims to 'create an environment congenial to Christian thinking, but without expecting it of everyone.'[51] Litfin contrasts the umbrella model with a more systemic one, where there is a sustained, deliberate attempt to ensure that Christian thinking is communicated in every aspect of university life and through the agency of every person employed, explicitly articulated in all policies. 'What marks off Systemic institutions from the Umbrella counterparts is that all of their faculty are drawn from those who embody the institution's sponsoring faith tradition.'[52] I think this would be neither possible in practice nor desirable even in theory for the healthy development of a Christian university. Even so, it behooves Christians to be constantly vigilant lest the umbrella fails to protect the institution from exposure to the corrosive weathering of the market mentality.

Of course, it is difficult to get the balance right in seeking to avoid a religious imperialism that imposes one point of view over others. Some forms of self-restraint can simply open the door to (what we believe are) wrong decisions (about what is permitted or prohibited) that damage students and our community, undermine virtue, and obstruct access to truth. If one is willing to be vulnerable, rather than self-protective of oneself, this should not entail abdication of the good of others. Despite the ambiguities that accompany power, as Stephen Sykes has recently argued, Christians should not shy away from responsible engagement with the levers of influence.[53] Despite past abuse of power by Christians and inevitable suspicion when they seek to influence policy, either in the public domain in general or more particularly in the university, there is no requirement that they enter the lists of debate and community politics naked or naively. By drawing on the treasury of their own ecclesial disciplines and wisdom they should be able to combine an appropriate blend of conviction and confidence on the one hand, and, on the other hand, humility, respect for and openness to those who differ from them.

Christian university scholars should relate their work to that of the church rather than consider it something quite separate. As Adriaan Peperzak has argued, they participate in the communion of saints as well as belong to the republic of letters.[54] Their work comes from within the church; it is for the church; it adds something to the thinking of the church; it helps the church to understand better the implications of the gospel as well as to communicate it more effectively. As Douglas and Rhonda Jacobsen say,

> one of the main goals of Christian scholarship is to make the best thinking of the academy available in the church. . . . [Christian scholars] assist the church in

---

[51] D. Litfin, *Conceiving the Christian College*, 14, 17.
[52] D. Litfin, *Conceiving the Christian College*, 18.
[53] See S. Sykes, *Power and Christian Theology*.
[54] A. Peperzak, *Philosophy Between Faith and Theology*, 43.

articulating the gospel in language and symbols appropriate to today's cultures. They share their knowledge and insights with the church about how to be more effective in the ministries of care that the church offers to the world. They provide technical and philosophical expertise to help the church reflect intelligently on the complicated moral issues of our day.[55]

Another way of expressing this might be that the Christian university prompts a reading of self, scholarship and faith that is generously outward-looking: the life of the mind for the good of the world. Such scholarship will be simultaneously supportive and critical of the academy, affirmative and iconoclastic with regard to the church.[56] Let me quote the Jacobsens one final time:

> The goal of Christian scholars is to use their minds each day to discover a bit more about how the world is put together, to ascertain what roles and responsibilities they might be called to play in the world because of their scholarly expertise, and to infuse all their scholarly efforts with a sense of generous care for the world that parallels God's own deep love for creation.[57]

Attention to Scripture can offer to the academy a fostering of sensitivity to the spiritual climate that is conveyed via the discourses being used. It can direct us towards an alternative set of verbs that can frame and channel our energies, giving us a new set of habits, one that helps to bridge the gap between instrumental and contemplative thinking. In addition to accepted academic ways of reading, which include analysing, synthesising, critique, being scientifically detached, observing, measuring, evaluating, endlessly questioning, frequently being ready to be suspicious and sceptical, regular reading of Scripture can help students and scholars to be persons who are dedicated, giving, devoted, and living for others. It can give us a heightened sense of the mystery and object of God's love that is present in those we speak to, and a deepened acceptance of the responsibility that accompanies our sense of who we are and where we are speaking from. It can, without doubt, reinforce in us an awesome awareness of the ultimate environment in which all our endeavours, ecclesial and academic, are carried out, that is, in God's presence. Philosopher Adriaan Peperzak speaks of 'rationality without receptivity,' a way of thinking that is not based on 'admiration, gratitude, and compassion, but rather on the celebration of human intelligence, possession, engineering, and mastery.'[58] He advocates a charitable style of communication, one which displays 'benevolence, care, generosity, humility, and patience' – all nurtured by belonging to a Christian

---

[55] D. Jacobsen and R. Jacobsen, *Scholarship and Christian Faith*, 162.
[56] D. Jacobsen and R. Jacobsen, *Scholarship and Christian Faith*, 164, 166.
[57] D. Jacobsen and R. Jacobsen, *Scholarship and Christian Faith*, 167.
[58] A. Peperzak, *Philosophy Between Faith and Theology*, 11.

community.[59] Detached academic thinking about a topic could thus, prompted by a reading of Scripture in the wider context of Christian living, be linked to concern, devotion and commitment. Peperzak refers to 'the vocation of all scientia to become sapientia.'[60] I think that this vocation is greatly assisted when we attend to God's word, dwell in God's grace, live in fellowship and communion with other Christians and engage in the life of the mind, not only in search of quality of life for ourselves, but also in order to serve the common good of others. With revelation grounding, guiding and raising up reason, students and scholars should be equipped for Christian formation or *paideia*, that is, learning about, learning from and learning to imitate Christ, who is the way, the truth and the life.

---

[59] A. Peperzak, *Philosophy Between Faith and Theology*, 27.
[60] A. Peperzak, *Philosophy Between Faith and Theology*, 63.

Bibliography

Barnett, R., *The Limits of Competence* (Buckingham: Open University Press, 1994)
—, *Beyond All Reason* (Buckingham: Open University Press, 2003)
Blondel, M., *l'Action* (Paris: Presses Universitaires de France, 1973)
Bramhall, E., and R. Ahrens, 'Academic Freedom and the Status of the Religiously Affiliated University' in *The Future of Religious Colleges*, ed. P. Dovre (Grand Rapids: Eerdmans, 2002), 304–31
Buley-Meissner, M., M. Thompson, and E. Tan, *The Academy and the Possibility of Belief* (New Jersey: Hampton Press, 2000)
Candler, P. *Theology, Rhetoric, Manuduction* (Grand Rapids: Eerdmans, 2006)
Cartledge, M., 'Christian Theology for Ministry and the Quality Assurance Agency Criteria: An Epistemological Critique,' *Discourse* 4 (2005), 26–42
D'Costa, G., *Theology in the Public Square* (Oxford: Blackwell, 2005)
Dumont, C., *Pathway of Peace* (Kalamazoo: Cistercian Publications, 1999)
Elias, J., *A History of Christian Education* (Malabar, FL: Krieger Publishing, 2002)
Griffiths, P., *Religious Reading* (New York: Oxford University Press, 1999)
Hadot, P., *Philosophy as a Way of Life*, ed. A. Davidson (Oxford: Blackwell, 1995)
Hedley, D., *Coleridge, Philosophy and Religion* (Cambridge: Cambridge University Press, 2000)
Illich, I., *In the Vineyard of the Text* (Chicago: University of Chicago Press, 1993)
Jacobsen, D., and R. Jacobsen, *Scholarship and Christian Faith* (Oxford: Oxford University Press, 2004)
Litfin, D., *Conceiving the Christian College* (Grand Rapids: Eerdmans, 2004)
Markus, R., *Signs and Meanings* (Liverpool: Liverpool University Press, 1996)
O'Malley, J., *Four Cultures of the West* (Cambridge, MA: Harvard University Press, 2004)
Peperzak, A., *Philosophy Between Faith and Theology: Addresses to Catholic Intellectuals* (Notre Dame: University of Notre Dame, 2005)
Pontifical Biblical Commission, *The Interpretation of the Bible in the Church* (Quebec: Editions Paulines, 1993)
Purves, A., *The Web of Text and the Web of God* (New York: Guilford Press, 1998)
Smith, L., 'The Use of Scripture in Teaching at the Medieval University' in *Learning Institutionalized*, ed. J. Van Engen (Notre Dame: University of Notre Dame Press, 2000), 229– 243
Stock, B., *Augustine the Reader* (Cambridge, MA: Harvard University Press, 1996)
Sullivan, J., 'Wrestling with Managerialism' in *Commitment to Diversity*, ed. M. Eaton, J. Longmore, and A. Naylor (London: Cassell, 2000), 240–59
—, 'Skills-based Models of Leadership' in *Religion in Education 4,* ed. W. Kay, L. Francis, and K. Watson (Leominster: Gracewing, 2003), 201–32
—, 'Scholarship and Spirituality' in *Spirituality, Philosophy and Education,* ed. D. Carr and J. Haldane (London: RoutledgeFalmer, 2003), 126–40

—, 'From Formation to the Frontiers: the Dialectic of Christian Education,' *Journal of Education and Christian Belief* 7 (2003), 7–24

Sykes, S., *Power and Christian Theology* (London: Continuum, 2006)

Williams, D., *Receiving the Bible in Faith* (Washington, DC: Catholic University of America Press, 2004)

Wood, S., *Spiritual Exegesis and the Church in the Theology of Henri de Lubac* (Grand Rapids: Eerdmans, 1998)

10

The Case for Empirical Assessment of Biblical Literacy in America
Byron R. Johnson

Introduction

Decades of solid survey research confirm that religion is important in America and that Americans consistently report high levels of religious participation, commitments and practices.[1] Yet at the same time it is common to hear clergy, religious advocates, and lay leaders lament that most Americans no longer read the Bible, and that today's youth in particular have little knowledge of the Bible. It is a widely held notion that daily Scripture reading or Bible study is a dwindling feature of America's distant past. Many have suggested that this pattern of decline regarding engagement of Scripture is a well-documented fact. But does the research literature really confirm such a downward spiral regarding the reading or understanding of the Bible? Is Bible reading or study of Scripture as rare a phenomenon today as many suggest? Similarly, is Bible knowledge or literacy at an all-time low? If so, is this lack of Bible literacy a pattern observed among particular groups or is it broadly representative across vastly different demographic categories? This paper seeks to address these and related questions by reviewing the research literature and by drawing upon relevant survey data. The paper offers some preliminary conclusions about this largely neglected area of inquiry and offers a Bible literacy research agenda that may be helpful in understanding and tracking future levels of Bible knowledge among Americans.

First, let us consider empirical evidence that will help to confirm or refute what appears to be a general diminishing of Bible literacy in America. Social science provides ample support for the common sense observation that 'things are not always what they seem.' Two current examples relative to the question might be instructive as we consider the issue of Bible literacy.

---

[1] A.M. Gallup, *The Gallup Poll Cumulative Index: Public Opinion, 1935–1997* (Wilmington, DE: Scholarly Resources, 1999).

Are Christians and Non-Christians Different on Key Social Outcome Indicators?

A recent and often quoted statistic is that there are no differences today between Christians and non-Christians with regard to divorce, crime, bankruptcy, and an array of other social maladies.[2] The implication of this often quoted statistic is that Christians are largely hypocritical and clearly do not practice what they preach. As one might expect, the book making this claim received a fair amount of attention and traction in both religious and non-religious circles. But does social science research actually support the conclusion of no difference between these two groups?

An exhaustive examination of hundreds of published studies in refereed journals from diverse fields confirms a remarkable and consistent set of findings with just the opposite conclusions from the statistic presented earlier on Christians (i.e., those who are religiously committed) and non-Christians (i.e., those who do not participate in religious activities). A systematic review of 498 published studies confirms that measures of religious commitment are inversely associated with levels of hypertension, depression, suicidal ideation, crime, delinquency and drug abuse.[3] To use social science jargon, religiosity is a significant and consistent protective factor that exhibits a buffering effect, insulating people from deleterious outcomes.

In addition to an observed protective effect, in a systematic review of 171 additional published studies, we find a consistent link between higher levels of religious commitment and increasing measures of hope, meaning, purpose and even educational attainment.[4] Stated differently, higher levels of religious commitment are associated with the promotion of positive attitudes or activities – what we social scientists often refer to as pro-social behavior.

In sum, we have an impressive and mounting body of evidence documenting that religiosity is consistently associated with protecting from harmful outcomes on the one hand, while promoting salutary outcomes on the other. However, both within and outside the Christian community, many accept as fact the faulty notion that Christians are no different from non-Christians on

---

[2] R.J. Sider, *Scandal Of The Evangelical Conscience: Why Are Christians Living Just Like The Rest Of The World?* (Grand Rapids: Baker, 2005).

[3] For a systematic review of these literatures see B.R. Johnson, *Objective Hope – Assessing the Effectiveness of Faith-Based Organizations: A Review of the Literature,* Center for Research on Religion and Urban Civil Society, University of Pennsylvania, and the Manhattan Institute, Center for Civic Innovation (New York, 2002); H.G. Koenig, M.E. McCullough, and D.B. Larson, *Handbook of Religion and Health* (New York: Oxford University Press, 2001).

[4] Johnson, *Objective Hope*; Koenig et al., *Handbook.*

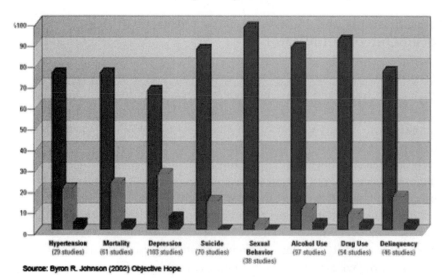

Figure 1. Research Examining the Relationship between Religion and Health Outcomes. *Eight Fields of Study (total of 498 studies reviewed).*

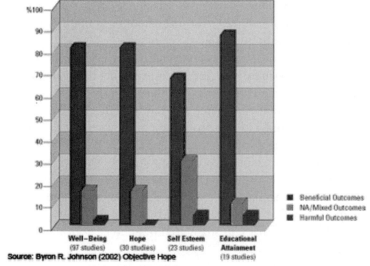

Figure 2. Research Examining the Relationship between Religion and Well-Being Outcomes. *Four Fields of Study (total of 171 studies reviewed).*

key social outcomes and indicators. The researcher who draws this faulty conclusion offers an inaccurate and, in fact, sophomoric presentation of survey data without any qualification whatsoever. Appropriate statistical analyses and controls were absent and thus the findings not only misrepresented the data, but unnecessarily misled readers.

Is America Becoming a Secular and Less Religious Society?

Another relevant example of things not always being what they appear to be is the ongoing debate regarding what is called the secularization hypothesis. Many scholars suggest that as societies develop and modernize, they become more secular and less religious since it becomes increasingly unnecessary to depend upon religion. Stated simply, religions are expected to weaken and gradually disappear as society progresses. Not surprisingly, many studies in the research literature have suggested that America, like Europe, is becoming increasingly secular and less devoutly religious. But is America – along with other countries – becoming more secular over time as various modernization theorists have posited?

It seems as if the enormous growth and vitality of religion in recent decades throughout much of the world would provide critical evidence to counter the secularization hypothesis. Interestingly, the global growth of religion is a fact that has gone largely unrecognized by many Western academics in spite of the fact that the phenomenal spread of Pentecostal and Evangelical churches in Africa and Latin America represent astounding social developments by even the crudest measures. The growth of Christianity in China and Korea are two more examples of religious growth and vitality that have been largely over-looked by scholars. Interestingly, on the rare occasion when such developments are mentioned by Western academics, it is typically in the context of discussion of the global rise of 'fundamentalism' – confirming the very bias that causes them to be amazed (or perhaps disturbed) by these movements that otherwise they neglect to study.[5]

This brings us to an important question, how can social science research help us to assess whether or not there is empirical support for the secularization hypothesis?

For decades, survey researchers have sought to answer this question by asking Americans to identify their religious affiliation as well as attendance. Respondents are typically provided a lengthy list of denominations from which to select a preference (e.g., Methodist, Episcopal, Assembly of God, etc.). As with many survey questions, respondents are given the option to indicate that they are not affiliated with any of the denominations listed, specifying 'none of the above' – what we call 'nones.' Alternatively, respondents may decide not to answer the question and simply leave the item blank before advancing to the next survey question. In instances where respondents do not fill out a response, we code them as 'missing.'

---

[5] J.W. Skillen, *The Secularization Hypothesis is Doubly Mistaken*, Public Justice Report (Washington, DC.: Center for Public Justice, 2000).

One of the most-respected surveys in existence is the General Social Survey (GSS), which regularly ask respondents about denominational affiliation and attendance. Conducted since 1972, it is a nationally representative survey that utilizes personal interviews of American households conducted by the National Opinion Research Center (NORC). Over the last several decades, approximately 15 percent of the U.S. population has indicated they have no religious affiliation. This figure is significantly higher than previous decades when approximately 10 percent of the U.S. population indicated no religious denominational affiliation. It is noteworthy that this finding in the GSS has been replicated in a number of other national surveys. The five percentage point increase in Americans who are no longer connected to congregations is clearly a very significant finding, and represents the main evidence scholars have used to support the claim that America is becoming more secular and less religious. As can be seen in Figure 3, the GSS finding of 15 percent 'nones' is essentially replicated once again in our recent Baylor Survey of Religion (BSR), where we find 16.5 percent 'nones.'

Modeled after the GSS, the BSR is a nationally representative survey of religious characteristics, orientations and attitudes of 1,721 adults in the United States.[6] A third of the survey is dedicated solely to religion items focusing on affiliation, identity, belief, experience, and commitment. Two-thirds of the survey is dedicated to topical modules which will be rotated in subsequent

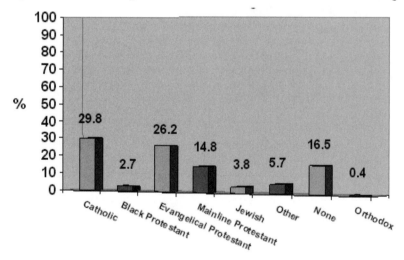

Figure 3. Religion Tradition. *(Total 1721 – Missing 556).*

---

[6] The BSR contains almost 400 questions pertaining to religious life, including measurement of religious identity, activity, belief, and experience, and a series of religion topical modules. The 2005 modules include questions concerning moral attitudes, political opinions, trust, civic engagement, religious consumerism, and New Age beliefs. We will repeat the Baylor Religion Survey every other year.

administrations. The BSR utilizes a mixed-mode sampling design and the first wave of data collection was completed in the fall of 2005, in partnership with the Gallup Organization.

As stated earlier, scholars have argued that the 5 percent increase in the 'nones' is an important empirical confirmation of increasing secularization and subsequent weakening of America's religious fabric. However, upon closer examination of the 'nones' and those cases typically coded as 'missing,' a different picture begins to emerge. In addition to asking respondents to indicate their denominational affiliation, we asked them to provide the actual name of their congregation as well as the specific address – a combination missing from other surveys. This methodological innovation allows us to systematically validate each respondent's full response. For example, although respondents may indicate 'none' or skip the question altogether, they may also write in the name or address (or both) of the congregation they attend. This additional data allows us to correctly recover denominational affiliation and to correctly identify and 'map' the locations of these congregations.

This methodological innovation allowed us to correctly classify many cases and to reduce the 'none' category from 16.5 percent to 11.1 percent. Instead of assuming that most 'missing' cases and 'nones' are either atheists or not affiliated with any religious body, as many have previously theorized, we are able to document many of these cases are, in fact, affiliated with congregations. And in the largest number of cases, they are affiliated with Evangelical churches. This 'corrective' finding is presented in Figure 4 and provides important empirical evidence that research over the last several decades has considerably overestimated the number of people who are not affiliated and underestimated the number of people who are affiliated with churches or houses of worship – especially Evangelical ones. This new finding provides important support for the notion that religious preference or affiliation in America has remained very stable and has not declined as previous research and scholars have claimed for a number of years.[7]

As a result of the corrective recovery of additional cases, we observe significant changes in the breakdowns presented from Figure 3 to Figure 4. Most prominent among these changes is the observed increase among Evangelicals from 26.2 percent to 33.5 percent. Interestingly, we witness an almost two-fold increase among Black Protestants.

---

[7] This important finding is not meant to imply that there is not decline in membership or attendance within different denominations. Many studies have confirmed that the significant growth among Evangelical and conservative denominations as well as the significant loss among mainline denominations.

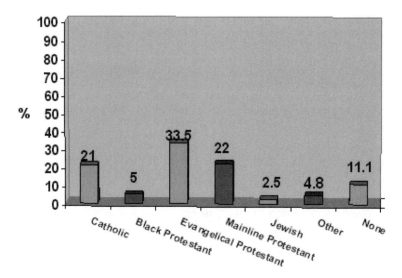

Figure 4. Religious tradition: agressive recovery of missing cases.
(Total 1721 − Missing: 42).

Data on Religion in America

For decades the Gallup Organization was about the only entity to collect data on belief in God and basic questions about religion in America. In fact, if it were not for Gallup and, in recent years, the Barna Group, there would be enormous gaps in our knowledge of national trends and patterns when it comes to indicators of faith, religion and spirituality in America. Within the academic community, C.Y. Glock and R. Stark completed in 1964 the first national survey dedicated to the topic of religion and religious practices in America. The 2005 Baylor Survey of Religion is the first nationally representative survey primarily focusing on religious beliefs and practices since the work of Glock and Stark, some four decades earlier.

It should come as no surprise, therefore, that social science has very little to offer in this important though largely neglected area of study. A preliminary review of the social science literature confirms that there are very few studies or even unpublished technical reports on the topic of Bible literacy. As one might expect, most of the work uncovered through a preliminary literature review on Bible literacy comes not from the social sciences, but from the humanities. The unfortunate reality, does not, however, preclude an empirical assessment of the available research addressing Bible literacy in America.

Is Bible Literacy Low and Declining in America?

As stated at the outset of this paper, many believe Americans no longer read the Bible. Further, it seems there is widespread belief that the retreat from Scripture engagement is backed by solid empirical evidence. But does objective research confirm the prevailing assumption of reduced levels of Scripture reading, studying, and even understanding?

In an important research paper entitled the *Bible Literacy Report*, Marie Wachlin interviewed a sample of award-winning English teachers regarding Bible literacy among American teens.[8] Wachlin found that 90 percent of high school English teachers said it was important for both college-bound and 'regular' students to be biblically literate. However, many of the teachers reported that among their students Bible illiteracy is quite common. The study also included the first extensive, nationally representative survey of the Bible and religious knowledge among American teens.[9] The survey revealed that only a minority of American teens appear to be 'Bible literate.' For example, one out of ten respondents indicated that Moses was one of the twelve Apostles. About the same percentage of teens were not able to identify what Easter commemorates. The study concludes that at least among American teens, Bible literacy is an obvious problem. Clearly, much more research in this area is needed, especially among youth and teens.

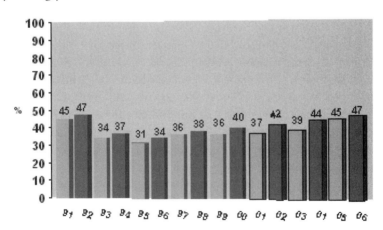

Figure 5. In the last 7 days, did you read the Bible (not including when you were at a church or synagogue)?

---

[8] M. Wachlin, *The Bible Literacy Report: What do American Teens Need to Know and What do They Know?* (Fairfax, VA: The Bible Literacy Project, 2005).

[9] Interviews of 1,002 teenagers between the ages of 13 and 18 were conducted by the Gallup Organization between May 20 and June 27, 2004.

The Barna Group may well be the only research organization to specifically ask about Bible literacy in their annual surveys. In Barna's recently completed national survey of religious behavior and beliefs,[10] they report a significant increase in religious activities on five of the seven core religious behaviors they track (Bible reading, church attendance, involvement in small groups, church volunteerism, and Sunday school attendance).[11]

Of the five religious activities to increase, the most significant increase was in Bible reading. As can be seen in Figure 5, Bible readership has been tracked by Barna since 1991. In 1995 Bible readership in America hit a low of 31 percent, and then began to slowly increase to higher levels, and finally returning to the 40 percent mark in 2000. After several years of no change, increases began again in 2004, continuing through to the present, when 47 percent of adults report reading the Bible during a typical week, other than when they are at church. According to the Barna tracking data, this is the highest readership level achieved since the 1980s. Over a sixteen-year period, the Barna tracking data provide very clear evidence that would seem to counter the claims that Bible literacy is both declining and at all-time lows. Interestingly, the pattern observed for Bible literacy over the sixteen-year tracking period looks very similar to that reported by Barna for church attendance (see Figure 6).

According to Barna, the recent growth in Bible reading has been most influenced by conservative Christians (up 17 percentage points from 2001), African Americans (an increase of 14 points), residents of the South (13 point increase), and people linked to non-Christian faith groups (15 point increase). The older a person is, the more like to read the Bible on a regular basis. The same pattern holds for women, African Americans, conservatives, and people residing in the South. Protestants are twice as likely as Catholics to read the Bible on a weekly basis (62 percent vs. 29 percent), and among Evangelicals the Bible is read regularly by 96 percent of respondents. In sum, the Barna tracking data are quite clear that Bible reading is not low or in decline. This clearly raises another point that we will revisit later in this paper, namely, what should be the criteria by which biblical literacy is determined?

Although much less reliable, a recent internet survey (weighted to be nationally representative) has also examined Bible literacy in America and provides unique insights about the characteristics of readers and non-readers.[12]

---

[10] George Barna, *The State of the Church: 2006. A Report from George Barna* (Ventura, CA: The Barna Group, 2006).

[11] The only two religious behaviors which did not reflect significant change were prayer and evangelism.

[12] Data were collected by Yankelovich MONITOR via the Internet-based FGI SmartPanel during the month of January 2005, with a sample 1,739 participants age 18 or older. The Yankelovich MONITOR is the longest continuously running study of attitudes and values in America.

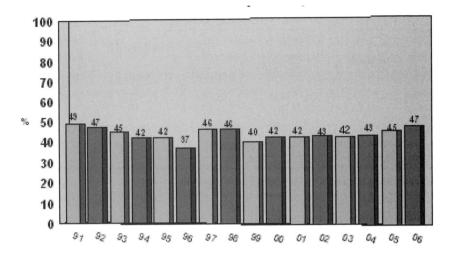

Figure 6. In the last 7 days, did you attend a church service (not including a special event such as a wedding or funeral)?

Analysis of the survey data reveals the factors associated with Bible reading among three distinct groups: (1) Frequent Bible Readers – those who report reading the Bible once a week or more often (n=481 or 28 percent); (2) Infrequent Bible Readers – those who report reading the Bible less often than once a week (n=684 or 39 percent), and (3) Non-Readers – those say 'never' when asked how often they read the Bible (n=574 or 33 percent).

Looking at specific Bible-related questions, Frequent Readers are significantly more likely to own a Bible than either Infrequent Readers or Non-Readers (99 percent, 87 percent, and 40 percent respectively). As might be expected, Table 1 reveals that Frequent Readers and Infrequent Readers are significantly more likely than Non-Readers to indicate that they spend too little time reading the Bible (73 percent and 69 percent vs. 38 percent).

Similarly, Frequent Readers and Infrequent Readers are significantly more likely than Non-Readers to agree with the statement 'the Bible contains insights and wisdom that can help me meet and overcome the challenges I am currently facing in my life.' Even though Non-Readers are significantly less likely to agree with this statement, it is striking that almost half (47%) agree that the Bible contains insights and wisdom that can help them. Finally, Infrequent Readers are more likely (46 percent) to report that they forget to read the Bible than either Frequent Readers (26 percent) or Non-Readers (16 percent). Finally, and perhaps most telling, Frequent Readers of the Bible are significantly more likely than Infrequent Readers or Non-Readers to report higher levels of spirituality and participation in religious activities. The link between

Table 1				
Question	**Bible Readership**			
	Total	**Frequent**	**Infrequent**	**Non-Readers**
I personally own a Bible	75%	99%	87%	40%
I spend too little time reading the Bible	20%	26%	21%	14%
The Bible contains insights and wisdom that can help me meet and overcome the challenges I am currently facing in my life.	73%	87%	85%	47%
I don't have enough time to read the Bible	20%	26%	21%	14%
I forget to read the Bible	30%	26%	46%	16%

religious commitments and Bible literacy is clearly an area ripe with research possibilities.

The recently conducted Baylor Survey of Religion (BSR) also asks of respondents 'how often they read the Bible, Koran, Torah, or other sacred book.' As can be seen in Figure 7, 28.4 percent read the Bible or a sacred text at least weekly. Approximately 6 percent read a sacred text 2 to 3 times a month. About 41.5 percent read Scripture a few times a year, and 24 percent indicate they never read any of these sacred books. It is noteworthy that Barna's tracking of Bible reading reports significantly higher levels of readership than that found in the Baylor Survey of Religion. This difference probably owes to the fact that the BSR asks respondents how often the Bible is read outside of religious services.

In order to obtain a more accurate picture of what we call 'religious consumption,' we asked respondents to indicate if they had read any of the books listed in Figure 8. As can be seen, almost 32 percent of the population indicated they had read *The Da Vinci Code*, followed by 20.5 percent indicating they had

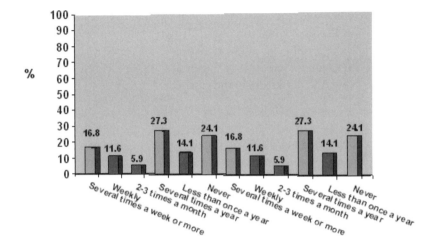

Figure 7. Outside of attending religious services, about how often do you read the
Bible, Koran, Torah, or other sacred book?

read *The Purpose-Driven Life*. James Dobson and the *Left Behind* Series were read
by 19.1 percent and 17.7 percent respectively.

Frequent Bible readers are far less likely than the average person to have
read *The Da Vinci Code*. About a third of those who never read the Bible (31.7
percent) and a third of those who read it infrequently (33.3 percent) have read
The Da Vinci Code. But fewer than 20 percent of those who read the Bible on a
weekly basis (19.4 percent) have read the book. The bestseller is very popular
with people who have also read *The Celestine Prophecy*. Nearly 68 percent

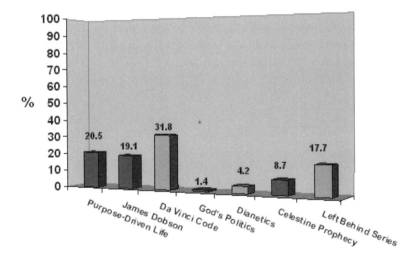

Figure 8. Have you read any of the following books?

(67.8) of those who have read *The Celestine Prophecy* have also read *The Da Vinci Code*. There was also substantial interest in Brown's book amongst those who have researched the prophecies of Nostradamus (38.6 percent) and those who expressed an interested in Scientology/Dianetics (48.9 percent). Half of those who visited a New Age bookstore in the past year (50.7 percent) have read *The Da Vinci Code*.

Conclusions

What can we conclude from this preliminary empirical assessment of bibical literacy in America? First, although biblical literacy is an important field of inquiry, it remains grossly understudied, especially in the social sciences community. Second, the best available research to date on Bible reading indicates that rates of reading are quite stable, and not in decline as many have suggested. Third, there is not yet sufficient evidence to document the claim that biblical literacy is at historic low levels as many have suggested. Fourth, we are in need of more quantitative as well as qualitative assessment of actual Bible reading habits in America, as well as the retention of biblical content by those who self-identify as Bible readers. Research of this kind will allow us more accurately to track Bible literacy over time. In short, this paper provides a preliminary review of the state of the social science literature on biblical literacy and offers initial insights that may be helpful in unraveling findings regarding Bible reading or the engagement of Scripture. It is obviously important to continue to search for additional research and relevant survey work that will help us better to evaluate biblical literacy. Only as research accumulates and a long-overdue body of literature matures, will we be able to speak more accurately about the state of Bible literacy in America as well as the implications of biblical literacy on an array of other important social factors.

11

'As if God Were Dead'

American Literature and the Question of Scripture

Roger Lundin

From the woods of northern Maine during the harsh winter of 1831–32, Mary Moody Emerson shot off a fiery letter to her nephew, Ralph Waldo Emerson, whose lukewarm relationship to the Christian faith had begun to rile his relatives and undermine his ministerial career.[1] She had taken a special interest in the son of her deceased brother and looked to him as the 'one minister remaining to be enrolled with the Mathers & Sewells' as a faithful minister of the gospel and promoter of the New England Way.[2]

Mary's nephew, however, was growing restive in the ministerial harness. Emerson had written to his aunt on Christmas day 1831, to explain his disenchantment with the standard form of Christian belief. It was the idea of God as a transcendent power that rankled him: 'What from the woods, the hills, & the enveloping heaven? What from the interior Creation, if what is within be not the Creator. How many changes men ring on these two words in & out.'[3] The death of his wife Ellen the previous February had triggered in Waldo a flood of spiritual self-confidence rather than feelings of despondency, and by the year's close, he confided to his family that he was thinking of leaving the ministry.

This news and the philosophical rationale Waldo sent along with it prompted Aunt Mary's heated response. 'And is it possible,' she began, 'that one nurtured by the happiest institutions whose rich seeds have been bedewed

---

[1] In dealing with the biographical details of Ralph Waldo Emerson's life, I will refer to him by the name his family used in conversation and correspondence: Waldo.
[2] M.M. Emerson, *Selected Letters*, 314.
[3] R.W. Emerson, *Letters*, 7:200.

by them – should be parrisidical!' Why, she demanded to know, was Waldo suddenly 'at war with that angelic office?' On what grounds could he possibly speak of 'a great truth whose athority you would feel is its own'? She claimed that in his Christmas letter he had asked, 'whether the heart were not the Creator' and to this implicit assertion, Aunt Mary could only offer a blistering critique: 'Now if the withering Lucifer doctrine of pantheism be true, what moral truth can you preach or by what athority should you feel it? Without a personal God you are on an ocean mast unrigged for any port or object.'[4]

After this outburst, long taken in Emerson criticism to be a sign of Mary's 'reactionary' theology,[5] there follows an absorbing meditation by the aunt on the vocation the nephew is about to renounce. She writes of her disappointment over the prospect of losing in her old age the pastoral correspondence of Waldo, which was meant 'to brighten & renew my wrinkled mind!' And what she terms her most 'childish antisapation' had involved envisioning the aged Waldo as 'an old venerable pastor in the most delightfull spot.' As his own life drew to a close, her nephew would be able to tell his 'grand children' that only miles from that spot 'reposed the ashes of pious ancestors – who preached the gospel,' including Waldo's own father, her brother. After the close of 'his last aspirations after the sovereign Good,' he would join that great cloud of witnesses – the Mathers and Sewells and others – who had stood in Boston's pulpits and hallowed this new world ground.[6]

As much as he respected the incandescent intellect and steely will of his aunt, Waldo spurned her advice. Within the coming year, he was to make his break with the church official by preaching the famous sermon that explained his refusal to administer the Lord's Supper. Freed from his pastoral duties and supported by a modest legacy from Ellen's estate, Waldo then embarked on a restorative trip to Europe in early 1833. He had left the ministry and the Christian faith behind him, and when he returned to Boston near the close of that year, he was about to become the herald of a new religion and the purveyor of a fresh revelation.

In taking this step away from historic Christianity, Emerson set the literature of the United States on the trail down which it continues to ramble almost two hundred years hence. To be certain, if it had not been Emerson, someone else would likely have pointed the way and set American literature on the same journey.

Yet Emerson remains, and his influence cannot be gainsaid. His decision to leave the church and become a public intellectual has come to be seen as the defining moment in the establishment of a distinct American literary tradition.

---

[4] M.M. Emerson, *Selected Letters,* 313–14.
[5] Cole, *Mary Moody Emerson,* 214–16.
[6] M.M. Emerson, *Selected Letters,* 314.

Emerson remains essential for understanding the subsequent fate of the Bible in American literature and its role in the academic study of that literature. Before him, the meaning of the Bible may have been contested in the literature of the United States, but its authority would rarely, if ever, have been denied; after Emerson, that authority could not be taken for granted.

What did remain for the literature of America was the undeniable symbolic resonance and associative richness of the Bible's stories, tropes and teachings. In several major writers from the nineteenth century, we can see the significant lines along which the use of the Bible in American literature and criticism would continue to develop. In the essays of Emerson and the work of Henry David Thoreau, we see the Scriptures appropriated to lend lustre and explanatory power to the primary drama of the human spirit and its fitful relationship to the natural world; in the fiction of Herman Melville, we find the Bible employed as an ironizing sourcebook for psychological understanding and narrative association; in the poetry of Emily Dickinson, the Scriptures serve as a storehouse of dramatically charged symbols and stories, waiting to be parodied or deployed in the interests of the needy spirit.

'As if God Were Dead': Emerson and Scriptural Authority

When she demanded an explanation for Waldo's belief in 'a great truth whose authority you would feel is its own,' Aunt Mary knew she was striking at the most sensitive spot in her nephew's spirit. The question of authority, writes Barbara Packer, made Emerson 'acutely uncomfortable,' and never more so than in the period leading up to his 1832 departure from the ministry of the Christian church and the faith it professed.[7]

As he prepared to leave the ministry, Emerson was acting upon doubts about theological authority that had been growing for years. Those doubts and uncertainties were, in part, rooted in personal sources involving a dark, tangled struggle with shame and the nature of parental authority. Yet they can also be traced to more conventional intellectual origins in the revolutionary philosophical ideas that began to germinate in Germany at the end of the eighteenth century and were being wafted across the Atlantic by the likes of Samuel Taylor Coleridge early in the nineteenth.

For Emerson, a direct link to continental ideas was established when his brother William travelled to Göttingen to study theology in 1824. William was following in the footsteps of other Harvard students who were to acquire

---

[7] Packer, 'Origin and Authority,' 67.

significant influence in the intellectual history of nineteenth-century America, including George Ticknor, Edward Everett and George Bancroft. They flocked to Göttingen to study with J.G. Eichhorn, J.D. Michaelis and other pioneers of the historical-critical study of the Bible.[8] With this method, the German scholars were seeking to subject the Scriptures to the same historical and literary forms of analysis applied to any other texts from the ancient world.

But there was a difference here, of course, for these Scriptures were the keystone in the arch that supported the Protestant cultural enterprise of modernity, just as they were for millions of believers an intimate final authority for faith and morals. With their questioning of the authenticity of the Bible, the source critics of the early nineteenth century were chipping away at the arch and undermining spiritual authority.

The new critical methods left William Emerson uncertain about the prospects of a ministerial career and dispirited about the possibilities of genuine Christian belief. By the fall of 1824, he had become so disenchanted with the consequences of his studies that he made a pilgrimage to Weimar to meet with Goethe, the great poet and sage. During his interview, William confessed his personal doubts and professional uncertainties. If he no longer believed in the truthfulness of the Bible, he asked Goethe, how could he return to America and preach its message to an unwitting congregation?

These doubts may have agonized William, but Goethe dispatched them with casual serenity. Many years later, William's niece Ellen (Waldo's daughter) said 'Goethe unhesitatingly told him that he could preach to the people what they wanted; his personal belief was no business of theirs; he could be a good preacher and a good pastor and no one need ever know what he himself had for his own private views.'[9]

Shortly after this meeting, William returned to the United States. He went to see his brother Waldo and immediately reported both his conversation with Goethe and the decision he had reached based on that advice. On the voyage home, there had been a great storm, during which William had been terrified by the thought 'that he could not go to the bottom in peace with the intention in his heart of following the advice that Goethe had given him.' He renounced the ministry and immediately took up the study of the law. 'Your Uncle William never seemed to me so great' as he did when he made that decision, Waldo told his daughter.[10]

That decision in 1825 may have solved William's problem of conscience, but it did nothing to assist his brother with the struggles he was already

---

[8] For the German background to nineteenth-century American debates over biblical authority, see Hurth, 'Sowing the Seeds,' and Brown, *Rise of Biblical Criticism*.

[9] As quoted in Barish, *Emerson: Roots,* 161.

[10] As quoted in Barish, *Emerson: Roots,* 161.

undergoing as he anticipated a life in the church. For the better part of the decade stretching between William's return and the beginning of his own post-ecclesiastical career as an essayist and lecturer, Emerson was to worry over the arguments of source criticism. To ground the spiritual life he wished to pursue, he sought sources of authority that could not be subject to the withering critiques of rationalist philosophy and textual study.

In that quest, the Unitarians of Harvard – Andrews Norton and the like – seemed more harmful than helpful. They were willing to concede too much to the purveyors of doubt and scepticism. Giving up on miracles here, forsaking historical accuracy there, the Unitarians had abandoned so much of the biblical landscape that little remained beyond a narrow stretch of shifting spiritual sands.

Emerson was looking instead for a rock upon which to build a new religion whose authority would withstand the storms of doubt and the winds of intellectual change. Particularly during his years as minister of Boston's Second Church, he worked through the issues raised by the higher criticism in the private domain of his journal and through the public forum of the pulpit. With a view of inspiration fashioned out of bits of the historical-critical approach and pieces from the works of Coleridge and the German Idealists, he developed a theory of the divine immediacy of the original utterance: everything that came after it, including the recording of that utterance in writing and its scribal preservation and textual transmission through time, was attenuated and imprisoning.

In 1830, a full two years before he left the ministry, Emerson wrote in his journal of his conviction that 'it is when a man does not listen to himself but to others, that he is depraved & misled.' The great figures of history, 'the teachers of the race, moralists, Socrates, Bacon, Newton' and the like, refused to 'take their opinions on trust, but explored themselves and that is the way ethics and religion were got out.'[11] The authority of the Scriptures, Emerson was coming to believe, did not support us in our quest for truth but merely put us off the trail of its true source:

> Internal evidence outweighs all other to the inner man. If the whole history of the New Testament had perished & its teachings remained – the spirituality of Paul, the grave, considerate, unerring advice of James would take the same rank with me that now they do. I should say as now I say this certainly is the greatest height to which the religious principle of human nature has ever been carried.[12]

In the coming year, the journal entries became even more heated in their denunciations of the idea of the authority of the Bible as traditionally

---

[11] R.W. Emerson, *Journals*, 3:199.
[12] R.W. Emerson, *Journals*, 3:214.

understood. 'Suicidal is this distrust of reason; this fear to think; this doctrine that 'tis pious to believe on others' words, impious to trust entirely to yourself,' he complained in late July of 1831. 'To think is to receive,' he wrote with evident disgust, and such a view of spiritual authority misses the fact that we can instead 'receive truth immediately from God without any medium. That is living faith. To take on trust certain facts is a dead faith – inoperative.' We hardly need the Bible to tell us anything significant about God, or ourselves for that matter, because 'it is by yourself without ambassador that God speaks to you. You are as one who has a private door that leads him to the King's chamber.'[13]

Since he had concluded that the members of his congregation could hear from God 'without ambassador' and enter his chamber freely when and how they wished, Emerson realized he had not only undermined the authority of the Scriptures, but he had also reasoned himself out of a job. In mid-1832, he wrote that he had come to believe 'that in order to be a good minister it was necessary to leave the ministry. The profession is antiquated,' and we who practice it 'worship in the dead forms of our forefathers. Were not a Socratic paganism better than an effete superannuated Christianity.'[14]

Shortly after he wrote this entry in his journal, Emerson notified his congregation that because of his views of the Bible, religious authority, and the nature of tradition, he could no longer administer the Lord's Supper in good conscience. He and a committee failed to reach a compromise on the matter, and on September 9, 1832, he preached his farewell sermon on the subject of the sacrament.

The sermon is a curious mix of elements. Among other things, it includes a relativizing discussion of the history of different theories and practices concerning observance of the Lord's Supper; Emerson examines at length the question of its authority and reasons on the evidence of the gospels that Jesus did not intend it to be a perpetual rite; and he closes with an argument of 'expediency,' and concludes that it is vain and fruitless for the church to require adherence to a 'certain form' while denying the deeper duties of the virtuous life. The church's institutions, Emerson tells his parishioners at the close of her sermon, 'should be as flexible as the wants of men. That form out of which the life and suitableness have departed, should be as worthless in its eyes as the dead leaves that are falling around us.' With a flourish of what Barbara Packer calls 'cosmic insouciance,' Emerson announces his final 'argument' against the sacrament: 'That is the end of my opposition, that I am not interested in it.'[15]

---

[13] R.W. Emerson, *Journals*, 3:279.

[14] R.W. Emerson, *Journals*, 4:27.

[15] R.W. Emerson, *Essays*, 1139, 1140.

Of this final sarcastic sally, Packer notes that the higher criticism had assisted many who sought 'to locate authority within the self rather than outside it, but the man who dismisses a sacrament because it bores him could probably have reached his conclusions without scholarly help.'[16] But in another sense, the footnotes and the fancy historical reasoning did serve a purpose. They covered an argument driven by the power of preference and poetic imagining with a patina of philosophical rigor and historical respectability.

From that point on in his career, Emerson rarely felt the need to offer elaborate scholarly support for his arguments, as he promoted a breathtaking vision of the future of poetry and piety in a post-Christian America.[17] Quickly establishing himself as a leader of this cultural project, Emerson wrote and delivered essays on a dazzling array of topics, almost all of which he presented by way of a single word title and theme, such as 'Self-Reliance,' 'Experience,' 'Compensation,' and 'The Poet.'

In his essays, Emerson drew upon the Bible's symbolic and narrative power, even as he repeatedly denied its authoritative status and revelatory claims. Both attitudes towards the Scriptures are on full display in one of his earliest and most influential essays, 'The Divinity School Address,' which was delivered at Harvard in the summer of 1838. With its caustic dismissal of the Unitarian efforts to cling to some remnant of scriptural authority and historical grounding for the faith, the address got Emerson into considerable trouble and led to his alienation from Harvard for several decades.

At the heart of the address lies Emerson's attack upon the 'defect of historical Christianity.' It has fallen into the error that corrupts all efforts to 'communicate religion' and pass a vital faith on to a coming generation. Modern Christianity, Emerson complains, preaches 'not the doctrine of the soul, but an exaggeration of the personal, the positive, the ritual. It has dwelt, it dwells, with noxious exaggeration about the *person* of Jesus. The soul knows no persons.' To the church's 'vulgar' portrait of a lordly Jesus Christ revealed through the Scriptures, Emerson opposes a simple theology with a single source: 'Obey thyself. That which shows God in me, fortifies me. That which shows God out of me, makes me a wart and a wen.'[18]

There is 'a second defect of the traditionary' interpretation of the Bible, Emerson argues. When the Scriptures are treated as an authoritative source, they become nothing more than debris blocking the flow of that 'Moral Nature' which

---

[16] Packer, 'Origin and Authority,' 83.
[17] In the case of Emerson and his cohort, 'post-Christian' did not mean 'post-Protestant.' For an examination of Emerson's role in the religious and philosophical transformation of late nineteenth-century American culture, see my *From Nature,* 41–70.
[18] R.W. Emerson, *Essays,* 80–81.

is the one true 'fountain of the established teaching in society.' In revering the rubble rather than drinking from the living waters, 'men have come to speak of the revelation as somewhat long ago given and done, as if God were dead.' The dogmas that the Christian church has drawn from the Scriptures over the centuries do nothing but 'mark the height to which the waters once rose.'[19]

As his address drew to what many of his hearers must have considered a startling close, Emerson exhorted the prospective pastors to reclaim 'the true Christianity, – a faith like Christ's in the infinitude of man.' They were to be 'newborn bard(s) of the Holy Ghost,' casting all conformity aside and acquainting 'men at first hand with Deity.' Warning against all efforts to turn the inspired, revelatory moment into the dead tradition of a 'Cultus with new rites and forms,' Emerson envisions the pulpits of New England stocked with poetic preachers whose quivering contact with an unmediated God leads them each week, each day, each moment to 'cheer the waiting, fainting hearts of men with new hope and new revelation.'[20]

It did not take long for Emerson's vision to establish in the literature of the United States a new and powerful tradition of distilling out of the Bible all the brackish elements of its particular claims and metaphysical judgments, so that only its poetic and structural essence remained. In Emerson's own lifetime, such exceptional writers as Henry David Thoreau and Walt Whitman seized upon the Emersonian inspiration, making use of the Bible's poetic resources and trading on the lingering authority the Scriptures still possessed in the life of the culture.

For Thoreau, in a work such as *Walden,* this entailed making frequent ironic use of scriptural images and confessional phrases. The goal for Thoreau was to draw upon the residual authority of the Bible in the verbal and moral traditions of the English-speaking world, even while resisting and subverting the theological vision that had once brilliantly informed and illuminated that verbal world. In Whitman's poetry, the use of the scriptural materials tended more to the grand and oracular than ironic, but he too followed Emerson's lead in refusing to grant authority to anything more than the evocative power of biblical language. He drew freely upon the riches of the Old Testament prophetic tradition and wisdom literature, and he never seemed to blush when, as frequently proved to be the case, he cloaked himself in the mantle of the suffering servant, the crucified and risen Christ. The role was there in the pages of the biblical prompt book, waiting to be enacted, and Whitman considered himself equal to the part.

Over the quarter century that stretched between the publication of Emerson's *Nature* (1836) and the start of the Civil War (1861), the scriptural

---

[19] R.W. Emerson, *Essays,* 82–83, 85.
[20] R.W. Emerson, *Essays,* 88, 89, 91.

borrowing in the Emersonian line was frequently earnest and uninflected by the allusive irony that would mark later usage. In particular, the fight against slavery created for pious evangelicals and post-Christian Protestants alike a common meeting ground. Here the language of the Old Testament, the Gospels, and the Book of Revelation could be deployed with moral vigor in a crusade against an evil practice. With the crucial exception of the African-American experience, however, neither the fervor nor the earnest use of the scriptural tradition could be sustained in the mainstream literature of the postbellum era and beyond.[21]

In the twentieth-century history of American literature, this tradition of biblical usage is evidenced both in the use of biblical allusion in poetry – in T.S. Eliot's *The Waste Land* and many of Robert Frost's lyric poems – and in the titles of novels – from *The Sun Also Rises* to *The Grapes of Wrath.* The emphasis is on the residual associative power of the biblical tropes. They are employed to lend seriousness to their subjects by providing a sense of symbolic extension and depth to an impoverished modernity.

In the academic study of literature in America, this set of practices developed into a loosely affiliated school of theory to which Frank Lentricchia has given the name, 'conservative fictionalism.' Lentricchia traces its origins to a domesticated American version of Friedrich Nietzsche's thought and to the poetry of Wallace Stevens.[22] Frank Kermode gave expression to its relevance for fiction in his 1967 study, *The Sense of an Ending,* and the entire career of Northrop Frye may be seen as an effort to construct a comprehensive literary system out of the allusive and associative instinct.

Near the end of his career, Frye wrote *The Great Code,* which dealt with the subject of the Bible and literature, but throughout his work, he focused on the symbolic mysteries of the Christian faith, in whose substance he no longer appeared to believe. Consider, for example, the opening chapter of his 1978 volume, *The Secular Scripture: A Study of the Structure of Romance.* In mapping out his theory of fiction as the surrogate scripture of our time, Frye is careful to distinguish between the products of the imagination and the objects of belief. 'Imaginative structures as such are independent of belief,' he asserts, and as far as the structure is concerned, it does not matter whether the implied beliefs are 'real, pretended, or denounced as demonic.'[23]

After all, new mythologies simply devour or absorb existing ones, and it is immaterial to the artist whether any of them is true. With the coming of

---

[21] For the intersection of Christian belief, the African-American experience, and the literature of the United States, see Stauffer, *Black Hearts,* and Bassard, *Spiritual Interrogations.*

[22] Lentricchia, *After the New Criticism,* 28–44.

[23] Frye, *Secular Scripture,* 13.

Christianity, 'classical mythology became fabulous, a branch of secular literature,' just as 'biblical mythology, as such, is rapidly becoming fabulous now.'
To Frye, it is obvious what needs to be done, in light of the collapse of 'biblical
mythology.' We must set about trying to 'look at secular stories as a whole . . .
as forming a single integrated vision of the world, parallel to the Christian and
biblical vision.'[24]

Whereas Emerson and Thoreau had believed in the human spirit's capacity
to discover a truth the biblical record had failed to transmit, Frye can only
vouch for the force of desire:

> There is a line of Pope's which exists in two versions: 'A mighty maze of walks with-
> out a plan,' and 'A mighty maze, but not without a plan.' The first version recognizes
> the human situation; the second refers to the constructs of religion, art, and science
> that man throws up because he finds the recognition intolerable.[25]

'The Secret of Our Paternity': Scripture in the School of Melville

In the end, as the advocate of a new religion that called upon its adherents to
generate the very revelation by which their lives were to be guided and their
destinies decided, Emerson was to have many admirers but few followers. One
of the considerable number who fell into the 'admiring' camp was Herman
Melville, whose first exposure to Emerson came when he heard him lecture in
Boston in 1849, only two years before the publication of *Moby Dick*. Although
Melville would differ profoundly with Emerson on key matters of theological
anthropology, his initial impression of the man from Concord was favorable.

'Now, there is a something about every man elevated above mediocrity,
which is, for the most part, instinctuly perceptible,' he wrote to a friend. 'This I
see in Mr. Emerson.' Let us call this great writer 'a fool,' Melville said, 'then had
I rather be a fool than a wise man. – I love all men who *dive*.' For near the surface any fish can swim,

> but it takes a great whale to go down stairs five miles or more; & if he don't attain the
> bottom, why, all the lead in Galena can't fashion the plumet that will. I'm not talking
> of Mr Emerson now – but of the whole corps of thought-divers, that have been
> diving & coming up again with bloodshot eyes since the world began.[26]

To the casual reader, it might appear that Melville is endorsing the Emersonian
system, replete with its call for a 'new revelation' and its celebration of a 'faith

---

[24] Frye, *Secular Scripture*, 14, 15.
[25] Frye, *Secular Scripture*, 30–31.
[26] Melville, as quoted in Brodhead, *Hawthorne*, 120.

like Christ's in the infinitude of man.' Yet in point of fact, Melville found much to disagree with in Emerson and admired him more for the brio of his manner than the substance of his thought.

For a way of looking at human nature and the human condition that would be amenable to his own post-Christian Calvinist yearnings, Melville turned to another key writer of his day, Nathaniel Hawthorne. At a picnic in western Massachusetts in the summer of 1850, these two struck up a brief friendship that would prove to be one of the most important in the history of American literature.

In the fiction of Hawthorne, who was fifteen years his senior, Melville found the traces of a genuine thought diver, and in this case, he was in sympathy with the thought as well as the style. Only weeks before their meeting, he had written a glowing anonymous review of Hawthorne's collection of short stories, *Mosses from an Old Manse*. Melville detected in the fiction 'a touch of Puritanic gloom,' and although he could not trace it to its ultimate source, he was confident 'that this great power of blackness in him [Hawthorne] derives it force from its appeals to that Calvinistic sense of Innate Depravity and Original Sin from whose visitations … no deeply thinking mind is always and wholly free.' For no matter what such sublime optimists as Emerson might believe, 'in certain moods, no man can weigh this world, without throwing in something, somehow like Original Sin, to strike the uneven balance.'[27]

At the time that he wrote this, Melville was in the throes of a sudden intellectual and artistic transformation that was to turn him from an author of modestly successful adventure tales into a daring allegorist of (eventual) international renown. Interestingly, the change that swept over him appears to have had less to do with circumstances in his personal life or station than with the program of reading he was undertaking at the time. Hawthorne was important here and Shakespeare preeminently so. Melville had begun reading Shakespeare in 1848–49, and his enthusiasm for the Stratford dramatist knew no bounds. He wrote to Evert Duyckinck:

> Dolt & ass that I am I have lived more than 29 years, & until a few days ago, never made close acquaintance with the divine William. Ah, he's full of sermons-on-the-mount, and gentle, aye, almost as Jesus. I take such men to be inspired. I fancy that this [moment] Shakespeare in heaven ranks with Gabriel Raphael and Michael. And if another Messiah ever comes twill be in Shakespeare's person.[28]

In commenting upon this breathless praise of the Christ-like Shakespeare, Nathalia Wright shrewdly notes that what attracted Melville most powerfully

---

[27] Melville, *Uncollected Prose* in *Pierre*, 1159.
[28] Melville, as quoted in Wright, *Melville's Use*, 3.

to the Bible and the bard was that the 'thought of both was couched in the early seventeenth-century idiom, the metaphysical strain of which is echoed in his most characteristic style.'[29] Audacious in its reach yet gentle in its comforting assurances, gnarled in its complexity and elegant in its simplicity, and balanced between the monosyllabic bluntness of the Anglo-Saxon sources of the English language ('he burst his hot heart's shell upon it') and the feline elegance of its Latinate roots ('an infinity of firmest fortitude'), this language fed Melville's new and voracious artistic appetite.

Wright's judicious study of Melville's use of the Bible, written more than half a century ago, nicely captures the fate of the Scriptures during and after the age of Emerson. She notes that the Bible was for Melville 'the earliest and best known' of all verbal resources. He knew it well long before he ever read a page of Shakespeare, or of Emerson and Hawthorne, for that matter. Even more important, she says, is the fact that his devotion to the language of the King James Bible 'bound him fast' to the Christian faith, even as he undertook a 'mature repudiation' of Christian doctrine: 'Though he rejected a good deal of substance of that background, he retained many of its forms virtually intact.'[30]

There is similarity here to the use of the Scriptures by Emerson and his followers, but also considerable difference. Whereas Emerson, Thoreau, Theodore Parker and others freely used biblical imagery within their romantic narratives of self-development and social transformation, Melville sought instead to bring grandeur to the drama of modern life by exploring its analogical relationships to the Scriptures. The point, obviously, was not to make definitive theological judgments about modernity but to trade upon the dynamic resonance of the language of the Christian tradition.

In so doing, Melville was participating in what critic Kenneth Burke has described as a massive modern effort to 'borrow back' the language of the Christian tradition for use in a post-Christian cultural project. 'Whether or not there is a realm of the "supernatural,"' Burke argued in *The Rhetoric of Religion,* 'there are *words* for it.' The words for this realm necessarily have come from 'the realm of our everyday experiences,' but after they have been appropriated and employed in the service of a complex theological system of reference, 'the order can become reversed. We can borrow back the terms from the borrower, again secularizing to varying degrees the originally secular terms that had been given "supernatural" connotations.'[31]

---

[29] Wright, *Melville's Use,* 3.
[30] Wright, *Melville's Use,* 4–5.
[31] Burke, *Rhetoric,* 7. In his exposition of Karl Barth's view of the being of God, Eberhard Jüngel offers a Barthian perspective on the transactions of which Burke has written here: 'The language in which revelation should be able to come to speech must, "as it were, be commandeered" by revelation. Where such "commandeering"

In this exchange, there is a considerable transfer of what we might call *associative energy*. As they draw upon the biblical materials, modern authors – such as Melville, Robert Frost, William Faulkner, and James Baldwin – depend upon their audience's devotion to the Scriptures, or at least their familiarity with them, to lend force to their own writing.

Melville believed the center of this power was to be found in the theological anthropology of the Bible. He relied heavily on the richness of biblical stories, from Abraham and Isaac to King Ahab, from Jonah to Jesus Christ. Early in *Moby Dick*, for example, we hear in Father Mapple's sermon that 'Jonah did the Almighty's bidding. And what was that, shipmates? To preach the Truth to the face of Falsehood! That was it!' On his first appearance before his ship's crew, 'moody stricken Ahab stood before them with a crucifixion in his face; in all the nameless regal overbearing dignity of some mighty woe.' And in its final sentence, the novel has a ship named the *Rachel* ('In Rama was there a voice heard, lamentation, and weeping, and great mourning, Rachel weeping for her children, and would not be comforted, because they are not' [Mt. 2:18 KJV]), '*that in her retracing search after her missing children, only found another orphan.*'[32]

This image of the orphan is instructive, because from Melville, through Faulkner, to the contemporary fiction of Kaye Gibbons and Toni Morrison, orphans haunt the post-Emersonian appropriation of the Bible in American literature. They symbolize the state of a humanity that has been abandoned to its fate by a dying or disappearing God. As Ahab himself frames the matter in *Moby Dick*, to be human is to pass 'through infancy's unconscious spell, boyhood's thoughtless faith, adolescence' doubt (the common doom), then skepticism, then disbelief, resting at last in manhood's pondering repose of If.' Where in all of this uncertainty, 'lies the final harbor, whence we unmoor no more?' And 'where is the foundling's father hidden. Our souls are like those orphans whose unwedded mothers die in bearing them: the secret of our paternity lies in their grave, and we must there to learn it.'[33]

For Melville, the Bible offered no satisfying clues as to the secret of that paternity. The best that it could do was to confirm the abandonment and comfort the orphan. It offered solace by providing heroic and tragic frameworks that could shape the formlessness of modern experience and lend it a coherence it would not otherwise possess. Even Bartleby, the listless man who desires nothing but only 'prefers not' to do, choose, or embrace anything ('Bartleby the Scrivener' [1853]), is wrapped within the symbolic presence of Adam and

---

of the language by revelation for revelation takes place, then there is a *gain to language*. The gain consists in the fact that God comes to speech as God' (*God's Being*, 23).

[32] Melville, *Moby-Dick*, 53, 109, 427.

[33] Melville, *Moby-Dick*, 373.

the promise of Christ; when the narrator of 'Bartleby' discovers the scrivener's lifeless body slumped against a prison wall, he says the hopeless clerk sleeps like Job 'with kings and counselors.'

In like manner, in Melville's final completed work, *Billy Budd,* the scriptural associations provide the resonant context for a tragic story of innocence, evil, and earthly power. The allegory in this story is strong, with Billy as the Adam/Isaac who becomes Christ, with John Claggart as the monomaniacal Satan, and with Captain Vere as a loving Abraham who becomes a forbidding God the Father. Yet as important as these associations may be, they belong to a romance that may satisfy the imagination's hunger for significance but has no grounding in reality. At the opening of *Billy Budd,* Melville terms his narrative 'an inside story,' and he counts on the fact that no discerning reader will take the scriptural analogies as anything more than the flights of fancy and longing that they are.

The one biblical doctrine for which Melville (à la Reinhold Niebuhr) believed there was something akin to empirical evidence was that of original sin. In attempting to account for the unmitigated hatred that Claggart has for Billy, the narrator of the story cannot find any satisfying explanation other than innate depravity. In Claggart, there was the 'mania of an evil nature, not engendered by vicious training or corrupting books or licentious living, but born with him and innate, in short "a depravity according to nature."'[34]

At one point in *Billy Budd,* Melville offers an ironic apology for such recourse to scriptural evidence and language:

Dark sayings are these, some will say. But why? Is it because they somewhat savor of Holy Writ in its phrase 'mystery of iniquity?' If they do, such savor was far enough from being intended, for little will it commend these pages to many a reader of today.[35]

Elsewhere in the manuscript, Melville slips in similar arch self-admonitions about using language 'tinctured with the biblical element' in a story written for an American audience at the end of the nineteenth century.

As he skewered a culture that liked to call itself 'Christian' despite its aversion to central elements of the biblical faith, Melville had greater prescience than did many self-professed Christians in the America of his day. In the final pages of *America's God,* Mark Noll wonders openly whether Emily Dickinson, Abraham Lincoln and Melville 'may have been pushed by the successes of "American Christianity" into post-Protestant, even post-Christian, theism.' In the last decades of his life, Melville took particular exception to those who

---

[34] Melville, *Billy Budd,* in *Short Novels,* 128.
[35] Melville, *Billy Budd,* in *Short Novels,* 128.

equated 'America's moral government of God with Christianity itself.' In reaction to them, to quote Noll, he, Dickinson, and others 'retained profundity at the expense of Christianity,' while at the same time, the postbellum commitment to Christian civilization began to 'trivialize the Christian theology that had brought it into existence.'[36]

Even as the Christianizers were trivializing the very theology upon which their spiritual lives depended, the secularizing academics were sealing off the wellsprings of the faith. By the late 1850s, writes Andrew Delbanco, Melville had concluded 'that the Bible was a collection of improbable fictions, and he cursed the secular scholars who had lately exposed it as an unreliable book compiled over time by fallible men rather than written by God.'[37]

Such conclusions about the fiction of the Scriptures dovetailed painfully for Melville with his fear that nature also had been silenced as a voice of God. Delbanco notes that Melville was writing *Billy Budd* 'at just the time when, in William James's phrase, the last vestiges of "tender-minded" faith in "the great universe of God" were fading away.' Not long after Melville died, James was to write of the curious fact that 'we carve out groups of stars in the heavens, and call them constellations.' The stars, 'if they knew what we were doing' might be 'surprised at the partners we had given them.' Yet, writes Delbanco, 'the stars know nothing. All knowing is the work of man. And so, for Melville, as for Vere, our fate as human beings is to live by norms that have no basis in divine truth, but that have functional truth for the conduct of life.'[38]

In *Billy Budd,* these functional truths require the reader to accept that in the welter of biblical allusions, there is no divine order to be found at work. Billy's death may be a Christ-like act of sacrifice, but 'Vere is no Pilate,' and Claggart – evil as he is – is just a man, a grubbing, grasping nineteenth-century man. More than anyone else, Vere resembles 'Abraham performing the sacrifice of Isaac.' According to Delbanco, the captain is 'torn to the depths of his soul' by the call of his duty and the demands of his fatherly love for Billy – 'except that in Melville's reprise of the father-and-son story from Genesis, there is no intervention by a merciful God. There is no God at all.'[39]

Melville was still touching up the manuscript of *Billy Budd* when he died in 1891, and it was to be more than three decades before his work finally came into print. Its initial publication in 1924 coincided with a revival of interest in Melville that has continued unabated to this day. Having died as an obscure and failed author, Melville's reputation was restored in good measure by the sobering realities of twentieth-century history and culture.

---

[36] Noll, *America's God,* 438.
[37] Delbanco, *Melville,* 257.
[38] Delbanco, *Melville,* 311.
[39] Delbanco, *Melville,* 314.

In the aftermath of World War I, talk of a 'mystery of iniquity' no longer seemed cranky or quaint. Indeed, as Reinhold Niebuhr brilliantly proved, in the middle decades of the twentieth century, one could parlay an intellectual passion for the doctrine of original sin into a highly successful theological career and an equally influential political program.[40] At the same time, from 1930 to 1970, several generations of literary critics combined a mixture of traditional poetics with Niebuhrian wisdom to plumb the ironic depths of poetry and fiction. In both the New Criticism and the burgeoning field of American studies, the symbolic vitality of Christian thought was accepted as a given, even if the practices of the faith were honored more in the breech than the observance.[41]

For the greater part of the twentieth century, criticism in the Melville line effectively viewed the human condition as an orphaned one and took the secret of our paternity to lie in the silence of the grave. Yet for many in this tradition, even if the documents left behind by our abdicating God have turned out to be forgeries or pale imitations, they at least give off enough light to illuminate some part of what Melville's friend Nathaniel Hawthorne called, in another context, 'the darkening close of [our] tale of human frailty and sorrow.'[42]

'An Antique Volume': Dickinson and the Limits of Scripture

Although we have no evidence that she ever read or commented upon Melville's fiction, we can be sure that Emily Dickinson would have resonated with his anxieties about matters scriptural and spiritual. To his troubled ruminations on divine paternity and human orphaning, she could have offered a number of her own poems in response. One, for example, sets the question in terms of a bloody dismembering of the divine. The perpetrator of this deed – was it history? the human race? God himself? – remains unknown. All we can tell for certain is that we are the orphaned inheritors of an abandoned world:

> Those – dying then,
> Knew where they went –
> They went to God's Right Hand –

---

[40] The decline of this neo-Niebuhrian school of literary criticism closely paralleled that of classic liberalism in the American political tradition.

[41] Of the many representative works in this vein, see Brooks, *Modern Poetry*; Matthiessen, *American Renaissance;* Smith, *Virgin Land*; Lewis, *American Adam*; Marx, *Machine in the Garden*; Delbanco, *Death of Satan*; and Kazin, *God and the American Writer*.

[42] Nathaniel Hawthorne, *Scarlet Letter,* in *Novels,* 159.

That Hand is amputated now
And God cannot be found –
The abdication of Belief
Makes the Behavior small –
Better an ignis fatuus
Than no illume at all – [43]

By the time she wrote this poem, a powerful intellectual current had pulled Dickinson away from her family's biblical anchorage. 'They are religious –' she wrote of the family in an 1862 letter, 'and address an Eclipse, every morning – whom they call their "Father."'[44] One force that made it difficult for Dickinson to worship the eclipse or find signs of the hand of God in her life was the same critical approach to the Scriptures that had vexed Charles and Waldo Emerson two generations earlier. By the time of her adulthood (the 1860s to the 1880s), many pastors no longer felt the need to heed Goethe's advice to conceal their doubts from their parishioners. Instead, they freely shared them. In the second half of the nineteenth century, explains James Turner, for many 'thoughtful men and women, the Bible was no longer an unquestioned source of religious authority' but 'itself needed defending,' and for a small minority, 'the Bible no longer provided evidence of anything but human religious longings.'[45]

We can sense the poignancy of these changes in Dickinson's account of a minor family drama of a kind that must have been unfolding in a number of late nineteenth-century American homes. In the summer of 1880, Emily wrote to a friend that she and her brother Austin had been 'talking the other Night about the Extension of Consciousness, after Death and Mother told Vinnie [their sister], afterward, she thought it was "very improper."' Alluding to 2 Timothy 3:16, Emily reported that her mother 'forgets that we are past "Correction in Righteousness –."' But the sister and brother concealed from their mother the clinching point behind their anxieties: 'I don't know what she would think if she knew that Austin told me confidentially "there was so such person as Elijah."'[46]

The mid-century revolutions in geology and biology had also eroded Dickinson's confidence in the Scriptures. When she was born in 1830, the argument from design ruled over a six thousand year-old earth; by the time she began writing poetry in the late 1850s, the earth had suddenly grown older. In the sixteenth and seventeenth centuries, Copernicus and Galileo had expanded the universe spatially, and now Darwin and others appeared to be stretching it

---

[43] Dickinson, *Poems,* poem #1581; hereafter each poem cited in the text by its number.
[44] Dickinson, *Letters,* 2:404.
[45] Turner, *Without God,* 150.
[46] Dickinson, *Letters,* 3:667.

far beyond its temporal limits. In one of her most perfect poems, Dickinson sets the brevity of human life within the newly discovered infinite expanse of geological time:

> Safe in their Alabaster Chambers –
> Untouched by Morning
> And untouched by noon –
> Sleep the meek members of the Resurrection –
> Rafter of Satin – and Roof of Stone –
>
> Grand go the Years,
> In the Crescent above them –
> Worlds scoop their Arcs –
> And Firmaments – row –
> Diadems – drop –
> And Doges – surrender –
> Soundless as dots,
> On a Disc of Snow – [#124]

Here the heavens move with a sickening slowness, death claims its victims relentlessly, and the human drama unfolds against a backdrop of absolute silence. The poem does not deny the possibility of resurrection but postpones it indefinitely and prolongs the wait almost beyond enduring.

'Science will not trust us with another World,' she wrote in an 1874 letter. 'Guess I and the Bible will move to some old fashioned spot where we'll feel at Home.'[47] Darwin in particular seemed to undermine her confidence in the Scriptures' story of a God-man whose sacrificial death and miraculous resurrection provided a release from bondage and the promise of eternal life. When a Dickinson neighbor complained in 1882 about an errant comment by a candidate for the governorship of Massachusetts – Benjamin Butler had referred to himself as a Christ-like figure – Emily wrote to a confidant: 'Mrs Dr Stearns called to know if we didn't think it very shocking for Butler to "liken himself to his Redeemer," but we thought Darwin had thrown "the Redeemer" away.'[48]

The higher criticism, evolutionary science, and a more diffuse historical skepticism worked in tandem, then, to deprive Dickinson of confidence in the same thing with which young Waldo Emerson had struggled earlier in the century: biblical authority. She told a friend in 1882 that 'the fiction of Santa Claus' always reminded her of 'the reply to my early question of "Who made the Bible" – "Holy Men moved by the Holy Ghost," and though I have now

---

[47] Dickinson, *Letters*, 2:511.
[48] Dickinson, *Letters*, 3:728.

ceased my investigations, the Solution is insufficient.' Santa Claus at least 'illustrates — Revelation,' while the Bible leaves its readers without a clue.[49]

There was more than intellectual disenchantment, however, behind Dickinson's struggle with scriptural authority. For she, like Emerson, Melville, and countless others in the nineteenth century, wrestled with the ethical and affective dimensions of the Bible's claims as much as with its historical assertions and miraculous reports. She was enough of a realist, for example, to understand what Melville was getting at with his briefs upon behalf of the explanatory force of the doctrine of original sin; yet she was also, like Emerson, too idealistic about human nature and human longing to accept as authoritative anything like a doctrine of innate depravity, as she explained poetically in the final year of her life:

> Of God we ask one favor, that we may be forgiven
> For what, he is presumed to know —
> The Crime, from us, is hidden —
> Immured the whole of Life
> Within a magic Prison
> We reprimand the Happiness
> That too competes with Heaven — [#1675]

To Dickinson, as to other heirs of the Enlightenment, the particularity of Christian claims about revelation proved to be a stumbling block. 'It always felt to me — a wrong,' she wrote

> To that Old Moses — done —
> To let him see — the Canaan —
> Without the entering —

Even though she doubts that a man named Moses ever gazed down from Pisgah, she is 'satisfied — the Romance/ In point of injury —' surpasses even the suffering undergone by Stephen and Paul in their martyrdoms. For they 'only' suffered death, while 'God's adroiter will' seemed to engage Moses in 'tantalizing Play/ As Boy — should deal with lesser Boy —/ To prove ability —.' If there was a fault in all of this, it 'was doubtless Israel's,' and rather than let Moses die in sight of the promised land, the poet says she would have ushered him, in his 'Pentateuchal Robes,'

> Upon the Broad Possession
> 'Twas little — He should see
> Old Man on Nebo! Late as this —
> My justice bleeds — for Thee! [#521]

---

[49] Dickinson, *Letters*, 3:756.

In Dickinson's mind, the ethical challenge of accepting scriptural authority was matched by the aesthetic difficulty of doing so. Only two years before she died, she wrote to a neighbor, 'thank you for "considering the Lilies." The Bible must have had us in mind, when it gave that liquid Commandment.' If only the rest of the Scriptures had appealed to our sense of beauty, instead of addressing us with imperious moral commands and incredible historical claims: 'Were all its advice so enchanting as that, we should probably heed it.'[50] This epistolary observation worked its way into a long Dickinson poem. In what might stand as a charter document for the 'seeker sensitive' movement, the poet demonstrates clearly that although she prized the Bible for its mysteries and assurances, she also sensed its unmistakable, alienating strangeness. The Scriptures spoke, she seemed at times to think, in an antiquated language about an attenuated faith:

> The Bible is an antique Volume – Written by faded Men
> At the suggestion of Holy Spectres –
> Subjects – Bethlehem –
> Eden – the ancient Homestead –
> Satan – the Brigadier –
> Judas – the Great Defaulter –
> David – the Troubadour –
> Sin – a distinguished Precipice
> Others must resist –
> Boys that 'believe' are very lonesome –
> Other Boys are 'lost' –
> Had but the Tale a warbling Teller –
> All the Boys would come –
> Orpheus' Sermon captivated –
> It did not condemn – [#1577]

The relationship to the Bible outlined in this poem is complex, and it points to what would become a highly influential line of approach to the Scriptures in American literature and criticism. The poem's opening lines are packed with images of insubstantiality and decrepitude; one can hardly have confidence in the authority of a book that had been 'Written by faded Men – /At the suggestion of Holy Spectres –.' The drama of the Bible reads like the playbill of a cheap traveling show, and it has become a 'lonesome' matter to believe this story in the modern world, because few are attracted by an ancient account of judgment. What the tale needs is a 'warbling Teller' to captivate the vast 'lost' audience. 'If you stage it,' Dickinson seems to say to the modern church, 'they will come.'

Yet for all its gentle sarcasm concerning the Bible and its stories, this late poem by Dickinson – written around 1882 – expresses an underlying

---

[50] Dickinson, *Letters,* 3:821.

admiration for the very world it parodies. We would do well not to confuse contemporary attitudes toward parody with the kind practiced by Dickinson. Rather than being simple and dismissive, her relationship to the biblical text remained, to the end, complicated and ambiguous. What drew her to Shakespeare and the Bible was the very strangeness that lent itself so well to parody and allusion. Those great texts offered her rich alternatives to the poverty of modern thought. In her poetry and prose, Dickinson both entered into their alien worlds, in order to experience their pleasures and learn their mysteries, and stood back from them, in order to subject them to quizzical critique.

Dickinson's attitude toward the Bible is similar to what Mikhail Bakhtin has described as the medieval style of parody. In the Middle Ages, according to Bakhtin, parody served the purposes of renewal. On feast and festival days, the serious language and ritualistic practices of the Christian faith were often treated with mirth and even ridicule. In Bakhtin's words, the purpose was 'to encourage laughter in the congregation – this was conceived as a cheerful rebirth after days of melancholy and fasting.'[51] Holy laughter provided a sanctifying counterpoint to the melody of sacred language and the liturgical year.

Bakhtin's caution against transferring our 'contemporary concepts of parodic discourse onto medieval parody' applies to Dickinson as well. 'In modern times,' he writes, 'the functions of parody are narrow and unproductive. Parody has grown sickly, its place in modern literature is insignificant.' Living as we do in a 'world of free and democratized language,' we find it hard to conceive of the 'complex and multi-leveled' language of the Middle Ages, which still permeates the world of Shakespearean poetry and King James prose. In Dickinson, parody is not sickly but wistful. Bakhtin writes that in great parody, 'it is often very difficult to establish precisely where reverence ends and ridicule begins.'[52] Emily Dickinson was astute enough to find in the Scriptures an incomparable verbal world, but she also knew how hard it would be to secure herself in the biblical world in a 'free and democratized' modernity.[53]

---

[51] Bakhtin, *Dialogic Imagination*, 72.
[52] Bakhtin, *Dialogic Imagination,* 71, 77.
[53] As pervasive as its presence has been in modern American culture, parody is more a matter of style than genre, more an issue of tone than substance. As a result, one perhaps would not speak of a 'school of parody' in the same way that I have described critical traditions in American literature that have followed from the Emersonian and Melvillean uses of Scripture. Instead, to provide a sense of what I mean in focusing upon the *parodic*, I will offer quotations from two important works from philosophy and literature in the 1970s. Both treat bodies of thought and texts, including the Scriptures, in a manner that emphasizes the derivative and ironizing nature of all interpretation. The operative term in both of the following passages

A Theological Response

The questions raised by Emerson, Melville, and Dickinson are representative of the dramatic shifts taking place in the nineteenth-century understanding of the Bible among America's cultural and intellectual elites. The new approaches fashioned and promoted by these writers exerted considerable influence over the development of fiction and poetry, and they also anticipated many dimensions of the academic study of literature in America. As James Turner has documented, the teaching of literature in the vernacular began in earnest only in the decades following the Civil War, when Emerson, Melville, and Dickinson were in the final stages of their careers.[54] The naturalistic consensus emerging at the close of the nineteenth century provided the impetus for the cultivation of a countervailing literary domain, and for much of the twentieth century an oppositional stance marked the literary response to science.[55]

What are the implications of these developments for a theological response to the stance taken towards the Scriptures in the American literary and critical traditions? I believe the answer requires addressing the root assumptions that

---

may be *parasite* rather than *parody,* but Bakhtin's critique would apply with equal force here.

First, from Richard Rorty: '[This] book, like the writings of the philosophers I most admire, is therapeutic rather than constructive. The therapy offered is, nevertheless, parasitic upon the constructive efforts of the very analytic philosophers whose frame of reference I am trying to put in question. Thus most of the particular criticisms of the tradition which I offer are borrowed from such systematic philosophers as Sellars, Quine, Davidson, Ryle, Malcolm, Kuhn, and Putnam' (*Philosophy,* 7).

Then, from J. Hillis Miller: 'To speak of the "deconstructive" reading of a poem as "parasitical" on the "obvious or univocal reading" is to enter, perhaps unwittingly, into the strange logic of the parasite, to make the univocal equivocal in spite of oneself, according to the law that language is not an instrument or tool in man's hands, a submissive means of thinking. Language rather thinks man and his "world," including poems, if he will allow it to do so....'

'The poem, like all texts, is "unreadable," if by "readable" one means open to a single, definitive, univocal interpretation. In fact, neither the "obvious" reading nor the "deconstructionist" reading is "univocal." Each contains, necessarily, its enemy within itself, is itself both host and parasite. The deconstructionist reading contains the obvious one and vice versa. Nihilism is an inalienable alien presence within Occidental metaphysics, both in poems and in the criticism of poems' ('Critic as Host,' 444, 447).

[54] See Turner, *Liberal Education*; and Roberts and Turner, *Sacred and Secular University*, 75–106.

[55] For a provocative and insightful treatment of this subject, see Rorty, *Consequences,* 139–59. I have discussed this issue in *From Nature,* 99–124.

our exploration of Emerson, Melville, and Dickinson has uncovered. It involves recognizing that Catholic, Protestant, and Orthodox thinkers of great stature have been engaging the culture on these fronts for the better part of the past century. With the likes of Barth and Balthasar, Bonhoeffer and Bakhtin, as well as MacIntyre and Ricoeur, having gone before us, there is no need to reinvent the theoretical wheel.

In this brief conclusion I wish to sketch several possible ways of interacting with the legacy of the nineteenth-century transformation of the concept of biblical authority. To do so, I will focus on three themes or tropes in contemporary theology. Although they may not seem at first to address specific attitudes towards Scripture, each theme or figure speaks to the underlying assumptions that began in the nineteenth century to undermine the Bible's authority and to cripple the capacity of its readers to hear in and through it the speech of God.

To Emerson's worries about the sources of spiritual authority, as well as to his angry attacks upon 'the personal, the positive, the ritual,' the Christian faith offers its witness to the particularity of the gospel and the personality of a God who appears in 'the figure of suffering man.' One of Emerson's greatest nineteenth-century admirers was Friedrich Nietzsche, of whom Barth observes, 'the new thing in Nietzsche' was 'the development of humanity without the fellow-man.' Christianity confronts the Nietschean 'superman' with 'the figure of suffering man.' According to Barth, it places before the Olympian man the 'Crucified, Jesus, as the Neighbour,' and in his person 'a whole host of others who are wholly and utterly ignoble and despised in the eyes of the world, the hungry and thirsty and naked and sick and captive, a whole ocean of human meanness and painfulness.' Christianity audaciously informs Dionysus-Zarathustra – and Emerson, one might add – that he is not a god, and it says that if he wishes to be redeemed, he must belong to the Crucified One and be in 'fellowship with this mean and painful host of His people.'[56]

In the American context, Emerson was a prominent source for the theology of experience that William James, Paul Tillich, and now, oddly, the likes of Richard Rorty have established as a powerful force in mainstream cultural life. At its best, this theology of experience illustrates the biblical account; at its worst, it supplants it. Barth repeatedly argued that an experienced-based theology can only be challenged through a renewal or reassertion of the doctrine of God and the doctrines of creation and reconciliation that flow from God's revelatory acts of self-disclosure. If critics in the Emersonian tradition, such as Frank Kermode and Northrop Frye, define literature as a coherent, self-enclosed imaginative realm that is 'independent of belief,' the Christian faith speaks of a God who breaks the bonds of our 'coherent' world system. It bears a

---

[56] Barth, *Church Dogmatics:* 3. 2:240, 241.

biblically-based witness to one 'who, though he was in the form of God, did not regard equality with God as something to be exploited, but emptied himself, taking the form of a slave, being born in human likeness. And being found in human form, he humbled himself and became obedient to the point of death – even death on a cross.'

In a similar fashion, the Christian faith addresses Melville's orphaned realists with a word of scriptural hope based upon the sacrificial acts of the triune God. No doubt the Melvillean orphans would have little trouble understanding George Steiner's recent observation that there is 'one particular day in Western history about which neither historical record nor myth nor Scripture make report.' This day 'is a Saturday. And it has become the longest of days.'[57] Though it stands between the two most important days of the Christian year – Good Friday and Easter Sunday – this is a day about which the Bible and Christian history have had precious little to say.[58]

This silence surrounding Holy Saturday troubles Steiner, and the day becomes for him the part that stands for the whole when he considers the modern condition. According to him, our age is an extended Holy Saturday; from within its boundaries, contemporary believers and atheists alike can look back upon on history and find ample evidence of the cruel truths revealed in the experience of 'the Cross.' Steiner sees the crucifixion of Jesus as a symbol 'of the injustice, of the interminable suffering, of the waste, of the brute enigma … of the human condition.' Pain, failure, and solitude mark 'our history and private fate,' and Good Friday embodies them all.[59]

Yet 'to the Christian,' explains Steiner, Easter Sunday signifies 'a justice and a love that have conquered death.' Sustained by faith in this reconciling love, believers can take comfort in the hope of eternal life, while unbelievers are left to grasp at an amorphous longing for 'a day of liberation.' In language that Melville, Dickinson, or Faulkner might have used, Steiner concludes that 'ours is the long day's journey of the Saturday,' where we live between the reality of suffering and 'unutterable waste,' on the one hand, and the 'dream of liberation, of rebirth, on the other.'[60] We survive in a time without end and are sustained by a dream that can never come true.

According to Steiner, this is the sober truth concealed at the heart of the modern experience. It is also an understanding of reality shared by many of America's most influential writers, critics, and thinkers. From Edith Wharton to Richard Rorty, from William James to Don DeLillo, these men and women

---

[57] Steiner, *Real Presences,* 231.
[58] In recent decades, Hans Urs von Balthasar sought to fill this void with several extended treatments of the theme of Holy Saturday. See *Mysterium Paschale,* 148–88.
[59] Steiner, *Real Presences,* 231–32.
[60] Steiner, *Real Presences,* 232.

have come to doubt the idea of a divinely given order to nature or an appointed end to time. They agree, as James reluctantly concluded, that our 'finite experience as such is homeless. Nothing outside of the flux secures the issue of it.'[61] St Paul may have believed that 'when the fullness of the time was come, God sent forth his Son' in order 'to redeem them that were under the law.' But the Melvillean and modernist mind knows better. It understands that there is no such thing as the 'fullness of time,' because time is nothing more than 'the mausoleum of all hope and desire,' in the words of William Faulkner's *The Sound and the Fury*. 'Christ was not crucified: he was worn away by a minute clicking of little wheels.'[62]

Once again, it is Barth who sounds a note of ringing scriptural assurance that appears strikingly different from the brooding rumblings of Melville, James, and Steiner. Barth says that naturalism of the kind Melville and Niebuhr embraced has deep roots in the theology of the Western church, which 'has a decided inclination towards the *theologia crucis*.' The 'theology of the cross' emphasizes the fact 'that He [Christ] was surrendered for our transgressions,' and under the considerable influence of naturalism, modern artists and intellectuals alike have found it easier to dwell upon this suffering than to imagine the glory of the risen Lord. Matters are different in the Eastern church, writes Barth, for it 'inclines towards the *theologia gloria*e,' which it 'brings more into the foreground the fact that He was raised for our justification.'[63]

According to Barth, both of these competing theological visions have their roots in the Bible, and they require each other to be complete. 'We ought not to erect and fix any opposition' between the suffering man and the risen god, for 'there is no Easter without Good Friday, but equally certainly there is no Good Friday without Easter!' If we focus upon the passage through sin, suffering, and death alone, Barth says we are likely to give way to a spirit of 'tribulation and sullenness' in which we speculate endlessly on the abstract concept of the cross – or as we have seen in the case of Melville, upon the forlorn plight of metaphysical orphans who find the Bible's only enduring truth to be its teachings about human finitude and the 'mystery of iniquity.' In focusing exclusively upon the experience of suffering and finitude, Barth says we run the risk of forgetting that 'the Crucified rose again from the dead the third day.'[64]

Such abstract speculation – on the cross or any other subject of interest – may, as the contemporary pragmatists like to say, 'keep the conversation going.' But it misses the point of that conversation, which in Christian terms is 'the real mystery' of both Easter and the scriptural narrative. The mystery is

---

[61] James, *Writings*, 601.
[62] Faulkner, *Sound and Fury*, 77.
[63] Barth, *Dogmatics in Outline*, 114.
[64] Barth, *Dogmatics in Outline*, 114.

'not that God is glorified in it [the resurrection], but that man is exalted, raised to the right hand of God and permitted to triumph over sin, death and the devil.'[65] If deprived of that ringing word of exaltation and triumph, the Christian Scriptures become just another commentary upon the human condition, one more voice in the never ending 'conversation of mankind.'

Finally, to the triumph of parody, which Emily Dickinson anticipated and contemporary culture has achieved, the Christian faith may answer with the alternative of eschatology. There, in a theology of hope, we may find justification for a way of playing with reality that renews rather than exhausts the language of Scripture and the Christian tradition.

'Art must be considered in an eschatological framework,' Barth argues in his *Ethics*, 'because it is the specific external form of human action in which this cannot be made intelligible to us except as play.' Along with humor, art is an activity of which 'only the children of God are capable,' and like humor, it is 'sustained by an ultimate and very profound pain' and is 'born of sorrow.' Art is the creation of children (1 Jn. 3:2ff.) who play away in a world "whose corruptibility they cannot overlook or ignore. . . . Only those who have knowledge of the future resurrection of the dead really know what it means that we have to die,' he reminds us.[66] This play is born out of the kind of deep pain and sorrow that Emily Dickinson and Herman Melville knew all too well. But it is also profoundly different from the glib cynicism and flippant sense of parody that inform the cultural productions of so many of their American descendants.

Although he would never have rested in Melville's 'pondering repose of If' or accepted Dickinson's sense of scripture and tradition as an 'ignis fatuus,' Barth would agree that art must recognize, as the Bible does, the essential homelessness of human experience east of Eden. 'The artist's work is homeless in the deepest sense,' he writes, and he presses the case so far as to claim that it is 'precisely in their strange and rootless isolation from all the works of present reality [that works of art] live so totally *only* by the truth of the promise' of God. By means of art, we learn 'not to take present reality with final seriousness in its created being or in its nature as the world of the fall and reconciliation.' In Barth's words, 'true aesthetics is the experiencing of real and future reality.' And to this extent, 'Art *plays* with reality' by refusing to let present reality 'be a last word' in its fallen and partial state:

[Art] transcends human words with the eschatological possibility of poetry, in which speech becomes, in unheard-of fashion, an end in itself, then to a higher degree – although we are still dealing only with the sound and tone of the human voice – with the eschatological possibility of song, and then – still with the intention of

---

[65] Barth, *Dogmatics in Outline,* 115.
[66] Barth, *Ethics,* 506, 507.

penetrating to what is true and ultimate, of proclaiming the new heaven and the new earth, but now using the voices of the rest of creation – with the eschatological possibility of instrumental music.[67]

In case the eschatological gravity of all this singing and versifying threatens to make us too serious, Barth reminds us that to the end of our lives we remain the *little* children of God. We play our parts in a drama whose Author and Finisher has revealed himself in the works of nature, the pages of the Scriptures, the sacraments of the church, and, supremely, in Jesus Christ. Whether we envision a transformed world in our poetry or seek to bring it into being through political struggle, we 'must not try to view our work as a solemnly serious cooperation with God.' Instead, we forever 'play in the peace in the father's house that is waiting for us.' At all costs, we strive to avoid allotting 'final seriousness to what we do here and now.' We play and we wait, 'because the perfect has still to come beyond all that we do now. . . . We cannot be more grimly in earnest about life than when we resign ourselves to the fact that we can only play.'[68]

But play we do, and play we will, throughout time and in eternity. At least that's what the Reverend John Ames believes we will do. He is the central character in Marilynne Robinson's recent, much-lauded novel, *Gilead*. Near the close of his life, Ames reports that he feels like 'a child who opens its eyes on the world once and sees amazing things it will never know any names for and then has to close its eyes again.' From his years of preaching from the Scriptures, he knows that this world is only a 'mere apparition' compared to the one to come, 'but it is only lovelier for that. There is a human beauty in it.' In fact, Ames refuses to believe that when we have all 'put on incorruptibility' we will somehow forget the fantastic drama of mortality and impermanence, 'the great bright dream of procreating and perishing that meant the whole world to us. In eternity this world will be Troy,' he believes, 'and all that has passed here will be the epic of the universe, the ballad they sing in the streets.' However great the future will be, he says, 'I don't imagine any reality putting this one in the shade entirely, and I think piety forbids me to try.'[69]

A genuine piety of this kind, one would think, would have the power to realize the difference between a restorative, playful interaction with the biblical materials and a corrosive post-Dickinsonian parodying of them. It would be able to recognize that the Bible points all of us Melvillean orphans to the cross, and that cross leads not to the 'mausoleum of all hope and desire,' but to the empty tomb and the Risen Lord. And to be certain, such piety would possess enough foolish wisdom to realize that the Scriptures do not tell us,   *pace*

---

[67] Barth, *Ethics*, 507–8.
[68] Barth, *Ethics*, 504, 505.
[69] Robinson, *Gilead*, 57.

Emerson, of 'a faith like Christ's in the infinitude of man.' Instead, as William Butler Yeats's 'Crazy Jane' explains, they proclaim the good news:

> 'But Love has pitched his mansion in
> The place of excrement;
> For nothing can be sole or whole
> That has not been rent.'[70]

---

[70] Yeats, *Selected Poems*, 149.

Bibliography

Bakhtin, M., *The Dialogic Imagination: Four Essays*, ed. M. Holquist, trans. C. Emerson and M. Holquist (Austin: University of Texas Press, 1981)

Balthasar, H.U. von, *Mysterium Paschale: The Mystery of Easter*, trans. A. Nichols (Edinburgh: T & T Clark, 1990)

Barish, E., *Emerson: The Roots of Prophecy* (Princeton: Princeton University Press, 1989)

Barth, K., *Church Dogmatics: The Doctrine of Creation*, vol. III. 2, ed. G.W. Bromiley and T.F. Torrance, trans. H. Knight, et al. (Edinburgh: T & T Clark, 1960)

—, *Dogmatics in Outline*, trans. G. T. Thompson (New York: Harper, 1959 [1949])

—, *Ethics*, ed. D. Braun, trans. G.W. Bromiley (New York: Seabury, 1981)

Bassard, K.C., *Spiritual Interrogations: Culture, Gender, and Community in Early African American Women's Writing* (Princeton: Princeton University Press, 1999)

Brodhead, R., *Hawthorne, Melville, and the Novel* (Chicago: University of Chicago Press, 1976)

Brooks, C., *Modern Poetry and the Tradition* (Chapel Hill: University of North Carolina Press, 1939)

Brown, J.W., *The Rise of Biblical Criticism in America, 1800–1870: The New England Scholars* (Middletown, CT: Wesleyan University Press, 1969)

Burke, K., *The Rhetoric of Religion: Studies in Logology* (Berkeley: University of California Press, 1970 [1961])

Cole, P., *Mary Moody Emerson and the Origins of Transcendentalism: A Family History* (New York: Oxford University Press, 1996)

Delbanco, A., *Melville: His World and Work* (New York: Knopf, 2005)

—, *The Death of Satan: How Americans Have Lost the Sense of Evil* (New York: Farrar, 1995)

Dickinson, E., *The Letters of Emily Dickinson*, 3 vols., ed. T.H. Johnson and T. Ward (Cambridge: Belknap, Harvard University Press, 1958)

—, *The Poems of Emily Dickinson*, ed. R.W. Franklin (Cambridge: Belknap, Harvard University Press, 1999)

Emerson, M.M., *The Selected Letters of Mary Moody Emerson*, ed. N.C. Simmons (Athens: University of Georgia Press, 1993)

Emerson, R.W., *Essays and Lectures*, ed. J. Porte (New York: Library of America, 1983)

—, *The Journals and Miscellaneous Notebooks of Ralph Waldo Emerson*, ed. W.H. Gilman et al., 16 vols. (Cambridge: Harvard University Press, 1960–82)

—, *The Letters of Ralph Waldo Emerson*, ed. R. Rusk and E.M. Tilton, 10 vols. (New York: Columbia University Press, 1939–96)

Faulkner, W., *The Sound and the Fury* (New York: Vintage, 1990 [1929])

Frye, N., *The Secular Scripture: A Study of the Structure of Romance* (Cambridge: Harvard University Press, 1976)

Hawthorne, N., *Novels,* ed. M. Bell (New York: Library of America, 1983)

Hurth, E., 'Sowing the Seeds of "Subversion": Harvard's Early Göttingen Students,' *Studies in the American Renaissance 1992,* ed. J. Myerson (Charlottesville: University Press of Virginia, 1992), 91–106

James, W., *Writings, 1902–1910,* ed. B. Kuklick (New York: Library of America, 1987)

Jüngel, E., *God's Being Is in Becoming: The Trinitarian Being of God in the Theology of Karl Barth,* trans. J. Webster (Grand Rapids: Eerdmans, 2001)

Kazin, A., *God and the American Writer* (New York: Knopf, 1997)

Kermode, F., *The Sense of an Ending: Studies in the Theory of Fiction* (New York: Oxford University Press, 1967)

Lentricchia, F., *After the New Criticism* (Chicago: University of Chicago Press, 1980)

Lewis, R.W.B., *The American Adam: Innocence, Tragedy, and Tradition in the Nineteenth Century* (Chicago: University of Chicago Press, 1955)

Lundin, R., *From Nature to Experience: The American Search for Cultural Authority* (Lanham, MD: Rowman & Littlefield, 2005)

Marx, L., *The Machine in the Garden: Technology and the Pastoral Ideal in America* (New York: Oxford University Press, 1964)

Matthiessen, F.O., *American Renaissance: Art and Expression in the Age of Emerson and Whitman* (London: Oxford University Press, 1941)

Melville, H., *Melville's Short Novels,* ed. D. McCall (New York: Norton, 2002)

—, *Moby-Dick,* ed. H. Parker and H. Hayford (New York: Norton, 2002)

—, *Pierre, Israel Potter, The Piazza Tales, The Confidence-Man, Uncollected Prose, Billy Budd,* ed. H. Hayford (New York: Library of America, 1984)

Miller, J.H., 'The Critic as Host,' *Critical Inquiry* 3 (1977), 439–47

Noll, M.A., *America's God: From Jonathan Edwards to Abraham Lincoln* (New York: Oxford University Press, 2002)

Packer, B., 'Origin and Authority: Emerson and the Higher Criticism,' *Reconstructing American Literary History,* ed. S. Bercovitch (Cambridge: Harvard University Press, 1986), 67–92

Roberts, J.H., and J. Turner, *The Sacred and the Secular University* (Princeton: Princeton University Press, 2000)

Robinson, M., *Gilead* (New York: Farrar, 2004)

Rorty, R., *Consequences of Pragmatism* (Minneapolis: University of Minnesota Press, 1982)

—, *Philosophy and the Mirror of Nature* (Princeton: Princeton University Press, 1979)

Smith, H.N., *Virgin Land: The American West as Symbol and Myth* (New York: Vintage, 1950)

Stauffer, J., *The Black Hearts of Men: Radical Abolitionists and the Transformation of Race* (Cambridge: Harvard University Press, 2002)

Steiner, G., *Real Presences* (Chicago: University of Chicago Press, 1989)

Turner, J., *The Liberal Education of Charles Eliot Norton* (Baltimore: Johns Hopkins University Press, 1999)

___, *Without God, Without Creed: The Origins of Unbelief in America* (Baltimore: Johns Hopkins University Press, 1985)

Wright, N., *Melville's Use of the Bible* (Durham: Duke University Press, 1949)

Yeats, W.B., *Selected Poems and Four Plays*, ed. M. L. Rosenthal, 4th edn. (New York: Scribner, 1996)

12

Biblical Literacy, Academic Freedom and Christian Liberty
David Lyle Jeffrey

In Whit Stilman's film *Metropolitan*, one of the characters defends his obtuseness by saying: 'Just because you haven't read a book, doesn't mean you can't have an opinion on it. I haven't read the Bible, and I have an opinion on it.' This sort of cheerful yet opinionated ignorance can be shared by some you might not suspect of it. I am concerned that not only the wider culture, but increasingly the subculture we call the church, has opinions on a book which, for practical intellectual purposes, it hasn't really read.

Ignorance of the Bible problematizes the work we are still pleased to call Christian education in a number of ways. One of these pertains to a great and generally celebrated ideal of all education – in respect of which it is often assumed nowadays that Christians, both individually and institutionally, are notably deficient. I refer to intellectual freedom.[1] The assumption of many, tacitly or explicitly, seems to be that a biblical worldview and intellectual or academic freedom are terminally at odds.

I wish to register my dissent to this prejudice, on the grounds that I have read the book. I propose, in fact, an alternative hypothesis in the form of a question: Are there in fact biblical resources that may help us to clarify current debates over the meaning and application of the principle of academic freedom? My answer to this question will be 'yes'.

A second question also prompts my excursus: Do those of us who claim a special interest in the Bible make adequate use of these resources? Here my answer will be, 'Not often enough, or well enough.' To the first question I will

---

[1] See *Academe,* the bi-monthly magazine of the AAUP (Jan/Feb 2006), which featured a series of articles on academic freedom and Christian profession in the academy, including counterpoised articles by K. Wagner, 'Faith Statements do Restrict Academic Freedom' and B. Olszewski, 'Critical Intellectual Inquiry at Catholic Colleges.'

come last, offering less an argument than one brief textual exposition. Regarding the second question I will argue here that we make poor use of our biblical resources, indeed that neither in our church-related institutions of higher learning nor in our churches are we now teaching the Scriptures sufficiently well that they rise to the level of becoming a true *intellectual* resource. Whether the current level of scriptural teaching allows them to become even a satisfactory *spiritual* resource is a question for others to answer.

Eclipse of Biblical Narrative

George Barna has recently concluded that only nine percent of the self-described 'born again' in America and only half of all Protestant pastors have anything that could be credibly described as a biblical worldview. Barna's surveys, howsoever adequately, attempt to reckon with a more widely remarked and embarrassing reality; namely, that the Bible has apparently lost authority in some churches once ostensibly most identified with the Bible. His research shows that 'even in churches where the pastor has a biblical worldview, most members of the congregation do not. More than six out of every seven congregants in the typical church do not share the biblical worldview of their pastor even when he or she has one.'[2]

We must not be content merely to understand why even the evangelical community in North America has – at least in significant sectors – apparently lost its appetite for coherent biblical teaching. We who work in Christian higher education may well need to discover a remedy for one of the consequences, for the decline has gone on long enough that biblical illiteracy can, on occasion, seem to be nearly as extensive among evangelical college students as within the general populace. This is a fact with pedagogical consequences.

In noticing this phenomenon I do not, of course, mean to suggest that evangelicals are uniquely apostate. Apostasy in North America is remarkably ecumenical. According to a recent issue of the journal *Current Issues in Catholic Higher Education*,

> Thirty two percent of lay presidents and 40 percent of religious [i.e., ordained] presidents [in Catholic colleges and universities in the USA] report contending with faculty and staff who are tradition illiterate, hostile toward, or simply disinterested in the Catholic mission and identity of the institutions in which they serve.[3]

---

[2] G. Barna, *Barna Research Online* (Jan 12, 2004), 3.
[3] M.M. Morey and D.H. Holtschneider, 'Leadership and the Age of the Laity: Emerging Patterns in Catholic Higher Education,' *Current Issues in Catholic Higher Education* 23 (Summer, 2003), 94.

I fear that at universities like my own, much the same sort of thing could be said. Even among regular church-going faculty, biblical literacy and theological competence is at a far lower ebb than might have been found a generation ago amongst rural Baptists and other evangelicals who never saw the inside of a college classroom. What they knew, and knew by heart, their college-educated children and grandchildren have largely forgotten. When Bruce Cole, Director of the NEH, speaks about 'American Amnesia,' he describes a cultural disorder that has infected 'People of the Book' as much as it has the great unwashed.[4]

Cole and I team-taught a course in medieval and Renaissance art history three decades ago at the University of Rochester. As a Jewish professor in a university with a large cohort of Jewish students, Cole once remarked to me on his disappointment at their typical lack of textual knowledge of their religious tradition. Biblical iconography in Renaissance painting which ought to have been obvious to reasonably taught Jewish students, was almost as opaque to them as to the majority of our shared students who were more or less cheerful pagans. I could relate to his frustration: teaching Chaucer's Miller's Tale, which depends for much of its humor on ironic misunderstanding of the Noah narrative in Genesis, I was getting blank stares at the mention of Noah. Only three of more than thirty students could say for sure they knew about the flood story and none could remember that 'God promised to Noah never to flood the earth again' – something Chaucer depends on for his laugh at the ignorance of the old carpenter who, you may remember, builds local churches, but is duped and even cuckolded by a 'seminary' student imposter because he has no knowledge of the foundation upon which the Church universal is built.

That was thirty years ago, and our faculty club grousing about biblical illiteracy in our students, to some of our peers, may well have seemed quaintly antiquarian. But, particularly for teaching Western art and literature in the secular university, the deficit has only grown more acute. Cole's thesis now is explicitly directed to political competence: he believes that amnesia (how we lost our story) is evidently culture-wide and a threat to American democracy.

I do not propose to reflect on such matters of political culture – they also lie well outside my competence. I restrict myself to the universities where, meanwhile, the devolution of humanities and social science disciplines over the last three or four generations has been determined both by general cultural trends and ideological fashions, in each case in several ways. In my own discipline, the loss of cultural memory and, specifically, of textual literacy, coupled with an elite diversion toward ideological fashions sometimes clumped for curricular purposes as 'cultural studies,' has amounted by now to a lamentable curricular

---

[4] Keynote Address, National Citizen Corps Conference, Washington, DC, July 29, 2003.

decadence.[5] In a *New York Times* book review of seven monographs on the subject, 'The Decline and Fall of English Literature,' Andrew Delbanco explains our demise as the corruption of a discipline that had once prided itself on replacing the narrowness of Christian preaching by the broad liberality of inspired, Emersonian principles. Matthew Arnold is, of course, likewise foundationally associated with the displacement of *God and the Bible* (1883) by modern literary criticism, abandoning curricular 'dogma,' as Arnold thought of it (*Literature and Dogma* [1873]), for secular literary study. Ironically, these critics are now worried about a tragic fall they themselves (or their guild) have helped to inspire, a flight away from primary literature toward theoretical dogmas so rigorously determinative of possible discourse as to marginalize literature itself as the subject and, it is feared, perhaps eventually the traditional study of literature as a discipline. When such a critique is made, their default position is perhaps unsurprisingly an Arnoldian apologetic, as when Delbanco insists that without the discipline the university would be 'left without a moral center'(35).

But to read this cliché now is to realize just how shop-worn the old apologia has become. In a 2002 presidential address to the Modern language Association, the eminent Renaissance scholar Stephen Greenblatt calls for literary criticism to promulgate the anti-religion of naturalist materialism, while he himself displays a displaced religious fervor in almost every sentence of his address. However narcissistic it must sound to the layperson or student, Greenblatt's final call is for a revival of the Lucretian doctrine of metempsychosis, in which frustrated critics get to live on as ghostly shades in the pages of their surviving work.[6] This is marginally better, one supposes, than coming back as a grasshopper or a bedbug, but a poor sort of confession *in articulo mortis* all the same, and not likely to inspire a general revival.

At the level of the American undergraduate curriculum, where enrollments in English literature over the last three decades have dropped by one third (National Center for Education Statistics), the CPR of last resort has been less often this sort of pseudo-religious rhetoric than a turn to kitsch. That one can satisfy distribution requirements in literature by courses in the History of Comic Book Art (Indiana), Rock Music from 1970 to the Present (Minnesota) or Campus Culture and Drinking (Duke) gives some sense of where recent Ph.D. topics in literature can lead the survivors of contemporary graduate programs.[7] That a critic such as J. Hillis Miller lectures on 'The Authority of

---

[5] A. Delbanco, 'The Decline and Fall of Literature.'

[6] S. Greenblatt, 'Presidential Address 2002: "Stay, Illusion"– on Receiving Messages from the Dead.'

[7] American Council of Trustees and Alumni, 'The Hollow Core – Failure of the General Education Curriculum: A Fifty College Study.'

Literature' – attempting to regain the lost authority while mirroring rhetorically older apologetics for the authority of the Bible[8] – shows well enough that what goes around comes around.

What I am suggesting, in brief, may be captured by my adapting a familiar title: English Literature is a *discipline* that has lost its story. The loss, as I have written elsewhere, was perhaps an inevitability following upon the choices made by my discipline's academic founders.[9] What Matthew Arnold and others too faintly recognized in their gesture to acknowledge the Bible as background or foundation literature, even while shearing it of its supernatural significance, is that cultural coherence in the inherently incoherent realm of creative expression depends on the possibility of reference back to a normative, anchoring central story. Socially, we know that to anchor a plurality of divergent stories to civil discourse and the pursuit of ethical formation you need to be able to appeal to some sort of *story* in the singular at the heart of a community. The same goes for a *curriculum*. Moreover, for such discourse to have abiding communal value the story must possess an authority and power proportional to some order of transcendence, as well as a certain intimate familiarity for those who read and write within its range. If I may be permitted a Tolkienesque metaphor, the common story must be as sturdy, and new–life–producing as the trunk of a tree from which springs, year after year, a surprising variety of secondary fruitful growth. Or one might think of a vine and its branches.

The problem of coherence in a humanities discipline such as English literature is not merely that one cannot adequately read the thicker branch texts of Shakespeare, Milton, Bunyan, or Eliot when one cannot recognize the DNA in their biblical allusions. The problem is that readers so bereft cannot relate any of these imaginative works to a coherent cultural conversation or ongoing dialectic across the disciplines, in which all the major works play a part. To put this in another way: such readers cannot 'see' the degree to which the greatest texts in English literature are already part of a conversation whose dialectical '*in principium*' was a Word from God.

To rephrase: contemporary incoherence in a core subject such as English literature results not merely from a disappearance of canonical authority, but from an absence of *any* replacement principle in terms of which either canon or authoritative judgment might be realized or recognized.

---

[8] J.H. Miller, 'On the Authority of Literature.'

[9] D.L. Jeffrey, 'Communion, Community and Our Common Book: or, Can Faustus Be Saved?'

Egotism and the Common Lot

One might press this observation still further by considering the most recently favored replacements for core intellectual principles and centering narrative: various postmodern advocacies of a particular agenda or, in some quarters, unfettered individualism which 'drowns all music but its own.' These forces almost invariably fragment. As cultures of personal preoccupation they reflexively suspect, indeed often scorn, any self-transcending or communal search for health, let alone the holy. In the end, no text by another person is really necessary, even, as once we might have said, as a pretext for critical utterance. As one of my students puts it, everybody wants to write like Madonna sings, autobiographically, and with self-adulating fervor.

But since this is a point on which the North American churches are now revealed to be nearly as confused as the general culture, we had better pause on it: in the postmodern literary world, poetry *has* largely ceased to be a communal artifact. A lot of it, you might think, has also pretty much ceased to be poetry. Think of this in AM Radio terms. Yes, there is the mostly low poetry of pop music: 'Big truck got my baby, / big truck got my baby, / big truck got my baby, / don't got no baby no more.' It alliterates, it scans, and it could even be said to rhyme. Christians in North America have their own baptized versions of such things. In the Church of the Blessed Overhead Projector they are sung regularly, Sunday morning echoes for many a Saturday night Nashville lament. But I hope you will allow me to suggest that not many of these ditties have much chance of attaining to enduring literary status in the manner of the hymns of Bernard of Clairvaux or Praetorius, Wesley, Watts, or Newton. That is, their poetry will not likely be reset to new tunes again and again as the fashions of music change. Little enough of it may, without special pleading, be said to voice with memorable eloquence a larger public dream or community vision. It is rather the lingo of private 'devotion' that tends to dominate, and along with it, a secular, often self-indulgent literary taste.

I do not wish to condemn all praise songs. I do wish to suggest that in their predominance something important to us as a thoughtful, worshipping community is at risk of being left out. Let me take you back to secular literary basics to try to suggest what this 'something' is. If we were to reflect back over even the basic Western survey syllabus that some of us have taught and nearly all of us studied, we might – any of us – readily produce a treasury of examples of poetry whose only purpose is celebration of the *common* life. Most of them, mind you, are from the first half of the anthologies. Not all are Christian. The opening lines of the *Odyssey* must here suffice to characterize the generality of literature surviving from the ancient world. Homer, as we call the narrator, begins:

Sing in me, Muse, and through me tell the story
Of that man skilled in all ways of contending,
The wanderer, harried for years on end,
On the proud height of Troy. . . .
Of these adventures, Muse, daughter of Zeus,
Tell us in our time, lift the great song again.

(trans. R. Fitzgerald)

The great song which must again be lifted is here a song too grand for any particularity of voice; it is a common story, the common property of a people
whose life and aspiration for *arete* it both characterizes and celebrates. The poet
is not the singular maker of this poem; he does not pretend to original invention. He is, as well as poets at least until the time of Dante, a servant for his own
time to a timeless tale, conferring cultural identity upon those who hear and
retell it. He is a spokesperson.

The similarity between the Greek and Hebrew notions of 'common story'
is striking. That voice which we identify with Moses in Deuteronomy 6 commands story telling in the same breath as it commands obedience to the law of
God: '*Shema Ysrael, Adonai Elohenu, Adonai echad*':

> And these words which I command you today shall be in your heart. You shall teach
> them diligently to your children, and shall talk of them when you sit in your house,
> when you walk by the way, when you lie down, and when you rise up.
>
> (Deut. 6:4–7, NKJV)

Persistence of the common story refurbishes and enhances the community
memory even as it defines what is still most to be loved. Told and retold, the
story shapes the community's future. Communal celebration of what their
God had wrought in Abraham, in Isaac and in Jacob, how above all He had led
them out of bondage into liberty, has been through long centuries of the diaspora the very sustenance of Jewish life, the lifeline of an improbable survival.
And if it has been able to overcome much more and form so many more mem-
ories than the song sung by Homer, this is at least in part because every parent
learned to tell it: their Homer was in every home.

Christians, grafted into the story, have sprouted their own fruitfulness. But
in the early stages of our growth especially, it was more than the narrative sap of
the root stock that gave rise to Christian poetry. It was, as well, the care to hold
in check the individual exuberance of each varying branch, pruning mere
quantity so as to enhance quality. An abundance of riches thus appeared in a
small space.

An apt literary example is afforded by the earliest Middle English lyric
extant, a flyleaf poem from about 1120 AD, deep in the depths of Norman
occupation and the official supremacy of another tribe and language. It has only

four lines – no epic to be sure. Yet in a way that confounds expectations tutored by the modern lyric, this poem parades no private fantasy, no aberrant or existential confession. It is rather, most deliberately, a public poem:

Myrie songen the monkes binne Ely
Whan Cnut Kyng rewe ther-by:
Roweth, knightes, neer the lond
And here we these monkes song.

[Merrily sang the monks in Ely abbey
When King Canute was rowing nearby
Row, knights, near the land
And let us hear these monks' song.']

(Anonymous, 12th-century)[10]

King Canute, you may remember, had already learned what many of his modern counterparts could well afford to: time and tide are not subject to the vanities of self-fashioning. No amount of mere political power will hold back the sea, which, in its own un-postmodern way, is as inexorable as the ordinance of God. But that part of reality is far too obvious to be this poet's subject; Canute's name alone is sufficient to conjure the image of self-restrained and therefore exemplary regality the poet wants. The king and his knights – rough-hewn warriors all – are out doing precisely what (in not so merry old England) their duty obliges: they are patrolling the estuary, guarding against surprise attack by perhaps even rougher Viking marauders. Inside the abbey church at Ely, the monks are doing precisely what, given their vocation, they should be doing: praying the sung psalms and intercessions of the office on behalf of the whole community. This was their complementary task, their *opus dei* – singing the new song, telling the old, old story. As Canute and his warriors head out upon the water, the king hears their sung prayers and has his craft brought in close to the abbey walls, so that his 'knightes' and he can pause quietly, drawing strength from the wafting and melodic words. It is an image of ideal social order as the anonymous poet cherishes it: the City of the World here corrects its course as it hearkens to the music of the City of God.

It has been a long time since we had anonymous poets. One of the least anonymous, William Carlos Williams, illustrates in a famous little poem ('The Red Wheelbarrow') the characteristic departure of modern poetry from a shared public vision:

so much depends
upon

a red wheel
barrow

---

[10] *One Hundred Middle English Lyrics*, 3.

glazed with rain
water

beside the white
chickens

So much depends. So much of what? The image is lovely, but, as Russell Peck
has shrewdly observed, what we draw from it is only what it conjures in the
subjectivity of our own private imaginations.[11] To say that this poem is impres-
sionistic would be imprecise; it offers not an impression (for that you want
Edna St Vincent Millay) but a bare image. Or perhaps, I should say, an image
'glazed' – it is not a form of realism exactly either. It is more like the vacancy of
Dada, the glazed emptiness of nature in the painting, let us say, of a Franz Marc.
Who can tell the meaning of it? Well, everyone, of course, and no one. The
meaning for you, to paraphrase Humpty Dumpty, is up to you – your private
fantasy as you reflect upon such a poem need not correspond to that of anyone
else, least of all the poet. In respect of any wider world of thought you have
almost perfect freedom – academic and otherwise – to think what you will.
The poem is, in its own way, merely a prompt for one's own fantasia, which is
another way of saying that it is representatively already postmodern. We may
suspect this has much to do with its popularity in the high school and college
curriculum. We may likewise suspect that the indeterminacy in such occasions
for private vision has contributed to the gradual decline of public vision as a
subject for literary treatment and reflection.

The Bible and Academic Freedom

Radical freedom: it sounds so good to the academic ear. Who could object to
it? Is it not nowadays indeed a kind of civic heresy to object to personal
freedom?

Well, let us try to pursue the rhetoric in these questions at a little deeper
level. The stance of postmodern literary criticism – over and against the canonical text – is to some appreciable degree analogous to the stance of professional
organizations such as ACCU and AAUP on defining *academic freedom*: the freedom claimed is increasingly an individualistic and subjective order of freedom.
To it, the idea of communal freedom – the freedom for some communities to
establish independent community norms, is often seen as a threat, perhaps
because it suggests a theoretical limit, namely, the possibility of reciprocal
accountability. In their attempts to elevate the individual over community,

---

[11] R.A. Peck, 'Public Dreams and Private Myths: Perspectives in Middle English
Literature.'

postmodern educators (whether legal or literary) have begun to resist ever more strongly the privilege of minority group counterbalance – of communal freedom for sub-communities to speak collectively. This, as most of you know, tends to apply especially when Christian religious or dissenting communities seek to define a communal rather than merely individualistic right with respect to state and federal statutes. (Other, often smaller but more vociferous 'communities' in the nominal sense, tend to get a pass.) This developing bias has enormous significance for Christian colleges and universities in particular, since in the United States and Canada at least, they need, for survival of their institutional missions, to be able to claim the right of a constituted community to 'act as a speaker,'[12] to be a voice among institutional voices in otherwise public education. It now appears that if they are to maintain religious exemption from a rigorous extrapolation of individually focussed rights in the secular sphere, Christian colleges and universities may need to defend their position with a much more coherently biblical (as distinct from secularist) reasoning than has typically been the case during the last century. That is to say, we may need to define our position in convincingly communal rather than individualistic terms. Succinctly: if Christian institutions are to defend themselves against the increasingly shrill charge that their hiring practices, curricular choices, and conduct policies exist simply to repress academic freedom as well as other forms of individual freedom (such as sexual freedom), they will need to rise above a definition of freedom which is, presuppositionally, as loosely subjectivist and individualistic as that of their postmodern antagonists. Those of us who help define these institutions will need to be able to show that we are people of a common Book – that we have read it, and seek to live by it.

The role of vernacular literary study as a university discipline in promulgating the cause of academic freedom, if not exclusively its development, is fairly well known. In this context, however, it may be worth noting how it connects to a pattern in which many writers and literary critics have tended to be rebels against the biblical traditions in which they were raised. English literature as a university discipline began in the nineteenth century in this fashion explicitly: one might think here again of Matthew Arnold and Ralph Waldo Emerson. This development was coeval with the emergence of avant-garde novelists writing against biblical ethical norms and taboos, as well as learned subversions of the Bible's theological authority: it may well be that such broader cultural challenges as the explicit anti-evangelicalism of novelists Samuel Butler, D.H. Lawrence, Theodore Dreiser and Sinclair Lewis, but also of Oscar Wilde and James Joyce in the Catholic context, as well, indeed, as Philip Roth in the

---

[12] See J.D. Gordon III, 'Individual and Institutional Academic Freedom at Religious Colleges and Universities,' 30; also M.W. McConnell, 'Academic Freedom in Religious Colleges and Universities,' 303, 305.

context of Judaism, have been the more influential. Defense of the works of such writers against censorship or religious scruple, especially in the classroom (e.g., *Lady Chatterley's Lover, Lolita*) have been signal battles in the emergence of statutes and policies respecting academic freedom. Resisters of such edgy texts have in the end almost invariably been cast as religious bigots and/or sanctimonious prudes. In response, Christians among the resisters have often been embarrassed, and some have fallen all over themselves, so to speak, to assure our critics that we aren't the prudes they assume.

If debates over the meaning and application of the principle of academic freedom tend to have the aura of old religious controversies, it may be in part because ranks of the professoriate in the literary disciplines have at least until the mid-twentieth century been rather more than proportionately filled with seminary dropouts and recanters of vows of ordination. Like Melville's Ahab or Joyce's Stephen Daedelus, such persons tend to take their ongoing quarrels with God quite seriously. One of the better known, Northrop Frye, has described the English curriculum as *Secular Scripture* (1976). It is a reasonable description. More recent literary theorists such as the rabbinically-trained Jacques Derrida have filled many volumes in an effort to show that no *écriture*, however, can be so authoritative as the opinions of the individual reader, and that, however ironically, preoccupation with the Word – or word – is futile. To all this spindrift Jonathan Culler has added a summarizing codicil; namely, that postmodern literary theory is 'an essentially anti-theological activity.'[13] Such positioning abounds.

I offer this thumbnail sketch merely to indicate to non-specialists something of the complex genealogy of academic freedom as a strategic initiative within the university, but as consistent with a subversion of traditional religious authority for which my discipline is, for good or ill, at least partly responsible. The sowing of wild oats by former clergy has for more than a century made literary study a kind of alternative catechism for many; it is this alternative catechism by which secular higher education and the judicial system have increasingly charted our wider cultural course. But this catechism is now undergoing a doctrinal development of its own, in terms of which Christian colleges and universities are increasingly prone to be challenged. It is about to become acceptable to partisans of academic freedom in some jurisdictions that at least one Book *should* be censored.[14]

---

[13] J. Culler, *On Deconstruction: Theory and Criticism after Structuralism.*

[14] The recent prominence of literary study of the Bible does not substantially alter the trajectory of this development, though it does seek to return the Bible to the foundation while insisting that it have a status precisely like that of any other text in the postmodern curriculum. See M.J. McManus, 'Should Public Schools Teach the Bible,' commenting on the recent Gallup poll on teen access to the Bible.

The Battle of the Books which lies behind contemporary arguments to exclude communities of a common book from 'privileging' their Book in either curriculum or law courts is a larger subject than we can satisfactorily consider within the scope of this essay. I must restrict myself here to suggesting avenues for further reflection.

Let me draw on the first two parts of this paper for one suggestion. Christian academics have been among those critics of postmodernist articulations of the inviolability of radical subjectivism who note its paradoxical, even self-contradictory character. For example, those who nominally advocate the most libertarian, even anarchic view of personal academic freedom tend to be those most prone to deny it to others – most notably to groups whose ideas of freedom have historically focussed on community as its locus and looked to self-transcending narratives as its defining exemplars (e.g., conservative and Anabaptistic Christians, Orthodox Jews and, more recently, Catholics).[15]

Yet all the while, in most Christian churches, universities and colleges, a secular, subjectivist, individualistic notion of freedom has become essentially institutionalized as if it also was a *Christian* norm! When this confusion is coupled with Scriptural illiteracy, the result, I believe, is destructive to a coherent biblical worldview. The injurious consequences that flow from failing to possess our own Book more securely are doubtless manifold, but surely they hurt us more than anyone. If our popular culture takes individual sexual freedom to be the highest good, and our educational culture thinks individual academic freedom is the highest good (these often go together), is our idea of freedom any better? In many cases, I think, not so much as we should wish.

Let me give one example, which here must stand for many of similar consequence to be found across the ecclesiastical landscape. I refer to that much celebrated parochial 'distinctive' of 'Baptist freedom.' 'What Baptist freedom means to me,' a leading spokesperson for the denomination in Texas is quoted as saying, 'is that as a Baptist I am free to interpret the Bible in any way I see fit.' This kind of statement apparently thrills the soul of some within the local constituency, but my own, Baptist upbringing notwithstanding, is not among them. Here is the reason: what has happened in many such expressions of interpretative freedom is that the authority of the Bible has given way *de facto* to the authority of the individual who reads some of it – or maybe just 'has an opinion' on it. As a radical extension of a shallow utilitarian and consumerist evolution of the doctrine of the 'priesthood of the believer' (not of 'the believers'), the effect can quickly become a full logical equivalent of some of the most 'will-to-power' postmodernism in literary and legal theory. I forbear to say it as a generalization about my own generation, but I am increasingly willing to say

---

[15]   See, e.g., E. Ottolenghi, 'The Stalinists of the AUT and How to Fight Back.'

it of the children and grandchildren who are our students: what such unreflective but frequently vigorous subjectivism would seem quite naturally to lead to, in practice, is neglect of the Bible altogether – even among the pious. In such a condition, 'soul competency' too readily generates into 'sole competency.' At that point, how relevant is the text? And absent a centering conversation in the teaching of Scripture, what is to keep our reflexive invocation of Christ from becoming an empty semantic gesture, even a psychological redundancy?

C.H. Spurgeon, the famous British Baptist preacher of a century ago, observed that 'instructed Christians recognize the value of the Lord's Word and warmly express it.'[16] By this standard, I suggest, we are not instructing our Christian undergraduates well enough before they come to college and university. Not only in matters of personal morality, but in respect of the way we demonstrate a sense of obligation to our neighbors, it can seem as if the Bible did not exist. In my literature classes I have found disappointingly few students who were not woefully ignorant of the Bible, both narratively and conceptually. I suspect that the problem is hardly unique to my university.[17] Though most would identify themselves as 'biblical Christians,' they most evidently do not possess their Book.

In what, then, do teaching and preaching in many of our churches consist? Well, far too often, they consist in 'relational,' 'how to succeed without really trying' injunctions, spiced with humorous stories (often the only real 'text'), references to movies and television shows, with perhaps a light scattering of verses from the more accessible Pauline epistles to 'authorize' the talk as some kind of sermon after all. Large numbers of biblical books are typically ignored in such preaching (the Gospels, universal letters, Acts, Romans, much of the Old Testament) because their content is unflattering or their thought too demanding. Scripture itself, in many churches, is now never read aloud in whole or discreet passages, partly because that would imply that the sermon which followed should in some measure be a 'reading' in common of the common text, partly because it would reduce the time available for musical entertainment and theologically hollow but emotionally gratifying praise songs, but mostly, I am told, because it is felt that the congregation can't 'follow it.' Meanwhile, in these musical 'moments' (and it may be that for many, orgasmic music itself is the actual object of worship), the subjective focus is often

---

[16] *The Golden Alphabet of the Praises of Scripture. . . Being a Devotional Commentary upon the One Hundred and Nineteenth Psalm.*

[17] See A. Crouch, 'Compliant but Confused'; also T.K. Beal, 'Seeking out Lives of Faith.' Beal, a professor of religion at Case Western Reserve University observes that the academic study of religion is 'a place where you'll find a great many ex-evangelicals, along with countless other lapsed or disaffected religious types.' This may help to account for the surprisingly small contribution of religion departments generally to the affirmative teaching of biblical texts.

overwhelming, distorting in a manner like unto entertainment of a purely secular, commercial kind.

In such a shallow spiritual environment it is a strange notion of Christian freedom that gets articulated. Essentially, I conclude, it is 'the freedom to be me.' But this is a neo-pagan, not a biblical, Christian notion of freedom. It is essentially individualistic, has no biblical or theological warrant, and while it may appear in the short run to correspond quite nicely to pop cultural clichés, or to the sort of academic freedom of the individual professor advocated by some of our contemporaries, it certainly does not correspond to 'the freedom wherewith Christ has made us free' (Gal. 3:1; Gk. *eleutheria*). As such, ironically, it is entirely inadequate to defend any claim of Christian colleges and universities to religiously distinctive practice, not to mention exemption from laws governing hiring practices and, ultimately, curricular choices and course content. That is, even though most of our schools do not permit radically individualistic sexual freedoms, our communal freedom to be different in other aspects of the moral life still may be in jeopardy. Indeed, who can now doubt that the communal freedom to hold to biblical rather than secularist sexual mores is itself insecure?

Vis-à-vis academic freedom, the urgent issue now is the right – or not – of religious communities to hold to internal norms in terms of which some kinds of behavior, including certain kinds of advocacy and even some kinds of research, may be deemed inappropriate, deficient in moral virtue or a transgression of basic communally held notions of rectitude – i.e., commitments regarding theological truth and ethical practice. It is evident that there is *no* ideal of communal freedom that does not entail some order of constraint upon individual freedom. And there's the rub both for church discipline and for religious exemption for colleges that wish to select and retain faculty in the light of essentially biblical norms.

In the Bible, which evangelical and other orthodox Christians take to provide the normative basis for both theological understanding and ethical practice, the Great Commandment is referred to also as 'the perfect law of liberty' (Jas. 1:25). Freedom is a communal virtue of a high order and, out of a prior respect for the biblical commandment, it seems to me that Christians ought to attach a high order of respect indeed to what is generally referred to as 'academic freedom.' But not as merely individualistically defined, à la mode.

Two years ago I took part in an event that was billed as a debate about academic freedom. My opponent posed a strategic question: 'There are two parties in a contest here,' he said, 'the Truth party and the Liberty party. I am of the Liberty party. Of which party are you?' The casual antithesis presupposed by this question has, in purely secular contexts, long ceased to be surprising. Yet in a biblical perspective the question asserts, of course, an obvious false dichotomy.

In the university, academic freedom is generally advocated as necessary to the pursuit of *truth*, and thus to an authentic learning environment. It is less frequently observed that, on this account, academic freedom is valued and defended as an *instrumental good*. Logically, it is not freedom *per se* but truth that is ultimately to be loved and sought as the chief end of intellectual inquiry.

But the confusions of our culture run deep – deep enough to be seen in casual public and sometimes patriotic quotations of John 8:32: 'the truth shall make you free.' Yet in this saying of Jesus, the relationship between freedom and truth is characterized as reciprocal, apposite rather than opposite: '*If* you continue in my Word, *then* shall you be my disciples, *and* you shall know the Truth, *and* [then] the truth shall make you free' (John 8:31). Here it appears that Truth is in fact a necessary condition for our freedom, or at least that the authentic experience of either requires both. That is, the grammatical construction renders explicit a set of consecutive and interactive conditions. If I may quote to this point a comment of the late John Paul II, 'Human freedom and God's law are not in opposition; on the contrary, they appeal one to the other' (*Veritas Splendor*, 30).

Here we see that the biblical notion of freedom refuses to abstract or isolate the experience of the individual from the Body. In community, none of us is, as a selfish wish might have it, absolutely autonomous, 'a law unto the self': Christian freedom is thus qualitatively different. When Jesus said 'You shall know the truth and the truth shall make you free' (Gk. *eleutheros*) he did not mean that the truth would make each of us independent – let alone autonomous. (He does seem to have meant that his truth would liberate us from myopic self-enclosure and tribal defensiveness alike.) On the biblical account, it is our agreement to live within a common accountability to a new common normative authority that creates the conditions in which true freedom may be experienced.

The instinct to defend oneself against this higher order of freedom is hardly novel, of course. Immediately after Jesus says these words in John's gospel his hearers respond defensively (and inadvertently somewhat humorously) by protesting, 'We are descendants of Abraham, and have never been slaves to anyone' (33) – conveniently forgetting not only Egypt and Babylon, but their rather painful current subjection and occupation by Rome (one can imagine well-armed Roman soldiers standing close by and unpleasantly attentive as they converse). Then, up from their defensiveness or repression comes the denial transposed, now predictably in the guise of a fearful aspiration concerning political liberation, 'What do you mean by saying "You will be made free?"' What Jesus says to them in reply is doubtless of some moment now also for us: 'The truth is that everyone who commits sin is a slave to sin. The slave does not have a permanent place in the household; the son has a place there forever. So if the Son makes you free, you will be really free (*ontos eleutheroi*)' (34–

36). The point of this saying of Jesus is not that the spiritual freedom which comes from grace and obedience does not have possible favorable consequence in forms of civic liberty, but rather that we cannot realize that connection until we have understood that our more formative bondage is spiritual. The narrative as a whole shows that when we become habituated to spiritual bondage we are likely to view the world and our place in it as solipsistically as those who, in whatever condition and relation to power, imagine freedom simply as a kind of independence or exemption from orders of law or obligation imposed by others. The specific force of Jesus' teaching is to show that one cannot achieve real personal freedom without a living, reciprocal relationship to truth, namely the Word of God – and to Truth, namely the Word of God Incarnate. After all, the reason that 'the Son makes free' is his own uncompromised obedience, his willingness 'freely' to 'obey.'

To summarize: when representatives of the wider academy defend academic freedom by arguing that it is essential to the pursuit of truth, they are ostensibly underscoring the value of academic freedom as an instrumental good; the higher good this freedom serves is evidently 'truth.' In effect, however, the terms have been collapsed, as if 'freedom' itself, individual and unrestricted freedom, were the only 'truth' worth having. By comparison, in Jesus' formulation the instrumental good is in fact concomitant to authentic discipleship, the faithfulness of which is its necessary condition; our abiding in the truth is the only sure means by which we can recognize and experience true freedom. But the character of this key difference, which presupposes the relationship of community to the possibility of true Christian liberty *and* personal freedom, has often been obscured in contemporary ecclesial discourse precisely to the degree to which an individualistic notion of freedom has usurped a biblical scope for the term. Many of us are very quick to see legalism as an enemy of *eleutheria*, much slower to appreciate that so also, and perhaps currently more deadly, is license.

So then, ought biblical Christians and their institutions to have a commitment to academic freedom? The answer is Yes, but not the sort of unbridled freedom so commonly insisted upon by our secular counterparts today. Christians do cherish freedom of speech both as a freedom from undue fear of temporal power and as a liberty of tongue and spirit to tell the truth (Eph. 3:12; Phil. 1:20 [Gk. *parresia*]). I do not doubt it can be shown textually and historically that it is from this biblical notion of freedom of speech that the provisions of the American First Amendment derive.

Should Christians accordingly regard academic freedom as an unqualified good, the *sine qua non* of intellectual integrity in the university? Not quite: we should regard academic freedom as a precious but nonetheless instrumental good which, to retain its value, must always be set in relation to the things which are above it, and prompt it, namely Truth and Love. That is why our own contribution to the international conversation in the academy and elsewhere on these matters should be patient in making the distinction between instrumental and ultimate goods, as between personal privilege and that more self-effacing, charitable concern for that order of the Good which in the very highest sense of the term, we call common.

Here is an instance then, where the literature of faith, principally the Bible, needs to be resituated more fully in the definition of our own community identity. Only then can we speak from the margins into the general culture in any very authentic way. On these particular issues, the biblical grand narrative must be appealed to more knowledgeably in our churches first of all. Only thereby can we hope to show that from the Decalogue forward in biblical tradition, law and liberty are closely linked (Ex. 20:1–2; Is. 48:18), and that the 'perfect law of liberty' (Jas. 1:25; 2:8) is a commandment to love the neighbor which is itself grounded in a prior commandment to love God with heart, soul and mind. That is, we have to return in a spirit of obedience to biblical exposition and orthodox biblical theology if we are to make our case against strident denigrations of the Bible by those who haven't read it but certainly have an opinion on it.

I want to suggest that the future of our coherent identity depends far more than we may have realized on recovery of the Scriptures (both narratively and theologically) across all disciplines of our thought. We need for ourselves, if we are not to ring hollow to our students and the world, an intellectual centering in our common story which is generous, capacious enough to permit a diverse body to have conversation around the prior Word. Our command of biblical resources needs to be deep enough that we cannot easily be confused – and thus confusing to others – about the meaning of Scripture's central terms and concepts, and so that we can readily articulate out of them our distinctive shared worldview.

If we reacquire this relationship to the Bible in our churches, in our private and communal reading, teaching and exposition, then it will come naturally to us in the articulation of our collegiate missions and the daily practice of our disciplines. Without that prior order of familiarity, I suspect, our connectedness to our biblical foundation will continue to be artificial, awkward, shallow, and fraught with embarrassment.

Bibliography

American Council of Trustees and Alumni, 'The Hollow Core – Failure of the General Education Curriculum: A Fifty College Study,' May 24, 2004, available at <http://www.goacta.org/publications/Reports/HollowCoreWeb.pdf>

Academe (bi-monthly magazine of the AAUP), Jan/Feb 2006, with articles including P.J. Hill, 'My Religious College, My Secular Profession,' K. Wagner, 'Faith Statements Do Restrict Academic Freedom,' L. Hardy, 'The Value of Limitations,' B. Olszewski, 'Critical Intellectual Inquiry at Catholic Colleges'

Barna, G., *Barna Research Online* (Jan 12, 2004), 3

Beal, T.K., 'Seeking out Lives of Faith,' *The Chronicle of Higher Education*, April 15, 2005, B6–10

Cole, B., Keynote Address, National Citizen Corps Conference, Washington, DC, July 29, 2003

Crouch, A., 'Compliant but Confused,' *Christianity Today* (April, 2004), 98

Culler, J., *On Deconstruction: Theory and Criticism after Structuralism* (Ithaca: Cornell University Press, 1982)

Delbanco, A., 'The Decline and Fall of Literature,' *The New York Review of Books* 46.16 (1999), 32–38

Gordon, J.D., III, 'Individual and Institutional Academic Freedom at Religious Colleges and Universities,' *Journal of College and University Law* 2 (2003), 30

Greenblatt, S., 'Presidential Address 2002: "Stay, Illusion" – on Receiving Messages from the Dead,' *PMLA* 118 (2003), 417–26

Jeffrey, D.L., 'Communion, Community and Our Common Book: or, Can Faustus Be Saved?' *Christianity and Literature* 53 (2004), 233–46

Marsden, G., *The Soul of the American University: From Protestant Establishment to Established Nonbelief* (New York: Oxford University Press, 1994)

McConnell, M.W., 'Academic Freedom in Religious Colleges and Universities,' *Law and Contemporary Problems* 53 (1990), 303–24

—, 'Religious Freedom at the Crossroads,' *University of Chicago Law Review* 59 (1992), 115–94

McManus, M.J., 'Should Public Schools Teach the Bible,' *Ethics and Religion* 237 (May 14, 2005)

Miller, J.H., 'On the Authority of Literature,' *Lectures on Modern Literature*, Baylor University, April 17, 2001

Morey, M.M., and D.H. Holtschneider, 'Leadership and the Age of the Laity: Emerging Patterns in Catholic Higher Education,' *Current Issues in Catholic Higher Education* 23 (2003), 83–103

One Hundred Middle English Lyrics, ed. R.D. Stevick (Urbana: University of Illinois Press, 1994), 3

Ottolenghi, E., 'The Stalinists of the AUT and How to Fight Back,' *National Review*, May 2, 2005

Peck, R.A., 'Public Dreams and Private Myths: Perspectives in Middle English Literature,' *PMLA* 90 (1975), 461–68

Spurgeon, C.H., *The Golden Alphabet of the Praises of Scripture...Being a Devotional Commentary upon the One Hundred and Nineteenth Psalm* (London: Passmore and Alabaster, 1907)

The Bible and the Academy

Some Concluding Thoughts and Possible Future Directions

C. Stephen Evans

I wish in this concluding essay to make some personal judgments about the other essays in this volume, including the relationships they have to each other and the possibilities they suggest for future work. These papers are far too rich and complex to be summarized in a brief manner, and so I will not try to do that. Rather, I will attempt to address a few main issues that one or more of the essays deals with, looking at them from my own perspective. My thoughts will be appreciative but also critical at places.

There is a large amount of agreement and common ground in the papers by Dallas Willard, William Abraham, Al Wolters, Scott Hahn, and Glenn Olsen, respectively. Let me begin with Dallas Willard. His paper tackles head-on what I would call the failure of nerve that has so often beset Christians in the academic world. Willard wants to challenge Christian scholars to affirm that Christians, through the Bible, actually gain knowledge. Our Christian faith is not merely opinion or conjecture or a set of preferences or values. We know something about the ultimate character of the universe, what it means to be genuinely happy or well-off, what it means to be good, and how a person can move towards achieving these fundamental goals. If these things are genuinely known by Christians, then they have a place in the university, if the university is the place where genuine knowledge is advanced and transmitted.

However, to many, perhaps even to many of us, Willard's claims will appear utopian. We can't imagine such knowledge claims being taken seriously in the contemporary university. This is particularly true of the secular university, but even at Christian institutions many of our colleagues will find lots of reasons to avoid making such claims. We are intimidated by our understanding that any such claims will be challenged and even dismissed as unfounded, dogmatic and overbearing. This is what I mean in referring to a failure of nerve among Christians in the academy. I think one line of thought that cripples us goes something like this: Genuine knowledge should lead to convergence and consensus. The conception of knowledge most of us take for granted includes a certain picture, at least partly mythological, of how things are supposed to go in science and mathematics. However, Christian claims to knowledge will essentially be contested in a modern pluralistic world, and if we think knowledge requires convergence, then we will be reluctant to claim that our Christian view of things amounts to knowledge.

Here is a suggestion for regaining our nerve. We need to recognize, as Willard says, that scientific knowledge is not the only kind of knowledge and that the presence of disagreement is not necessarily a sign that knowledge is lacking. If we think of politics or economics, each of us can probably think of some convictions we have that we are willing to claim amount to knowledge, even though we know that many others, equally knowledgeable, will disagree with us. I think, for example, that George Bush's decision to start a pre-emptive war of choice against Iraq was unjust, and I think this is not merely an opinion but something I know. Yet I also know that there are many people, Christians as well as non-Christians, who will disagree with me about that. But that realization does not shake my conviction that this amounts to knowledge. I know and acknowledge my fallibility; I realize I could be wrong. But that is a feature of the human condition, not a reason to become a sceptic. If this political example does not move you, think of a case where one person in a family recognizes that another member of the family is manipulatively taking advantage of the family's good will, even though others in the family have not yet recognized this. The fact is that all of us know some things that others who should be able to know as well disagree with.

Why is this so? It is because knowledge, contrary to Enlightenment epistemology, is not merely conditioned by evidence and logical relationships, but by the character and skills and situation of the knower. This thought brings me to the other four papers I have grouped with Willard's, all of which in some way are rooted in this insight. William Abraham wants to help us see that the way we modern Christians think about the Bible obscures rather than clarifies the way the Bible functions as a source of knowledge. Abraham argues that the Bible should not be thought of primarily in epistemic terms, as a foundation or criterion that supplies or certifies religious knowledge. One might think that this claim contradicts Willard's paper, but I do not think it does. For Abraham wants to say that we do gain knowledge through God's revelation, and I would guess he surely would want to say that the Bible either is or can be a form of revelation, or at least plays a key role for most Christians in giving us such a revelation. My suggestion is that Abraham is not really arguing that the Bible does not give rise to knowledge, but that it does not do so if we conceive of it simply as providing *data*, a set of foundationalist facts to support theological theorizing. Instead we need to think of think of the Scriptures as functioning soteriologically, and we need to reclaim them for the Church. However, it seems to me that when we do this we will recognize that the Bible is indeed a source of knowledge, though I agree fully with Abraham that the fact that we gain knowledge through the Bible when it functions salvifically as God intended is more certain than any particular epistemological account of how this happens, just as the reality of the atonement seems to me more certain than any particular theological theory of how the atonement works.

Although I agree with what I take to be Abraham's main point, I do have some worries about the separation of the soteriological and epistemological function of Scripture. If the Bible does indeed give us knowledge, there is a sense in which it can properly be said to be an epistemic norm, and one of the areas where the Church should do some more thinking concerns the way in which this is so. Abraham seems to think that once we understand the soteriological nature of Scripture we can embrace the critical scholarly work of the modern biblical scholar. However, it is not clear to me whether the conclusions of some biblical scholars do not in fact undermine the soteriological work of Scripture, and in so doing cripple its value as a source of knowledge as well.

Al Wolters' paper, from my perspective, continues to advance this line of thought by giving us insight into what it means for the Church to reclaim its Scriptures. One thing it means is recognizing that biblical scholarship is not a neutral, objective science, but itself reflects substantive commitments. Such commitments are of diverse kinds; some of us might disagree with Wolters' taxonomy of various kinds of assumptions Christians bring to Scripture, such as is found in his discussion of various ways of thinking about the relation of nature to grace. However, I think he is surely right to say that some of these commitments we bring to the Bible are themselves religious in character, and it is important to unmask those religious commitments that hinder or even outright block us from discerning what God wants to say to us through the Bible.

I myself would want to argue that the most significant differences in these assumptions no longer run along denominational fault lines. There are likely still some Thomists around who may have a two-stage theory of nature and grace, with grace supplementing nature, and I agree with Wolters that this view of the relation between nature and grace is less than satisfactory if we take it as a general model. However, it is a mistake to think that this is 'the Catholic view,' in contrast to Protestant views. I have discovered there are many Baptists who think of nature and grace in this way as well, and that there are many Catholics who have a much richer view of such things. And even if the 'grace adding to nature' model is deficient when taken by itself or as a general model, it nevertheless can have value in some contexts, as a way of affirming the goodness of the created order.

I would also want to raise a question about the role of extra-biblical philosophical assumptions. Granted, when Augustine employs Plato, or Aquinas uses Aristotle there is a risk that the Gospel will be distorted. But there is also a possibility that elements in the biblical revelation will come into sharper view, and I believe that in the providence of God this sometimes happens.

Scott Hahn's reading of the exegetical views of Benedict XVI in some ways could be seen as a kind of synthesis of the papers of Willard, Abraham, and Wolters. With Willard, Hahn argues Benedict thinks we actually can come to know things through Scripture. With Wolters the current Pope thinks that, though historical work is valuable, it is crucially important that we be critical of philosophical assumptions that may hamstring biblical interpretation. And with Abraham, Benedict, on Hahn's reading, wants to see biblical interpretation as the province of theology, not just biblical scholars, and theology itself as something that must be done in the context of the Church. Furthermore, theology is a task not just for the theologians, but in some sense must be undertaken by all of the faithful gifted by God with intelligence and education to seek understanding.

Glenn Olsen's paper, in my view, completes this section by giving us some concrete thought on some of the implications of taking the Bible to be God's word, a word properly interpreted and understood by the Church in the context of prayer and worship. Olsen properly argues that a 'spiritual sense' does not have to be understood as an alternative to taking seriously the historical context of biblical texts, but rather as providing us with new layers of meaning. Far from being an arbitrary imposition on the text, such a reading of the Bible is inherent in Christianity, which begins with just this kind of reading of the Old Testament. I would just want to add that anyone who finds such a reading of the Scriptures problematic would do well to reread 'Second Meanings,' chapter 10 of C.S. Lewis's *Reflections on the Psalms*, which is full of Lewis's typical good sense and clarity.

The second group of papers I want to discuss focus on more specific areas of the academy in relation to the Bible. Byron Johnson's paper seems to me most important simply in helping us see how little research has been done on what people actually know about the Bible and in suggesting a large number of possible fruitful areas for empirical research. Of course the raw data that could be collected will itself be in need of interpretation and here the Church will once more need the biblically informed scholar who does not merely have biblical information but knows how to think and assess things from a Christian perspective.

I found Robert Roberts' attempt to put what we might call New Testament psychology, focusing on the concept of the heart, in conversation with contemporary psychological theory and research, to be inspiring. Biblical scholars and theologians may have their criticisms of the way Roberts reads the New Testament; that is well and good and he is certainly open to correction. But my challenge to such critics would be this: Go thou and do likewise. It is high time for our theologians and biblical scholars to be addressing psychologists and economists and other scholars rather than mainly their own guilds. As someone who has himself written a book about the quest for the historical Jesus as well as a book about what Christian psychology might be like, I am well aware of how risky it is to cross disciplinary barriers. However, until the job is done by those better qualified to do it, I suspect we will find philosophers and others stepping into the breach. We need much more conversation across the disciplines and much less worry about what other people in our own guilds or the others will think.

Robert Cochran's paper is an important exploratory survey of the bearing of the Bible upon our thinking about human law. It is cautious in some ways but bold in others, and shows good sense in both of these respects. Cochran embraces some of the tenets of natural law thinking, but is cautious in applying these principles to our own concrete situation, recognizing that it is one thing to have an insight into a principle, but another to see what that principle implies for a particular situation. His paper thus exemplifies the legal virtue of wisdom that he affirms is present in a good judge – one who draws on tradition in interpreting the law, but nevertheless must apply legal principles to particular cases.

David Smith and John Sullivan both give us papers that address education itself, both as a part of the university where we teach people to teach, but also as something that goes on in the university as a whole. Smith gives a powerful reading of Comenius's use of the biblical image of a paradisal garden, both to help us understand Comenius and to help us see how the Bible informs our thinking not merely though propositions and narrative but through fruitful and productive metaphors. These metaphors both suggest lines of inquiry and patterns of thinking and also help us grasp what the propositions and narrative may really be saying. Though I personally have some worry that Comenius may have needed a more robust sense of the nature of human sinfulness, there is little doubt that Smith's reading of Comenius provides a point of departure for some fresh thinking about the educational process, perhaps steering us away from the sterile debate between Rogerian child-centered views of education and traditional views that focus on the transmission of information.

Sullivan gives us, I think, a lovely account of the powerful ways Christian character and themes can shape reading habits, and contrasts this with a devastating account of the contemporary dehumanized university where reading seems to be becoming a dying art. He couples this with a helpful warning that Christians must be careful about the character and style of their intervention in the secular academic world and careful not to allow the forms of power to corrupt the content of the Christian message. All of this I would affirm, though I would take issue with the blanket claim that this might suggest to some, namely that Christian institutions should favor what Duane Litfin calls an umbrella approach to education rather than a systemic approach.[1] I think we must, as a rule, avoid blanket claims and recognize that the model one favors in a specific time and context must reflect the history of that institution and the nature of the cultural context. Certainly, it is unrealistic to expect an umbrella to stand very long if those huddling under the umbrella wish to destroy it. I believe that we need to value and cherish a Christian presence in higher education in many forms: in secular universities, in schools that have a diverse faculty under a Christian 'umbrella,' as well as in schools that attempt to have a Christian identity that permeates all of the campus and every aspect of its life.

Roger Lundin's essay provides a metonymic history of the alienation of the Bible from its place as the cultural authority for nineteenth-century America. He shows us in Ralph Waldo Emerson in particular a man whose journey from the seminary and pulpit, via the biblical criticism of the German academics, took him to a strident secularist podium from which he would seek to make the reading of Scripture intellectually disrespectable. In Lundin's account, Emerson's project was both enormously successful in its own time and formative for the rise of literary study as an alternative or antidote; he offers a trenchant account of how modern literary criticism tried to set itself up as a discipline that would give guidance and meaning to human life by reading texts informed by the Bible, even after faith in the biblical message had been lost. However, there is much reason to doubt, and Lundin shows this powerfully, whether such a discipline can survive in the long run. For it is seems central to the discipline as it has been progressively conceived that it function to 'deconstruct' the biblical foundations of the texts that are studied. But what happens when this process of deconstruction is complete? In that case the texts that were rooted in the biblical narrative themselves become unintelligible and inaccessible, and the discipline that unseats that founding narrative by exploring those texts is left without a clear *raison d'etre*. There is nothing left to deconstruct and the texts by which the deconstruction was accomplished no longer make sense apart from the communal norms against which they were reacting.

David Jeffrey's essay provides further evidence for this judgment about the role the Bible has played in the discipline of English literature. Jeffrey begins with the sad state of contemporary biblical literacy (or the lack thereof), and he then connects this problem with the crisis literature departments face, in which political activism often substitutes for the reading and study of texts. The

---

[1]　See D. Litfin, *Conceiving the Christian College* (Grand Rapids: Eerdmans, 2004) for an explanation of the ideas of a 'systemic' Christian college versus an 'umbrella' model.

problem seems to be that no one is sure what texts should be read or why they should be read; the freedom to deconstruct the Bible as the foundational narrative for English literature has led to aimlessness. This in turn leads Jeffrey to some deep questions about the meaning of freedom, both in the Church and the academy.

There is little doubt that individual freedom is seen as something close to the highest good by many in the academy; such a view can even be found in some forms of Christian faith. Jeffrey does not wish ultimately to question the value of individual freedom; indeed, he claims at one point that such a conception has biblical roots. However, the value of individual freedom must be qualified in several ways.

First of all, he argues, individual freedom is an instrumental good, not an intrinsic good. The scholar desires freedom to seek the truth; the Christian values freedom because he or she sees that genuine love and devotion to God must be voluntary and cannot be coerced. In both cases freedom is valued because freedom makes possible something greater than freedom: truth and salvation. Freedom is good and necessary because it makes it possible to achieve these goods, but a freedom that is merely a freedom 'to do what I want' is simply a tragically missed opportunity.

Second, the freedom of the individual must be qualified by the freedom of the community. Human beings are social beings and cannot be fulfilled and fully human apart from communities in which we participate. To belong to a community to some degree requires the individual to commit to communal norms and values. If I want to join a bowling club, I must be willing to bowl. If I want to join a Baptist church, I must be willing to forego the rule of Bishops and the comforts of having my infant children baptized. An individual who insists on individual freedom of choice on such points while also insisting on being part of a community that cannot survive the choices the individual makes is, paradoxically, working against his or her own freedom. For this individualist is, consciously or unconsciously, working to undermine the existence of distinctive communities, and thereby reduces individual freedom of choice. I cannot choose to be part of a community that does not exist.

Jeffrey wants to argue that a biblical view of freedom must take both of these qualifications into account. The Christian recognizes that freedom is an instrumental good, and also recognizes that the freedom of the individual must be set in the context of the needs of the community. Christian churches and Christian universities have an identifiable character that requires communal freedom.

The preservation of such distinctive communities of character in the present situation may be doubly important. The Christian scholar or student who is living and witnessing in the secular university badly needs a community of Christians who can articulate a vision of meaning and hope that is grounded in the biblical narrative. Such Christian communities are not valued in the secular university, and they are certainly not nourished there. Christian colleges and universities then may play a key role, not only on their own campuses and for their own students and alumni, but also as places of refuge and encouragement for Christian scholars in the broader academic world. They may come to function much as the monasteries did in the so-called 'dark ages,' places that preserve and nourish a vision of scholarship informed by the grand biblical narrative.

In sum, then, if there are major lessons to be drawn from the tapestry of essays in this volume, they surely include the following:

1. In the grand tournament of narratives, we Christian scholars must not lose our nerve. In Christian institutions this narrative can and should define the institution. In a secular context our goal should be to make the Christian story a worthy competitor.

2. To do this we must read the Bible whole and we must read it as the Word of God. This does not mean the rejection of historical study. But it does mean that the ultimate meanings of texts cannot be simply handed over to the critical biblical scholar.

3. This is because 'knowing' is a function of the whole person, not just the intellect, and it is shaped by communities and practices. This is particularly true for moral and religious knowledge.

The University of Gloucestershire

We are glad to see the Scripture and Hermeneutics Seminar come to its completion in the present volume. The University of Gloucestershire has been closely involved with the project from its inception. We were privileged to host two of the Consultations; many colleagues have participated in various ways over the years. We owe a special debt to Craig Bartholomew and Rosemary Hales, who undertook much of the formative work here.

We are also deeply appreciative of the participation of our partners in the project. The British and Foreign Bible Society gave indispensable support throughout. And the project received fresh impetus with the addition in due course of Redeemer University College and Baylor University, each of which hosted a successful Consultation. It was fitting to round off the series at Baylor in June 2006, with the highly stimulating papers offered in the present volume. We are most grateful to David Lyle Jeffrey and C. Stephen Evans for hosting the Baylor Consultation and editing the present volume.

The topic of the 2006 Consultation, and the volume, represents an apt climax to the series. The University of Gloucestershire has a Christian foundation yet sits within the public sector, and therefore seeks ways of expressing its Christian origins in a highly diverse community. It was in this context that our commitment to the project had its beginnings. And so the present volume, with its wide-ranging engagement of the relationship between Theology and the broader life and curriculum of the university, is visionary in a way that we find particularly resonant.

Professor Gordon McConville
Department of Humanities
University of Gloucestershire
Swindon Road
Cheltenham
Gloucestershire GL50 4AZ
UK

British and Foreign Bible Society

The first volume in this seminal series was published in 2000 under the title 'Renewing Biblical Interpretation.' That has been a fitting ambition for the whole project the first phase of which now draws to an end with this volume, 'The Bible and the University.' Each of the seminars has led to a high quality of debate, enlarged understanding and a scholarly volume and this last one was no exception. In many ways we are pushing the boat out further even than before in suggesting a relationship between the Bible and disciplines beyond the realms of Biblical Studies and Theology. Yet the timing may be right as some of the barriers erected by the culture of Modernity crumble and as the force of the rivers of postmodern thought penetrates the dam.

For too long the Academy has operated as though the universe is a closed system and each academic discipline a closed box within it. In truth, just as no man is an island, so no thought is isolated particularly from the underlying assumptions and beliefs held by the thinker. This seminar and the ensuing volume is a bold attempt by scholars from a range of disciplines including Biblical Studies and Theology to think outside their box. To those who hold on to old ways of thinking it will appear to be subversive but to many of us it represents the way forward if we are to preserve the fruits of these past centuries in a future which in the words of one scholar 'may otherwise belong to the barbarians.'

BFBS has been honoured to be the major sponsor of the Scripture and Hermeneutics Seminar which has included employing Rosemary Hales to whom this volume is dedicated. It is a fitting tribute to all her hard work and organisation over the years. We also want to commend the vision of Craig Bartholomew without whose persuasion many of us may not have met and formed the deep relationships which have been a welcome by- product of this initiative and will endure well beyond it. Baylor University proved to be a more than suitable venue for the climax of the project and thanks must go to David Lyle Jeffrey and Stephen Evans who had to do more work than anticipated to pull it together. It was a job well done. As ever, we have been grateful too for the partnership with the University of Gloucestershire and Redeemer University College, Ontario.

My predecessors had a dream that included 'the hermeneutical recovery of the diverse and variegated traditions of the biblical story in the context of an equally diverse, plural and multicultural society.' This continues to be our agenda and we hope that having engaged in these seminars and by producing, with Zondervan and Paternoster Publishers, these volumes we have put it on yours. Only time will tell!

Canon Ann Holt OBE, BA, PGCE
Executive Director of Bible Society (England and Wales)
Stonehill Green, Westlea,
Swindon, SN5 7DG
UK

Baylor University

Baylor University is honored once again to have been able to join with the British and Foreign Bible Society, Redeemer University College and the University of Gloucestershire in support of the Seminar on Scripture and Hermeneutics. As a university with more than 160 years of continuous commitment to Christian higher education, as well as the largest Baptist university in the world, we are deeply interested in the kinds of issues to which Scripture and Hermeneutics Seminar has directed its attention. This present volume arose from the consultation held at Baylor University in June of 2006, an event that we were privileged to host and in which many members of our own university community were enriched by the depth and range of the presentations and conversations that occurred.

It is rather widely apparent that the relationship between formal biblical criticism and the life of Scripture in the churches has come to be at best tangential and at worst adversarial in our times. Despite a now longstanding institutionalized separation, more recently it appears that within the guild itself there have arisen uncertainties about even the residual implications of possible relationship and, further, pressing questions about the justification for biblical studies in the curriculum of contemporary universities and colleges. In the light of these considerations the essays in this volume have a heightened relevance to one of the most pressing issues of university education in the Christian tradition, namely moral development, and thus to the ongoing development of curriculum in the humanities, social science and law. What emerges from this book is a rich demonstration of the continuing pertinence of the Bible for the self understanding of our larger intellectual tradition, and a cumulative suggestion that we may well prove unable to do justice to the intellectual culture we inhabit without access to it as part of our ongoing educational formation.

We congratulate the partners and participants in this consultation, and the work of the Scripture and Hermeneutics Seminar in general over the past decade. Since this is projected at present to be the last volume in the series, we want to take this opportunity to congratulate and thank Craig Bartholomew for the leadership he has provided to his colleagues across the continents and around the English-speaking world as this project has progressed. The achievement has been remarkable, and it is our honor to have had a small part in the collective effort.

David Lyle Jeffrey, FRSC
Distinguished Professor of Literature and the Humanities
Baylor University
Waco, TX 76798-7122
USA

Redeemer University College

Redeemer University College is honoured to have been associated in the past decade with the Scripture and Hermeneutics Seminar, to have given it a home for a period, and to have worked with our older partners – the British and Foreign Bible Society, the University of Gloucestershire, and Baylor University – who have given support to this important international project.

We are grateful for this eighth and culminating volume: *The Bible And The University*. We are most thankful also for the vision, generosity, and determination of David Lyle Jeffrey in ensuring that this volume would go to press. The spread of topics is wide, touching on the relationships between the Bible and the concerns of the university, including not just theology but psychology, law, philosophy, teacher education and American literature. These essays, and the introduction to them, capture something of the spirit of the entire project, demonstrating that the Bible is not a book that can be shunted off to the margins of thought but is one of the foundations of Western culture. (It is likewise increasingly apparent that modern Africa and China cannot be fully understood without recognising the role of the Bible in shaping some aspects of popular and intellectual culture in those parts of the globe.)

The essays in this volume evidence careful scholarship. They also illustrate the conviction of Dr. Craig Bartholomew, the guiding spirit behind the entire project, that academic professionals ought not to leave their faith commitments outside the door of the academy. Indeed, it is an assumption in this volume, as it is in the rest of the series, that faith is intrinsic to the human condition and always a motivating factor in academic discourse, as is recognised by figures as diverse and as historically removed from one another as St Augustine and Fyodor Dostoevsky.

Redeemer University College is proud to identify with, and to do its modest share to push forward this project. Redeemer University College is a confessional university – rooted firmly in the catholic creeds of the Christian Church and the distinctive features of the Reformed theological and philosophical tradition. Open and confident about its moorings, Redeemer is committed to engaging the intellectual currents in our culture. That is what this volume, and the entire Scripture and Hermeneutics series, is likewise committed to doing.

Jacob Ellens
Academic Vice-President
Redeemer University College
Ancaster, Ontario L9K 1J4
Canada

Scripture Index

Old Testament

Genesis
1:1 162
1:26 162
2 188
2:15 193
2:16–17 163
25:11 116
41:41–57 163
47:21 163

Exodus
1:8 163
1:16 163
5:7 163
18:15 167
19:4 164
19:6 165, 174
20:22–21:1 172
21:1 165
21:2–11 166
22:21 166

Leviticus
19:9–10 166
19:18 165
19:22–23 166
19:34 166
25:8–17 166
25:44–46 166

Numbers
5:6–7 166

Deuteronomy
4:13 165
5:30 172
5:33 165
6:4 210
15:1–5 166
24:1–4 171
24:17 164
24:19–22 166

2 Samuel
12 148

Job
23:9–10 35
26:14 35

Psalms
1:2 164, 167
19:7 165, 167

Proverbs
31:10–31 66–67

Isaiah
5:5–7 197–98
6:10 147
10:1–2 167
42:1–4 170

Ezekiel
36:35 196

Name Index

Subject Index